THE SPLENDID VISION

Centennial History of the
National Council of Women of Canada
1893 ❧ 1993

N. E. S. GRIFFITHS, F.R.S.C.

THE SPLENDID VISION

Centennial History of the
National Council of Women of Canada
1893 ✤ 1993

ALTIOR

by
N. E. S. GRIFFITHS, F.R.S.C.

CARLETON UNIVERSITY PRESS
Ottawa, Canada
1993

Printed and bound in Canada

CANADIAN CATALOGUING IN PUBLICATION DATA

Griffiths, N. E. S. (Naomi Elizabeth Saundaus), 1934-
   The splendid vision : centennial history of the
National Council of Women of Canada : 1893-1993

(Carleton women's experience series ; 4)
ISBN 0-88629-198-4 (bound) -
ISBN 0-88629-199-2 (pbk.)

   1. National Council of Women of Canada–History.
I. Title. II. Series.

HQ1907.N338G74 1993   305.4'06'071   C93-090187-8

CARLETON UNIVERSITY PRESS   Distributed in Canada by:
160 Paterson Hall
1125 Colonel By Drive   OXFORD UNIVERSITY PRESS CANADA
Ottawa, ON Canada   70 Wynford Drive
K1S 5B6   Don Mills, ON Canada M3C 1J9
(613) 788-3740   (416) 441-2941

COVER DESIGN by Sally Gilmour. Cover photograph: the National Council of
Women of Canada annual meeting, Calgary, June 1921, taken by W.J. Oliver. It is
provided kindness of the Glenbow Archives, Calgary, Alberta / NA 4875-1.
INTERIOR DESIGN AND TYPESETTING by Victory Design.

Acknowledgements
   Carleton University Press gratefully acknowledges the support extended to its
publishing programme by the Canada Council and the Ontario Arts Council.
   The Press would also like to thank the Department of Communications,
Government of Canada, and the Government of Ontario through the Ministry of
Culture, Tourism and Recreation, for their assistance.

To

I.L.D.

In the writing of this volume the author has been given full and generous cooperation by the National Council of Women of Canada, including full access to those relevant papers in the possession of the National Council of Women of Canada. The inferences drawn, however, and the opinions expressed are those of the author herself and do not necessarily represent the opinions of the National Council of Women of Canada.

TABLE OF CONTENTS

FOREWORD   ix

PREFACE   xiii

LIST OF ILLUSTRATIONS   xvii

INTRODUCTION:
Unacknowledged Strength   1

CHAPTER ONE:
An International Idea Finds a Canadian Expression, 1893-1894   13

CHAPTER TWO:
Establishing a Presence, 1894-1899   47

CHAPTER THREE:
Expansion and Development, 1900-1913   79

CHAPTER FOUR:
From the Eve of the Great War to the First Year of Peace, 1914-1919   111

CHAPTER FIVE:
Searching for a New Dispensation, 1919-1929   145

CHAPTER SIX:
Confronting the Depression, 1929-1939   181

CHAPTER SEVEN:
War and Aftermath, 1940-1950   211

CHAPTER EIGHT:
Reorganization and Continuity, 1950-1960   243

CHAPTER NINE:
Towards the Royal Commission, 1960-1969   275

CHAPTER TEN:
Reaction and Resolution, 1970-1980   309

CHAPTER ELEVEN: Years of Ambiguity, 1980-1988   343

CHAPTER TWELVE:
Continuity and Change   383

APPENDICES:

A: Presidents of the National Council of Women of Canada   419
B: The Foundation Fund   420
C: Affiliated Societies of Local and Provincial Councils, 1956   422
D: Terms of Reference for the Standing Committees, 1956   430
E: Local Councils of Women, 1893-1993   435
F: Nationally Organized Societies Presently Affiliated with the NCWC   439
G: Present Provincial and Local Councils   440
H: Excerpts from the Current Constitution and By-Laws of the NCWC   441

INDEX   445

FOREWORD

ARRIVING AT THE venerable age of one hundred is bound to generate a variety of emotions: some surprise; quite a lot of pride; and perhaps a bit of anxiety about what the future holds. Those of us who are NCWC members probably experienced all these emotions as we approached 1993, our Centennial Year. But one thing was clear: we were pleased to have arrived at this landmark. And like other centenarians, we wanted to spend some time looking back at our past and its achievements.

It was at least six years ago when the Officers of the National Council of Women of Canada first began to make plans for the one hundredth birthday of the Council. They wanted to mark the occasion in some significant and lasting way, and decided that this might best be done by the publication of a new history of the Council. The last history of National Council had been written in 1957; it was clearly time for a new one. A committee was struck to explore ways and means, to find a publisher, and, most important of all, to find the right author. We are fortunate indeed that they found in Dr. Naomi Griffiths a historian who brought a lively understanding and sympathy to this story of the women and organizations who make up the National Council of Women of Canada.

The National Council of Women began one hundred years ago as an association of women's groups who believed that they would have a more effective voice if they worked together rather than separately on issues affecting women, families, and communities. Much has changed in the intervening hundred years. Now the Council is but one amongst a

multitude of voices urging government action. Single interest groups
have emerged as effective advocates for change. The Council operates
in a world shaped by the influence of the media and by the technology
of instant communication, where family patterns have altered and where
the majority of women are in the work force. Its challenge is to come to
terms with these changes while maintaining its emphasis on the quality
of life for women, families, and communities.

The strength of National Council still comes from the Local
Councils and the affiliated National Organizations which make up its
membership. It is their delegates who come to the Annual General
Meeting, held each year in a different part of Canada. Much time at this
meeting is devoted to debate on resolutions which have already been
considered at the local and provincial council level. Once approved, the
resolutions form the basis of new Council policy and of the Annual
Brief to the federal government. This process has served Council well
over the years but is undeniably slow and somewhat cumbersome. Task
Forces have now been set up to look for new ways of establishing policy
which will allow Council to respond more quickly to emerging issues,
while retaining the integrity which comes from grass roots participation.

The National Council of Women provides a vehicle for empowering
women, through education and debate, to participate in the process of
forming public policy. Additional members can only strengthen its
voice, and it will always welcome as new members national voluntary
organizations which share its interests and concerns.

In 1993 the National Council consists of twenty-four local Councils
of Women, four Provincial Councils of Women, and twenty-seven
Nationally Organized Societies. It continues to be an active member of
the International Council of Women (ICW); Canadians on the Executive
of ICW in 1993 include the Treasurer, four International Convenors of
Standing Committees, and two Consultants to Committees, as well as
the National President.

In this centennial year those of us who are current members of the
National Council are particularly aware of the contributions made by
our predecessors, and delighted that their story is being told in this history. As one who has had the good fortune to be president of National
Council during its one-hundredth year, I am especially grateful to those
who began planning for the writing of this book. They include Mary
Howell and Rosslyn Tetley, as well as past presidents Doreen Kissick

and Joan De New and former Executive Secretary Pearl Dobson. I am sure that as you read *The Splendid Vision* you will agree that they planned well.

RUTH BROWN
President of the National Council of Women of Canada
August, 1993

PREFACE

I AGREED TO write The Splendid Vision in the fall of 1988. At that time I knew very little about the National Council of Women of Canada except that it was an organization run by women who gave time and energy to volunteer work. My interest was captured because I have long felt that women's philanthropy has been consistently overlooked and undervalued. Far too often even the most committed feminists have accepted the idea that what is socially and politically valuable has to be something done within the institutional structure of the polity and done for money.

Over the past five years my suspicion that volunteer work by women played a crucial and significant role in the emergence of Canadian society has been more than amply confirmed. Women who worked through the Council, during these hundred years, were responsible for the founding of the Victorian Order of Nurses and the establishment of the Canadian Consumers' Association; they fought for women's suffrage and for women's rights as parents; they supported the battle for decent working conditions in factories and in shops and they lobbied for proper enforcement of government regulations in these areas. In the area of municipal life, members of the Council led those demanding better sewage systems, water purification plants, and properly inspected abattoirs and controls to ensure clean milk and bread. Without the work of this organization many towns and cities in Canada would be without a museum, an art gallery and a music program.

In writing about their work I have had one major worry. This has come from the knowledge that even in a book of some 150,000 words I have had to leave aside so much. I have barely mentioned the work done for the Canadian National Exhibition by the Council; I have skipped far too quickly through the ways in which this Council has supported Canadian artists. For these sins of omission, and others, I beg forgiveness.

Forgiveness which I am confident I will receive from present-day members of the Council because one of the most important sources of support for my efforts has been the intelligent interest shown by these women in *The Splendid Vision*. During the summer of 1991 I was welcomed from Victoria to Truro by Council women who met me in airports and at ferry terminals, housed me, fed me, gave parties for me and talked, with honesty and enthusiasm, about the reasons why they work for Council. I owe a great deal to all those I met, but in particular and working from West to East, I wish to thank those who were in charge of local arrangements: Kay Armstrong, Victoria; Bette Pepper, White Rock; Joy Scudamore, Vancouver; Evelyn Fingarson, Burnaby; Freda Hogg, New Westminster; Marjorie Norris, Calgary; Florence Romanchuk, Edmonton; Lynda Newson, Saskatoon; Ann Sudom, Regina; Elizabeth MacEwan, Winnipeg; Pearl Dobson, Ottawa; Catherine Sly, Montreal; and Marjorie Bulmer, Truro. To them, and many others, unnamed but nevertheless deeply appreciated, who ferried me about and talked wittily and wisely of their visions of Council. I owe more than I can say, and I hope this work is to their taste. I also hope they will forgive me for not always including every achievement of their own locality! Throughout the months, I have been sustained by the enthusiasm of those members of Council who had some responsibility for the project of this Centennial history. In alphabetical order I would like to thank the following for their consistent encouragement of my efforts: Ruth Brown, Pearl Dobson, Doreen Kissick, Joan De New, and Rosslyn Tetley. The willingness of past Council presidents to provide me with autobiographical information must also be mentioned, and I cherish the long — sometimes, not long enough — letters I received from Ruth Brown, Ruth Hinkley, Margaret MacGee, Elizabeth MacEwan (about her mother), Mrs. Turner Bone, Joan De New, and Amy Williams. Katherine Tait, the present Executive Assistant of Council, has helped me without stint by looking up all kinds of details of past Council activity and never making me feel unwanted when I interrupted her work with a question.

I must also acknowledge a debt of gratitude to a number of people, who are not Council members, without whose work this book could not have been completed. Many Canadian historians took a considerable chance in working on the history of women's experiences in Canada, when such study was neither easy to do nor particularly appreciated. I have benefitted very much from work done by Veronica Strong-Boag, who wrote her doctoral thesis on the early years of the National Council of Women. As well the work of Alison Prentice and Susan Mann Trofimenkoff has been most illuminating. To these, and many others, I owe a debt of gratitude. However, the work that needs to be done on the lives and achievements of Canadian women remains very great. In presenting the lives of Council members I have often been unable to give birth dates, since the public record of their work does not record this information. During the last century, most middle class women did not choose to disclose their age and their birthdates are still hidden in parish registers. There is a dearth of easily available biographical information about women who have helped shape Canadian society. In writing about them I have tried to present as much of this data as possible and to refer to them in the way the contemporary records did. There is a considerable variation of address: some will have their marital status stressed and be given their husband's initials, not their own. Others will have their own first name, and occasionally, their own family name. It is hoped that, as a result, the reader will come to see the women, whose work is the subject of this volume, as individuals and not just as members of a category.

I also wish to thank, most particularly, a number of people without whom this book would never have been finished, this year or any other. Heather Phaneuf and Kerry and Sue Badgeley worked as research assistants, putting in much longer hours than the monetary recompense warranted. Dr. Olena Heywood spent three days of her holidays working in the National Archives of Canada to make certain I had the correct information about the connection between the Council and the Consumers' Association. Enid King worked, out of friendship, very long hours trying to uncover biographical information about Council members. Further, she provided me with many welcome dinners, and she and her husband listened with considerable patience as I discussed how I wanted to shape a particular chapter. Margaret Wade Labarge also fed me, and listened with interest providing thoughtful comments concerning women and volunteer work. Carol Strong gave unstinting help with the index. My colleagues at Carleton University were helpful with positive comments about the task. In particular, S.F. Wise read the manuscript from beginning to end and wrote a lengthy, thoughtful, and witty appraisal, without which this book would have been very much the poorer. To all these, and many others, I am deeply grateful. Whatever errors

---

1   Veronica Strong-Boag, *The Parliment of Women: The National Council of Women of Canada 1893-1929*, National Museum of Man Series, History Division Paper No. 18, A Diamond Jenness Memorial Volume, (Ottawa, 1976).

there may be in this work, however, are my own responsibility.

Finally, for financial aid, I wish to thank John ApSimon, Dean of Graduate Studies, Carleton University, and Joan De New, both of whom provided research monies which enabled me to travel across Canada, and to photocopy archival material. Terresa McIntosh of the Documentary Art and Photography Division of the National Archives of Canada provided scholarly help, at very short notice, on available photographic resources of Council. And it would not do to conclude without mentioning that the staff at Carleton University Press have done all in their power to ensure that the book appears before the public in the best possible form. Anne Winship, Madge Pon, Jennie Strickland, and Sue Stott showed much patience with an author more and more tense as publication date drew near. Finally, Noel Gates, the copy editor, struggled with my idiosyncratic punctuation and strove mightily to make sure my words reflected my thoughts clearly. The flaws in this work are the author's own unaided achievements.

LIST OF ILLUSTRATIONS

1. Lady Ishbel, Marchioness of Aberdeen and Temair, President 1893-1898   19

2. Washday   41

3. Mrs. Adelaide Hoodless   53

4. Emily Howard Stowe   67

5. Lady Aberdeen (right) and Lady Taylor, President 1899-1902, 1910-1911   75

6. Mrs. Clark Murray, founder of the Imperial Order of the Daughters of the Empire   81

7. Lady Taylor, President 1899-1902, 1910-1911   87

8. Mrs. Robert Thompson, President 1902-1906   95

9. Lady Edgar, President 1906-1910   109

10. Mrs. F.H. Torrington, President 1911-1918   113

11. Mrs. W.E. Sanford, President 1918-1922   119

12. Mrs. Laura Jamieson, the first woman magistrate in the British Empire   127

13. Carrie Derick   141

14. Miss Caroline C. Carmichael, President 1922-1926   147

15. Mrs. J.A. Wilson, President 1926-1931   153

16. Mrs. Irene Parlby   161

17. Miss M. Winnifred Kydd, President 1931-1936   191

18. Mrs. George O. Spencer, President 1936-1941   201

19. Mrs. Edgar D. Hardy, President 1941-1946   225

20. Mrs R.J. Marshall, President 1946-1951   237

21. Mrs. Turner Bone, President 1951-1956   253

22. Mrs. Rex Eaton, President 1956-1959   263

23. Mrs. G.D. Finlayson, President 1959-1961   269

24. Mrs. Saul Hayes, President 1961-1964   283

25. Mrs. M.F. Steen, President 1964-1967   297

26. Mrs. S.M. Milne, President 1967-1970   303

27. Mrs. John Hnatyshyn, President 1970-1973   317

28. Mrs. Gordon B. Armstrong, President 1973-1976   327

29. Mrs. Ruth (Charles) Hinkley, President 1976-1979   337

30. Mrs. Amy (Jack) Williams, President 1979-1982   351

31. Mrs. Margaret (Arthur) Harris, President 1982-1984   361

32. Mrs. Margaret MacGee, President 1984-1987   371

33. Mrs. Doreen Kissick, President 1987-1990   377

34. Mrs. Joan De New, President 1990-1992   391

35. Ruth Brown, President 1992 to the present   401

36. The National Council of Women of Canada 100th Annual Anniversary meeting.
    Carleton University, Ottawa, May 17, 1993.   411

INTRODUCTION

Unacknowledged Strength

FOR A HUNDRED years the National Council of Women of Canada has served as a coordinating voice for women in volunteer organizations. It has been a continuing presence in Canadian life, involved deeply in the debates over major Canadian social and political issues at all three levels of government, municipal, provincial and federal. Council has provided women with ideas and information about public matters, given them a forum for debate, and organized the presentation of their concerns to official bodies of all kinds, of all types and in all places. Further, because the Council of Women of Canada has been linked to the International Council of Women since 1897, many Canadian women have found that Council has given them an opportunity to support international efforts for the improvement of women's lives.

Considering the place of women in the community it is interesting how often work in volunteer organizations is overlooked. This is, perhaps, because one of the most pernicious half-truths about the content of women's lives has been the idea that, in the past, it had no public component and no impact upon the judgement and development of community affairs. The truth, in this half-truth, is obvious: discrimination against women has been at its most blatant in their exclusion from direct political power and in continuing attempts to circumscribe their employment world to the home. What the perception ignores and covers up, however, is the way in which women have always had a public voice, through their work for the social and cultural welfare of the communities in which they lived. Visiting the sick, comforting the dying, succouring the poor- these activities might be carried out by priests and ministers, by members of the male religious orders and by the male-directed political institutions of a community. But charitable work has always been undertaken by women, as individuals or as members of a group.

Further, women's direct contribution to the development of large public charitable enterprises, such as hospitals and orphanages, began to be highly visible with the emergence in the Catholic Church of the active religious orders of women in the seventeenth century. During the eighteenth century, Protestant women such as Lady Margaret Spencer (1737–1814) organized their own philanthropy and were often called upon by local and national governmental bodies for help and advice in welfare matters.[1] By the early years of the nineteenth century women, on both sides of the Atlantic, had carved out a place for themselves in the area of public charitable enterprises.

The work of Elizabeth Fry (1780–1845) for prison reform in England, during the eighteen-twenties, is only one of a number of similar public careers. Protestant women, in particular, joined together as the nineteenth century went on, in organized groups of volunteers, both in Canada and elsewhere. In the United States Anne Parrish, a Philadelphia Quaker, is often credited with the initiation of organized charitable works. In 1793 she organized her friends into a "Friendly Circle" to cope with the impact of a yellow fever epidemic. In 1811 her group became officially incorporated into "the Female Society of Philadelphia for the Relief and Employment of the Poor."[2] Such groups played a crucial role in mitigating the poverty of the burgeoning industrial-urban world. This type of volunteer work paved the way far for the establishment of national women's organizations such as the National Council of Women in Canada.

The movement that would lead to the foundation of this Council became visible to the public in 1888, in which year fifty-three different national organizations, founded and run by women, came together in New York, represented by forty-nine delegations from England, France, Denmark, Norway, Finland, India, Canada and the United States.[3] Two particular developments supported the emergence of such a movement. The first was the extraordinary growth of women's volunteer activity during the nineteenth century and the second, was the growth, in the course of that activity, of a strong convic-

[1] Donna T. Andrew, "Philanthropy and Property: The Charity Letters of Margaret, Countess Spencer, 1760–1814, to appear in John Brewest and Susan Staves eds., *Early Modern Conceptions of Property*, (Routledge, 1993).

[2] Mary Bosworth Treudley, "The Benevolent Fair: A Study of Charitable Organization Among American Women in the First Third of the Nineteenth Century," *The Social Service Review*, XIV, no. 3, (Sept 1940), pp. 509–22.

[3] Anon., *Women in a Changing World: The Dynamic Story of the International Council of Women Since 1888*, (London, 1966), p. 14.

tion on the part of women of the need to cooperate, as women, to bring needed change to society.

The volunteer movement was by no means restricted solely to the material needs of the community. Local societies of women for libraries, for intellectual and cultural activities and for missionary aid joined those established for penal reform and for aid to orphans and the indigent old. Nor were women alone in banding together in voluntary associations of varying types and kinds. As Veronica Strong-Boag has pointed out, the development of women's associations in general, and the National Council of Women of Canada in particular, was part and parcel of a widespread proliferation in late nineteenth century Canada of alliances and associations formed to confront provincial and national difficulties.[4] The eighteen-nineties, in particular, saw the emergence of all kinds of groups, people coming together to find common ground for action, businessmen and manufacturers as well as farmworkers and industrial employees.

It must be remembered that this was an era in which the structure of the modern state, as we know it, was only beginning. The complex web of government institutions which regulates so much of late twentieth century life hardly existed in the eighteen-nineties. What is called today "the social net" did not exist at all. Its place was partially filled by the emergence of a very great variety of organizations, voluntary associations with self-regulating membership, formed for very diverse purposes. The word "club" became used to cover a multitude of organizations, associations, societies, confederations, fraternities and sororities. Some were organized to promote religious aims: societies to aid and encourage the faithful to lead the life that faith enjoined, or missionary societies to spread the truth believed. Some were formed for charitable purposes, some for aesthetic and cultural aims. Many were linked to political objectives and perhaps as many were established to promote business contacts.

Whatever its declared purpose, a club brought together like-minded people in pursuit of a common aim. To be a member of a club required spare time and, almost always, some financial ease. The latter requirement was considerably less important for church-centred associations, such as the women's auxiliaries which were formed by most denominations at the parish level; for those clubs, however, whose aim was self-improvement or volun-

[4] "Setting the Stage: National Organization and the Women's Movement in the Late 19th Century," in Susan Mann Trofimenkoff and Alison Prentice, eds., *The Neglected Majority: Essays in Canadian Women's History*, (Toronto, 1977), p. 87.

tary action for the good of the community, membership tended to be drawn from the ranks of the middle class. A certain life-style is implied by membership in a morning music circle or a reading union. Benevolent associations, which were centred upon visits to the sick and charitable enterprises in general, also tended to have a membership of the leisured and the comfortably circumstanced. The leadership of almost all such associations, male or female, was usually drawn from the middle class urban elite.

But while associations, such as the Women's Institute and Young Women's Christian Association, might be founded and organized by women from the middle class, a considerable part of their support came from a much broader spectrum of society. The Young Women's Christian Association, in particular, brought together young women throughout the Dominion — shop-girls, servants and factory workers.

By the end of the century, the number of such societies in existence, run by and for women, inspired the publication of somewhat pejorative articles on "the club woman."[5] This person was depicted as a woman of "privilege," a wealthy woman freed of economic and family responsibility. She was seen as having a "problem of leisure,"[6] and any activity she undertook was, therefore, seen as a matter of self-indulgence, no matter how laudable the enterprise might be. Not only were such women barred by contemporary beliefs of their class from full participation in their societies; the lives they did live have been too often dismissed as an unimportant reflection of the status of their male relatives. This view seems to have two sources. The first is an enduring prejudice against middle and upper class women whose lives were based upon the family. There is, apparently, an unwillingness to allow them the usual variation of individual human personalities and range of circumstance common to other categories of people. Secondly, there seems to be a refusal on the part of their contemporaries and, too often, of later historians as well, to recognize the work done by these women for the community, because it was neither paid employment nor the result of a position held through a public electoral process.

These critical attitudes had little impact on the growth of women's volunteer associations in the western world generally or in Canada in particular.

5   F. Stuart Chapin, "Social Institutions and Voluntary Associations," *Review of Sociology,* Joseph B. Gittler, ed., (New York, J. Wiley and Sons, 1957), Anne Farnham, "A Society of Societies: Associations and Voluntarism in Early Nineteenth-Century Salem," *Essex Institute Historical Collections,* 113, no. 3, (July 1977), pp. 181–90.

6   F. Stuart Chapin, "Social Institutes and Voluntary Associations," in Joseph B. Gittler, ed., *Review of Sociology,* (New York, 1957), pp. 264–65

This was as much due to the long tradition of Christian philanthropy as to the obvious need for the work done by voluntary associations. In a world without a welfare net, the emergence of volunteer societies dedicated to coping with those whose lives were poverty-stricken was welcome. What, at the close of the twentieth century are matters for government departments and state-funded social welfare agencies, were, in the nineteenth century, the concern of a group of private individuals.

In Ottawa, for example, between 1890 and 1910, volunteers organized and funded the Protestant Home for the Aged, the Refuge Branch of the Protestant Orphans Home, the Home for Friendless Women and the Ottawa Maternity Hospital.[7] There is no doubt that the present welfare provisions in Canada are built upon, and take much of their character from, the achievements of this type of volunteer activity.[8]

The obvious link of such activities with religious institutions deflected some of the criticism directed against women meddling in matters better left to men. Another bulwark against reproach was the strong development of women's missionary societies. It was difficult for a polity that was explicitly Christian, to criticize work done in the name of Christian living and the bringing of the Christian message to those who knew it not. By 1885, Baptist women had 123 societies, scattered through the small towns and villages of the Maritime provinces alone. The Presbyterian Woman's Foreign Missionary Society, with branches established throughout Canada, including Quebec, was founded in 1876. The Methodists created their association in 1881 and, while Methodist women did not achieve an independent organization until 1911, the Anglican women took steps to form a similar organization in 1885.[9]

These associations were very definitely organized, directed and controlled by women, who raised remarkable amounts of money for the projects which they, themselves, decided to support. The leaders of these associations, those who became their presidents and members of their executives, were most often the social counterparts of the men who went into politics, ran small businesses, were lawyers and doctors. However, it is at least

7. On this see Sharon Anne Cook, "A Helping Hand and Shelter: Anglo-Protestant Social Service Agencies in Ottawa, 1880–1910," unpublished M.A., History Department, Carleton University, 1987.

8. On this see, in particular, Kathleen Woodroofe, *From Charity to Society Work in England and the United States*, (1962) and Walter I. Trattner, *From Poor Law to Welfare State: a History of Social Welfare in America*, (New York, 1974).

9. Alison Prentice, Paula Bourne, Gail Cuthbert Brandt, Beth Light, Wendy Mitchinson, Naomi Black, *Canadian Women: A History*, (Toronto, 1988), p. 171.

arguable that at the parish and congregation level the involvement of women of all social backgrounds took place. Without bake sales, sewing bees and other community activities, as well as special collections, weekly donations and the sale of pamphlets — all of these being activities organized by the women of the particular locality — the associations would never have prospered. A very substantial proportion of this work was done by women who ran their homes on their husbands' weekly wages. If individual contributions were made the money had to be found, more often than not, from money given to women for housekeeping and a husband's approval would usually be necessary for its disposal in this fashion. Yet "in 1899 Presbyterian women from the Western Division collected no less than $45,513 from 21,000 members; in 1900 Baptist women collected $10,000 in the Maritimes alone."[10] It was multiple donations of small amounts rather than the few substantial gifts that built these impressive totals — money urban women could gain by an extra load of washing or an extra cleaning job, rural women from "egg money."

The experience gained from membership in such societies helped many women to find the vision and courage to create other associations whose purpose was broader than the advancement of just one particular interpretation of Christianity. For example, the first Canadian branch of the Women's Christian Temperance Movement was founded in 1874 by Letitia Youmans.[11] The strict teetotalism and strongly Protestant character of this association restricted its attraction to like-minded individuals. On the other hand, its essentially practical nature, which centered upon care for the women and children of broken homes, appealed to many. By 1891 there were 9,000 members of the association throughout Canada, and Ontario by itself had 175 branches.[12]

By that time, there were other nationally organized, inter-faith associations of women in Canada, such as the Young Women's Christian Association, which had established its first branch in Saint John, New Brunswick in 1870. Both the W.C.T.U. and the Y.W.C.A. were concerned with lobbying for major legislative reform programs. There were also orga-

---

[10] Prentice, et al., *Ibid.*, p. 171.

[11] She was born Letitia Creighton in Hamilton Township, 3 Jan. 1827, and died in Toronto, 18 July, 1896. At the age of 23 she married a widower with eight children. She was a Methodist and she taught Sunday school. The impact of alcoholism on the lives of her young students was the spur for her involvement in the temperance movement.

[12] Ontario numbers from Veronica Strong-Boag, *The Parliament of Women: The National Council of Women of Canada 1893–1929*, (Ottawa, 1976), p. 61.

nizations whose major concern was improving the immediate living conditions of young girls and women. Often these associations had a more restricted membership, both ideologically and geographically, than the W.C.T.U. and the Y.W.C.A. Examples are the Girls' Friendly Society and the Dominion Order of the King's Daughters, both centred in Ontario. Both were established from parent bodies in other lands, and kept their subsidiary status for many years. The Girls' Friendly Society was a British off-shoot and fundamentally Anglican. It came to Canada in 1882. The Dominion Order of the King's Daughters had American roots and established itself in Ontario in the eighteen-nineties. It was more broadly based than the Girls' Friendly Society and included women from most of the Protestant denominations.

It is against the background of such organizations, which were also coming together in the United States and in Europe, that the International Council of Women was brought into being.[13] Much of the original energy for such an enterprise come from two remarkable American activists, movers and shakers in that country's suffragist movement: Susan Anthony (1820–1906) and Elizabeth Cady Stanton (1815–1902). They were convinced that an international association could bring together the different organizations of women that were already in existence and dedicated to changing society for the better. The vision was above all a vision of consensus, a belief that the provision of a neutral arena, in which women of good will could meet to find common solutions to commonly acknowledged problems, would result in a new and positive influence on world affairs.

The first plans for making this vision a reality were placed before the Annual Convention of the National Women's Suffrage Association by Susan Anthony in New York in 1887. This organization was a major player in the early days of the planning of the International Council of Women, but it was one of its executive members, May Wright Sewall, who ensured that the suffrage should be only one among many other concerns for the new association. The founding convention took place in Washington in 1888 and brought together forty-nine delegations, representing fifty-three different national organizations of women and nine countries: England, France, Denmark, Norway, Sweden, Finland, India, Canada and the United States.[14] These delegates decided that what was required was an institution that had a

---

13 One of the best short accounts of its inception is that by Edith F. Hurwitz, "The International Sisterhood," in Bridenthal and Koonz, eds., *Becoming Visible Women in European History*, (Boston, 1977), pp. 328–342.

14 Anon, *Women in a Changing World*, p. 3.

real and effective connection to the work of women at the local level, in the various countries which would be its members. It was not to be an organization of individuals but an organization of already established associations. Its structure was to be flexible, allowing each country an internal liberty with respect to the constitution of its own Council. Neither particular political or religious philosophies, nor even specific priorities of reform, were to be the guiding force of the international body. Its foundation was to be a common consensus about the way human beings should treat one another, rather than about shared beliefs as to the nature of human society. The preamble to the constitution which was accepted by the delegates in 1888, stated that the International Council of Women was founded in the belief that "the good of humanity will be advanced" by women binding themselves "in a confederation of workers to further the application of the Golden Rule to society, custom and Law: Do Unto Others as Ye Would That They Should Do Unto You."[15]

The shape and form of the International Council of Women, as opposed to its ambitions, are to be found in Articles I and II of its constitution. These stated that there were two objectives for the organization: firstly, the provision "of a means of communication between women's organizations in all countries;" secondly, the organization of:

opportunities for women to meet together from all parts of the world to confer upon questions relating to the welfare of the commowealth and family.

Article II announced that:

This International Council is organized in the interests of no one propaganda and has no power over its members beyond that of suggestion and sympathy; therefore no National Council voting to become a member of the International Council shall render itself liable to be interfered with in respect to its complete organic unity, independence or methods of work, or shall be committed to any principle or method of any other Council or any utterance or act of this International Council, beyond compliance with the terms of this constitution.

---

[15] *Ibid.*, Appendix I, p. 329.

What is clear from these provisions is that the Council movement was indeed a movement of women, constructed in the belief that women had their own views and ideas that needed expression and that society as a whole needed to hear. The Council's method of operation was to be very different from the main-stream political practices then current among western peoples. Exchange of information and exchange of opinions among members was given greater importance than explicit prescriptions for action. This, of course, arose naturally from the fact that Council was an umbrella organization, content to allow each member society that affiliated to design and carry out the particular program of reform which its circumstances, in its view, dictated. The Council had an obligation to move only when consensus was clear and on matters which its members decided were important. As an organization it was analogous to the Manufacturers' Association or the professional societies of doctors and lawyers. The Council movement was quintessentially, from the outset, an educated lobby, composed of people with interests which, in the majority of cases, would seldom coincide.

The papers given at that founding meeting in 1888 showed the broad concerns of the women for the problems of humanity as a whole, and not only for the difficulties they faced because they were women. Philanthropic work, temperance movements, legal and political struggles, prison reform, hospital work, missionary work, industrial work, all these topics and more were debated in 1888 in Washington. The founding meeting concluded with plans for action to secure for women greater access to higher education and professional training, with equal wages for equal work, and with the respect for identical social standards of "personal purity and morality for men and women." This last goal opposed the idea that prostitution was both a necessary evil and the result of the inherent flaw in women's souls, the inheritance from Eve as temptress.

The immediate result of the 1888 meeting was a pause, during which only the United States structured an effective Council at the national level. Over the next five years, from 1888 to 1893, the movement was mainly American in funding and action. May Wright Sewall had been elected president and she worked tirelessly to promote a vision of international action by women. The major result of this activity was the meeting of the International Congress of Women at the World Exposition held in Chicago in 1893. On 19 May 1893, the International Council of Women was more formally established and Lady Ishbel, Countess of Aberdeen was elected as its President, a position she would hold, except for two short intervals, until 1936. She was twenty-nine at the time and her husband had just been appointed Canada's

Governor General. Her impact upon the Council of Women movement was, as will be seen, extraordinary, and she would play a crucial role in its growth.

There had been a good Canadian representation at this First Quinquennial meeting of the International Council of Women. Mrs. Mary Macdonell and Mrs. Willoughby Cummings were elected as provisional vice-president and secretary respectively to promote the formation of a Canadian National Council.[16] Within the year the National Council of Women of Canada had been founded. In the Constitution, as published in the Act of 1914 incorporating the National Council, its object was stated as being to "unite in a Dominion federation for the betterment throughout Canada of conditions pertaining to the family and state, all societies and associations of women interested in philanthropy, religion, education, literature, art or social reform." All were to be welcome in a constitutional embrace which sought to include the established church groups, both Protestant and Catholic, Jewish groups, women's self-help groups, temperance groups, child welfare groups, groups working for women's suffrage, groups working for better urban conditions, groups working for family aid, philanthropic groups, groups interested in art and literature, groups that were defined by the male association to which they were an auxiliary, any and all groups that provided women with a way to bring their influence to bear on public life.

Over the next hundred years, the National Council of Women of Canada succeeded, to a remarkable degree, in fulfilling the aims of the women who brought it into being. Never tied to one ideological wheel, concerned to find the "common ground," the Council has represented the ideas and wishes of women who wanted to "do something, right now" about problems that they met daily. It has helped to form the Canadian social conscience and, because its structure allowed great autonomy, it has had a profound regional importance in addition to its considerable national presence.

It should never have worked. An organization with no single aim a priority, except the most general agreement that a problem existed, ought to have collapsed the moment the debate was joined over what actually ought to be done. But women vowed to temperance and women whose money came from the sale of alcohol, women who thought that their vote would be the

[16] Rosa L. Shaw, *Proud Heritage: A History of the National Council of Women of Canada*, (Toronto, 1957), p. 4. Further biographic details on the Canadian delegation will be found in Chapter One.

solution to all social distress and women who did not believe that females should vote, talked and talked until they could agree that a first step towards change should be a better water filtration plant for the town, or women inspectors in factories to insist on laws being enforced, or women in the justice system to ensure that women prisoners were not subject to a particularly hostile environment. The vision of Council has been, above all a vision of consensus, a belief that the provision of a neutral arena in which women of good will could meet to find common solutions to commonly acknowledged problems would result in a new and positive influence on world affairs.

Even so, Council should never have lasted. Once women were granted the vote and given access to educational and professional opportunities, it ought to have faded away. Yet Council had a membership of 150,000 women in 1919, 500,000 in 1940, and today represents nearly 700,000 women. Council continues, affiliations disappear, but new ones emerge. Council continued to bring together those who first acted within their communities in pursuit of a very specific ambition — the aftercare of prisoners, or the continuance of their local church, or the needs of a hospital — and then find the energy to add one more meeting to their lives: the local council, dedicated to helping organizations combine on those issues on which they can agree.

It ought to have split apart long ago. When those who want to solve problems by state action meet those who think that the individual ought to have the greatest possible freedom, including the freedom to starve, and debate how welfare budgets should be spent, meetings should end with the dissolution of Council. Yet Council meetings have continued to be held. The recognition of a problem leads to lengthy debates and studies of the nature of the problem, before the position paper emerges. This makes it possible for a Council resolution to be something that can be supported by very different associations.

The public issues discussed by the National Council have covered a wide range, from the 1917 Conscription crisis to the present need for soup kitchens, from the need for a federal department of health to the need for better government departments concerned with the environment, from the rights of union workers to rights of women farmers, from the rights of native women to the way in which the justice system handles rape. For a hundred years Council women have investigated and commented on public issues. They have spoken to municipal councils and provincial ministers. They have organized petitions and public meetings. They have held press conferences and met with the federal Cabinet. Sometimes their ideas were accepted, sometimes not, but always the women who joined Council were opinion makers. They were the concerned. They made themselves informed. If they were divided over what should be done, they were rarely divided over the seriousness of the issue raised. Above all, they were people who wanted an issue intelligently discussed and debated.

Council has been an invisible strength to Canada: pragmatic, problem-oriented, ideologically always disunited, rarely working for a single cause, almost always seeking for the solution of a particular dilemma. The history of this body reflects the history of the country itself, its tensions and its angers, its visions and its dreams. It is the story of women who worked because they felt they must, within the communities that were, indeed, theirs to build. It is about some women's political space. Those who have worked with Council over the years have been a diverse and lively crew. They have included the sane, the balanced, the conventional, the commonsensical. They have also included those obsessed by a cause, stunted by an overwhelming need to achieve one very particular aim, willing to work within and without social conventions, and having no moderation in their pursuit of their good.

Women whose lives built this organization, were, and are, a very varied segment of humanity. The importance of National Council has often been summed up as that of a commentator, the voice of much significant female opinion within Canada. Others have described its importance as that of an enlightened lobbyist for the formation of social policies directed towards the needs of women and children. Both these views are correct in themselves, but Council has had a further importance. For many Canadian women it has been an organization for their political and social education, regardless of the value of its activity within the life of the community. Council was not only an organization that helped a considerable and important section of Canadian women to a public voice; it also provided them with information on which to base their opinions, gave them an arena for debate on their differing views, and taught the principles of cooperative action between those of different beliefs. It gave women a way to shape important Canadian policies and institutions, when they were excluded, either through legal disability or social prejudice, from direct influence on the process of Canadian politics. To dismiss them as "ladies in hats and gloves" is not only to dismiss "ladies in hats and gloves" as being an easily categorized group of women, it is to define women by their role — yet one more time. As the next chapters show, women who worked through Council deserve to be known in detail and their work deserves acknowledgement in full.

CHAPTER 1

An International Idea finds a Canadian Interpretation
1893-1894

LESS THAN A generation before the National Council of Women of Canada was established, Canada itself came into being. As the eighteen-nineties opened it was still very much open to question whether Confederation was more than just carpentry, a structure nailed together rather than a living, growing community. Wilfrid Laurier, then Leader of the Opposition, wrote: "We have come to a period in the history of this young country when premature dissolution seems to be at hand ... How long can the present fabric last? Can it last at all? All these questions which surge to the mind, and to which dismal answers only suggest themselves."[1] Ever since the hanging of Louis Riel in 1885, relations between English-speaking and French-speaking Canadians had been strained and acrimonious. In the words of one historian of the period: "Provincialism, unequivocally supported by the Judicial Committee of the [British] Privy Council in the nineties, threatened the delicate fabric of unity, with a cancerous decentralization, dissolution or annexation as the price of its triumph."[2] Maritime satisfaction with Confederation was minimal and the developing West was uncertain as to what, if any, possible benefits there could be in Ottawa's authority. Religious and political partisanship ran bitter and deep. During the decades that saw Canadian federalism become a reality, the founding and growth of the National Council of Women of Canada was of major importance for the unity of the country.

The Council was first and foremost a communication net between

---

[1] Cited from the Laurier papers. See John T. Saywell, "The 1890's," in J.M. Careless and Craig Brown, eds., *The Canadians 1867-1967*, (Toronto, 1970), p. 109.

[2] *Ibid.*

Canadian women. It was made up of two groups: local councils, themselves umbrella-organizations bringing together the societies and associations that existed in their locality, and national associations, such as the Girls' Friendly Society and the Women's Art Association. Most branches of an affiliated national organization would join the local council, if one existed, but the local councils also included branches of national organizations that were not affiliated. For example, the W.C.T.U. at times rejected national affiliation; yet its branches were frequently enthusiastic local council supporters. Local council meetings were usually held monthly, or bi-monthly from September to June. The National Council as a rule met once a year, bringing together delegates from all the local councils and from those associations affiliated at the national level. The Executives at both levels met more frequently. Between the annual meetings of the National Council, contact among members was carried on through visits of the President, correspondence from the Head Office, and a complicated, and frequently revised, committee structure.

As the Standing Committees of the National Council were established, information about particular social problems, and proposed solutions, was sent from one end of the country to the other by the Convenors. Such information was intended to be the grist for the local council meetings, where the particular issue would discussed and debated, and the discussion then reported to each of the affiliates of the local council, through the delegate that the individual affiliate sent to local council meetings. It was expected that each local affiliate would discuss the matter in question, and that its delegate would report its views to the local council meeting. The next step was for the person appointed by the local council, as the corresponding member of the National Council's Committee on the issue, to send the results of the local council's debate to the National Convenor in question. She would prepare a written report for the annual meeting, detailing the questions discussed and any resolutions which local councils suggested for consideration.

The usefulness of this activity depended firstly, upon the efficiency with which the National Convenor of the Committee sent out information, questionnaires and summaries of reports received; secondly, it was a function of the energy and breadth of membership at the local level. Ideally, all local councils would have members appointed to correspond with each of the committees established at the national level. For many local councils, however, the two- or three-member executive handled correspondence with all the national committees. When this method of action worked, which was more often than one might think, it brought together women whose religious beliefs, political affiliations and economic status divided them as they went about their daily lives in the towns and villages of Canada. The local council meetings provided a forum in which social differences could be mitigated, and urgent and obvious contemporary needs could receive attention.

The actual formation of the National Council of Women of Canada in 1893 was the result of two equally important influences. The most obvious of these was the impact upon Canadian women of the international movement, which had seen the foundation of the International Council of Women in Washington, D.C. in 1888. The second, less dramatically visible, influence was that of the tradition of cooperative action by women in Canada. This tradition had already led, by the 1890s, to the establishment of the Women's Christian Temperance Union, the Young Women's Christian Association, the Girls' Friendly Society, the Dominion Order of the King's Daughters and — one of the most significant associations for Canadian women — the Dominion Women's Enfranchisement Association, which was effectively constituted under the Presidency of Dr. Emily Howard Stowe[3] in 1889.

The international influence in the founding of the Council was a striking and, at first sight, an uncomplicated force. After all, the National Council of the Women of Canada was founded explicitly as an organization that would be affiliated with the International Council of Women. The connection is plain. Canadian women were instrumental in founding the international body. The records of the Washington meeting, which founded the International Council of Women, identify six delegates from Canada: among them Dr. Emily Howard Stowe, representing the Dominion Women's Enfranchisement Association and Bessie Starr Keefer, delegate from the Women's Christian Temperance movement.[4] In addition, Mrs. Willoughby Cummings, Mrs. Foster, Mrs Hardy and Mrs. Mary Macdonell are named as being present. Further, the woman who was to be President of the international organization for forty-three years, Lady Aberdeen, arrived in Canada as the wife of the country's Governor General in 1893. This was the year in which she was elected for her first term as President of the International Council of Women.

---

3   Née Jennings. She was born in Norwich, Upper Canada, 1 May 1831 and died in Toronto, 30 April 1903. She married John Stowe in 1856. His illness, and the need to support him and their three children, led her to seek medical training in the United States. She enrolled at the New York Medical College for Women, Graduated in 1867 and set up practice in Toronto. She was instrumental in organizing the Women's Medical College in 1883 and in 1867 she founded the Toronto Women's Literary Club, Canada's first women's suffrage club.
4   Shaw, *Proud Heritage*, p.2.

Thus the impact of international events on the establishment of the National Council of Women of Canada is clear, especially when the personality, character and prestige of Lady Aberdeen are considered. She had been born in London, England, 15 March 1857. She would die in Aberdeen, 18 April 1939. Her grandfather had been a senior partner in Coutts Bank and Queen Victoria's banker. Her father, Edward Majorbanks, was a successful businessmen and was elected to Parliament for Berwick-on-Tweed, as a member of the Liberal Party. Ishbel's mother, Isabella Hogg, was the oldest daughter in a family of seven daughters and seven sons. One of her brothers was Quintin Hogg, the founder of the London Polytechnic Institute. Isabella married Majorbanks in 1848. Ishbel was the third of five surviving children and the youngest daughter. She married John Campbell Gordon, 7th Earl of Aberdeen, 1st Marquess of Aberdeen and Temair, in 1877. Lord Aberdeen was born in Edinburgh, 3 August 1847 and would die in Tarland, Scotland, 7 March 1934. He was educated at St. Andrews University and University College Oxford. He entered the House of Lords, as a supporter of the Liberal party, in 1870.

The Aberdeen marriage had followed a somewhat lengthy and involved courtship, but it developed into a close partnership between two people equally interested in religion, politics and social reform. There were five children, born between 1879 and 1884. Four lived to adulthood: three sons and a daughter. During the early years of their marriage, the Aberdeens were known as social reformers of great piety, and in later years Ishbel would look back with amusement on Gladstone's comment that they were "an edifying couple."[5] However it is clear that, from the outset, the Aberdeens were deeply interested in social issues and it was during these years that they established the "Household Club" for their own servants. This gave rise to persistent rumours that they "ate with the servants" and led to much criticism by their acquaintances of their radical ideas. The "Club" was the beginning of the Onward and Upward Association, an organization for servant girls that eventually comprised "115 branches and 8,280 members across the Scottish countryside."[6] In both cases the aim was as much the creation of a supportive and healthy social life, for those away from family and birthplace, as it was for self-improvement through correspondence courses.

Lord Aberdeen's career was that of a British aristocrat in the days of Empire. Before coming to Canada he had served as Lord Lieutenant of

---

[5] Doris French, *Ishbel and the Empire: A Biography of Lady Aberdeen*, (Toronto, 1988), p. 54.
[6] *Ibid*, p. 53.

Ireland in 1886, a position he would hold again from 1905 to 1915. He was
Canada's Governor General from 1893-1898. Ishbel proved herself a brilliant political hostess and an intelligent, if occasionally partisan, diplomat.
Beautiful, witty and intelligent, self-educated, socially poised, she considered women a great unused civilizing force for the world. Her diaries, begun
when she thirteen, reveal a woman of lively mind, very wide interests and a
capacity for pithy commentary on the life she led.[7] She had an extraordinary
ability to make herself loved and admired by acquaintances and a great
capacity for mediating conflicting views. She was well aware of her own
social standing, and never hesitated to use her social position to advance
views she considered right. Her abiding life-long passion was for the right of
women to be able to contribute fully to the lives of their communities, and
her support of the National Council of Women of Canada in its early years
was of enormous importance for its development and growth.

Canadian women were, however, not merely a passive community living
on the edges of world events and responding to an outside stimulus. The
future of Confederation might be in doubt in the early eighteen-nineties but
Canada did exist as a political entity and one with its own traditions. It is
true that the Canadian women in Washington in 1888 were not there as representatives of a national association of Canadian women, but were either
delegates from particular associations, such as the Dominion Women's
Enfranchisement Association, or as private individuals, but their participation in the discussions was important. They were citizens of a country that
had an acknowledged place within the western world and Canada was no
more exempt than any other country from concerns about the problems of
late nineteenth century society.

Indeed, by the late eighteen-eighties, in common with other urbanized
industrial states, Canada had experienced a sufficient growth in towns and
cities, and a large enough industrialization of the economy, to be confronted
with massive and inescapable problems of social and political injustice. By
1890 nearly 32% of all Canadians, some one and a half million out of a population of not quite five million people, lived in towns.[8] It was not only in
England and France, but also in Montreal and Toronto, that back-to-back
housing was built. Child labour was a commonplace in the textile factories

[7] See Journals 1870 to 1884, Haddo House Collection, Aberdeenshire, Scotland, "Canadian
Journals, 1893-1898," National Archives of Canada, Ottawa. Much of the latter published in John
T. Saywell, ed., *The Canadian Journal of Lady Aberdeen, 1893-1898*, (Champlain Society, Toronto,
1960).

[8] O.J. Firestone, *Canada's Economic Development, 1867-1953*, (London, 1958).

of Canada, as it was in the United States and in England.[9]

Further, in common with most of the other western countries Canada endeavoured both to understand and to find remedies for ills perceived. While there was little unanimity about what to do, there was considerable general agreement about the need to do something. Government after government instituted enquiries and commissions to study what was called in the papal encyclical of Leo XIII written in 1891, "the misery and wretchedness pressing so unjustly on the majority of the working class." There was a widespread consensus that "It is neither just nor human so to grind men down with excessive labour as to stupefy their minds and wear out their bodies." Throughout the eighteen-eighties Canada had seen a whole series of Royal Commissions established to consider what state action was required to ameliorate working and living conditions. Two of the most important were the Royal Commission on Mills and Factories (1882) and the Royal Commission on the Relation Between Capital and Labour (1889). The most important private enquiry of the time was that made into "Conditions of Female Labour in Ontario," an investigation published in 1892.[10]

Many Canadian women were directly involved in the work which resulted from the findings of these deliberative bodies. They became thoroughly acquainted with the inequalities of the society in which they lived, and convinced of the need for social and political action. All denominations of Christianity in Canada, as well as the representatives of Judaism, had, by the mid-nineteenth century, organizations of women dedicated to the social welfare of their fellow believers in particular, and of their community in general.[11] It is in these associations of volunteers that the beginnings of community responsibility for the disadvantaged are to be found. Women such as Henrietta Edwards, who founded the Working Girls' Association in 1875, were actively involved in presenting the need for social reform to the general public.[12] Partly, although not entirely, because they were barred until 1918 from direct participation through the major political representative institutions, women came together in a wide variety of associations, dedicated to

9   D. Suzanne Cross, "The Neglected Majority: The Changing Role of Women in 19th Century Montreal," in Trofimenkoff and Prentice, eds., pp. 66-84.

10 Jean T. Scott, "The Condition of Female Labour in Ontario," (University of Toronto,Studies in Political Science, #3, Toronto, 1982). See also Alice Klein and Wayne Roberts, "Beseiged Innocence: The 'Problem' and Problems of Working Women, Toronto 1896-1914," in *Women at Work in Ontario 1850-1939*, (Toronto, 1974), pp. 211-260.

11 On this see, for example, Patricia E. Malcolmson, "The Poor in Kingston, 1815-1850," paper presented before the C.H.A., Kingston, 1973.

12 She was born in Montreal in 1849. In 1917 she was the Provincial Council Vice-President for Alberta.

1. Lady Ishbel, Marchioness of Aberdeen and Temair, President 1893-1898

influencing the course of public policy. As Hurwitz has pointed out,

> Women reformers in those years fell into two categories, those with
> purely political goals and those with purely social goals. Exclusion
> from the vote symbolized to the political reformer second class citi-
> zenship of women. The social reformers promoted temperance,
> higher education for women, charitable work, women's self develop-
> ment and more career opportunities in professions such as law and
> medicine. They judged the political goal alone to be too narrow.[13]

Many women belonged to a variety of differing organizations, being
interested in both political and social reform as well as the cultural life of
their communities. Within a diversity of groups from the Ladies'
Educational Associations to Civic Improvement Leagues, from the Women's
Missionary Societies to the Women's Christian Temperance Movement,
from the Young Women's Christian Association to the nascent organizations
of professional women, doctors, lawyers and journalists, women came
together to represent publicly their views and ideas on the needs of their
time. At the time that the International Council of Women was founded,
Canada possessed a wide range of women's organizations dedicated to group
action for the improvement of women's lives. It is against this well-established activity that the impact of the International Council of Women — and
of Lady Aberdeen — on Canada must be placed.

The first quinquennial meeting of the International Council of Women
was held in conjunction with the World Congress of Women and the World
Columbian Exposition in Chicago in May 1893. One of the Canadian
women who attended, and one who would work very hard for the establishment of the National Council of Canadian Women, was Adelaide Hoodless.
She had been born on 27 February 1857 at "The Willows," a clapboard farm-
house on Blue Lake Road near the village of St. George, Ontario.[14] Her
mother was the former Jean Hamilton and her father was David Hunter. She
had a rural childhood and a fairly secure adolescence. Education was prized
and she attended a ladies' college in Gainsville for some period of time. It
was in Gainsville, at Zion Church, on the 14 September 1881, that she married John Hoodless, a Hamilton business man three years her elder. When
she was contemplating this marriage, she discussed the matter with her cler-

---

13 Hurwitz, "International Sisterhood," p. 329.
14 Cheryl Macdonald, *Adelaide Hoodless: Domestic Crusader*, (Toronto, 1986), p.13.

gyman. She is reported to have said: "Here I am, a strong Presbyterian and a Whig planning to marry a man who is not only an Anglican but a Tory. What should I do?" His reply was: "My dear, you can be a good Christian in any Church, but stick to your politics!"[15] Adelaide Hoodless would demonstrate this recommended religious tolerance throughout her life. Like tolerance would enable the National Council of Women in Canada to survive bitter sectarian debates during its early years, and to make the local councils extraordinarily effective nets of communication between people holding very different theological beliefs.

In a report she made to the *Hamilton Times* on her return, Adelaide Hoodless remarked that "Canada was about the only country — representing advanced civilization — not officially represented through an official body of women ... There were only five Canadian organizations officially represented at the Congress, the Dominion Women's Christian Temperance Union, the Young Women's Christian Association, the Missionary Society of Canada, the Dominion Order of King's Daughters and the Women's Enfranchisement Association .... You will readily see how unfairly Canadian work was represented, and in order to prevent a repetition of such mistakes the Canadian delegates called a meeting then and there to discuss the question of forming a National Council for Canada. Each of the above mentioned societies had three delegates present, which were supplemented by several Canadian women who were attending the Congress, making in all about twenty-two in attendance."[16]

By late May, 1893, this company of twenty-two women was back in Canada. They included, amongst others, Emily Howard Stowe of the Dominion Women's Enfranchisement Association and Emily Willoughby Cummings of the Anglican Women's Auxiliary. Mrs. Emily Willoughby Cummings was a widow and a working journalist. Whatever term one might use to describe these women, it would not be leisured wives of prosperous men. None had more than moderate financial resources, but through a summer of travelling and correspondence, they helped to organize the founding meeting of the National Council of Women of Canada.

That meeting, held on 27 October 1893[17] in the Horticultural Pavilion in Toronto, was a mass gathering of some fifteen hundred women and a few men. It had been organized basically by women in Toronto, who had sent out

[15] Cited in *Ibid.*, p. 16.
[16] *Ibid.*, p. 30, cited from *Hamilton Times*, ca. November 1893.
[17] This is the date given for the founding of Council in the first *Yearbook*, p. 18. There is some confusion as to whether it was the 26th or the 27th but evidence points to the 27th.

"two hundred special invitations to the presidents and principal officers of all the large Associations of Women in Quebec, Montreal, Kingston, Ottawa, Hamilton and London ..." It was pointed out that invitations were not sent to the "distant provinces" because the shortness of time would not permit attendance.[18] As the *Globe* noted "It was a meeting of women, for women, managed by women." The report took pains to point that nearly every women's association was represented and that "it was an audience not of sharp-featured man-haters, denouncing mankind and scolding the course of civilization" but of "pleasant faced women" representative of "motherly womanliness."[19] It was above all a gathering of people concerned to find ways to promote effective action by women.

The Countess of Aberdeen was elected as the first President of the Council, an office she held until 1899. Her opening speech concluded with the following motion:

> Resolved:- that this meeting do heartily endorse the formation of a national council of women for Canada, believing that by means of such a federation a more intimate knowledge of one another's work will be gained, which will rely in large mutual sympathy, greater unity of thought, and therefore, in more effective actions, especially in matters that may arise from time to time which command a general interest.[20]

When the vote was called, every women in the room stood up to support the motion.

The meeting ended with an Executive being chosen. In addition to Lady Aberdeen as President, Mrs. Macdonell from Toronto, who had served as interim president since May, was elected vice-president for Ontario; Mrs. English, from London, became the recording secretary, Mrs. Hoodless, as treasurer and Mrs. Cummings, another Toronto resident, was appointed the corresponding secretary. There were two honorary vice-presidents-at-large: Lady Thompson, the wife of the Prime Minister and Madame Wilfrid Laurier, the wife of the Leader of the Opposition. The wives of the lieutenant governors were to be honorary vice-presidents for their provinces.

The first meeting of the Executive was held the next day, October 28,

---

[18] *Yearbook*, 1894, p. 19.
[19] *Globe*, 28 October 1893.
[20] *Ibid*.

1893, and work was begun which would lead to the first general meeting of the National Council in Ottawa in April 1894. There were an extraordinary number of difficulties to be faced. The idea of organizing women to work together for the betterment of society was the idea which had aroused such enthusiasm. Now form had to be given to the vision and specific objectives outlined. The enthusiasm had to be channelled and harnessed. Lady Aberdeen had requested the Clerk of the House of Commons, Dr. — later Sir John — Bourinot, to draft constitutions for both the National Council and for the local councils. These constitutions were not only the basis for the work of the Executive but also the key to the successful creation of local and provincial councils. Both constitutions reflect the influence of the constitution and by-laws of the I.C.W., the general goals envisaged by the Canadian women involved and the means they considered appropriate to achieve the desired goals. The texts are to be found in the first yearbook of the National Council which was published in 1894.[21]

The preamble to this first Constitution of the National Council reads:

We, Women of Canada, sincerely believing that the best good of our homes and nation will be advanced by our own greater unity of thought, sympathy and purpose, and that an organized movement of women will best conserve the highest good of the Family and State, do hereby band ourselves together to further the application of the Golden Rule to society, custom and law.

The tone that is struck in this preamble, which some critics have considered to be one of naive idealism, would prove to be one of the strengths of the Council. The assumption implicit in this wording, is that it is possible to provide a framework for cooperation among women who, as individuals, are working for a wide variety of different causes, with very different, if not precisely competing, sets of priorities. It was the affirmation of a broad faith in the possibility of mutual respect and action, arising from according to one another the courtesies each one required for the pursuit of particular goals. The very diffuse expression of good intentions allowed the Council to avoid defining its aims as inextricably linked either with the suffrage movement, or with any particular interpretation of religious faith. What can be easily seen as a woolly-minded piety became a foundation for an organization aimed,

---

[21] *Yearbook,* 1894, pp. 22-27.

above all, at getting its various members to know one another, and to unite for such common purposes as would emerge from this knowledge.

The second article of the national constitution emphasized this deliberate avoidance of partisanship. It is a very close paraphrase of Article II of the constitution of the ICW and reads:

> This council is organized in the interest of no one propaganda, and has no power over the organizations which constitute it beyond that of suggestion and sympathy; therefore, no society voting to enter this council shall render itself liable to be interfered with in respect to its complete organic unity, independence or method of work, or be committed to any principal method of any other society, or to any act or utterance of the council itself, beyond compliance with the terms of this constitution.

Reading the preamble and this article in combination will make the assumptions behind the formation of the National Council quite clear. Firstly, as was the case with the foundation of the International Council of Women, there was the belief that an organization of women was a good in itself. Secondly, there was a clear belief that Canadian society had an ideal of womanhood and that this ideal would be a powerful weapon for the betterment of society.

Much has been written about the prevalence of this second idea in western civilization at the end of the nineteenth century. One Canadian historian has referred to the International Council of Women itself as "a gigantic maternal union."[22] Unquestionably there was, as the nineteenth century closed, a generalized belief among many, both men and women, working for the reform of social ills, that women were naturally endowed with a finer nature, a more spiritual outlook, than men. Those who spoke for the ambitions of the International Council of Women, in 1888 and 1893, had emphasized, again and again, that their purpose was to use what one delegate, Madame St. Croix from France, called "the motherheart of the world.[23]"

This idea was reiterated in the introduction to the first *Yearbook* of the Council, which was published in 1894 with the title *Women Workers of Canada; Being a Report of the Proceedings of the First Annual Meeting*

22 Strong-Boag, *Parliament of Women*, p. 74.
23 Hurwitz, "International Sisterhood," p. 331.

and Conference of the National Council of Women of Canada. The introduction was probably written by Mrs. John English, and she quotes from an
anonymous source as follows:

> It seems plain that the drift of things is in the direction of the devel-
> opment of womanhood and the virtues and Christian graces which
> woman represents, and that the great factor in the future evolution of
> Society must by the nature of things and by all the traditions of the
> world's past, by all the laws of nature, by all facts of science, be the
> ascent of woman.

The Introduction continues: "Happily there are abundant signs that this
ascent will be for the benediction of humanity."

The idea of certain innate human characteristics being the exclusive
property of either women or men is an idea that has lost much authority in
the years since the late eighteen-nineties. That this is so should not lead to an
undervaluation of the importance of what the vision of women's role as a
moral force meant in the eighteen-nineties. Further, as the years passed and
the notion of an inborn humane feminine characteristic diminished in importance, those involved in the National Council of Women of Canada began
the far more difficult task of working to ensure that a value system for their
efforts was brought into existence. If women were not naturally gifted for
motherhood, then the qualities which good mothering demanded should be
analyzed and women helped to acquire them. If women did not have a natural aesthetic appreciation, then the value of the beautiful must be explained,
defined, and defended. If there was no general code of righteousness and
purity to which women had an inherent and privileged understanding by the
very fact of their sex, women must set about discovering what were basic
social requirements in this field. Such a philosophy would make possible
coherent action by the National Council, and enable the organization to provide an essential forum in which women could debate fundamental issues of
Canadian social policy.

In 1893, the National Council was not yet confronted with the necessity
of making such complex arguments. Convinced that womanhood was something that existed, and that it embodied an innate good, those who founded
the Council were equally convinced that this belief was generally held in
Canada and would make the new organization immensely powerful. Mrs.
Emily Cummings, the Corresponding Secretary who helped to establish a
local council in Hamilton, drew this point to the attention of those who gath-

ered to found that branch of the association on November 17, 1893. She cited:

> ...the case of protests recently made by the women of British Columbia against the horrible practice of selling Chinese women which prevails along the coast with the full knowledge of the Dominion Government. This protest was supported by all the Mission Boards..and..was pigeonholed in the Customs Department and no further notice taken of it. Now had such a protest emanated from a National Council of Women it would at least have been thought worthy of notice and might have been successful.[24]

The constitution proposed for the local councils reiterated the axioms embodied in the senior document. The preamble to the former reads:

> ....believing that the more intimate knowledge of one another's work will result in larger mutual sympathy and greater unity of thought and therefore in more effective action, certain Associations of Women interested in Philanthropy, Religion, Education, Literature, Art, and Social Reform, have determined to organize Local Councils...

Similarly, Article II of the constitution proposed for all local councils noted that:

> The aim of a Local Council is to bring the various Associations in [name of town] into a closer relations [sic] through an organised union; but no Society entering a Local Council shall thereby lose its independence in aim or method, or be committed to any principle or method of any other Society in the Council, the object of which is to serve as a medium of communication and a means of prosecuting any work of common interest.

Whatever a skeptical mind of a later age might say, there is no doubt that these broadly framed principles of attitude and action proved immediately popular.

---

[24] Cited from the *Hamilton Times*, in Macdonald, *Adelaide Hoodless*, p. 37.

At 10 o'clock on the morning of Wednesday April 11, 1894 the first annual meeting of the National Council of Women of Canada was brought to order by the President, Her Excellency Lady Aberdeen. She herself made the opening speech. During the months since the founding meeting in Toronto, Lady Aberdeen had seen more than enough to convince her of the continuing necessity for social reform in the country. Her visit to Toronto for the founding of the National Council had given her the opportunity to ask plain questions about the poverty in that city. When the Directors of the Y.M.C.A. told her that the city of 181,215 had more than 800 applications from the destitute for aid, she noted in her diary "So much for the common saying that there are no poor here."[25] Her diary entries, during her visits to Quebec City and Montreal over the next months, reveals the growing strength of her opinion that organized philanthropy was essential to the well-being of society.[26] At the same time, the beliefs she had expressed at the founding meeting concerning the need to break down barriers between competing faiths within society, were actually reinforced by the open hostility she experienced to this very idea. Appearing in London at the Opera house in February 1894, before a crowd of two thousand, she had to face Mrs. Thornby, the president of the W.C.T.U. Mrs. Thornby and Lady Aberdeen were not particularly empathetic to one another, since Lady Aberdeen had already informed the Association that she and husband were not abstainers "and could not be in accord with some of their methods..."[27] In the public meeting Mrs. Thornby asked whether the Council was going to include societies "not acknowledging God and Christ." Lady Aberdeen wrote in her diary that she replied:

We were to include all societies and institutions. Most seemed quite satisfied...but she will doubtless give trouble and would not mind excluding R.C.'s, Jews, Unitarians and Quakers..[28]

The result of such experiences showed in her opening remarks to the conference in 1894. She began her speech by emphasizing the common religious faith of those present. "We represent here different creeds, different churches, different races, different views and schools of thought," she said,

---

[25] "Canadian Journals," 25 October 1893.
[26] *Ibid.*
[27] *Ibid.*, 13 September 1893.
[28] "Aberdeen Diaries," 14 February 1894.

"but we are all children of the same Father and we have a right to approach Him in the way which we feel would be the most real and true, remembering that God is a spirit and they who approach Him must approach Him in spirit and truth." She went on to say, "Therefore I think that our Executive is right in inviting this National Council this morning to commend themselves and their work to our Heavenly Father in silent prayer." By this action Lady Aberdeen made possible the continued affiliation of Jewish and Roman Catholic women. It was an act of courageous and far-sighted leadership in a decade when religious debate was particularly bitter in Canada. Nevertheless it caused much criticism, and would engender considerable controversy in the local councils over the next thirty years. Tolerance was the aim but was not to be easily achieved.

Lady Aberdeen's opening remarks were followed by a welcoming speech from the President of the Ottawa Local Council, Lady Ritchie,[29] and a *Report* from the Executive on the growth of the Council.[30] This growth was not only an indication of the strength of support from individual women for the organization, but also evidence of the extraordinarily diverse nature of the societies which the local councils brought together. The number of women who came out to the meetings that resulted in local councils was certainly impressive, and has often been commented upon. Lady Aberdeen was present for the first meetings of all the local councils formed between October 1893 and April 1894, except for that of Winnipeg. It could be argued that the presence of the Governor General's wife made such occasions a social event and that Lady Aberdeen's role as President of the National Council was a secondary matter. But there is no doubt that the idea of the Council itself aroused enthusiasm. As striking as these figures of individual attendance at the founding meetings may be, the assortment of societies that were drawn in to meet one another was even more remarkable. It is this wide variety of organizations that actually affiliated at the local level which reveals the force of the idea of cooperation among women across bar-

---

[29] She was the daughter of Thomson Nicholson and Amy Gardner and married, as his second wife, the Hon. William Johnston Ritchie, a judge of the Supreme Court of New Brunswick. He was made Chief Justice of that province in 1865, a Judge of the Supreme Court of Canada in 1875, and the Chief of Justice of Canada in 1879. His knighthood was bestowed in 1881. He died in 1892. Lady Ritchie's volunteer interests encompassed both the Woman's Humane Society and the Women's Canadian Historical Society. She was a founding member of the Ottawa Local Council of Women.

[30] This Report, summarized here, is printed in *The First Yearbook of the National Council of the Women of Canada, 1893-4*, pp. 18-21. The NCWC has published an annual account of its work since it began. Sometimes these accounts have been called "Yearbooks," sometimes "Reports," and sometimes "Proceedings" and, occasionally, "Women Workers of Canada" (1896). Hereinafter, this publication will be referred to as *Yearbook*.

riers of divergent beliefs.

Lady Ritchie has often been severely criticized for the insensitivity of the remarks she made in her speech of welcome at the First Annual meeting. In attempting to underline the fundamental intent of cooperation between those of differing ideas, she remarked that "The Golden Rule furnishes the basis of union, making no surrender of our own convictions, claiming respectful attention for the interest we represent and liberty to enjoy our own belief. Justice impels us to offer in return the same respect for what others hold to be truth and duty." She continued: "Catholic, Protestant, Jew and Gentile may here join hands in a practical Christianity." Insensitive she may have been, but her speech was a step in the development of a non-sectarian approach to social problems. Religious partisanship was, along with its political counterpart, to be a major concern for the Council at both the local and national level for many years. That it could be overcome at all in the local councils is both a testimony to the ideals proposed, and to the importance attributed to work of the Council by those who joined. People were willing to act in concert with what Lady Ritchie affirmed as a basic principle later on in her speech, the maxim that "a difference of opinion on one question must not prevent us from working unitedly in those on which we can agree."

Toronto was the first city to form a local council. The founding meeting was held on 2 November 1893 bringing together more than 200 women who represented some forty-nine different societies.[31] Within a month sixteen societies had federated; the first quarterly meeting was held on 11 December, at which fifty-six of their elected representatives were present. A considerable encouragement was giving to the fledgling organization in February 1894. On the 19th of that month, in the Horticultural Pavilion, a general meeting assembled in Lady Aberdeen's presence to hear an address by Dr. Lelia Davis on "The Condition of the Unemployed." 3,000 women attended and the following resolution was passed:

> That the Council desire to express their sympathy with the many persons suffering from the want of employment, and request the delegates to bring the matter before their several Societies, with a view to their taking action toward the amelioration of the condition of the unemployed.[32]

---

[31] Anon, *Nothing New Under the Sun: A History of the Toronto Council of Women*, (Toronto, 1978), p. 28.
[32] *Yearbook*, 1894, p. 30.

In reporting this action to the first annual meeting of the NCWC, Mrs. S.M. Grant and Mrs. Dignam — respectively President and Recording Secretary — went on to recount that the memorial was presented and

> a Civic Employment Bureau was opened at the City Hall with as little delay as possible. The first morning four hundred persons, including teachers, book-keepers, accountants and all kinds of mechanics and domestic servants registered as desiring work.

By March 1894 another seven affiliates had joined, and the Executive were already coping with problems related to voting by members who were delegates of more than one society, it being decided that such delegates would only have one vote on questions before Council. By spring 1894, therefore, the Toronto Local Council was truly in being. Its membership included eleven associations that considered their work philanthropic, namely the Infants' Home and Infirmary; the Convalescent Home; the Humane Society; the Girls' Industrial Institute; the Moses Montifiore Benevolent Society; the Boys' Home; the Toronto Relief Society; the Industrial Rooms Association; the Orphan Girls' Home. Two societies were listed under the title "Literature and Art": the Women's Art Association and the Women's Literary Society, Toronto University. There were seven religious organizations: the Church of England Auxiliary to Missions; the Methodist Women's Missionary Society; the Primary Sunday School Teachers' Union; the Young Women's Christian Association; the Women's Christian Temperance Union; the Roman Catholic Woman's Work and the Young Women's Christian Guild. Under the heading "Not Classified" were listed the Working Woman's Protective Association; the Toronto Union of King's Daughters; the Ministering Children's League and the Women's Enfranchisement Association. In their report, the Toronto Local Council said that it considered that:

> Six of the federated Societies have for their object the benefit of children; one...the consideration of Social problems; one, Sunday School Work; one, Temperance; one Woman's Enfranchisement; and three, work in the interests of Industrial Reform.[33]

---

33 *Ibid.,* p. 31.

Hamilton, following Toronto, organized its branch on 17 November 1893 with thirty-two federated societies. As well as most of the organizations Toronto had assembled, Hamilton also included within its philanthropic organizations the Society for Prevention of Cruelty to Animals. The Hebrew Women's Society was listed among the religious groups, and Hamilton brought together a number of societies under the heading "Educational": the Senior Section of the Hamilton Teachers' Association; the Third Book section of the Hamilton Teachers' Association; the Second Book Section of the Hamilton Teachers' Association; the Kindergarten Department of the Hamilton Teachers' Association and the Wesleyan Female College. In the "Unclassified" section Hamilton listed, among others, the Newsboy Club; the Women's Stenographic Club; the Librarians and Civil Service Association; the Wentworth Historical Society and The Press.

In Montreal, the Victoria Armouries were packed on the night of 30 November 1893 when that city's local council was established.[34] This founding meeting brought together thirty-two societies, most of them very similar to the societies which had come together in Toronto and Hamilton. The list of philanthropic societies, however, was headed by the Women's Protective Immigration Society and none of the societies listed were either Catholic or French. A Madame Thibaudeau was, however, elected as a vice-president. The Ladies' Aid Society of Spanish and Portuguese Jews and the Ladies' Sewing Society of Spanish and Portuguese Jews were among the Church societies listed. During the first months of its existence, the Montreal Council spent considerable time on drafting its by-laws and committee structures. It decided that it would have four committees, each one of which would report monthly on its work. They were called:

Committee of Report of Philanthropy and Benevolence
Committee of Report on Work for Women and Children
Committee of Report on Work by Church Societies
Committee of Report on Music, Art and Education.[35]

The Ottawa Local Council was established on January 16, 1894 and brought together twenty-seven federated societies. This council added an important clause to the constitution for local councils. It read:

34 "The Countess' Busy Day," *Montreal Gazette*, 1 December 1893.
35 *Yearbook*, 1894, p. 31.

Any woman representing various organizations, which by reason of internal regulations cannot affiliate, and which it is at the same time desirable to have represented, may be invited by the President and Executive to join the Committee.

It was under this clause that six Roman Catholic ladies were elected to the Council. They represented the Convent of the Good Shepherd; St. Patrick's Orphan Home; St. Bridget's Sewing Society; L'Asile Bethlehem; The Orphanage of St. Joseph and La Congregation de Nôtre Dame.

The organization of the London Local Council began on January 16, 1894, with "one hundred representative ladies" gathered together to consider the matter. Mrs. English was appointed Provisional President and it was decided to call a public meeting. Lady Aberdeen agreed to attend on the appointed day, February 14, and, as the report to the NCWC annual meeting stated:

Long before the hour arrived the Opera House was filled to over-flowing, it was estimated that fully two thousand persons were present and at least one thousand disappointed ones were turned home.[36]

This local council was the first to challenge the rules that had been laid down by the founding meeting of the NCWC. It proposed to change the pre-amble of its constitution by inserting the words: "Certain Associations of Women who believe in God and in His Son our Saviour, the Lord Jesus Christ." Lady Aberdeen reacted immediately and, as the Report of the Local Council of Women of London to the NCWC noted:

As soon as Her Excellency learned of the change she explained that the Local Councils could not alter the Constitution in such a manner, and at our first meeting, held on the 6th of April we adopted the original Preamble as offered by the Executive of the Dominion Council of Women.[37]

At the annual meeting, London reported ten affiliated societies.

The Winnipeg Local Council was brought together on February 24 and

---

[36] *Ibid.*, p. 40.
[37] *Ibid.*

the six societies affiliated were: the Children's Home; the Woman's Hospital Aid Society; the Central Woman's Christian Temperance Union; the Free Kindergarten; the Women's Christian Union; the Young Woman's Christian Temperance Union and the Lady Aberdeen Association. The Quebec Local Council barely existed, having been brought together on April 3, 1894 and having appointed both English and French Secretaries. At the time of the annual meeting it existed only on paper. Kingston organized its council immediately following the first Annual General Meeting. In addition to the eight affiliated local councils, the Executive reported that the following nationally organized societies had joined the Council: the Woman's Art Association of Canada; the Girls' Friendly Society of Canada; and the Dominion Woman's Enfranchisement Association.

The first Annual General Meeting had allowed time for the local councils to report their activities over the past months. One can smile with considerable sympathy at the unselfconsciousness of these first accounts. In reporting on the Winnipeg Local Council, for example, Mrs. Schultz, the wife of the Lieutenant-Governor of Manitoba and President of the Winnipeg Local Council, remarked that she had not been aware she would have to speak, and while she could recollect some of the societies that had affiliated, "the names of all the other societies I cannot at the moment remember, as I am not accustomed to speak this, and have forgotten them at the moment." In future years these reports would convey the reality of the grass-roots work of the Council, but in the spring of 1894 there was little to note. Likewise, the reports from the national associations that had joined the Council were short, a compendium of good wishes rather than requests for endorsement of action.

A good deal of time was spent by this first annual meeting on the actual functioning structure of Council. Agreement was reached on details of the clauses in the constitution dealing with the appointment of officers, membership rules, frequency of meetings, fees, the possibility of patrons and the way in which constitutional amendments could be brought about.[38] The question of fees, and of the possibility of patrons, would be discussed over and over again during the life of the NCWC. Since the Council was, at both levels, essentially a federation of volunteer organizations the need for it to be self-financing was obvious from the outset. The fees were $5 per annum for each local council and $2 for each nationally organized association federated to

---

[38] *Ibid.,* pp. 23-27.

the National Council. Patrons were also solicited, and, if found acceptable by the Executive Committee, would be charged a $10 fee for an annual membership, and a $100 fee for a life-time membership. Individuals, it was decided, could also become members of Council by payment of $1 annually. This would entitle such a person to participate in meetings but not to vote. Individual membership in Council was never very great. Within a short time, at both the local and national level, it was decided that this category of membership should be restricted to less than 30% of the total membership of a particular Council.

As to the election of officers, only one nomination was made for any of the positions in 1894 — Corresponding Secretary, Recording Secretary and Treasurer — so no ballot was necessary. The Executive Committee included the Honorary Vice-Presidents, who were the wives of the Lieutenant-Governors of the Provinces, the Presidents of the local councils already founded, and the Presidents of the nationally federated associations, the Women's Art Association of Canada, the Girls' Friendly Society of Canada and the Dominion Women's Enfranchisement Association.

Adelaide Hoodless was the Treasurer and her Report was simplicity itself. It showed that the Council had gathered in receipts, between October 10, 1893 and April 12, 1894, $187.65. It had disbursed the same amount, mostly on office supplies. However $3 had been spent on January 8, 1894 for flowers.

While a great deal of time at this first Annual General Meeting was devoted to the minutiae of organization, substantive matters were also addressed. There a were number of "Public Conferences", seminars on matters the Executive had decided were of importance to Council; a plenary session devoted to resolutions concerning action to be taken about certain issues; an evening public meeting which was attended not only by His Excellency the Governor General, but also by other leading personalities, including His Honour the Lieutenant Governor of Manitoba, Sir John Christian Schultz, and the Right Honourable Sir John Thompson, the then Prime Minister of Canada, the Reverend G.M. Grant, Principal of Queen's University, and Mr. Justice Adolphe Routhier of the Superior Court of Quebec. Wilfrid Laurier, Leader of the Opposition, sent his regrets. This occasion was a very important demonstration of the support for the National Council by leaders of the Canadian political and religious elites.

Just as the constitutions adopted by Council at the national and local level convey something of the ideals of the founders, and the opening speeches of the Annual General Meeting illustrate the convictions of leaders

of the movement about the principles on which it was being developed, the
conferences themselves provide information about problems the Council
members considered of prime importance. The afternoon sessions of April
11, 1894 were three in number and dealt with questions of cooperative
action. The first centred upon "Co-operation in work and its advantages"; the
second upon "Women's clubs and their benefits" and the third upon "The
Relation of parents and children, and its responsibilities." The most radical
discussions of the first session were those resulting from a paper given by
Lady Aberdeen on "The Co-operation of Working Women for Protective
Purposes." She used material she had obtained from the President of the
Women's Protective Union in Toronto, and gave the meeting a vivid descrip-
tion of sweated labour. In part her speech reads:

> ...the conditions and surroundings of many of the factory girls, and
> the low wages that many of them receive; some as low as $2.00 a
> week, $3.00 being the general ...it would be very difficult for these
> girls to support themselves... a woman is only given 14 cents for a
> boy's coat with three pockets in it, 35 cents for a waistcoat, which
> takes a day and a half to make, and 50 cents a dozen for small arti-
> cles, thread having to be supplied by the workers.[39]

In the debate which followed women argued over what caused the situation.
Lady Aberdeen had concluded her communication by asking her audience to
consider whether "when we are trying to get bargains, to rush after cheap-
ness, we are not getting them at the price of our sisters' lives." Mrs. Tilley,
vice-president of the London Local Council, remarked that "the craving for
bargains is at the bottom of the whole thing."

The session devoted to "Women's Clubs and their benefits" included
papers about topics which were to become a very important area of action
for local councils: that of associations aimed at supporting artistic and cultural activities. The papers presented and the topics discussed show a high level
of critical thinking. Mrs. Dignam,[40] President of the Women's Art

---

[39] *Ibid.*, p. 61.
[40] She was of United Empire Loyalist descent, born at Charlotteville, Ontario, January 13, 1859 to
Byron and Margaret (Ferguson) Williams. She died in 1940. She pursued artistic studies in the
United States, France, Italy and Holland. She married John Sifton Dignam, March 2, 1880. They
had three children. She was a considerable painter with exhibitions in New York, Chicago,
Philadelphia, Paris and London. She was as important to the International Council as she was to
the Canadian Council.

Association in Toronto did not hesitate to attack what she called "the greatest decorative craze that ever struck this country."[41] She commented most unfavourably on the "indiscriminate decoration of milk-stools, butter-bowls, pots, pans, draintiles and fabrics of all kinds, with birds, fish, fowl and reptiles, landscapes, flowers and fruit..." Her paper continued with sharp criticism of sentimental paintings and a plea for recognition of the strength of simple design. She had obviously been much influenced by a sojourn in Europe and acquaintance with the works and ideas of William Morris.

The final sessions that Wednesday afternoon focused upon ideas about bringing up children. Mrs. Emily Stowe, President of the Dominion Women's Enfranchisement Association, said that she had been deeply impressed by the papers on the management of children, but she went on to remark that:

> .... the principles laid down in the paper by Miss Laidlaw are excellent, but there was not a word said about girls, and with one exception the pronouns "he" and "him" were used exclusively.[42]

Whatever else the sessions provided in the way of hard information, the discussions following the papers were what has become known, in the late twentieth century, as consciousness raising.

The afternoon sessions of April 12, 1894 were concerned with problems of women's work and were again divided into three: the first concerned itself with "Women's Work in connection with social reform"; the second with "Women's work in connection with the sick"; the third with "The problem of domestic service." It is interesting that among the papers given in the first session was one given in French by Madame Routhier,[43] who was the President of the Quebec Local Council. The tone of all three papers in the session concerning social reform was one of exasperated frustration. The theme of Madame Routhier's paper (which is given in both French and English in the Yearbook) was illegitimacy. Her survey of conditions in Quebec paid as much attention to the distress and despair of the young mother as to the demands of the new child. Her paper did not suggest anything more than a continuance of philanthropic work as a solution to the problems she described. It was followed by one presented by Henrietta Day Smith, the

---

[41] *Yearbook,* 1894, p. 77.
[42] *Ibid.,* p. 97.
[43] She was the wife of Mr. Justice Adolphe Routhier.

President of Hamilton's branch of the Women's Christian Temperance Union. Her solution for Canada's ills was abstinence from alcohol and tobacco.

The most interesting note was struck in papers which dealt with the question of women and nursing. It was the general consensus that the public should be better educated about medical matters. The paper given by Mrs. Tilley, from London, Ontario, was entitled "Nursing the Poor in their own Homes." Much of the paper was descriptive, relating what "visiting the poor" meant in terms of the provision of actual nursing and social welfare. The first meant everything from bathing the sick, changing bed linen, providing simple medical treatment, ranging from massage to midwifery care, including the provision of "all articles needed by mother and infant, including sheets, pillow cases, and towels." The latter entailed "teaching and directing the children" how to help, providing and cooking food, and cleaning house. It is in this address that the idea of a "corps of trained nurses" for such work is mentioned, something that lay behind the development of the Victorian Order of Nurses by the National Council some years later.[44]

The second paper, by Mrs. Hodgins of Toronto, dealt with "The Benefit of Emergency Lectures." It is clear that the speaker is praising something very much like the present-day short courses on cardio-pulmonary resuscitation techniques and first-aid, generally taught by organizations such as the St. John Ambulance Society and the Red Cross. During discussion at the close of the papers, there was a general exchange of views on how best to resuscitate a drowning victim, how to make poultices and bandages for the head, and how to cope with fainting fits and heart attacks.

The third and final session raised an issue that has discomfited many a late-twentieth century feminist: "The Problem of Domestic Service." The very idea that the National Council of Women of Canada should devote a session to the issue of domestic servants has often been harshly criticized. It is seen as essentially a class-based, self-serving pre-occupation.[45] It needs to be considered in some detail here, because the work of the National Council of Women of Canada has often been dismissed as the work of an association

---

[44] *Yearbook*, 1894, p. 144.

[45] One of the clearest commentaries on this issue, from this point of view, is that of Veronica Strong-Boag who wrote:The Council's efforts to encourage working class women to enter domestic service complemented its drive to legitimize the expansion of the feminine sphere beyond the home. Domestic emancipation,however, was implicitly reserved for the upper classes. New opportunities for club members and their friends depended not on the repudiation of the domestic myth but on the substitution of different personnel of the same sex in the house.Strong-Boag, *Parliament of Women*, p. 212.

of "Lady Bountifuls," basically pursuing self-serving ambitions. To have employees dedicated to running your personal household conveys the image of the wealthy, powerful and insensitive exploiting the poor, powerless and suffering — an exploitation, moreover, that could be avoided. To many such commentators, the use of servants seems an immoral, unnecessary self-indulgence. Marilyn Barber expresses something of this point of view when she remarks that "middle class women could extend their activities to include social reform because they had servants to do the work at home."[46]

Such a judgment seems to be an over-simplification. Firstly, it implies that middle class women were the only people who employed servants, overlooking men as beneficiaries of domestic service. It ignores the fact that men always formed the largest percentage of servants in the work-force, even if the work of the male servant was less obviously under the continuous and direct supervision of the employer.[47] The work of the male servant was more frequently outside work: handyman, gardener, the care of horse and carriage. It also demanded fewer "rituals of deference" from the employee. Nevertheless, men were also servants in the house: scullery lads, boot-boys, valets, butlers and cooks. But the principal thrust of the criticism is that civic responsibilities and community service carried out by the women who paid to have household work performed, is somehow tarnished.

Secondly, it is a judgment that overlooks the norm of Canadian social mores at the close of the nineteenth century. To Council women before 1914, the problem was both less and more perplexing than for today's feminist. It was a less complex matter because having daily help in the home was much more widespread than it is now, and the institution of domestic service was less questioned. Before 1914, it was a common enough practice for Canadian farm households, with minimum resources, to employ a hired girl as well as a hired man. In towns, even the moderately circumstanced were accustomed to hire household servants. In 1881 the proportion of female servants to households was 1 to 16.2 (800,410 households); in 1891 it was 1 to 11.3 (900,080 households); in 1901, 1 to 13.0 (1,058,386 households); in 1911 it was 1 to 15.1 (1,482,980 households) and in 1921, 1 to 21.4 (1,897,227).[48] Or, to put it another way, in 1891, this category represented 41% of the female work force. In 1921 domestics were only 18% of all employed women.[49]

---

[46] Marilyn Barber, *Immigrant Domestic Servants in Canada*, (Canadian Historical Association Booklet No.16, Ottawa, 1991), p. 8.

[47] Sixth Census of Canada Volume III - Population, p. 3, vol. IV - Occupations pp. 2-3, (Ottawa, 1927).

[48] Table given in Genevieve Leslie,"Domestic Service in Canada, 1890-1920," in *Women at Work, Ontario, 1850-1930*, (Toronto, 1974), p. 75.

[49] *Ibid.*, p. 71.

The change in these statistics was largely attributed to the availability of other work for women, but also to improvement in domestic technologies which diminished the demand for domestic servants. The work required to run households, whether urban or rural, was greatly reduced by the application of electricity to the home, the development of efficient wood and coal stoves, which demanded less back-breaking work before they produced both heat for cooking and warmth for the house, and improved plumbing, which meant that clean running water was available for all the usual purposes of personal hygiene, as well as the household laundry and general cleaning. Changes both in the style and availability of manufactured clothing also diminished household work. Voluminous garments, made from linen, cotton and wool, demand techniques of sewing, washing, starching and ironing that are time-consuming even with present-day washing and drying machines and electric irons. At the turn of the century, the washday was not only a day of exhausting labour as water was boiled, household linens, shirts and socks, blouses and underwear, diapers and bed-clothes were soaked, washed, rinsed, wrung out, and put out to dry; it was also the prelude to hours of ironing, with tools that demanded a fire even in the hottest weather. Dusting, sweeping, polishing and cleaning, washing pots and pans, scrubbing bathrooms with soap, soda and beeswax, the main aids to the tasks, took skill as well as energy and strength. One might wish to be critical of women employing other women to help run their houses, but one cannot deny the work-load that gave rise to the practice.

At this first annual meeting of the National Council "The Problem of Domestic Servants" was addressed by Mrs. Boomer,[50] Mrs. Helliwell, and Mrs. Stowe. The paper-givers understood clearly enough that household work was as onerous as it was necessary, and that good help was a boon. The possibilities for the exploitation of servants in a class-conscious society were recognized. In her paper, which was entitled "From the servants' point of view" Mrs. Helliwell, Toronto Local Council, said, "I am speaking of the general servant...her lot is usually a hard one, her room often the worst in the house, her furniture, her bed etc., of the cheapest and commonest kind, and

50 Mrs. Harriet Boomer had emigrated from England to the Red River Settlement with her widowed mother, Mrs. Mills, in 1851. The latter was head of a ladies' school there but the two returned to England for five years in order for Mrs. Mills to take up an appointment as the head of Queen's College, Harley Street, London. Harriet married Alfred Roche and went with him to South Africa. Widowed, she married Dean Boomer, of the diocese of Huron, Ontario, in November 1878. She was a representative for the Mother's Union on the London Council.

she often, I grieve to say, after working hard all day, goes tired out to a cold, comfortless room to rest or sleep in."[51] Domestic work could be as soul-destroying as any employment in a factory.

The National Council of Women members were well aware that there was a considerable difference, for servants, between the household that employed more than one domestic, and the one that relied upon "a general" who would stoke a coal range at 6 a.m., and spend the next seventeen hours fetching, carrying, washing dishes, cleaning rooms, and helping to cook and care for children. Mrs. Boomer in particular showed an awareness that those who employed servants would be best served if they remembered that servants were people first, servants second. Mrs. Stowe considered that much of the difficulty lay in the refusal to acknowledge the importance of domestic work. "Housewifery" she remarked, "is of all the industries the most neglected in its preparation. The most degraded because of this neglect, the most shunned because the most degraded."[52] For her, and for many another Council member, the solution was training, the establishment of domestic science courses, and the organization of apprenticeships for women.

In the final analysis, the attitude of Council towards the conditions of employment for women in the homes of the middle class was very much the same as its attitude towards the employment of women generally: conditions ought to be humane. There is no doubt that status concerns and class consciousness were present at the meetings of Council, nor that the majority of those who worked at both the local and the national level accepted the social hierarchy of the times, and were from the ranks of the comfortably circumstanced. There is also no question that the possibility of society without individual servants, or servants as part of the working class, would have seemed implausible to many of these women in the last decade of the nineteenth century. They were, for the most part, concerned about the functioning of their society rather than the creation of a new world. They were, by upbringing and through their marriages, the counterparts of the established male elites. It is not surprising that many of their reforms centred upon the better ordering of what existed, rather than the initiation of a new social order.

Two afternoons of the annual meeting had been given over to papers, and only a single morning to the consideration of resolutions and actions to be taken by the National Council as a whole. However, the Thursday morning session set the work of the Council afoot in a number of extremely

---

51   *Yearbook*, 1894, pp. 160-163.
52   *Ibid.*, p. 164.

2. Washday

important areas of Canadian life. As well, the desire for the promotion of patriotic feeling led to the establishment of a prize of $2000 (a very considerable sum of money) for the publication of a Dominion school history. The work was to be

> furnished with full, accurate maps on which every place mentioned in the letterpress is given, the history to be written in a clear, simple, captivating style, the author with skill and power combining the whole record of Indian romance, French chivalry and British endeavors to confer the boon of constitutional Government upon its people, into one complete and powerful record of colonial development, which shall be a delight to all students.[53]

Unfortunately, nothing seems to have resulted from this initiative.

Turning from the work of strengthening the sense of Canadian unity, the meeting went on to consider petitioning the provincial governments "for the appointment of women inspectors for the factories and workshops where women are employed." This was passed unanimously, as was the motion that followed, respecting the appointment of police matrons. Such resolutions were moved, in the first place, to improve the environment of working women, and of girls caught up young into criminal activity. But the implementation of such resolution had the unexpected result of opening up professional occupations for women, thereby offering the possibility of better training and better jobs.

The issue of women's education was more directly addressed by the next resolution presented, and sparked considerable discussion. The motion was presented by Adelaide Hoodless, and read as follows:

> This National Council of Women of Canada do all in its power to further the introduction of Manual Training for girls into the Public School System of Canada, believing that such training will greatly conduce to the general welfare of Canadian homes...[54]

What Hoodless was fighting for was practical instruction that was linked to probable future occupation. Such a seemingly simple ambition was one that would lead the Council, in future debates, through a very complex set of issues, particularly in the General Meetings of 1896 and 1897. Underneath

---

[53] *Ibid.,* p. 104.
[54] *Ibid.,* p. 114.

the field of work which Adelaide Hoodless made a life's preoccupation, lay a quagmire: the whole issue of whether men and women should be trained for "separate spheres." In 1894 Hoodless was quite clear that housekeeping was a field of knowledge, a pursuit demanding intelligence, talent and expertise. She cited in her speech an American statistic as to the amount of food wasted annually in the United States because of bad management and ignorance. Against a background in which refrigeration was rare and labour-saving devices for preparation and cooking few and far-between, her proposals for training had considerable force. Moreover, she did not confine her syllabus proposals to cooking. She also wanted instruction to be given in needlework, sewing and mending and garment making, knitting, and practical advice on cleanliness and house furnishings and kitchen gardens. The resolution was passed and signalled the beginning of interest in the "right" education for women, and many a debate on that subject at annual meetings of the National Council. Decisions about the time and place of the 1895 annual meeting concluded the morning's business.

A final public meeting took place that Thursday evening, April 12, 1894 in the Assembly Hall of the Normal School in Ottawa. Its importance should not be underestimated. It was much more than an occasion where expressions of goodwill were uttered by a number of important men. It was a demonstration of the social power that the National Council of Women of Canada had managed to mobilize. The early eighteen-nineties had not only been years of bitter political and religious partisanship, they had also seen the arrival of a major economic turn-down in 1893, which led to growing misery in town and countryside. Wage rates were depressed and class consciousness grew sharper. There was mounting popular criticism of the way in which businessmen conducted their affairs, as the trends towards monopolies, combines and price-fixing, already apparent in the eighteen eighties, continued to strengthen. In these circumstances little sympathy was found for what the editor of the Christian Guardian called, in 1894, "the lower classes." As far as he was concerned, the antagonism felt by such people was "to some extent the outcome of the feeling of the lower classes and the needy against those who are successful and comfortable."[55] In an ambience of political division, religious tension and economic distress, the public meeting of the fledgling National Council of Women on April 12, 1894 was a major triumph with great potential force.

---

[55] Cited in Saywell, "The 1890s," p. 116.

On this occasion the Council received explicit endorsements of the respectability of their purposes. Lord Aberdeen's presence brought a very public profile to the movement. It was, however, the letter sent by John Walsh, Archbishop of Toronto, which provided a greatly needed commendation for the enterprise. His letter, expressing his regrets at being prevented from attending, said in part:

> ...I am thoroughly in sympathy with the objects which Your Ladyship proposes to attain and promote the organization and development of the National Council of Women of Canada. The purpose of this Council, as I understand it, is to bind and consolidate into a great confederation the various associations in this country which are the care and management of women, each association retaining its own autonomy and independence, acting out its own religious principles and pursuing its own special objects; only the representatives of the various associations and cities are required to meet, from time to time, in friendly conference, to discuss their various works and projects, and to encourage one another by mutual sympathy, advice and emulation.[56]

Similar letters of regret were sent by Bishop Bond of Montreal, Bishop Hunter Dunne of Quebec and Reverend Dr. Carman. While the presence of these gentlemen would have been a testimony to Christian tolerance, their written regrets gave the Council important, and necessary, support.

The Prime Minister, the Right Honourable Sir John Thompson, opened his remarks by saying that he felt proud that it was in his period of office that "this National Parliament of the women of Canada has assembled." He then went on to make particular mention of the possible work for social cohesion that the National Council could perform. He said in part:

> Let me say that no class in this country could appreciate more than public men the benefits that are aimed at in this movement. One other and great and inevitable result will be that besides helping forward all the charitable institutions of the country, it will bind together in sympathy and close citizenship those who are interested in charitable work — it will take them out of the influence of the thou-

---

56   *Yearbook,* 1894, p. 174.

sand and one influences which divide our people. Any movement which tends to bring together the people of the various provinces, of different opinion, politics and beliefs will be patriotic in its aim and in its work and Divinely blessed in its results.[57]

The public support of churchmen, statesmen and politicians would help the National Council enormously in the years to come.

However, Principal Grant of Queen's University offered the Council a word of far-sighted caution. He warned that "every movement has persons connected with it who say foolish things, and the critics take them up as true representatives of the movement and they call out loudly at every unfortunate speech uttered and say I told you so." He supported the actions undertaken fully, in spite of the behaviours of "a few foolish women." He stated explicitly that "Mind is the same in men and women," and noted that as universities open their doors to women "we see nothing but good resulting from this action." "Men," he remarked, "cannot but be dwarfed if women are dwarfed." Such forthright advocacy of the right of women to be considered as foolish and wise just as men are foolish and wise, would be particularly important in the coming years, as the argument continued to burn over the proper social roles for women.

On Sunday, April 15, 1894 the Reverend W.T. Herridge preached a sermon on "Woman: her Place and Work," the text of which was printed in the first Yearbook. Herridge was the Minister of St. Andrew's Presbyterian Church, the parish church of many wealthy Anglo-Protestant Ottawan families. His point of view was one widespread at the time. In its essence, it was a defence of women, but of women as different from men, woman as "man's helpmate, not his rival in the stern battle of life." "In exceptional cases," Herridge admitted, "she may do men's work and do it well." He continued:

She may be a prophetess like Miriam or Deborah, a patriot like Judith, a philosopher like Hypatia, a soldier like Joan of Arc. In all likelihood, we have not yet discovered how well she could walk, if need be, in many avenues which "the lords of creation" now tread alone. But she has a distinctive ministry which she can not only discharge better than man but which in many cases he could not discharge at all. Whatever may be the developments of the future, her

---

57 *Ibid.*, p. 186.

immediate business is to estimate aright the value of the duty which lies nearest to her.[58]

At the close of the evening service conducted by Mr. Herridge, the women attending the first Annual General Meeting of the National Council of Women of Canada, would have been prey to some very mixed emotions. Urbanization and industrialization in Canada had led many people to consider the home as something women would manage, toward providing an oasis of peace in troublous and changing times. It was this vision of home that would become a confusing icon to those involved in the National Council of Women of Canada, framed as it was in terms of families that could manage without wages earned by the wife, and for workers whose occupation was close to their living quarters, not in factories located many streets away from their homes. It was not a vision that applied to life on the farm, whether in the Prairies or in Ontario. It certainly had little in common with the life actually lived in Newfoundland fishing hamlets or the fishing ports of Nova Scotia and New Brunswick. It would be only a dream to the urban poor of Montreal and Toronto who, men, women and children alike, all had to work to buy food and shelter for the family.

Whatever the future held, however, the spring of 1894 had seen an organization founded which would provide Canadian women with two very important tools. Firstly, a communication network had been established for the exchange of ideas and opinions about matters that were of particular concern to them. Secondly, there had been a general acknowledgement that the views gathered together by this network should be given consideration by the rest of society. Over the next five years, its activities would be strengthened and developed.

---

58   *Ibid.*, p. 240.

CHAPTER 2

Establishing a Presence
1894–1899

THERE WERE TWO immediate, major tasks facing the Council and one long-term, critical obstacle that it would have to overcome. First, there was the need to grow: the seven local councils and three associations, which had come together in Ottawa, must recruit others if the Council was to become truly national. Then, there was the problem of action. The meeting in Ottawa had defined an agenda for the local councils. How was this work to be carried out? Finally, and most importantly, there was the overall problem of the evolution and development of the idea of the Council from an inchoate vision to something which would have a concrete reality in Canadian social and political life. The all-encompassing nature of the constitution and by-laws could very easily produce an organization that was less a net to hold diverse and conflicting elements together for common aims, than one whose mesh was so broad nothing would be achieved.

During the months following the Ottawa meeting, the problem of growth proved to be no problem at all. By the spring of 1895, when the National Council held its second annual meeting in Toronto, nine more local councils had been organized. All the major urban centres of the young Dominion had established a Council. This was thanks in great part to the energy and the social prestige of Lady Aberdeen, who was present at the establishment of every one, but it was also due to the fact that women saw the organization of a local council, as something important and useful.

Kingston Local Council was the first to be added on April 26, 1894. Saint John Council, New Brunswick came into being on August 14, 1894; the two Nova Scotia Councils were also summer born, Halifax Council on August 24, 1894 and Yarmouth Council on August 28, 1894. The visit to the

West that year by the Governor General and his wife resulted in the forma-
tion of the Council of West Algoma on October 14, 1894, and a short-lived
Council established in Edmonton in the same month. In British Columbia,
the Council of Vancouver came into being on November 10, and the Victoria
Local Council was also founded in that month. The Council of East
Kootenay was organized in January 1895.[1] At the national level, the
Dominion Order of the King's Daughters joined with the Council in October
1894 and the Aberdeen Association joined at the same level on May 27,
1895.

Growth continued during the next four years, but at a slower pace. The
building brick of the Council movement was, and is, a collective association
of societies at the local level. While, as will be seen, the Council does reach
into rural life, its primary context is that of a town. Thus, once a collection of
associations and societies has been banded together in a particular locality,
the resulting council may grow but new councils will be slower to appear.
Once the major towns have established their councils, any further increase in
the number of these bodies will depend on the growth of new urban centres.
By the time of the third annual meeting, held in Montreal in 1896, four more
councils had been established: Regina, October 16, 1895; Vernon, also in
October 1895, and Brandon, on the 29th of that month. Rat Portage (Kenora)
established its local council on December 3, 1895. Thus, two years after the
first meeting of the National Council, there were twenty local councils in
existence, Edmonton Local Council having decided to discontinue its activities for the moment: lack of volunteers was given as the reason. The number
of federally associated organizations remained at five, the same as in 1894.

In January 1898, Charlottetown, Prince Edward Island organized its
council. By the sixth annual meeting of the Council, held in Hamilton in
1899, three more locals had been established: Nelson, British Columbia,
June 22, 1898, New Westminster, July 1898 and East Pictou County Local
Council in Nova Scotia, organized May 1899, making a total of twenty-one.
Moreover, in 1899 the Victorian Order of Nurses, an association founded
through Council work, joined the Council in its own right, bringing the number of national associations federated to the Council to six.

This proliferation of local councils has often been skipped over, attention
being centred upon the work done during the annual meetings at the national

---

[1]   There is some argument over the precise dates when local councils were founded. I have taken
      those given in the *Yearbooks*, and, in particular, for the Councils mentioned above, the *Yearbook*
      of 1895, pp. 5–6.

level. But the National Council of Women of Canada was not just one more nationwide association, attempting to find "a collective solution to the similar problems of the Dominion's 'island communities.'"[2] At both the national and local levels, the Council was an association of associations, whose very existence depended upon the previous establishment of other societies and organizations.[3] All other contemporary women's associations were defined either by a clear common aim or by an equally clear adherence to a common religious creed. The aims of such bodies as the Women's Christian Temperance Union and the Dominion Women's Franchise Association are expressed in the titles of the organizations. The common ground shared by church groups, and by political parties, is equally apparent.

The creation of the National Council brought neither a radical new challenge to the established norms of Canadian political beliefs in the eighteen-nineties nor a startling new set of demands for social reform. Its *raison d'être* was to make the work done by community-minded women more efficient, and improve their already established power. Its genesis was the result of a very widespread conviction among such women, already members of voluntary associations, that cooperation among the various associations would be profitable for each one of them. From the moment of its birth, however, the Council had to cope with a fundamental division of opinion between women (and men too): should the goal of such cooperation be the removal of all barriers to women's full and equal participation in political, religious and social life, or the continuation of women's action as an indirect influence on the course of events?

The solution chosen in the eighteen-nineties by Council was based on agreement that women, as women, had something to give to society as a whole. In her address to the annual meeting of 1894, Lady Aberdeen had struck this note. "We come together as women," she said, "...who are...earnestly desirous to make their work more effective for the common good by taking counsel with one another as to the carrying on of women's grand mission."[4] The Council was to be the effective organization of women to confront very particular problems; it was about the action and influence of groups of women in society, rather than about the pursuance of any particu-

---

2 Strong-Boag, "Setting the Stage," p. 87.
3 Parallel umbrella organizations were few. Perhaps the most important of them was linked to sport: see Wise, "Sport and Class Values in Old Ontario and Quebec," in W.H. Heick and Roger Graham, eds., *His Own Man: Essays in Honour of Arthur Reginald Marsden Lower,* (McGill-Queen's Press, 1974), pp. 93–115.
4 *Yearbook,* 1894, pp. 10–11.

lar program of reform. At no point was the Council presented as an alternative to the women's suffrage movement, and it did not collapse when women obtained the vote at the federal and provincial levels.

The most important person during the first five years of its life was Lady Aberdeen, and although she did not work single-handedly or without enthusiastic support, her ideas and beliefs greatly affected the development of the Council.[5] She was its president during these years and she was also linked to the development of the International Council of Women, the first of her many terms as President of that organization running from 1893 until 1899. Without question, she was a member of a privileged elite. Her priorities and goals were not a new social order but the better ordering of the accepted and the known. In many ways Lady Aberdeen was the conservative counterpart of Fabian socialists such as Beatrice and Sidney Webb. In giving her support to women's suffrage, to the advancement of religious toleration, to measures which would reduce the obstacles created by class barriers and improve the lot of the poor, she worked deliberately, as did the Fabians, for reform, not revolution. Many socialists found inspiration for their work in the contemplation of a future without poverty and crime, rooted in a society where privilege and religious hierarchies were without power. Lady Aberdeen, and those who followed her leadership, also dreamed of a society without poverty, where the sick had proper care, where the lot of factory worker and the shop-girl was bearable.[6] However, their dream had its setting in a society where privilege had its duties and religion comforted.

This essentially conservative stance was the source of much of the success of the National Council of Women of Canada, both at the time of its founding and later. Its most attractive element was its very positive definition of women, a definition based upon the reality of the way the majority of women lived, as people having the family as a predominant force shaping their life-cycles. It must be remembered that marriage was then, and continues to be, the norm for most Canadian women. In 1891, 90.6% of women between the ages of 45 and 49 were married. This statistic declined slightly to a low point of 88.3% in 1951 and rose to 94.2% in 1981.[7] Mrs.

---

5   On this see Wendy Thorpe, "Lady Aberdeen and the National Council of Women: A Study of a Social Reformer in Canada, 1893–1898," (M.A., Queen's University, 1973) and Joanna Dean, "Lady Aberdeen's Vision for Canadian Women: A Study of Evangelism, Liberalism and the Woman Question," (M.A., Carleton University, 1989).
6   "Presidential Address," Yearbook, 1896, pp. 121–22.
7   Ellen M. Gee, "The Life Course of Canadian Women: An Historical and Demographic Analysis," in Arlene Tigar McClaren, ed., Gender and Society: Creating a Canadian Women's Sociology, (Toronto, 1988), Table 2, p. 190.

Drummond, President of the Montreal Council in 1894, spoke for many when she said that "home will ever be our chosen kingdom, but that we shall order our homes with greater wisdom...[by] taking a woman's part in helping the great world."[8] But the logic of those involved in Council activities, at whatever level, meant that if the home was seen as the principal theatre for women's activity, it was not the only one. Mrs. Drummond herself was renowned during her life-time as a tireless worker for those causes she chose to support, among them the Home for Incurables in Montreal, the Women's Historical Association, the Aberdeen Association and the Anti-Tuberculosis League, as well as work at both the local and national level for the Council of Women.[9]

In her presidential address in 1896 Lady Aberdeen articulated clearly the reasoning that linked the place of women within the home to work in a wider sphere, the basis for what has since been labelled "maternal feminism." Because women were responsible for child-rearing in their own homes, the responsibility for the "work of education in the schools; the work carried on by church societies and philanthropic organizations; the efforts to promote literature, art and music are largely in the hands of women and the social life wholly so."[10] An ideal of marriage which saw it as a basis for work within the larger society, rather than as a confining ghetto might be idealistic, but it was an ideal that many thought attractive, reasonable and attainable, above all because marriage was an accepted life experience for them.

In sum, Council presented a fundamental, necessary and developing, if traditional, role for women in Canadian society that reflected the reality lived by a great many Canadian women. It did not seek a revolution in that experience, in the sense of a radical alteration. It did seek the realization of the best possible conditions for women, based upon the assumption that marriage would be, if not inevitable, then highly likely. Thus the whole question of the legal aspects of marriage, of women's rights in marriage, became a matter of crucial and continuing interest to Council. This was not the support of the cult of domesticity, a propaganda for marriage as a "a world of care without/world of strife shut out."[11] It was support for women's rights within

---

8   *Yearbook*, 1894, p. 219.
9   Biographical details from Henry James Morgan, ed., *The Canadian Men and Women of the Time: A Hand-book of Canadian Biography*, (Toronto, 1898), p. 346.
10 *Yearbook*, 1896, pp. 127–8.
11 Dora Greenhill, "Home," in *The Cornhill Magazine*, Sept. 1863: cited in Leonore Davidoff, Jean L'Esperance and Howard Newby, "Landscape with Figures: Women and Community in English Society," in Juliet Mitchell and Ann Oakley, eds., *The Rights and Wrongs of Women*, (London, 1976), p. 139.

marriage. As time passed, Council would press for equal grounds for divorce and for equal parental rights for women, for the married woman's right to choose to retain her own nationality instead of being automatically considered as having acquired her husband's. Council would support equality for all women before the law, for a woman's right to engage in paid labour outside her home, and finally, for a wife's right to a share in the assets of the family because of her work as a partner. This development of the attitude of Council over the years came because, at the outset, it was a body willing to accept as members those who challenged the opinion of the majority. Again, in Lady Aberdeen's words, this time to the International Council in Washington in 1899: "We want to make it absolutely clear that women holding the most opposite views and ideas on [any] subject can join the organizations; however much their views may conflict, they can join our Councils; we desire to represent in our Councils every possible phase of work and activity and thought existing among women..."[12] Every effort was made to hew to Article II of its Constitution, which stated that "The Council is organized in the interest of no one propaganda and has no power over the organizations which constitute it except that of suggestion and sympathy..."

The organization of Council, through representation of groups already formed, was a positive reinforcement of choices women had already made. The leadership of the Women's Christian Temperance Union and the Dominion Women's Enfranchisement Association might regret that they could not swing Council, at either the local, national or international level, into whole-hearted endorsement of their particular agendas. Yet at all levels of Council meetings, such organizations received acknowledgement of the legitimacy of their aims. In her address to the Second Triennial Conference of the International Council of Women, which met in Washington in May 1895, Lady Aberdeen quite unselfconsciously underlined this function of social approval when she said, "in Local Councils, we have, I think, in nearly all cases, the most representative women of the city or the district, taking the lead in all sections." [13]

Two years later, in 1897, as part of her annual address as President of the Canadian Council, she put this point even more clearly. "In every one of our Councils," she said, "a number of the most prominent women workers of the districts have been brought into direct relations with manifold other sets of

[12] *Yearbook,* 1895-97-98, p. 9.
[13] "Address by the Countess of Aberdeen...March 2, 1895..." (Boston, 1898). Bound in combined *Yearbook,* NCWC, 1895, 1897, 1899. p. 6.

3. Mrs. Adelaide Hoodless

workers and other sides of life and thought, of which they had previously no experience. 'I should never have known you, you dear, if it had not been for the Council,' said one woman to another of a very different class, as they sat side by side listening to an address on the results of the Council.'[14]

One of the paradoxes of clubs is that, in bringing like-minded people together, they also, frequently, divide the community into mutually exclusive groupings. The social prejudices expressed by the restrictive membership rules of many business and social clubs, until very recent times, frequently sharpened divisions within a community. For women, the local councils were a place where some of the barriers, some of the time, were overcome. The place of these bodies as unifying forces within a community becomes startlingly obvious when their composition is considered. In Montreal, which by 1901 had a population of 328,172, and Toronto, whose population that year was 209,892[15], the social mixing that occurred through local councils might not have as much impact as it would in small centres, like Kingston— population of 17,961—or New Westminster, with 6,499 that year.[16] Yet even in the large urban centres, the variety of societies federated in the local council made it a powerful pressure group on the municipal council, its very diversity being a large part of its strength and reflecting the particular character of the locality. The intense sectarian strife among Christians of that period made the cooperation of, for example, Anglicans, Baptists, Methodists, and Catholics in Charlottetown a remarkable achievement. Charlottetown in 1901 had a population of just over 10,000, and common cause in a relatively small society among people of different and strongly held religious opinions is rare.

During the first five years of its existence, the emollient action of local councils on their communities was much needed. The eighteen-nineties were a period in Canadian history of obvious economic difficulties, coupled with bitter political and social antagonisms. The census of 1891 had shown a net loss of people to the United States. While reasonable harvests marked the years 1891–93, an economic downturn began in 1893 which did not end until early in 1897. At the same time, some made a great deal of money and divisions between rich and poor became more and more apparent.[17] A royal commissioner commented in 1889 that "there seems to be no idea of any

---

[14] *Yearbook*, 1897, p. 36.
[15] *Census of Canada*, 1931, p. 9.
[16] *Ibid.*, p. 8.
[17] On this see Saywell, "The 1890's," p. 109 and Desmond Morton, *A Short History of Canada*, (Edmonton, n.d.), p. 132, *et. seq.*

obligation existing between the employer and his operatives, any more than the mere payment of wages. To obtain a very large percentage of work with the smallest possible outlay of wages appears to be the one fixed and dominant idea.[18] The context for these economic problems was a public mood that was irritable and discordant. In the view both of contemporaries, such as Lord Minto, Governor General in 1899, and of later historians, such as Jack Saywell and Desmond Morton, the times were out of joint. "Between English and French Canada," Saywell has written, "lay a gulf of incomprehension bridged only by the necessities of politics. Bigotry was widespread, finding outlets in the traditional French-English and Catholic-Protestant conflicts, in hostility to any strangers in the land, and in sharp rivalries among Protestant sects."[19]

This distemper makes the cooperation at the local council level the more remarkable. By 1899, the affiliations of the local councils brought together a very broad spectrum of organizations. Ottawa Local Council, and the Victoria and Vancouver Island Local were the largest, with twenty-eight affiliated organizations. Ottawa had representation from three Roman Catholic institutions. Montreal Local Council had twenty-seven affiliates, and was one of the councils with Jewish representation: the Ladies' Hebrew Benevolent Society, the Ladies' Sewing Society of Spanish and Portuguese Jews and the Ladies' Aid Society of Spanish and Portuguese Jews. Hamilton had twenty-two affiliated societies, including a branch of the Trades and Labour Council, the leading organization of the Canadian union movement. Saint John, New Brunswick had twenty members, including the Seamen's Mission and several branches of the Women's Christian Temperance Union, as well as the Women's Enfranchisement Club. The Halifax and Dartmouth Local Council had seventeen affiliates, with the Catholic Children of Mary Society a full member, as were the Woman's Work Exchange, the School for the Blind and the Women's Enfranchisement Society. Toronto gathered up seventeen societies including the Industrial Room Association and the Catholic Young Ladies' Literary Society. Kingston's membership was fifteen, and, like Montreal, included a Jewish organization, The Jewish Society of Kingston. Charlottetown, with fourteen member organizations, was basically a grouping of religious societies, including, as has been said, both Catholics and Protestants. Vancouver and Winnipeg both had fourteen affiliates, Winnipeg including the Francophone and Catholic St. Boniface Ladies'

---

[18] *Ibid.*, p. 115.
[19] *Ibid.*, p. 109.

Aid Society. London and West Algoma each had thirteen affiliates as did Rat Portage. New Westminster brought together twelve, Brandon, Manitoba and Nelson, British Columbia each had a membership roll of eleven. East Pictou Local Council in Nova Scotia had seven, as did Quebec City. Regina had six affiliates and Vernon, British Columbia had five.[20]

In reporting their memberships most local councils divided their affiliates into categories. Ottawa, for example, reported that there were twelve "Philanthropic" member organizations which included: the Ottawa Orphans' Home, Home of the Aged, Visiting Committee of the Protestant Hospital, Home for Friendless Women, Ottawa Humane Society, Young Women's Christian Association, Women's Christian Temperance Union, Maternity Hospital, King's Daughters, Children's Aid Society, Victorian Order of Women and the Aberdeen Mutual Benefit Association. Eight associations were grouped together under the heading "Educational": The Harmon Schools, the Presbyterian Ladies' College, The Model School Association, the Women's Morning Musical Club, The Aberdeen Association, the Froebel Union, Women's Educational Union, and the Women's Canadian Historical Association. The "Church Aid and Missionary Societies" included: the Ladies' Aid Society, First Baptist Church; Home Missionary Society, St. Andrew's Church, Women's Foreign Missionary Society, St. Andrew's Church; Dorcas Society, St. George's Church; Ladies' Aid Society, Dominion Methodist Church; Ladies' Aid Society, St. Andrew's Church, and the Women's Alliance, Unitarian Church. The representatives of Roman Catholic institutions were associated with the following societies: the Convent of the Good Shepherd, St. Patrick's Orphan Asylum and L'Asile Bethlehem. In their Annual Report to the National Council, Ottawa also listed the Mutual Benefit Association of Working Women as a member. There is no doubt that volunteer organizations supplied the major part of the social welfare provided by the Ottawa community for its citizens at the close of the nineteenth century. This city of less than 60,000 supported not only those affiliated to its local council but a number of others as well.[21]

This gathering together of numerous affiliates at the local level highlighted three characteristics of the Council movement which would give it great strength in the coming decades. Its structure, as an association of associations, meant that it would reflect the current political and social forces at work in a community. Clubs joined and left a local council as support for

---

[20] These figures compiled from *Yearbook*, 1899, pp. 6–27.
[21] Ottawa's population would reach 59,928 in 1901. *Census of Canada*, 1931, p. 6.

their distinct purposes developed or dwindled. Council drew in those who were committed to working for particular, urgent and contemporary needs. The very imprecision of Council's stated aims of communication and support, as distinguished from particular reform agendas, allowed for a flexibility of development that would prove to be powerful for several generations. The gathering of local councils at an annual meeting, where discussion resulted in resolutions for study as well as for action, was a mechanism for defining areas of community life in need of attention. It was a communication net, to and from the centre and periphery of the country. Finally, the support at the national level of the distinctive nature of each local council gained it the loyalty that it might have lacked in the absence of a precise reform agenda. As the reports of the annual meetings show, Council managed to organize effective strength to influence policy at the provincial and national levels while accepting, and indeed encouraging, very different organizations of priorities at the local level. It was an extraordinarily successful mode of action, for it resulted in very definite successes in shaping policy at the national level and equally visible achievements with specific, but often quite different, enterprises at the local level.

The National Council not only expanded as an association during the years 1894–9, it also improved its internal organization. Its financial situation, in terms of current receipts and expenditures, had altered little except in scale. Mrs. Hoodless was still Treasurer and in 1899 she reported receipts of $1,021, mainly from membership fees of one kind and another. There were expenditures of $809, primarily for printing and reporting.[22] However in 1898 a fund had been established to meet the rent of an office for the National Council and the salary of a secretary. This special fund was guaranteed by Lady Aberdeen, with the aim of raising $3,000 over three years; $1,005 had already been received at the time of the annual meeting in 1899.[23] It was considered impossible to rent an office and employ a secretary on less than $1,000 a year and it was hoped that, by 1902, the general membership funds of Council would be sufficient to carry these expenses.

The need for the central office and an organizing secretary was spelt out in detail in the meeting of October 23, 1899. Lady Aberdeen noted that there had always been plans for a Standing Committee on Finance, on "which there should be a member from each local council." She went on to say that many councils "have forgotten to appoint any members to this Committee"

---

[22] *Yearbook*, 1899, pp. 56–7.
[23] *Ibid.*, Appendix iii-vi.

and therefore, it had not met. It was unclear whether Lady Aberdeen considered that this committee should have an actual representative from every established local council, or whether it should be staffed by executive nomination and have corresponding members in each of the local bodies. What was clear was that, unless the Finance Committee was taken seriously, the organization would not be able to fulfill any of its dreams. Lady Aberdeen put her finger on what would be an enduring issue for Presidents when she said that "we know it is a very difficult matter to get money for organization, since it is not an attractive thing." "Expenses of typewriting, printing, circulating information and so forth," she said, "do not at all appeal to people, but still on these matters of routine, the success and effectiveness of the work of Council very largely depend."[24] As a result of her own generous contribution to the special fund, and the earnest plea for a functioning Finance Committee, Lady Aberdeen managed to place the finances of Council on a firmer footing than had been the case in the first five years of the organization.

Equally important for the future was the work that was done at this sixth annual meeting of standing committees at the national level, and the orderly presentation of reports at the annual meetings. The *Yearbook* of the annual meeting of 1899 was the first that listed various committees at the national level and presented the reports of their convenors in any discernible order. The Council was not particularly precise on the difference between ad hoc and standing committees but at least, at the 1899 meeting, it was clear that committees were to be the major working instruments. Eleven committees were listed, three of them with the word "discontinued" after their titles. These were the committee concerned with "the Length of Working Hours for Women and Children," the committee for the "regulation and methods of election of Boards of School Trustees" and the "International Council Committee." The committee on "Literature and Home Reading" was invited to turn itself into a nationally organized society and then join Council. The committees on the "Raising of Loans for Dhoukhobor [sic]," for "Aid for the Transvaal Contingent"— Canada's expeditionary force to the South African War — and the committee for the "Canadian Women's Handbook to be prepared to the Paris Exhibition" were obviously ad hoc committees. The remaining committees on the list were those of: Laws for the Better Protection of Women and Children; Pernicious Literature; Custodial Care of

---

[24] *Ibid.*, p. 171.

Feeble-minded Women; Care of the Aged Poor; Provision of work for the Unemployed; Finance; Immigration; Press; and Bureau of Information.

While the convenors of the committees were selected, at this time, as much by subtle pressures within the organization as by any form of election, the procedures for determining membership of each committee were more clearly established. Each local council was expected to name a person who would "serve" on the committee in question and act as liaison between that committee and her local council. Service would mean attending a committee meeting annually and carrying out other work by post. It was the convenors of the national committees who were expected to decide what work should be done, to direct the flow of material, and report to the annual meeting not only what had been initiated at their level, but what any local council might have done in the same field.

Over the years, the names of these committees were altered to reflect changing agendas of investigation and action but the topics they covered remained relatively unchanged. All of the committees interpreted their mandates very broadly, and there has rarely been a period when a committee has considered it would be out of order to cover a topic which, logically, would have been better dealt with under some other heading. Further, local councils were rarely clear about the path to follow in reporting their activities. It took considerable time and patience to persuade local council members that requests for information by the convenors of the national standing committees ought to be fulfilled.

In 1899, only three standing committees presented reports: "The Committee on the Better Protection of Women and Children"; the "National Home Reading Union-Canadian Branch"; and the "Committee on Employment for the Poor." The main issue raised by the committee for the Better Protection of Women and Children was the need to raise the age of consent for marriage of young girls from fourteen to sixteen. The convenor of the committee had written to the Minister of Justice on the issue, asking that the "age of absolute protection for girls be raised from 14 to 16 [i.e. the legal age of marriage]....and qualified protection from 16 to 18 [the age of marriage with the consent of a parent]." The Justice Minister expressed sympathy but nothing was immediately achieved.[25]

The National Home Reading Union defined its aim as the promotion of reading and the discussion of books. A reading circle could consist of "a few

---

[25] *Ibid.* pp. 91–2.

friends...members of churches, clubs, literary and scientific institutes, co-operative societies, labour unions, grouped together and meeting periodically..." It reported that it had expanded its circles from British Columbia to Halifax, with a total membership exceeding five hundred. The committee on the Employment for the Poor announced that most of the effort in this area was carried on through Relief Committees in Winnipeg, Kingston and Montreal, by the St. Vincent de Paul Society in Quebec and Montreal, through the organization of associated charities in London and Ottawa, and through the Salvation Army shelter in several towns. Only Charlottetown had organized a Labour Bureau. None of these reports presented resolutions for discussion, and all complained that the local councils gave them less than full support.

In fact, the effective work of the National Council between 1894 and 1899 had been carried out by the Executive Committee and reported through general resolutions at the annual meetings. The 1894 meeting had concluded with the direction to local councils that they were to work in their respective provinces for: (1) the appointment of police matrons; (2) the appointment of female factory inspectors; and (3) the introduction of manual training into the public schools. As with almost all the groups of resolutions which were adopted at the annual meetings of the NCWC, these particular resolutions were implemented piece-meal and province by province. The work for appointment of police matrons was part of a very general concern by a number of local councils about the treatment of girls and women by the law. In this first instance success was limited, but the resolution placed the idea of the impact of the penal system on women firmly on the agenda of local councils, and led the way to cooperation with the Prisoners' Aid Association. For example, in 1896, the Toronto Local Council reported work in this area,[26] as did Kingston[27] and Halifax.[28] The aim was as much the improvement of living conditions in penal institutions as the moral improvement of prisoners. While this enterprise was not wholly successful, it did lead, like so many other actions, to education of the general public about the need for reform. From their inception, local councils proved excellent at public relations, and newspaper coverage of their actions was generally very thorough. In the case of the work done for the appointment of prison matrons, historian Veronica Strong-Boag considers it was the needed preparatory step to the

[26] *Yearbook,* 1896, p. 40.
[27] *Ibid.,* p. 50.
[28] *Ibid.,* p. 52.

introduction of female officers into police forces at the time of the First World War.[29]

Council's efforts to place female government inspectors in factories was more immediately successful, at least in Ontario, the most heavily industrialized province. There an appointment was made within the year, and the Ottawa Local Council remarked that "it was not obtained without a great deal of labor by all Councils, and others, and so I presume we can all report our joy at the success of this united effort."[30] The Toronto Local Council followed up this achievement by gathering, during 1895, the signatures of fifty ratepayers, asking the Toronto City Council to make an "appointment of a woman inspector for shops and places other than factories."[31] It was the belief of the Toronto Local Council, as reported to the NCWC, that:

> By the law of Ontario such an appointment after such a petition must be made within a given time, and the Toronto City Council acknowledging the obligation, entrusted the selection of the Woman to the City Health Officer.[32]

The appointment being made, whether because of legal requirements or as a matter of common sense, the City Health Officer acknowledged its usefulness. He informed the Toronto Local Council that "many details have been brought to his notice that could not have reached him through ordinary channels...and his consequent action thereon, the health and comfort of girls in certain establishments are more carefully considered than formerly."[33]

Councils in other parts of the Dominion paid less attention to this resolution than Ontario did, but when the question of the working hours of women and children was raised the previous year, at the annual meeting in 1895, there had been a vigorous response from one end of the Dominion to the other. Not all cities had experienced marches of the unemployed during the eighteen-nineties, such as that which took place in Toronto, on February 11, 1892, when 300 people assembled and formed a procession to city hall, behind a flag bearing the motto "Work or bread."[34] But urban poverty was

---

[29] Strong-Boag, *Parliament of Women*, p. 191.
[30] *Yearbook*, 1896, p. 45. It should be noted that the institutional organization of the Council in its first five years was occasionally deficient.
[31] *Ibid.*, p. 39.
[32] *Ibid.*,
[33] *Ibid.*
[34] Charles Lipton, *The Trade Union Movement of Canada 1827–1959*, (Toronto, 1973), p. 90.

visible from the Atlantic to the Pacific and the problems of slums, sickness and unemployment were clear even to those whose circumstances were comfortable. The study in 1896 by a young Montreal businessman, Herbert Brown Ames, of that city's particular situation was not matched by equally penetrating contemporary studies elsewhere in Canada,[35] but knowledge of dilapidated, over-crowded housing, inadequate and polluted water supplies, and sewage arrangements that were even worse, were the common grist of municipal politics.

The contribution of wretched employment circumstances to the general misery of much of the working class, in particular the conditions of work for women and children, was the aspect on which the National Council focussed its attention. The matter was raised by the Kingston Local Council at the 1895 annual meeting, the motion being introduced by Agnes Maule Machar[36] as follows:

> Proposed..that on account of the injurious consequences which naturally result from the present length of working hours, during which girls and women may be and often are employed in factories and stores, the Legislature be respectfully petitioned by the National Council of Women of Canada to limit the legal hours of such employment of women and girls and also children, to at most nine hours a day, and also to provide that a forewoman — who should always be employed to superintend female employees — should arrange for occasional rest and change of position, if not work, during each division of the working day.[37]

The fate of this resolution illustrates both the strength and weakness of the Council with respect to labour legislation. There is no doubt that the conditions of work of women and children exercised Council at both the local and national level, but the motion was amended when proposed, and a request made for further information on the subject to be gathered. This meant that at the annual meeting of 1896 a report was presented by a sub-

---

[35] See Terry Copp, *The Anatomy of Poverty The Condition of the Working Class in Montreal, 1897–1929*, (Toronto, 1974).

[36] She was the daughter of the Rev. John Machar, the second Principal of Queen's University, and had an interesting career as a novelist. She worked for the Kingston Humane Society and was a member of Council at both the local and national level, as a representative of this organization.

[37] *Yearbook*, 1895, p. 36.

committee, leading to a general discussion of the matter. The report was introduced by Lady Aberdeen and was seconded by Mrs. Drummond, who has already been quoted in this chapter as representing the views of many who thought that a woman's chief role was that of wife and mother.

This introduction to the report is an honest reflection of the ambivalent position in which the sub-committee found itself. It was admitted that the members of the committee had had great difficulty in deciding what to recommend for:

> On the one hand they recognize that sudden and violent changes in the direction of compulsory restriction of working hours, even when undertaken with the object of defending the defenceless, may, by ignoring the other interests involved, prove injurious to the community, and ultimately provoke reaction; on the other hand, believing that the true wealth of the community lies in the health and strength of body and mind of its members, they find that present working hours and present working conditions taken as a whole not only sacrifice unnecessarily the health and strength of the workers, and thus degrade the community, but also correspondingly impair and reduce the industrial output and power of the country.[38]

The resulting discussion revealed the depth of both the concern and the disagreement. Agnes Machar remarked that when she had moved the resolution the previous year she "had no idea that it would meet with opposition."[39] She went on to quote from the recent Report of the Royal Commission on Labour, which had recommended the reduction of the working week in factories to fifty-four hours. Mrs. Drummond voiced the concerns of those who opposed the resolution by remarking that "there has never been any doubt or difference of opinion among us as to the desirability of the shorter working day."[40] She contended that "further discrimination as is hereby proposed would lend countenance to the popular assumption of an inferiority that does not exist; and to a prevailing disparity in wage which has no proportionate foundation in fact." She was quite clear that for a woman, "every protection or privilege which is accorded to her womanhood is also an injury and a disability to her as a worker and wage earner."[41] The solution that she proposed

---

[38] *Yearbook,* 1896, p. 354.
[39] *Ibid.,* p. 358.
[40] *Ibid.,* p. 361.
[41] *Ibid.,* p. 362.

was that the working day be made shorter for both men and women.

An interesting aspect of the debate on the resolution was the intervention of the President of the Montreal Trades and Labour Congress, Mr. Ryan, a silver-tongued Irishman. This organization had been established in the summer of 1883 and had, since that date, held a series of conferences on the problems confronting labour in the Dominion.[42] In 1895 the Trades and Labour Congress decided to appoint in all cities, where it was appropriate, a representative to work with the Local Council of Women. Mr. Ryan's comments were very clear on the point that working hours were, in general, too long for both men and women, and that "if a woman does the same work as a man, she ought to receive the same remuneration."[43] His speech went on to describe, chapter and verse, conditions experienced by women in laundry work and shoe factories. He outlined the practice whereby a proprietor could obtain a permit "from the Factory Inspector which allows him to work his employees twelve and fifteen hours a day; while during the other portion of the year he closes the factory down."[44] In spite of the obvious sympathy of many in his audience, the resolution was defeated.

This did not mean the end of Council's concern with the problem. Year after year the issue came back for discussion at the national level. In 1897, for example, Mrs. Dennis, representing the Halifax Local Council, spoke for the shortening of women's working hours not only in factories but also in shops; she also addressed the problems of child-labour.[45] She, and many others, also made it quite clear that a law was only as good as the provisions made to enforce it.

The efforts of the National Council in this area have been criticized. Their refusal to back the resolutions brought forward by the Kingston Local Council and supported by the London Local Council is seen as rooted in class interest. This may be so, but it is a judgement that does not take into account what was achieved. The issue of working conditions for women was discussed within Council and by all local councils, not only in 1895 and 1896 but in the years that followed. Sometimes it would be raised in connection with education, sometimes as a matter of protection necessary for women and children, sometimes with respect to the conditions of employment of both men and women. While the National Council would rarely sup-

---

[42] Lipton, *Trade Union*, p. 72.
[43] *Yearbook*, 1896, p. 365.
[44] *Ibid.*, p. 367.
[45] *Yearbook*, 1897, pp. 45–46.

port a resolution for immediate action of a particular type in the field of labour legislation, it did support continued investigation of working conditions. The reports drawn together for the annual meetings were forwarded to the relevant government departments. This kind of activity resulted, both immediately and in the long term, in the exercise of particular pressures from some Councils regarding the general working conditions of women, servants and shop-girls, as well as those of factory women. In 1897, the Ontario Local Councils, with the support of the Trades and Labour Congress, successfully petitioned to have the provisions of the Factory Act of that Province extended to shop-girls.[46] The Montreal Council worked along these lines, as did the Halifax Council. Very often the task at the national level was to identify where reform in society was needed, to set about gathering information on the problems perceived, and to lead discussions permitting expression of various current opinions about these issues.

Now and again there would be a direct, legislative result of National Council work, but more often the successes were of a less dramatic kind. In her presidential address in 1898, Lady Aberdeen made a summary of what she considered to have been achieved over the past five years. She began by noting that the third resolution of the first National Council, the introduction of manual training into public schools, had been successfully implemented in Ontario and that this meant "an emphasis to the same movement in other provinces."[47] This was not as controversial a matter as working hours, but it provoked debate. Adelaide Hoodless led the discussion. She was to found the Women's Institute in February 1897 at Stony Creek, and it was her practical nature which led her to propose resolutions concerning what was taught in public schools. Characteristically, she stated clearly at the outset what sort of support she hoped to gain from Council. She introduced her ideas by saying, "it is not my purpose in this paper to enter into the details [of possible schemes of manual training]...but to draw the attention of the Council to the different points to be considered so that we may unite, together with our Local Councils in forming some feasible plan that may be presented to the Departments of Education in the various provinces."[48]

Adelaide Hoodless was of the view, then widely held across the United States and Europe (as she herself remarked), that schools should not only

---

[46] "Presidential Address at the fifth annual meeting of the National Council of Women of Canada," *Yearbook*, 1898, p. 1.
[47] *Ibid.*, p. 2.
[48] *Yearbook*, 1894, p. 118.

teach reading and writing but also domestic arts. She particularly approved of the Belgian system, which taught knitting and the rudiments of sewing in Grade One, cutting and making underclothes, darning and mending and embroidery in Grade Two, dressmaking and shirt-making in Grade Three.[49] Within three years she had a clear notion of why she wanted these subjects taught and of how they should be developed at the secondary level. In 1896 she argued that manual labour ought to be elevated to "the equally honoured position hitherto occupied by the more intellectual pursuits." Mrs. Hoodless believed that domestic science ought to include "agriculture..dairying, poultry-raising, bee keeping..."[50]

One of those who opposed the ideas of the Hamilton reformer was Mrs. Archibald, President of the Halifax Local Council,[51] not because she objected to the idea of domestic science courses, but because she did not wish to see education of this kind restricted to young women. She opened her remarks by saying that she had no patience with a woman who was "willing to work in a factory or stand long weary hours behind a counter yet consider herself disgraced and degraded if compelled to do housework."[52] On the other hand, she objected strongly to "boys being taught carpentering unless the girls are."[53] The debate over the issue was further confused by the suspicion that proposals for practical training for girls and young women were thinly disguised training schools for servants. In other words, those who worked in favour of teaching domestic science in the schools system were seen as being as interested in preparing girls to be good servants, as in equipping them to run their own domestic lives.

While Lady Aberdeen opened her address to the fifth annual meeting of the NCWC by commenting on the success of efforts to have manual training included in the public school curriculum in Ontario, this was only the beginning of a long list of other Council achievements and activities between 1894 and 1898. Her second and third points were the appointment of women factory inspectors in Ontario and Quebec, and the extension of the provisions of the Factory Act to the Shop Act in Ontario. The rest of her list

---

49 *Ibid.*, p. 119.
50 *Yearbook*, 1896, p. 384.
51 This was Mrs. Edith Jessie Archibald who was a staunch supporter of the W.C.T.U. She had been born in Newfoundland, the daughter of Sir Edwin Mortimer Archibald, and married Charles Archibald, a cousin. She wrote a biography of her father, *The Life and Letters of...* (Toronto, 1924) and also a novel, *The Token* (London, 1930). She would work hard throughout her life for hospitals and child care. She died in Halifax in 1934.
52 *Yearbook*, 1896, p. 390.
53 *Ibid.*, p. 392.

4. Emily Howard Stowe

included the appointment of women to the boards of school trustees in New Brunswick, and amendment of the School Act so that women could be elected in British Columbia; changes in arrangements for women prisoners in various places, notably Quebec City, where matrons were being placed in charge of women, while young girls were sent to a separate institution; the organization of cooking schools and classes; a call to all members of Council to unite in efforts for the protection of animal and bird life from useless destruction in the interests of fashion; efforts to promote systematic instruction in art design adaptable to industries and manufactures, towards opening up a field full of opportunities for women.[54] Lady Aberdeen concluded her remarks by bemoaning the fact that there were far too few young members of Council. This plaint would echo and re-echo down the decades.

Almost all other topics of achievement and concern mentioned by Lady Aberdeen would continue to spur action and debate in succeeding years. These matters fall under three headings: firstly, main policies which were above all the result of action initiated and developed at the national level; secondly, the work of one or more local councils which addressed subjects of grass-roots importance; thirdly, actions which came about because Council existed, and which otherwise would not have been undertaken.

There were six major polices in the first category. One of the most effective of these national policies related to the appointment of women to boards of school trustees, school commissions, advisory boards and boards of education. At this time most of these were not elected. By 1898 Nova Scotia, British Columbia, and New Brunswick had appointed women. Secondly, the National Council supported organization through local councils, boards of associated charities, precursors of the United Way. Thirdly, the Council backed the examination of available literature and, in particular, wished to control the circulation of "Impure Literature."[55] As part of activity in this area they helped inaugurate "the Home Reading Union to promote habits of good and systematic reading." Fourthly, they launched an inquiry into "the Laws for the Protection of Women and Children" and brought together a number of suggestions which were presented to the Minister of Justice. Fifthly, National Council set on foot yet another enquiry, this time into the "Care and Treatment of the Aged Poor, so many of whom," Lady Aberdeen

---

[54] *Yearbook*, 1898, pp. 2-4. This volume is bound in an odd fashion and includes that of 1895, and also the ICW *Report* for that year.

[55] On this see Mariana Valverde, *The Age of Light, Soap and Water: Moral Reform in English Canada, 1885–1925*, (Toronto, 1991).

noted in her report, "now find their only refuge in the jails for want of any other provision for them." She went on to say that "on the authority of the Chief Inspector for Provisions for Ontario, some 60% of the jail population of that province belong to the infirm, aged, destitute or feeble-minded class."[56]

The sixth, and perhaps most important achievement, was the establishment of the Victorian Order of Nurses as a result of National Council action.[57] The resolution establishing the Order was passed at the meeting of the National Council in Halifax, in July 1897, as an effective way of honouring Queen Victoria's Diamond Jubilee. The idea had been sparked by the Vancouver Local Council in 1896, who had brought the "dire need that exists in the outlying parts of the Dominion for medical aid" to the attention of the National Council.[58] In the speech proposing the resolution Lady Aberdeen listed five main aims for the Order:

1. to provide skilled nurses in sparsely settled and outlying country districts;
2. To provide skilled nurses to attend the sick poor in their own homes in cities;
3. To provide skilled nurses to attend cases in cities at fixed charges for persons of small income, the charges being paid to the funds of the Order;
4. To provide small lying-in rooms or wards in cottage hospitals or homes;
5. To provide trained nurses thoroughly qualified to carry out these objects.[59]

The growth of the Order within two years was phenomenal. In 1899 it reported to the National Council that nurses were being trained especially for its service in Halifax, Montreal and Toronto. Branches of the Order were established (in chronological sequence) in Montreal, Toronto, Baddeck, Cape Breton, New Richmond, Regina, Vernon, Hamilton and Saint John. Nurses had either been sent, or were in process of being sent, to Mattawa, North Bay, Thessalon, Port Arthur, Fort William and Fort Francis.[60] As well as listing the expansion of the Order, the report gave details about what each

---

56 *Yearbook*, 1898, p. 4.
57 On this see John Murray Gibbon, *The Victorian Order of Nurses for Canada: Fiftieth Anniversary 1897–1947*, (Toronto, 1947).
58 *Yearbook*, 1897, p. 44.
59 *Ibid.*, p. 110.
60 *Yearbook*, 1899, p. 314.

new establishment meant. "One of the physicians at Regina," it was remarked, "said that two-thirds of the fifty patients who had been cared for would surely have died had it not been for the good nursing they received."[61] There is no doubt that the new service met a very great need.

It is, in fact, at the level of grass-roots action, and in particular in the field of medical care, that work at the national and local levels was most successfully joined at this time. From work by the Halifax Council for the establishment of a children's hospital to work by women in Vernon, Rat Portage (Kenora) and Regina for the establishment of a hospital for the community as a whole, the associations joined together in Councils worked to give their towns an infrastructure of medical care. Some of what this meant can be gleaned from the terse report of the Rat Portage Local Council in 1899. At that time the settlement's population was somewhere between 4,000 and 5,000. Its population would be 5,273 in 1901. The local council had thirteen affiliated societies in 1899: the Humane Society, the W.C.T.U., the Zion Church Ladies' Aid, St. Alban's Ladies' Aid, Knox Church Ladies' Aid, Women's Foreign Mission Society, Methodist Church, Presbyterian Church, St. Agnes Guild, Christian Endeavour Society, Epworth League Society, Sacred Heart of Jesus Society, and the Ladies' Aid Society. Alicia Robinson, who was affiliated to the local council through the Sacred Heart Society, opened the relevant section of her report to National Council by saying that a hospital had been the particular thrust of the work of the local council since its inception. "Such an institution," she went on,

> had been sorely needed in the town; for being a mining and lumbering centre, hundreds of men are there employed whose homes are far away from their labors. Upon becoming ill, or injured through accident, they were usually obliged to fall back upon the limited and inadequate resources of hotels and boarding houses.
> There were previous to the formation of the Council, no resident trained nurses in the town; and the nearest Hospitals were those at Winnipeg, 135 miles distant.[62]

The Royal Victoria Jubilee Hospital was opened on June 24, 1897, eighteen months after the organization of local council.[63] Within two years "between

---

[61] *Ibid.*, p. 152.
[62] *Ibid.*, p. 68.
[63] *Ibid.*, pp. 68–9.

three and four thousand patients" were treated. Like success was reported in that same year, 1899, by Regina, whose "Cottage Hospital" had by then been in active operation for over ten months.

The work of local councils was, however, always varied, and much of it a specific response to the needs of the particular centre. In Montreal, for example, the most impressive work was through its "Standing Committee on Philanthropy."[64] At the end of the nineteenth century, Montreal's child mortality rate was one of the worst in the world, not merely one of the worst in the western world. As Terry Copp has pointed out, "Between 1899 and 1901, 26.76 per cent of all new born children [in Montreal] died before they were one year old. This was more than double the figure for New York City and it was customarily cited as being lower than only one large city — Calcutta."[65] Starting in 1895, the local council made the preservation of child life one of its most important missions. In 1896 the Council reported that its actions were as much about the education of mothers as about the distribution of aid, although that too was carried out by many of the affiliated societies. What was both innovative and effective was the preparation by women doctors of "health cards for wall hangings" which gave "in brief compass clear directions for the care of infants in health and in sickness."[66] The distribution of these publications was carried out door-to-door and at meetings in the poorest districts, where talks were given in both English and French on the health needs of children.

Other local councils followed equally original paths, defined by the particular character of the community. Toronto tended to spend the major part of its energy on translating the resolutions of the National Council into action within the Province. Hamilton and Ottawa paid great attention to artistic and educational activities. Ottawa's particular enterprise at this time was the establishment of a public library. In reporting on the enterprise, the representative of Ottawa's Council said she thought "our Local Councils stood to the cities in which they were established very much in relation of wife to her husband." She went on to remark that, "Perhaps if that be the case the wife of the City of Ottawa need not be discouraged if on the first application she finds her husband a little disinclined to put his hand in his pocket for what he

---

64 On this see Lynn S. Lavery, "Infant Mortality and the 'Gouttes de Lait': The Montreal Council of Women's Campaign for a Comprehensive Preventive Public Health Programme," (M.S.W. Thesis, Carleton University, 1989).
65 Terry Copp, *The Anatomy of Poverty: The Condition of the Working Class in Montreal 1897–1929*, (Toronto, 1974), p. 26.
66 *Yearbook*, 1896, p. 42.

deems a needless luxury. But after all such a wife does not take the first 'no' as final."[67] This imagery of how the Council should lobby is a common pattern in Council discussions throughout its existence: the idea that the community was merely a home writ large formed the basis of much of the strategy and planning for Council work. Women questioned why the values that were ascribed to domestic life ought not to applied to the general arena of public affairs, and used the rhetoric of a caring and well-established home to demand compassionate and enlightened care for their cities.

Toronto was, after Montreal, the most efficiently organized Council, with committees established to consider Immigration; Pure Literature; Preventable Causes of Insanity; Better Protection of Women and Children; Care of Teeth and Eyes of School Children; Care of the Aged and Infirm Poor; and Home Topics. Like several other local councils, including Winnipeg, Saint John, and Charlottetown, Toronto Council spent time discussing the formation of a precursor to the United Way: a bureau of "Associated Charities." Toronto was able to persuade Goldwin Smith to pursue the matter.[68] The London Local Council had turned its attention to fund raising for a Children's Pavilion for the new General Hospital. It raised $5,000. The enterprise was unusual for a local council; raising money was never a major role for a local council in the way it was for their affiliates. West Algoma reported with pride that it had held its annual meeting in January 1899, despite the fact the thermometer registered 26 degrees below zero. Papers were read at this meeting on "Our relations as a Council to the Public Schools, "How our Towns are Governed" and "Manual Training for Schools."[69] This type of educational enterprise was an important part of Council activity in these early years.

Quebec's Local Council was primarily concerned with literary and cultural endeavours. Halifax Local Council gave a report that emphasized it had achieved little, but it was given in a rhetoric of determination. "In surveying the past year's work," the corresponding secretary wrote, "we are forced to acknowledge that although much has been hoped, asked and fought for, but little has been accomplished by us as a Council during these many months; yet we trust that time, the radical leveller and distributor of results, will bring to the light of day our mustard grains of effort, thus proving that our toil and

---

67 Pamphlet, *What the NCW of Canada Has Done*, (Ottawa, 1896), in "Papers of the NCWC," vol. 151, file 5, National Archives of Canada.

68 *Yearbook*, 1899, p. 60.

69 *Ibid.*, p. 67.

talk have not always fallen on stony soil, and that the reforms for which we are striving are yet to furnish and benefit those they were intended to bene-fit."[70]

The local councils in Victoria and Vancouver were deeply involved in civic issues relating to the governance of the city and the working conditions of women and children. All councils, from New Westminster to Saint John, remarked on the difference that the arrival of the Victorian Order of Nurses made to the treatment of the sick. Vancouver Council made a special point of supporting the work of the nurses and reporting on the difference they had made to the Klondike.

The final category of Council achievements includes those that are due to its very existence. Dramatic examples were reported both in 1898 and 1899. The 1898 Report is given in full:

> ...last year (1897) Canada was shocked one Monday by hearing that the town of Windsor,in Nova Scotia, had been totally destroyed by fire and that thousands of its inhabitants were homeless. Next day it learnt that in addition to the measures being taken by Provincial and other authorities for the relief of the sufferers, that a number of ladies from New Brunswick were already on the spot with supplies of food and clothing. Why were they there? Just because the President of the Local Council of St. John, Lady Tilley, whom we rejoice to see amongst us, summoned the Local Council immediately she heard the sad news. The Local Council, representing as it does, every class and all sections of society, were ready for the emergency, knew at once where to turn for help, and by the co-operation of the railway authorities were able to be on the spot with assistance within a few hours. They were joined within a day by the Halifax Council, who were able to take like prompt measures and to whom was entrusted a sum of public money by the Municipal authorities for the purposes of relief."[71]

In 1899 information about a similar activity was given in the report to the National Council from Vancouver concerning "the disastrous fire at New Westminster on Sunday, September 11, 1898."[72] The Vancouver Local Council immediately met and its organization "proved a most useful focus

---

[70] *Ibid.*, p. 74.
[71] *Yearbook*, 1898, pp. 9–10.
[72] *Yearbook*, 1899, p. 81.

for the practical sympathy of our citizens, especially where sufferers were women and children." The support organized by both these local councils was obviously more quickly brought together, and more effectively delivered, than would have been the case had they not existed.

Besides these achievements of Council, there are two other aspects of the meetings at the national level which deserve remark. The first of these is the presentation of reports by the nationally affiliated societies at the annual meeting, and the second is, once again, the explicit link reported at the annual meetings between the National Council of Canada and the International Council of Women. The presentation of the reports of nationally affiliated societies in 1899 included the report of the "Women's Art Association of Canada"; the "Report of the Girls' Friendly Society of Canada"; and the "Report of the Dominion Order of the King's Daughters and Sons." Quite apart from their actual content, the importance of these reports lies in the communication of women's activities to one another. There was, of course, a great deal of cross-membership among the associations, some women being at the same time members of cultural associations, philanthropic associations, church groups and political associations. However, listening to, or reading, the reports of associations of which one was not a member meant the acquisition of knowledge about what was being done across a broad spectrum of community enterprise. It signified the ability of women to call on a network of people whose interest was in particular causes and problems, and to decide, on occasion, to develop a particular association in their own communities.

The link of the Canadian Council to the International Council enabled Canadian women to participate in international meetings dedicated to obtaining information "regarding the position [of women] in education,..work...and some account of the history of various movements in connection with the women's question and how they are faring."[73] At the time of the Quinquennial Meeting of the International Council in London in 1899, its actual membership consisted of the United States (1893), Canada (1897), Germany (1897), Sweden (1898), Great Britain (1898), Denmark (1899), Australia (1899) and the Netherlands (1899). In addition, some twenty-eight other nations sent representatives. The main resolutions passed, and recorded in a six-volume publication, dealt with equal pay for equal work; the need for access to all professions according to aptitude and not to sex; the need for

---

73   *Ibid.*, p. 116.

5. Lady Aberdeen (right) and Lady Taylor, President 1899-1902, 1910-1911

radical improvement of conditions in the nursing profession; the need for state-paid maternity maintenance; the need for the appointment of female factory inspectors; and the need for the participation of women in trade discussions in order to defend their rights. There was a resolution in favour of the protection of all workers, passed with the proviso that protective legislation in favour of women must never go so far as to exclude them from the work in question. Finally, there was a request that those who supported industrial research should consider the need for the development of modern household machinery to relieve women from household drudgery.[74]

Both the reports from the nationally affiliated associations and the lengthy report and discussion of the meeting of the International Council of Women,[75] reinforced women's sense of their own right to speak in public about matters that concerned them. It is interesting to note how they reported the compliments they received regarding their abilities as public speakers and capable administrators. Further, the approval of such work by Queen Victoria, shown by her reception of three hundred of the delegates at Windsor Castle, was taken as a welcome affirmation of the rights of women. Some of the rhetoric reported had a sardonic modern tinge. The American delegate, Susan Anthony, remarked that her watchword had always been "Educate the women," although she did not now despair "of the possibility of educating men."[76] There is no doubt that the International Council of Women was, to a much greater extent than the NCWC, a meeting place for upper class women. The financial operations, which made each delegate's expenses the responsibility of herself or her National Council, virtually ensured this. Nevertheless, it was a meeting that showed itself concerned with a very broad range of problems and took a feminist stand on most of them.

The 1899 meeting of the National Council of Women of Canada was the last at which Lady Aberdeen presided. She was made the Council's Advisory President, and she thanked the assembly for the honour, saying that "one of these days I shall hear of a debate in which you discuss means for getting rid of me."[77] This was the annual meeting, to use the Churchillian phrase, that saw "the end of the beginning." Over the past six years, from the time of the first organization of local meetings in 1893 to the founding Council in 1894,

---

74 Anon., *Women in a Changing World*, p. 23.
75 *Yearbook*, 1899, the report and discussion of the London meeting is given on pp. 115–146.
76 *Ibid.*, p. 121.
77 *Ibid.*, p. 151.

and from the resolutions of that year to the establishment of a complex system of Standing Committees in 1899, the National Council had developed and expanded within the Canadian framework. During the next fifteen years, it would become a very important force in the country.

CHAPTER 3

Expansion and Development
1900-1913

IN 1898 LADY Aberdeen left Canada with her husband, whose term as Governor General had concluded. She retained a link with the National Council of the Women of Canada throughout the rest of her long life, (she died on April 18,1939). Her leadership had been so important to the National Council since its inception that many predicted her departure would mean its rapid demise. But while her inspiration had been indispensable in the founding years, and would be of great importance for the National Council movement throughout the world during her lifetime, she left behind her a situation propitious for further growth. Her extraordinary gifts and her social position and prestige had enabled her to exploit fully her talents, her energy and her vision; but what mattered most was that she was fortunate enough to articulate ideas and beliefs at a time when they found ready acceptance among her contemporaries.

The women who had joined her in establishing the Council, while they accepted her leadership, had brought their own ideas, talents and knowledge to the enterprise. Since Council was, and remains, primarily an umbrella organization, those who were members, and especially those who accepted executive positions at either the local or national level, usually had a considerable background in community affairs. It took time for a woman to make her mark in her chosen volunteer association, then sent to the local council and finally to become a member of its executive. Throughout the years, women have complained that it is not only the middle class that runs the Council network, it is also the middle aged. Yet this is almost inevitable. Most young wives are also mothers, and young children limit the amount of time available for volunteer activities. Moreover, the natural progression to positions of authority within volunteer organizations has always taken time, and although there were a few members of Council who were without any other affiliation, the majority represented some organization to which they had a prior commitment. They were women who were activists, involved with the public life of their day, working through a broad variety of associations for ideas they considered important.

While most of the prominent figures of the Council have belonged to middle and upper class elites they have not been mere blank-faced copies of one another, certainly no more than a similarly circumstanced group of men would be. Council members came from very different organizations, whose interests and priorities were diverse and, as with male associations, spanned social class.[1] Members of Council were people whose views differed on many issues: the annual meetings were forums where issues of social policy and political action were matters of lengthy debate, ending with agreements to differ. While the rhetoric of debate might be neither rancorous nor acrimonious it was, as this history will show, clearly expressive of deeply felt philosophical and political divisions.

Those who were on the national executives of such organizations as the Dominion Women's Enfranchisement Association (member of the National Council in 1894), or of the women's life insurance society called the Ladies of the Maccabees (member of the National Council in 1902) were women used to organizing their ideas and expressing their minds. Those leading the local councils, whether they represented a church auxiliary, a philanthropic organization or a cultural society, all had experience of bringing together diverse people for a common purpose. In fact, in one sense the local councils had a more disparate group of affiliates than did the National Council, for bodies such as the Women's Christian Temperance Union, which would not join the latter, were frequently members of the local organization. Thus the women who worked in towns and cities from coast to coast were used to persuading others to accept their own particular views, and accustomed to working hard to bring about action based upon consensus. There was a strong bond of common experience amongst those who gave time and effort to Council, but this fact should not be allowed to obscure the very real contrasts of background that existed.

The expansion and development of the National Council of Women of Canada between 1900 and 1914 proceeds at the rhythm of the expansion and

---

[1] Wise, "Sport and Class Values," p. 93.

6. Mrs. Clark Murray, founder of the Imperial Order of the Daughters of the Empire

development of the country as a whole. The work of the Council, at the local and national levels, becomes intelligible and interesting when it is seen for what it was: an integral part of the building of a nation. During these years Canada was transformed and the Council had to meet the demands of a rapidly evolving society. Between 1901 and 1911 the total population grew by more than two million, a 34% increase.[2] Two new provinces, Saskatchewan and Alberta, were established. Or, to make the same point slightly differently, "from 1896 to 1913 one million people moved into the three Prairie provinces, where the population increased from seven to twenty percent of the Dominion total."[3] A significant part of the population increase was due to immigration.[4] From local council actions in ports of entry across the country, Halifax to Vancouver, to the resolutions of National Council, the records of the organization show it to have been deeply involved in discussions and actions concerning the recruitment, reception, and assimilation procedures for immigrants.

This population growth produced a transformation of society which signified something greater than just an enlargement of what was already there. As the twentieth century opened, Canada was struggling to integrate its separate regions and its disparate communities, and facing problems that increasing prosperity and improved communications made increasingly evident. Canada in 1914 was not just the Canada of 1891 more or less doubled. "The Great Boom," as many have dubbed the years 1900-1914, moved the country from a predominantly rural way of life to a rapidly growing city environment. On the eve of World War I, Canadian writers were already portraying, with nostalgia, the life of small towns and country farms in the Maritimes, Quebec and Ontario. Once a dominant model for Canadian society, such patterns of livelihood were now giving way to urbanization, industrial development and large-scale agriculture. There are two well-known works, one in English and one in French, that express the longing for the past. Stephen Leacock's *Sunshine Sketches of a Small Town* was published in 1912. In Quebec, where the transition, though less sharp, was also occurring, that classic of rural Quebec life by Louis Hémon, *Marie Chapdelaine*, was published in 1917. Neither of these works celebrated the now and the future:

---

2   F.H. Leary, ed., *Historical Statistics of Canada* (2nd edition, Toronto, 1983), Series A 78-93, Population by age and sex. 1901: total population 5,371,000; 1911: 7,207,000; 1921: 8,788,000.
3   John A. Stovel, *Canada in the World Economy*, (Harvard University Press, Boston, Mass., 1959), p. 105.
4   On this see Firestone, *Canada's Economic Development*, pp. 43-51. The question of the relationship between immigration and emigration is discussed in these pages.

both described a world of dwindling importance, retreating before the tumultuous advance of modern life. As O.D. Skelton pointed out long ago, "From 1900-1910 the farming population decreased in every eastern province except Quebec (and Quebec farms were notably less well to do than the Dominion average.)"[5] Yet this transformation had much more to do with changes in farming technology, and with the emergence of agricultural life in western Canada, than it did with agricultural depression. During the nineteen-hundreds, the organization of the dairy industry, for example, was precisely what that term implies: the organization of an industry and the production of milk, butter and cheese for the growing cities proceeded apace, with more productivity and less labour than dairying had demanded ten years earlier.

Like all other changes during these years, the alteration of country life in Ontario and Quebec was no simple matter. Its complex nature was reflected in the action and policies of organizations such as the Women's Institutes, many of which were affiliated at the local level to Council, and also in the attention paid to rural problems by the annual meetings at the national level. The relationship between town and countryside, as well as the ratio of rural and urban dwellers, was altering, and by 1914 the coming of the automobile meant that "highways and roads began to slice up the landscape more systematically than in the days of the horse, the buggy, the carriage and the sleigh."[6] The population of cities over 5,000 increased very rapidly. From 1900 to 1910 the urban population grew from 38 to 45 per cent of the total population.[7] Montreal's population was 328,172 in 1901 and 490,504 in 1911.[8] The population of Toronto was 209,892 at the opening of the period and 381,833 at its close. The figures for Winnipeg are 42,340 and 136,035. Vancouver grew from 29,432 in 1901 to 190,847 in 1911. New towns were established and some died while others flourished. Local councils brought together the volunteer associations, such as those supporting hospitals, relief societies, and training societies, who were coping with the social needs of new communities, and the associations attempting to unite the citizenry in projects for cultural development. At the national level, the affiliation of organizations such as the Dominion Women's Enfranchisement Association,

---

5   O.D. Skelton, "General Economic History, 1867-1912," in *Canada and its Provinces*, A. Shortt, ed., IX, pt. II, (Toronto, 1914), p. 246.
6   Robert Craig Brown and Ramsay Cook, *Canada 1896-1921: A Nation Transformed*, (Toronto, 1974), p. 1.
7   Stovel, *Canada in the World Economy*, p. 173.
8   For all four cities the figures are from *Historical Census of Canada*, Table 8, p. 9, (Census of Canada, 1931).

Canadian Women's Press Club, and the Victorian Order of Nurses created a network of information for women about the concerns and beliefs of a broad sector of the Canadian populace. By 1914 the Council had developed both confidence in its value, and the means and methods of attending to the problems and issues its membership considered important.

Ramsay Cook has pointed out that the "emerging industrial and urban society was founded on the success of the wheat economy."[9] The expansion of the railways was as essential to this development as the growth in population. Railway construction grew "from less than 500 miles per annum in 1900 to almost 2500 miles per annum in 1913."[10] "Railways," as Blair Neatby has written, "made prairie settlement possible... Only railways could bring in the food, fuel and equipment on which the settlers depended; only railways could move out the millions of bushels of wheat that they grew."[11] Two new transcontinental railways were chartered during these years, and new settlements flourished or died according to where and when new tracks were laid. Almost a third of the newcomers who travelled to settle the newly opened western lands and to swell the populations of those burgeoning cities, Montreal, Toronto, Winnipeg and Vancouver, brought with them an intellectual and cultural heritage that was from neither the English- nor the French-speaking world. As Canada coped in these years with changes brought about as much by worldwide as by internal developments, the National Council played a significant role in events at both the local and federal levels.

Four women held the office of President of the National Council of Women of Canada between the departure of Lady Aberdeen and the outbreak of World War I. Lady Edgar was the acting president briefly, from 1898-1899. Her husband died in 1899, cutting short any further service to the Council at that time. She later became President in her own right in 1906, serving until 1910. Lady Taylor, who was President from 1899 to 1902 also returned for a second term of service, from 1910 to 1911, following the unexpected death of Lady Edgar. Mrs. Robert Thomson was President from 1902 to 1906, and Mrs. F.H. Torrington from 1911 to 1918. While they had a considerable amount in common, they were very much individuals in their own right with divergent priorities.

---

9   Ramsay Cook, "The Triumphs and Trials of Materialism (1900-1945)," in Craig Brown, ed., *The Illustrated History of Canada*, (Toronto, 1987), p. 379.
10 Stovel, *Canada in the World Economy*, p. 106.
11 H. Blair Neatby, "The New Century," in J.M.S. Careless and Craig Brown, eds., *The Canadians 1867-1967*, (Toronto, 1967), p. 144.

All four were women whose parents had had some social status and whose husbands pursued successful careers. Lady Edgar was perhaps the most advantageously connected. Both her own family, and her husband's, were part of Upper Canada's elite. She was born into a Loyalist family in 1844 and christened Matilda, after her mother, Matilda Ann Bramley, her father's second wife.[12] He was Thomas Gibbs Rideout, whose career was linked to the Bank of Upper Canada. He was the third son of the Honourable Thomas Rideout, the Surveyor-General of Upper Canada from 1810 to 1820. Her family was deeply enmeshed in Ontario politics and her childhood training gave her social poise and a developed intellect. She became an historian of note and her *Life of General Brock*, published in 1904 as part of the "Makers of Canada" series is still worth reading. In 1865 she married James David Edgar, a barrister and later a knight. He was one of the leaders of the Ontario Liberal party for many years and was appointed as Speaker of the Dominion House of Commons in 1896. They had eight children, five sons and three daughters. Lady Edgar's life allowed her to pursue not only her own intellectual interests, but her opportunities for political and social pursuits. She began her charity work with the Infants' Home in Toronto. She would be President of the Women's Canadian Historical Association and President of the Women's Art Association. As well, she was Vice-president of the United Empire Loyalist Association.[13] Undoubtedly Lady Edgar gained status from her husband, but her own energy and talents, and her wish to become involved in associations that later elected her into executive positions, brought her particular distinction. Her work with the International Women's Council, during her second term as President, revealed traits for which she was praised as "a woman of clear intellect and graceful tact."[14]

Lady Taylor was the daughter of a Hamilton lawyer, Hugh Vallance. She married Thomas Wardlaw Taylor in 1864. He was a Scottish immigrant, born in Auchtermuchty in 1833. He had taken a B.A. at Edinburgh University, graduating at the age of twenty-one, but he completed legal studies at Osgoode Hall, and was called to the Bar in 1858. He was Master in Chancery in Ontario from 1872 to 1883, when he became a justice of Queen's Bench. Margaret Vallance was his second wife. They had no children. His career took him to Manitoba and he was the Chief Justice of the Province from 1889 to 1899. Lady Taylor's interests were in the Aberdeen

---

12 Robert J. Burns, "Ridout, Thomas Gibbs," in *Dictionary of Canadian Biography*, vol. IX, p. 661.
13 James Henry Morgan, *Types of Canadian Women*, (Toronto, 1903), p. 103.
14 Morgan, ed., *Men and Women*, (1898), p. 103

Association, the Victorian Order of Nurses and the encouragement of the missionary work of the Presbyterian Church.

Mrs. Robert Thompson, her successor, was the first Maritimer to hold the office of President of Council. She was the daughter of a Presbyterian minister, the Reverend William Donald, who was, at the time of his death, pastor of St. Andrew's Church, Saint John, New Brunswick. Louisa A. Donald married, in October 1870, Robert Thompson, a successful New Brunswick merchant and steamship owner. He was a native son of Saint John, being born there in June 1842, but he always considered himself as being of "Scottish origin."[15] He was a man of wealth and influence, receiving an appointment as German Consul in the city. In 1908 the order of the Red Eagle was conferred on him by the German Emperor. His wife's interests were her church, the Women's Canadian Club, (which she served as Vice-President at one point), the Victorian Order of Nurses and sundry philanthropic organizations, such as the Protestant Orphans' Asylum and the Home for the Aged in her city.

Mrs. F.H. Torrington, who would become the National President in 1911, was born in Ireland and came to Canada in 1869. Little is known of her family and her early life. She became the second wife of the English-born musician F.H. Torrington in 1878. He had come to Montreal as an organist in 1857, and he remained there until 1869. After four years as organist and musical director at King's Chapel in Boston, Massachusetts, he was appointed to the same positions for the Metropolitan Church in Toronto. The couple had two sons, and Mrs. Torrington established herself as a journalist concerned with social questions. She belonged at one time or another to the Board of the Y.W.C.A., the Toronto Playgrounds Association, the Women's Welcome Hostel, the Toronto Women's College Hospital and Dispensary Board, and in 1906 she became President of the Toronto Local Council.[16]

In terms of the life of the organization, these presidents struggled with the very same problems as their successors: financial needs, the running of the national office, the attendance of members at meetings and the recruitment of new associations to the Council. In 1901 the Executive faced severe financial troubles. It was pointed out that "the backwardness of the federated associations to send in their fees" had resulted in the inability of Council to pay its way during the first six months of the year.[17] Not for the last time, the

---

[15] Noted as such in various official c.v.'s: Morgan, *Men and Women*, (1912), p. 1100.
[16] Anon., *Nothing New Under the Sun*, p. 35.
[17] *Yearbook*, 1901, p. 21..

7. Lady Taylor, President 1899-1902, 1910-1911

Executive agreed to ask for additional "Council Aid" from the Federated Societies.

Throughout the twentieth century the Council would never be without financial problems, hovering somewhere close at hand. Basically, it lived on three funding sources: membership fees, of varying types and kinds, donations, and specific fund drives. Life memberships had been established in 1899, carrying a fee of $25. Further, local councils had been required in that year to provide a per capita sum of "two cents for each member of their affiliated Societies or Branches." Funds from these sources usually provided enough money for the general expenses of the National Council. The situation was, however, always precarious, and a constant source of worry to the national executive. Since neither at the local nor the national level was the Council itself a charitable organization, fund raising was always difficult. The Council's most pressing need was for money for the least popular purposes: the support of head office, the expenses of postage and printing, and charges for executive travel. While it might, at both levels, act as fundraiser for a specific charitable purpose, its own financial requirement was to pay for a bureaucracy. The President and her executive officers might consider "the estimated yearly expenditure most moderate and satisfactory," in the words of the 1901 *Yearbook*, but the membership would never look with enthusiasm on a demand for greater contributions to support organizational needs. It must be re-emphasized that members would always have a prior loyalty to another organization, in most cases a charity, whose fundraising and monetary demands would almost always be directly linked to an explicit human need. To any member, at any time, the debates of Council in 1902 as to whether meetings should be triennial instead of annual, in order to economize, will sound a sympathetic chord.

If financing the Council would be a perennial problem so would the efficiency of the National office, which was run from the very beginning on a mixture of paid and unpaid labour. President after President will thank her helpers, apologize for the "late" arrival of the Annual Report and beg local councils to be efficient and business-like correspondents. Similarly, the continuing problems of membership attendance were noted by Adelaide Hoodless as early as 1901. She had been with the Council since its inception in 1893. That year she decided to resign the post of Treasurer she had held so far, as she wished to give more time to the organization of the Women's Institutes, ten of which had been founded to that point. Her farewell address is notable, as much for the style of her criticism as for its content.

She opened with praise, noting that she looked upon the "Council as a

National School of Economics, offering a five year course in the study of social conditions, at the end of which time the diligent student should have a far broader view of life and its vital questions." "She herself," she continued, "had taken a post-graduate course of three years, in consideration of which fact she hoped to be pardoned if, in a spirit of friendliness, she ventured to point out what she thought one of the weaknesses of the Council, namely, its system of irresponsible representation, both at the Executive and Annual meetings."[18] Few members were as forthright as Mrs. Hoodless but the uncertainty about levels of commitment to Council would plague its leadership throughout ensuing decades.

Finally, both early and recent presidents have had to confront the problem of recruitment. In the years before the First World War, however, the problem was less urgent than it later became. As has always been the case, some local councils disbanded and others, having lapsed for a number of years, re-emerged. Quebec City disappeared in 1901, (it would be re-established in 1920) as nobody was willing to undertake the presidency.[19] In 1903 local councils were formed in Port Hope, Whitby, Guelph, Lindsay and Ingersoll.[20] Some of these had a very brief span of existence. Lindsay disappears in 1914, for example, but others such as Guelph and Ingersoll would disband only to be resuscitated a number of years later. A council was established in Fredericton, New Brunswick in 1904, although it ran into difficulties in 1908. Rat Portage (Kenora) died in 1907. Brantford was organized in 1908, largely due to the efforts of Mrs. Boomer.[21] Edmonton re-established itself that same year. A local council appeared in Renfrew in 1909, due to the efforts of Mrs. Adam Shortt. The *Yearbook* of 1909 states that the Council had twenty-five local branches.[22] In 1910 two local councils were established, Walkerville, Ontario (this appears to be the eleventh local council in that province) and Strathcona in Alberta. Charlottetown collapsed in 1910, but Chapleau was established in 1911 as were Sudbury and Sydney, Nova Scotia. Calgary began again in 1912 and Truro was founded that year. Peterborough emerged in 1913 as did Sarnia. Councils founded in 1914 were Pembroke, Ontario and Yarmouth, Nova Scotia, Lethbridge and Medicine Hat, Alberta.

This list of local councils, compiled from the annual reports of these

---

18 *Ibid.*, p. 126.
19 *Ibid.*, p. 22.
20 *Yearbook*, 1903, p. 14.
21 *Yearbook*, 1908, p. 10.
22 *Yearbook*, 1909, p. 4.

years, provides a very bony skeleton for information about the growth and activity taking place. It has to be remembered that there were a number of Councils that had only a brief existence. Those who were Council members, after all, were members because they were already committed to another association or club. Individual members, while welcome, have never been the real core of Council strength. To exist at all there had to be both a critical mass of associations and societies whose executives considered joint action useful in their community, and also individuals willing to take up the work that Council membership required. This work was above all that of a delegate: the concerns of the affiliate had to be properly presented at local council and the questions and problems that Council raised for discussion had to be reported back to the affiliate for commentary. Establishment of a local council in a community meant, first and foremost, that the local association membership agreed to a general forum for discussion of issues important to that community. The continued existence of a local council meant that the women of the community found the local council an aid in pursuing their own agendas. The proliferation of local councils says much about the way in which women found the organization a useful forum for social and political action. It is noteworthy that outside of Montreal, local councils are almost unknown among Francophone Canadians. The leadership of the Council movement has been overwhelmingly, but *not* exclusively of Protestant and Anglophone background and this reality has shaped the growth of the organization and its policies.

At the national level, the growth in the number of affiliate associations between 1900 and 1914 was impressive. All but one of the new associations continued their membership beyond these years. The Alumnae Association of the Ontario Medical College for Women affiliated in 1901 and the Ladies of the Maccabees in 1902. The Women's Institutes of Ontario joined in 1902. In 1906 both the National Historical Society and the Peace and Arbitration Society joined, but the National Historical Society let its membership lapse in 1909. That was the year in which the Imperial Order of the Daughters of the Empire affiliated, as did the Canadian Women's Press Club, the Canadian Society of Superintendents of Training Schools for Nurses and the Women's Branch, Independent Order of Foresters. The fact that the International Council held its triennial meeting in Canada in that year was a spur to affiliation, but most of those who joined in 1909 remained part of the Council for at least the next decade. In 1913 the Single Tax Association became an affiliate and in 1914 the Ontario Horticultural Association joined.

These years of growth changed the Council, in much the same way that

expansion changed Canada during the same era. The change was evolution-
ary rather than revolutionary. It involved a clearer understanding of how
Council could marshal its resources most efficiently, and of the role that the
National Council should play in informing and directing public opinion. The
period 1900-1914 was a time in which Council built a recognizable public
profile of its aims and concerns both by way of intelligible political statements about issues of the day, and effective lobbying for particular causes.
They were also years in which the Council moved from defensive arguments
concerning the benefit of women's influence in society to a confident assertion of women's right to be heard because of their fundamental role in society. Whereas in the early years the annual meeting had heard a great deal of
comment as to why the point of view of Council should be considered by
government, the 1914 *Yearbook* lists without apology the four main issues
about which Council had made representations to Parliament during the past
year. These were the question of a universal Penny Postage (in order that
costs of communication among peoples should kept to a minimum); the
appointment of competent matrons on Indian reserves (to teach sanitation,
hygiene and domestic science); a petition regarding non-support of deserted
wives; and a general comment on needed changes to the Criminal Code.[23]

The issue of effective mobilization of the strength of Council was considered at the annual meeting of 1903, held in Toronto from May 20 through
May 26. Mrs. Hoodless presented an address on the matter. She is so often
seen as the moving spirit behind the Women's Institute that her work with
the National Council has been, if not overlooked, not given the importance it
warrants. She was typical of women whose contribution to Council was
enduring but whose major sphere of action lay in work for their particular
affiliate. In her address, which was entitled "Suggestions for the work of
Local Councils,"[24] Mrs. Hoodless outlined both the extraordinary and enduring strength of Council's structure and its equally enduring weaknesses. She
was completely clear in her mind as to what Council meetings ought to be
about. She declared bluntly that annual meetings were not "a kindergarten
where members learn by doing but a legislative session where intelligent
women meet with carefully studied plans for the welfare of their sex and
society at large." This expectation demanded an effective administration so
that local councils would be prepared to speak intelligently at annual meetings. For Mrs. Hoodless one of the most important functions of the Council

---

[23] *Yearbook*, 1914, pp. 18-19.
[24] *Yearbook*, 1903, p. 71.

was its work as a forum for intelligent discussion of the issues of the day, and her desire was to prevent it being used in "any chaotic manner." She was quite clear that "irresponsible and uninformed representation at the Annual Meeting is not conducive to the work of the Council."

Certainly the situation in 1903 needed remedy. Mrs. Hoodless listed seventeen Standing Committees of the National Council, covering the following subjects: Laws for the Better Protection of Women and Children; Pernicious Literature; Custodial Care of Feeble-minded Women; Care of the Aged and Infirm Poor; Finance; Immigration; Press; Bureau of Information; Publication; Domestic Science and Manual Training; Agriculture for Women; Promotion of the Industrial and Fine Arts; Women on School Boards; Vacation Schools and Playgrounds; Promotion of a Uniform Standard of Education and Dominion Registration of Teachers; International Committee; Committee of Revision. "These Standing Committees," Mrs. Hoodless went on to point out, "are composed of one member, elected by each Local Council, when they do elect them, and meet once a year the day before the annual meeting of National Council." "Can you imagine," she concluded, "any logical discussion of a subject under such conditions?"[25]

For Mrs. Hoodless the work of the Council as a conduit to inform and consult "an organized body of representative women in many of the chief cities and towns of the Dominion"[26] was seriously hampered by the very characteristic that facilitated this consultation: the unfettered liberty of action allowed local councils with regard to their formation and functions. She suggested three remedies: that local councils adopt a form of organization that would mirror the pattern of standing committees at the national level, and that they set their agendas so as to provide a proper time for the study of questions that the National Council considered important. Acceptance of this latter idea would require compliance at the national level with her third suggestion, that important resolutions be presented to the Executive at the first meeting after each annual meeting. This would make it possible for an agenda to be sent out to local councils in order that views would be presented "in organized fashion" at the national level. Over the years, Council came to conduct itself in line with her suggestions. Nevertheless it had to wrestle continuously with problems of organization, as well as with those of finance and membership.

Revisions to the Constitution and by-laws, and reorganization of

25   *Ibid.*, p. 72.
26   *Ibid.*, p. 73.

Standing Committees were all recurring phenomena, as much testimony to the ability of the Council to adapt to changing societal patterns as to any inherent weakness of Council structure. Any organization made up of local bodies, themselves composed of affiliates of which only some would also be linked through their head offices to the National Council, and of national associations, which might or might not be linked to other local councils, would inevitably encounter problems. In 1903, for example, local council memberships varied from the thirty-one affiliates which the Montreal Council encompassed, to the six bodies affiliated with the Regina Council. Council at both the national and local levels would establish its role as an organizer or facilitator rather than an innovator. Its most important objective was not the initiation of innovative and radical reform programs but, in Mrs. Hoodless's words, "to prevent overlapping of work." There is no doubt that Council did evolve policies, at the national and local level, which represented a Council initiative, a Council voice. On the whole, however, the organization functioned in these early years as a study-group, as a clearing house, and as a market-place for information. As has been mentioned, the National Council was called "the Parliament of women" at its founding meeting by the then Prime Minister of Canada, Sir John Thompson.[27] At a time when women's voting rights in Canada were restricted to participation in certain municipal elections, this assembly provided women with an alternative to the established political systems. But the issue of women's suffrage was only one of its many concerns, and when suffrage was achieved, Council did not disappear. It became a place where women were given priority because of gender. The limits placed on women's actions in the broader society, the particular difficulties they faced in life because of their sex, became the essential subject matter of Council action. Throughout its existence, however, the organization has avoided close identification with particular feminist ideologies, be it those of the "Moral Majority" or the National Action Committees. Both nationally and locally, members have been concerned with a broad spectrum of issues which have appeared particularly important to women, and, in some instances, to men also. Veronica Strong-Boag consider that Council women were "largely middle-class women who were moved by humanitarian, class and egalitarian concerns to attempt the redemption of their society."[28] I would amend this description only to the extent required to make it clear that the organization was the creation of people who were

---

[27] *Yearbook*, 1893, p. 184.
[28] Strong-Boag, *Parliament of Women*, p. vii.

women, concerned not so much with redemption of society as with its functioning effectively in their lifetimes and the lifetimes of the generation to
come. This might mean desire for reform, it might mean desire for repen-
tance, but it always meant concern for the contemporary scene, what A.R.M.
Lower called "the day to day questions that affect society."[29]

The actual agendas of Council, at both local and national levels, changed
over the decades as circumstances of Canadian life altered. They were
moulded by events of the times, by the extent to which a particular affiliate
could get its own program adopted by Council, and by the demands of local
councils that particular issues be addressed. The resultant activities can best
be illustrated by a detailed review of some of the issues brought forward for
consideration in each of these three categories.

Immigration was as much a major issue for the Council as for the
country as a whole. The growth of the population of Canada at the opening
of the twentieth century, from just over five million in 1901, to over seven
million on the eve of World War I and to nearly nine million in 1921,[30]
focused much public attention upon general questions surrounding the kind
of society and culture that the people of Canada wanted to build. While
natural increase was obviously responsible for part of this growth the dramatic change — a 34% increase during the decade 1901–1911 and a further 22% increase between 1911 and 1921[31] — was largely due to immigration. The massive influx of newcomers was the result of the migration
of people to Canada, under many different circumstances, from all parts of
the globe. Close to a third of the migrants, during these years, were
Americans: farmers' sons, among others, went north as the free homestead
lands of the American West filled up. Men came, from China and India,
almost always without their families, to be part of the labour force necessary to build the transcontinental railways. Farming families emigrated
from the Austrian empire, "nearly 6,000 in 1900, over 10,000 five years
later, over 21,000 in 1912-13."[32] Others came from Russia. Emigrants from
Britain came, after 1905, in ever increasing numbers, some in family
groups, others, both men and women, alone. In 1912-13, 150,000 people
left those islands for a new life on a continent.[33] The total number of immi-

29 A.R.M. Lower, *Canadians in the Making*, (Toronto, 1958), p. 314.
30 The best source for population data during this period remains Leary, ed., *Historical Statistics*.
    New work based on the release of the census returns is continually being published.
31   Cook,"Triumph and Trials," p. 183.
32 Brown and Cook, *Canada 1896-1921*, p. 63.
33 *Ibid.*, p. 57.

8. Mrs. Robert Thompson, President 1902-1906

grants in that year was 400,870.[34]

This influx was a considerable challenge to the Canadian sense of community.[35] When the new migrants began arriving there was no explicit statement about the extent to which they, as new Canadians, were expected to conform to the norms of the society already established. However, there was a policy implicit in services provided by provincial and federal governments to new migrants at the opening of the twentieth century, a policy made explicit in many statements from opinion leaders. Canada was about "peace, order and good government." Society was to be built and developed on the basis of beliefs about English values, and outside of Quebec migrants were expected to assimilate and become part of "English Canada." In the early decades of the twentieth century, no one in Canada held a brief for multiculturalism.

From 1900 onwards, the Council supported its constituent bodies as they worked to give new immigrants knowledge about the country they had joined. In particular, it acted as a link between the various societies promoting the immigration of single women. The British Women's Emigration Society, which had been formed in 1884, despatched some 16,000 single women to Canada during the years leading up to 1914. From 1903 to 1914 the Salvation Army helped another 15,000 single women emigrate to the Dominion.[36] Montreal had established a home to welcome female immigrants as early as 1882.[37] Winnipeg followed suit in 1897, and that year the National Council supported the action initiated by the Toronto and Montreal Councils for the establishment of the Women's Protective Immigration Societies. Local Councils of Women were behind the organization of other homes of welcome in Toronto, (1905), Calgary (1906), Halifax (1909) and Regina (1910).[38]

At the annual meeting of 1903, which was held in Toronto, Council gave the general issue of migration considerable prominence. While migration was considered from a regional standpoint, the issue of immigrant women for domestic service was also emphasized. Three position papers were delivered: "Immigration to the Eastern Provinces," written by Mrs. John Cox, member of the Montreal Local Council for the Women's National

[34] John Herd Thompson, "Ethnic Minorities During Two World Wars," C.H.A. Series "Canada's Ethnic Groups," Booklet No. 19, (Ottawa, 1991), p. 3.
[35] On this see Reg Whitaker, *Canadian Immigration Policy Since Confederation*, C.H.A. Series, "Canada's Ethnic Groups," Booklet No. 15, Ottawa, 1991.
[36] Barber, *Immigrant Domestic Servants*, pp. 10-11.
[37] *Ibid.*, p. 10.
[38] *Ibid.*

Immigration Society, and read by Miss Reid; "Immigration" written by Miss Fowler, member of Winnipeg's Local Council, and read by Mrs. Cooper; the final paper was "Immigration from a western point of view,"[39] written and read by Mrs. Skinner, member of Vancouver Local Council from the Young Women's Christian Association. All three papers considered the general problems of immigration: employment opportunities, the ways in which immigrants were welcomed into the towns and villages where they settled, the provision of educational, and religious and medical services to the new-comers; but the theme that surfaced repeatedly was the lot of the single woman migrant and her prospects in domestic service.

A considerable amount of time at the meeting was spent discussing the different types of work that servants could be expected to do in Canada, and the difference between the life of a servant in Canada and in England. The distribution of wealth within the two societies, the relative number of the wealthy in each, the difference between the lifestyles of the cities and the countryside, were all matters which the Council members saw as having an impact on the nature of service. It was pointed out that there were few homes in Canada which had more than two servants, whereas the wealthy upper middle class and aristocracy in Britain often employed six or more. Further, on the farms and in the countryside, servants were often enough a couple, the man working as a farm labourer and the woman inside the home. The category of "domestic help," the general maid-of-all work, was probably the most common category of domestic service for women in Canada.[40]

The immigrant woman employed for such work was, as Mrs. Halliwell remarked, not often "foreign" [i.e. those from countries other than the British Isles] since for the most part these people "emigrate in families." But for women from the British Isles, the prospect of domestic service in Canada and the existence of agencies recruiting for this work meant that they could emi-grate with assistance and without the ties and burdens of family. According to Marilyn Barber, "by 1911, over one third of female domestics in Ontario and three quarters of those in western Canada were immigrants." [41]

In her paper, Mrs Skinner linked the view that domestic service was the best job market for women with general prospects for women's employment in Canada. She noted that there was "a certain demand for girls to act as clerks in stores, some typewriters and stenographers."[42] She went on to point

[39] *Yearbook*, 1900, pp. 104-121.
[40] *Yearbook*, 1903, p. 111.
[41] Barber, *Immigrant Domestic Servants*, p. 8.
[42] *Yearbook*, 1903, p.114.

out, however, that while "nurse or housemaid work paid better, often girls preferred to work in shops." In her view this was "first because they have more freedom; and, secondly, because it is to them a step up in the social scale."[43] Mrs. Skinner had placed her finger on the central issue concerning the employment of women, both immigrant and native Canadian, as servants. Neither employer nor employee really believed domestic service to be either a trade or a profession. It was an occupation of long hours and little privacy and no one considered it an important part of the nation's economic life. Even today, in the nineteen-nineties, housework is only just being taken into account as a contributing factor to the gross national product. At the opening of the twentieth century domestic service, especially in the cities, was considered by employer and employee alike, as the lowest form of "respectable" work. It was rarely entered upon, consciously, as a lifetime job and in fact was, for the majority of both men and women, whether Canadian or immigrant, usually a temporary occupation. It was, even more rarely, a lifelong occupation in one particular place for one particular employer.[44] The essence of the "servant problem," in the eyes of the employer, was the mobility of the servant, the high turnover of employees, and the marked preference of women, in particular, for other work. Domestic service was a stepping stone: an occupation that allowed the immigrant to learn how the new land functioned, to take time to look around for something better.

The debates at the National Council meetings about the employment of immigrant women as domestics continued until the First World War. There is no doubt that the women who were members of the Council at the national level, as well as most of those who represented one or another of the many volunteer organizations that came together to form local councils, employed servants. However, it would be a travesty of history of Council to present this issue as the essence of Council's reaction to immigrants.

There were in fact other aspects of immigration in which Council took a major interest, and a striking example of the way in which the National Council and local councils interacted was the issue of child immigration. It has been estimated that during the last thirty years of the nineteenth century some thirty thousand youngsters, boys and girls, between the ages of 12 and 14, were sent to Canada from Britain.[45] Given that there were already poor children in Canadian cities, most of these youngsters went to the country-

---

[43] *Ibid.*

[44] See Del Muise, "The Industrial Centre of Inequality: Female Participation in Nova Scotia's Paid Labour Force 1871–1921," in *Acadiensis*, vol. 22, no. 2, (Spring 1991), pp. 3-31.

[45] Jack A. Blyth, *The Canadian Social Inheritance*, (Toronto, 1972), p. 22.

side. While there were undoubtedly good and kind employers, the exploitation of these young immigrants became a matter of common knowledge and was directly responsible for the founding of the Toronto Children's Aid Society, in 1891, and the passage, in 1893, of the Ontario Children's Protection Act. Moreover, the need for continued public action in this area became obvious, and in 1896 representatives of local councils in London and Kingston presented instances of careless exploitation of young children at the annual meeting.[46] The National Council set up a committee to address the issue and make presentations to both the provincial and federal governments. At the same time, local councils were urged to take cognizance of the situation in their own localities. This led to action in London, Toronto, Montreal, Kingston and Halifax.[47] Activity also centred at the national level, where the Council expressed its concern, year by year, regarding "the urgent necessity of increasing the inspection and other precautions used in connection with the immigration of pauper children into Canada."[48] The effort to protect children who immigrated alone came to an end in the nineteen thirties, when this type of immigration ceased, due, in very large part, to the vigorous campaign conducted by Charlotte Whitton, a member of the Council.

In a similar fashion, particular needs of specific groups of adult migrants were considered at the behest of local councils. In 1899, for instance, the plight of the Doukhobors drew the attention of Council.[49] Some 7,400 members of this Russian sect had come to Canada in 1898 and the majority were settled on three blocks of land in the northwest, near Yorkton, Saskatchewan.[50] The particular needs of the migrants were examined, the Council being informed that the women were engaged in building their homes from logs and "a plaster which the women themselves make, treading it out in a large pit."[51] The speaker, Mrs. Fitzgibbon, was immediately questioned on what the men were about and the answer was that "the men were working on railway construction and on the farms. They have had to go out to earn a little money for the coming winter." A committee was struck to consider the matter. Money was raised to buy sewing machines for the women and local councils in the West undertook to look after the sale of work produced.

---

46 *Yearbook,* 1896, pp. 470-486.
47 Shaw, *Proud Heritage,* pp. 12-17.
48 *Yearbook,* 1897, pp. 167-68.
49 *Yearbook,* 1899, p. xii.
50 Brown and Cook, *Canada 1896-1921,* p. 63.
51 *Yearbook,* 1899, p. 266.

The demography of migration underlay most public issues in Canadian life between 1900 and 1914 but it was by no means the only area which demanded attention. The migrants were arriving in a political system that was already in operation and had to solve a wide range of problems, including the consequences of rapid urbanization and the manner in which the country conducted its external relations. Within the framework of the National Council the local councils took the lead in working out approaches to the needs of communities, as they sought to build social nets in their localities. The functioning of the organization was dependent on a two-way transfer of concerns. The National Council informed local councils of the topics of concern to be addressed in any given year, the selection having been made by the Executive at the time of the annual meeting. Local councils in their turn, presented the National Council with topics they wished to have considered in the coming year. But local councils were also required to make annual reports to the National Council and these formed part of the published Yearbook (Annual Report) of the National Council. This publication, partly a calendar of events, partly an overview of past achievements and present problems, made the concerns of each local council matters of general knowledge. No local council was restricted to the agenda proposed by the National Council and, very often, work done in one community would spark investigation and discussion elsewhere. For example, the interest which Ottawa Local Council showed in the problems faced by women alcoholics in 1903 was debated in Toronto and Hamilton within the year.

By 1900 a typical Council pattern had taken shape: a problem is identified at the local level and referred to the National meeting. It is accepted as a matter for general concern and study committees are organized at both the national and local levels. Reports go back and forth, leading to the passing of resolutions in favour of action, usually in the form of lobbying the appropriate authority. In an age without radio or television, the distribution of material by Council provided a common body of knowledge in widely separated communities. The way in which the National Council drew together ideas and resolutions grew increasingly more effective, and the lobbying work displays increasing sophistication as members of the Executive came to know who ought to be lobbied over particular issues.

Not all local problems were repeated elsewhere and the diversity of Canada is reflected in the differing ways in which local councils emerged and developed. In general, the National Council did not recruit effectively within Quebec, except in Montreal. This was due in part to the suspicion French-speaking women felt for an organization that was predominantly, but not exclusively, Anglophone. It was due, also, to the view taken by the Catholic hierarchy of a body that was essentially, though not exclusively, Protestant in character. The major reason was, however, the place of the women's religious orders in Quebec. It is an over-simplification to conclude that the Catholic women's active religious orders, those concerned with education, health and general social service, obviated the need for secular activity. Nevertheless, as Marta Danylewycz has pointed out, "Francophone women who joined active (as opposed to contemplative) religious orders to work for the benefit of society behaved like lay women elsewhere who organized charitable work."[52] In Montreal these orders made a major contribution to the social well-being of the city. "One-sixth of the 6,500 nuns working in the province of Quebec at the turn of the century ministered to the needs of Montreal's growing female population."[53] While these orders were by no means the only organization in the city for French-Canadian women concerned for the betterment of society, they were by far the most important and were seldom linked to Council activities.

From the outset some upper class French-Canadian women had participated in the National Council. In particular, Joséphine Dandurand, the editor of a pioneering women's magazine *Le Coin du Feu* and Marie Lacoste-Gérin-Lajoie, a self-taught legal expert, enthusiastically joined in the founding meetings of the National Council in 1893.[54] It was to a large extent due to these women that the intense interest of the Montreal Local Council in coping with the obvious problems of poverty was combined with a concern for the broader issue of women's suffrage.

On the other hand, Montreal's ethnic mix helped to bring support to its local council and, while Catholic organizations, Francophone and other, did affiliate on occasion, its primary membership was Anglophone and

---

52 Marta Danylewycz, "Changing Relationships: Nuns and Feminists in Montreal, 1890-1925," *Histoire Sociale/Social History*, vol. XIV. 28, Novembre-December 1981, p. 413.
53 *Ibid.*, p. 414.
54 Joséphine Dandurand was born in St. Jean, Quebec and died in 1925. She was the daughter of the Hon. Félix Gabriel Marchand, who was premier of Quebec, 1897-1900. She married, in 1886, Raoul Dandurand, who was appointed to the Senate in 1898. In 1893, Madame Dandurand became editor of *Le Coin du Feu*, a magazine aimed at raising the prestige of women in Quebec. In 1898, she became the first Canadian woman to be appointed an Officier de l'Académie by the government of France. Marie Gérin-Lajoie, née Lacoste was born in Montreal 19 October 1867 and died in 1, 1 November 1945. Her father was Sir Alexandre Lacoste, Chief Justice of Quebec from 1897-1910. She was self-educated, and through reading her father's library she became aware of the legal disabilities of women. She was one of the founders of the Fédération nationale des sociétés St-Jean-Baptistes in 1907 and she worked throughout her life for better conditions for women. She wrote two major law texts: *Traité de droit usuel* (1902) and *La femme et le code civil* (1929).

Protestant or Jewish. It may be noted here that in 1901 the composition of Montreal's population, with respect to its origins, was as follows: 63.9% French, 31.6% British, 1.9% Jewish, .6% Italian and 2.0% "other."[55] In the 1903 *Yearbook*, Montreal listed thirty-three affiliates.[56] Its report made a distinction between those projects which were undertaken by an affiliate alone and those for which the prime responsibility was the Montreal Local Council itself. Some of the projects of the latter kind, such as the appointment of women on school boards, were long-term endeavours initiated by resolutions of National Council. Others, such as the work for the provision of pure milk and the sponsorship of "Health Talks" in different areas of the city, were matters of particular concern to Montreal. Certain activities, such as the provision of philanthropic aid to the poor, were a reflection of the unique ethnic heritage of the city. Many similar ventures were also undertaken in the other major Canadian cities, but the particular balance of French, English and Irish, Protestant, Catholic and Jew, which became apparent in Montreal at the turn of the century, gave the work of the local council a very particular flavour.

There is no doubt that local councils were the moving force behind community action, building a network among the separate volunteer organizations, with their very specific agendas. A problem identified would always bring the local council into action. Ottawa Council, for example, not only provided immediate and organized relief when a major typhoid epidemic struck the city in January 1911. It also organized meetings, in March of that year, to discuss the health needs of the city and to persuade the provincial government to prod Ottawa City Council into action.[57] This response to local disaster was typical of the work of councils during these years.

Equally typical were the drives to establish hospitals and libraries, the performance of a function of mediation between differing religious denominations, and the provision of a forum for public discussion of competing interests. One of the activities most consistently maintained was the organization of information sessions on participation in public meetings. As the Toronto Council noted in 1904 "it was felt by Council that many members

55 Michael D. Behiels, *Quebec and the Question of Immigration: From Ethnocentrism to Ethnic Pluralism*, C.H.A. Series, "Canada's Ethnic Groups," Booklet No. 18, (Ottawa, 1991), p. 2.
56 *Yearbook*, 1903, pp. iv-viii.
57 Ottawa City Council Records, vol.2, Book 3, p. 53, National Archives of Canada. Cited in Diane Reid, Anita Penner, Slidon Nesmith, Paulette Dozois, *A Bridge to the Future: A History of the Council of Women of Ottawa and Area*, (Ottawa, 1970), n.p.

did not understand the elements of parliamentary procedure."[58] Many local councils followed the example of Toronto and organized a "Speakers Committee," charged with the duty of organizing a program that would help members become better public speakers. Council provided an invaluable training for women in the conventions of joint action. Considering the education received by most women in Canada at this time, even those of the middle and upper class, in this training in public life was of inestimable benefit and indeed indispensable.

With regard to general goals for community betterment, high on the list of most local councils, was the establishment of child care centres, kindergartens and nurseries. By 1913, Veronica Strong-Boag has noted, "more than 13 local councils had active committees organizing playgrounds throughout their cities."[59] As the work of the Vancouver Council demonstrates, local councils paid considerable attention to the essential details of children's lives.[60] Along with most of the Ontario Councils during these years, Vancouver's Local Council lobbied the City Council for the improvement of the sanitary provisions in school buildings. In an country where a high standard of public sanitation is today accepted without question, and the water-closet has made the disposal of human waste a matter of clean invisibility, the problems of one- and two-room schools, with fifty to sixty children in attendance, no running water and no proper sanitation, is now difficult to envisage.

Councils in all provinces, but particularly in Ontario, also provided much of the political lobbying necessary for the establishment of the Children's Aid Societies. The troublesome question of a dividing line between childhood and adulthood led the National Council to consider the problem of the definition of the juvenile. In 1906 Council celebrated the enactment of the Juvenile Delinquents Act, which forbade, in almost all cases, the imprisonment of any young person under sixteen.

In the pre-war era, a local council could bring to bear an astonishing amount of informed and organized volunteer labour. At their peak of activity, some local councils numbered over a hundred affiliates. During these years however, young councils such as Calgary and Regina usually numbered some twenty to thirty affiliates while Councils such as Vancouver, Toronto

---

58   Anon., *Nothing New Under the Sun*, p. 36.
59   Strong-Boag, *Parliament of Women*, p. 269.
60   Vancouver Council of Women, Correspondence and Minutes: Seventeenth Annual Meeting, 5 February 1912.

and Montreal counted approximately fifty affiliates. The structure of local councils was the usual organization of executive, standing and ad hoc committees. The Standing Committees before 1914 were most often those dealing with finance, immediate civic questions and, after 1909, suffrage. The ad hoc committees were most frequently struck to cope with demands for comment and action required from the National Council. The adoption of an issue by a local council meant that support for the action in question would be organized throughout most of the important religious and volunteer associations of women existing in that town. Given this basic pattern of action it is not surprising that local councils became involved in most public issues relating to women.

The context of women's lives, from birth to death, childhood to child-rearing, becomes the context for the work at the local level. From clean water to wrapped bread, from conditions of women's employment to support for those caught up in the justice system, from the representation of women on public boards — school, prison, hospital — to their appointment on public commissions, a diversity of topics presented themselves to local council members, regarding which they felt a duty to comment, advise and criticize. The many efforts of organizations such as the women's auxiliary branches of local churches, the local chapters of the Ladies of the Maccabees,[61] and the Salvation Army were coordinated through local council meetings. It is easy to forget that while the Council organization worked hard at obvious social ills it was also involved in the support of cultural activities. Most local councils included societies dedicated to the promotion of music, painting, reading and general appreciation of the arts. The establishment of free public libraries was a continual subject of debate and Ottawa Local Council was particularly concerned with this objective. Interest in things aesthetic extended to town planning and most local councils had a standing committee charged with commenting on the amenities of their town and on the development activities envisaged. Members might be divided in their opinion as to where maximum effort should be placed: on local issues or on national problems, on long-term reform projects or on immediate crises, on curfew laws to control adolescents (Calgary) or on the provision of free dental care for children (Toronto and London), but despite these diversions they made the opinions of a considerable number of women a factor that had to be taken

---

[61] Which defined itself in 1906 as a fraternal beneficial society, founded in Great Britain with a membership of 141,000 and an outstanding protection on the life of its members of over $96,000,000. *Yearbook*, 1906, pp. xxiv-xxv.

into account.

The tact and diplomatic art necessary to make local councils work were also required for the management of the Council at the national level. It is remarkable that Council was able to function with considerable agreement, even in areas where its membership held strong and divergent views. It rarely became locked into uncritical adherence to the program of a specific group. Despite much pressure, for example, it resisted the appeal of the Women's Christian Temperance Movement to become itself a temperance organization. In its advocacy of women's rights, the Council began moving extremely cautiously. At the annual meeting of 1906, for example, Mrs. Augusta Stowe Gullen moved for the establishment of a standing committee to work for "Political Equality."[62] Her motion was supported by 52 votes against 22. In the following year, 1907, a resolution was carried to the effect "that all institutions of learning and professional instruction (in the best interests of humanity) be as freely open to women as to men; that opportunities for industrial training be as generally and as liberally provided for one sex as for the other, and that in all avocations in which both men and women engage equal wages shall be paid for equal work."[63]

The first local council to endorse suffrage was Victoria, in 1908, yet it was the impact of the meeting of the International Council of Women, held in Toronto in 1909, which brought the National Council of Women of Canada, in 1910, to support votes for women, by a majority, but not unanimously. It was at the Berlin Conference in 1904 that the International Council had affirmed its support for female suffrage. At that time its membership was fifteen, Italy (1900), New Zealand (1900), Argentina (1901), France (1901), Austria (1903), Switzerland (1903) and Norway (1904) having become members since 1899. Now in Toronto, five years later, this stand was confirmed. Belgium (1906) and Greece (1908) had joined in the previous five years. The International Council voted unanimously in favour of the resolution that "women ought to possess the vote in all countries where representative government existed."[64] The public support of Lady Aberdeen for this policy, in speeches given at the University of Toronto on June 20 and 21, 1909 was probably as important for the National Council of Women of Canada as the stand taken by the International Council itself.

---

[62] *Ibid.*, p. 68.
[63] *Yearbook,* 1907, p. 80.
[64] L. Cleverdon, *The Woman Suffrage Movement in Canada,* (Toronto, 1950), p. 31.

Canada gave strong support to its National Council for this meeting in
1909. Receptions were organized for the delegates in Quebec, Montreal and
Ottawa and there were more than a hundred of them, representing twelve
countries. The Dominion government set up a temporary post office for the
occasion on the grounds of the University of Toronto. The railways reduced
their fares to Toronto from all parts of the United States and Canada, as well
as providing excursion fares for those delegates wishing to visit western
Canada. All kinds of dignitaries addressed the gathering, from the Lieutenant
Governor of Ontario to the Mayor of Toronto. The latter quoted the
Canadian Prime Minister as saying that "if the National Council of Women
had done nothing else than to bring together women from the east and from
the west, they had done a great deal towards the unification of the country
with its diverse races and creeds."[65]

The main business of the conference turned upon the question of
women's suffrage, of women's equality before the law, better working conditions for women and children, better public health and international peace.
As far as suffrage was concerned it was announced in the report of the
National Council of Finland that in the elections of 1907 nineteen women
had been elected to the Finnish Diet: "one lady student, teachers, authors, a
clergyman's and a peasant's wife." The report went on to say that "the nine
social-democratic women members were all without exception, seamstress-
es, former servants, factory hands and working men's wives."[66] It is interesting to note that the Argentinean women requested that the tone of the resolutions of the International Council be restrained, because of the opposition of
the Catholic bishops to suffrage matters.

Whether the greatest impact upon the policy of the Canadian Council
came from the particular example of Finland, the urging of the American
women, or the public stance taken by Lady Aberdeen is a matter for debate.
In any case at the annual meeting of the National Council in 1910 the resolution reading "That the National Council of Women of Canada do hereby
place itself on record in favour of the enfranchisement of women" was
passed 71 to 51.[67]

The debate had been lengthy and heated. The opening speech in favour
of the motion was delivered by Dr. Margaret Gordon on behalf of the
Medical Alumnae of Toronto University. She based much of her argument

[65] Lady Aberdeen, ed., *International Council of Women: Report of Transactions of the Fourth
Quinquennial Meeting held at Toronto, June 1909*, (London, 1910), p. 70.
[66] *Ibid*, p. 398.
[67] *Yearbook*, 1910, p. 104.

on the view that women "seem to be using their influence for the moral advancement of society, and there is no reason to believe that when women receive a direct voice in affairs they will change." The President, Lady Taylor, felt that the resolution would divide the Council and that many Councils, Halifax for example, would break up because of it. According to the *Yearbook*, Miss Ritchie, speaking for the Halifax Local Council, "emphatically, earnestly and with quiet humour, showed that this would not be the case."[68] The most reasoned speech reported was that of Carrie Derick, an outstanding Montreal feminist.[69] In the precis of her words it is noted that she contended that "it is a waste of energy to go from legislator to legislator in order to press our reforms...not having the authority carried by the power of the vote, we are frequently deserted by the very men who are supposed to represent our cause...The homesteading law, the laws dealing with hours of labour for women, etc., had all been lost because women did not have the direct method of voicing their opinions."

The franchise was still in the distance in 1910 but many women knew precisely why they wanted it. The argument for women in public life was shifting away from the theories of maternal feminism to the viewpoint that women, qua women, had rights. This view was clearly put by Sonia Leathes in 1913 at the annual meeting of the National Council:

> ...women today say to the governments of the world; you have usurped what used to be our authority, what used to be our responsibility. It is you who determine the nature of the air which we breathe, of the food which we eat, of the clothing which we wear. It is you who determine when, and how long, and what our children are to be taught and what their prospects as future wage earners are. It is you who condone or who stamp out the white slave traffic and the starvation wage. It is you who by granting or refusing pensions to the mothers of young children can preserve or destroy the fatherless home. It is you who consider what action shall be a crime. And since all of these matters strike at the very heart strings of the mothers of all nations, we shall not rest until we have secured the power

---

68 *Ibid.*, p. 101.
69 She was born in Clarenceville, Quebec, Jan. 1862. Her family was United Empire Loyalist. She was a student in McGill's Botanical Department between 1887 and 1890, graduating with the gold medal in natural science. She took her M.A. there in 1896, and went on to study at the University of Bonn, Germany. She was the first woman on the staff of McGill University, being appointed a demonstrator in botany in 1891. In 1906 she was promoted to assistant professor and later became Professor of Evolution and Genetics. She was a lifelong Council member.

vested in the ballot...[70]

Nevertheless, if the argument for woman's right to vote was no longer solely based upon her moral worth, her "innate" maternal attributes were still, on most occasions, offered as *the* justification for the extension of the suffrage. Even Carrie Derick used the argument that "...the spirit which animates the [suffrage] movement is not self-seeking. It is rather, a maternal spirit aroused by infant mortality,the exploitation of child labour, the evils of prostitution, the hardships of the sweated worker, and the greater value placed upon property than upon the persons of women."[71]

In 1913 the National Council of Women of Canada had been in existence for twenty years. In 1914 it would finally be incorporated by Act of Parliament. Its existence makes nonsense of the idea that women in these years had no public voice. Although not exercised in the same manner as that of men, the point of view of many women on public issues found a channel through Council. To ignore the work of this body is to refuse to acknowledge a major contribution by women to the building of Canada. The exercise of power, in the National Council and at the local level, was less direct for women than the exercise of power through the electoral process was for men. It was wielded in a more restricted area, major questions of fiscal policy and of foreign affairs were not addressed through the mechanisms of the Council. But influence and power were wielded by women and had a far-reaching impact upon the fabric of Canadian life. What was addressed, through the Council movement, was a set of issues regarding local community needs and national policies affecting women and children. If there was disunity among the women — and the *Yearbooks* present a record of very differing views among the delegates on most issues — it was no greater than that found in the male associations. Further, it is arguable that the needs of working class women were given at least as much attention by the councils as was accorded to the needs of working class men by those males elected to the various legislatures.

In the positions it took, the National Council of the Women of Canada had been neither particularly innovative, nor radical, nor even consistent over the decades. At both the national and the local level, however, it accomplished a great deal. At the national level, it had worked effectively for better child care, better conditions for shop-girls, better treatment for women

---

[70] *Yearbook,* 1913, p. 74.

[71] Carrie Derick, "The common cause," in *Montreal Herald,* "Women's Edition," (Nov. 23, 1913), 4, cited in Strong-Boag, *Parliament of Women,* p. 277.

9. Lady Edgar, President 1906-1910

caught up in the justice system and improved educational opportunities for women. By the establishment of the Victorian Order of Nurses, the National Council provided a major component of the development of community health care throughout Canada.

Its influence on the migration policy of the federal government is difficult to estimate; that on the reception of immigrants, however, is undeniable. The work in this area was achieved through the local councils, and it is when their activities are considered that the achievements of the organization become most obvious. Disaster relief, hospital construction, school inspection, educational initiatives and cultural ventures were all part of the programs undertaken by local councils. They were the centre of an information net which reached across the country and the hub of debates among women about the questions of the day.

The annual meeting of any local council turned upon both local and national issues and was attended by a broad spectrum of women active in community life. The preparation of the annual local council meeting was a rigorous matter. Its agenda was laid down by the National Council and included the submission of an annual report on the activities of every auxiliary. The meeting was a gathering of women concerned in the running of their city and the shaping of their country. Resolutions led to the lobbying of municipal and provincial authorities, as well as to memoranda to the National Council, for consideration and action at that level. The establishment of a local council gave strength to community action by women. As members of an individual association, the Business and Professional Women's Association, for example, or the women's auxiliary of a particular church, women might find their views summarily dismissed by men in power, as being representative of a very small sector of female opinion. The impact of a local council resolution upon the male institutions of the community was much more considerable. This became particularly obvious as the councils learned to use the press, and personal relationships, as tools of persuasion.

In sum, the National Council of Women of Canada had, in its first twenty years, built an alternative network for the organization and expression of women's views on major public issues. Elitist, conservative in a very fundamental sense, a mediator rather than an innovator in policy and program, at both the national and local level, councils provided a forum for women in which each could learn what others thought important and to evolve, wherever possible, common platforms to present to those who held overt and direct political power. It was for this reason that the winning of the vote did not lead to the demise of Council.

CHAPTER 4

From the Eve of the Great War to the First Year of Peace
1914–1919

IN 1914 THE National Council of Women of Canada counted its membership at 150,000. At the national level there were twenty affiliated associations:[1] Women's Art Association of Canada (1894); Girls' Friendly Association of Canada (1894); Canadian Suffrage Association (1906), first affiliated as the Dominion Women's Enfranchisement Association in 1894; Dominion Order of the King's Daughters (1894); Aberdeen Association (1894); National Home Reading Association (1894); Medical Alumnae of the University of Toronto (1910), first affiliated as the Alumnae Association of the Ontario Medical Council for Women (1901–09); the Victorian Order of Nurses (1897); Ladies of the Maccabees (1902); Women's Institutes of Ontario (1903); Peace and Arbitration Society, sometimes known as the Peace and Arbitration Association (1906); Imperial Order of the Daughters of the Empire (1909); Canadian Women's Press Club (1909); Canadian Society of Superintendents of Training Schools for Nurses (1909); Women's Branch, Independent Order of Foresters (1909); Agnes Baden Powell Girl Guides (1912); Single Tax Association (1913). The Ontario Horticultural Association joined in 1914 as did the National Union of Women's Suffrage Associations.[2]

This increase in affiliation of associations at the national level was matched by a like increase in local council participation. By 1914, there

---

[1] The date in the brackets, which follows the title of the Association, is the year of affiliation. There are conflicting tallies of the number of associations affiliated at the national level printed in *Yearbook*. The listing which follows is the author's best estimate.

[2] This catalogue is based upon the *Yearbook*. V. Strong-Boag's listing is somewhat different.

were at least thirty-two local councils. It is difficult to be quite certain that all the local councils in existence that year have been listed, since even the records of the National Council are incomplete. The National Council criteria for recorded membership was the payment of dues and sometimes local councils were more than eighteen months in arrears. The geographical distribution of local councils in good standing, from east to west, was:[3] in Nova Scotia there were councils in Halifax (1894), East Pictou (1899), Sydney (1911), Truro (1912), West Pictou (1914), Yarmouth,(1914). In New Brunswick the Council at Fredericton had lapsed in 1908 but Saint John (1894) continued to flourish. Quebec City had lost its council in 1900 but Montreal (1893) prospered. In Ontario there were councils at Hamilton (1893), Toronto (1893), Kingston (1894), London (1894), Ottawa (1894), West Algoma (Port Arthur) (1894), Ingersoll (1903), Brantford (1908), Renfrew (1909), Sudbury (1909), Chapleau (1911), Peterborough (1913), Sarnia (1913). Manitoba had local councils at Winnipeg (1894) and Brandon (1895). Saskatoon (1895) was the sole member in Saskatchewan, and in Alberta the Edmonton Local Council came into being in 1908, Calgary announced its rebirth in 1912 and Lethbridge was established in 1914. For British Columbia there were Councils at Victoria (1894), Vancouver (1895), Vernon (1895), Nelson (1898) and New Westminster (1898).

While the local councils of smaller centres, and those more recently formed, usually had no more than ten or twelve affiliates, the long-established councils such as Halifax, Montreal, the southern Ontario councils, Winnipeg, Saskatoon, and most of the British Columbian Councils could count on forty or fifty affiliates. In 1913, for example, the Vancouver Local Council of Women reported fifty-two federates and ninety-three individual memberships, making a total membership for that Local Council over 5000.[4] An exception to the rule that the number of affiliates of recently formed councils tended to be low was Calgary, which within a year of formation had forty-three federated societies.[5] It was at the local level that many major associations of women, such as the Business Women's Association, the Women's Christian Temperance Union and the Red Cross, held membership.

3   This listing is compiled from the *Yearbooks* for 1899 and 1919. Newfoundland was, of course, not part of Canada at this time and the Local Council of Women of Charlottetown had folded in 1910. The dates given for the founding of some of these councils are inconsistent. The author has rationalized the data.

4   Margaret Lang Hastings and Lorraine Ellenwood, *Blue Bows and the Golden Rule-Provincial Council of Women of British Columbia: An Historical Account,* (Vancouver, n.d.), p. 27.

5   *Yearbook,* 1913, p. 13.

10. Mrs. F.H. Torrington, President 1911–1918

It was also at the local level that the associations of Jewish women joined
and that Catholic organizations were represented. Membership of the
Councils was increased by the number of women's auxiliary groups that
affiliated, representing hospitals, general charity organizations and cultural
societies, as well as the auxiliaries of local church congregations.

The major concerns of the National Council of Women of Canada on the
eve of war were very diverse. The resolutions embodied in the "Women's
Platform," which had been endorsed in 1912, and recommended to both federal and provincial legislatures for adoption, centred upon control of prostitution and the rights of women as parents.[6] The policy of the National
Council concerning prostitution was in conformity with a widespread movement within English Canada for "Moral Purity," which had its roots in the
late nineteenth century.[7] Many of the affiliates of local councils strongly supported the ideas which were expressed by the phrase "Moral Purity." To a
very large extent, the "Methodists were the leaders in both theoretical and
practical purity work,"[8] but it was a movement which had an influence at all
levels of political life. Both its aims and its supporters were diverse, and
there were as many suggestions on priorities as there were on policies of
action. In general, however, the eradication of prostitution, brothels and
drunkenness, as well as gambling, obscene publications and Sunday commerce were the most generally accepted goals.

Much of this program was based upon Methodist interpretations of
Christianity, but the movement was closely linked to the broad concern for
social justice among both Catholics and Protestants of the time. Moreover, the
movement gained support because of general public concern about the problems of urban life in early twentieth century Canada and, in particular, the
concern felt by medical men and women with regard to the proliferation of
sexually transmitted diseases. In an age without penicillin and other antibi-
otics, syphilis and gonorrhea were major scourges. Women such as Carrie
Derick and Emily Murphy[9] were appalled, not only at the suffering of the
infected individuals but also at the hereditary impact of venereal diseases.[10] It

---

[6]   *Yearbook*, 1912, pp. 112–123.
[7]   On this see Valverde, *Age of Light.*
[8]   *Ibid.*, p. 53.
[9]   Born in Cookstown, Ontario, March 14, 1868; died in Edmonton, Alberta, 27 October, 1933. This
      renowned reformer, the first woman appointed to be a police magistrate in the British Empire—in
      Edmonton in 1916—was linked to Council through the Women's Institute.
[10] On this see Carol Bacchi, "Race Regeneration and Social Purity: A Study of the Social Attitudes of
      Canada's English-Speaking Suffragists," *Histoire Sociale/Social History*, xi, 22, (November, 1978),
      pp. 460–74.

was known by 1905 that syphilis could be transmitted from infected mother to unborn child. Emily Murphy estimated that "one in three prisoners in Alberta's provincial jail had to be treated for syphilis and gonorrhea." In the minds of a number of women attached to Council, the regulation of sexuality was as much about public health as morality. In sum, there was a broadly based public concern linking various Protestant churches, as well as associations such as the Women's Christian Temperance Union, the Salvation Army and the Young Women's Christian Association in agreement over a wide spectrum of issues, including the regulation of alcohol, the regulation of sexual activity and the definition and control of obscene publications. The National Council of Women reflected many of these preoccupations, but its main endeavours were concentrated on gathering information and lobbying for legislative change, rather than on direct social action. The latter was the principal aim of the affiliates of local councils, such as the Salvation Army Social Workers (a Toronto affiliate) and the Hamilton Health League.

As to the rights of women as parents, the common law provisions in 1913 stood as follows: "The right of the father, whether he keep the children under his control or place them with a third person, is an absolute one, even against the mother, although the child be an infant at the breast."[11] The National Council considered that equal guardianship of the parents ought to be established and that the primary right to custody of children under 12 ought to be vested in the mother.[12] The Council was also concerned with unsupported wives and families. It asked that the prison wages of those jailed for desertion be used for the support of their children, both legitimate and illegitimate.

The resolutions of the annual meeting of 1913 endorsed, once more, the general principles of the "Women's Platform," but were also concerned with women's rights as citizens, wives and parents; the employment conditions of women and children; the appointment of women factory inspectors; the representation of women on committees dealing with immigration; gun control; and the pasteurization of milk.[13] The "Reports" of local councils centred upon civic enterprises. For example, Vancouver, New Westminster and Victoria councils reported that year that "important work [was] done in the field of better housing, immigration, health, immoral literature, the care of the feeble-minded and laws relating to women and children."[14]

11 *Yearbook*, 1911, p. 37.
12 *Ibid.*, p. 37; *Yearbook*, 1913, p. 4, Women's Platform 1912, "Provincial measures," clause 2.
13 *Yearbook*, 1913, pp. 19–21, 94–116.
14 Hastings and Ellenwood, *Blue Bows*, p. 27.

The resolutions at the national level of Council seem, at first sight, to be
no more than a reflection of many of the issues which exercised mainstream
politicians at this time: employment, public health, the position before the
law of women and children, town planning and immigration. But while
Council often recommended policies in these areas that had much in common with proposals put forward by political parties, its overarching consideration for women and children frequently resulted in a different order of
priorities for the actions proposed. Employment, for liberals and conservatives alike, was an economic issue, to be discussed in terms of labour, capital
requirements and trade and tariff considerations. From the perspective of
Council, interest in employment meant, above all, concern with the conditions of work for women and children, such as light, heat and sanitation;
length of hours worked; the link between wages paid and the life those
wages made possible. The resulting activities constituted the agenda of the
Standing Committee of National Council on "Laws for the Better Protection
of Women and Children."

It is this focus on the conditions of the workplace, rather than on the
broader issues of capitalist society, that has led some commentators to dis-
parage National Council's record and call it little more than an ineffectual
statement of *noblesse oblige*.[15] If this view is correct then the work of the
major political parties in this field must be similarly characterized. Council
efforts were those of mainstream women in Canadian society to work within the limits of the accepted "way things are." Their reforming drive was
framed largely within the existing general pattern of daily life, indicating
their desire for the continuation of the society they knew rather than for its
radical change. Council actions and policy took two forms: lobbying for the
enforcement of existing legislation and pressure for new laws. The demand
for the enforcement of existing legislation was behind the repeated requests
for the appointment of women factory inspectors. The 1913 Annual
Yearbook was typical, in that it recorded the decision to bring it to the
attention of governments, yet again, that "more women Factory Inspectors"
were necessary to ensure compliance with legislation on conditions of work
for women and children.[16]

Under the second heading, regarding new legislation, the major concerns

[15] V. Strong-Boag, for example, concluded that Council was guilty of "near inertia on industrial questions." She remarked that the Yearbooks "failed to mention women workers in the Bell Telephone
Strike of 1907 or in the clockmakers' strike at Eatons in 1912," *Parliament of Women*, p. 256.
[16] *Yearbook*, 1913, p. 19.

were shorter working hours and the removal of barriers against women's entry into particular occupations. In pursuit of the latter aim, Council worked predominantly through demands for equal educational opportunities for women, toward allowing them to obtain the necessary certification to enter professional life. As to the former objective, the *Yearbooks*, in the years immediately before World War I, repeatedly mention the progress of various bills calling for an eight-hour workday. In order to lobby effectively for such bills, Council set up investigatory committees and prepared reports to the appropriate government bodies at both federal and provincial levels. Information on general conditions of working women and children was routinely packaged at the national level and sent out to local councils. One of the most impressive collections of such information was despatched in 1910. It contained "a digest of the Factories and Shops Acts, the Children's Protection Acts, and Compulsory School Attendance Acts, as they relate to labour, the Mechanic's Lien Acts, the Workingmen's Compensation Acts, the Criminal Code as it relates to women employees, and various other Acts."[17] Council women helped to publicize issues affecting women in employment and consistently exercised pressure for particular improvements in their working conditions. Like any other lobbying group, such as the Trades and Labour Congress, the National Council of Women, besides preparing information for its members, organized public meetings, drew up and circulated petitions, wrote to government officials at all levels, issued press releases and generally attempted to call public attention to those issues considered important and to induce public opinion to accept Council proposals as a basis for action.

Where public health was concerned, Council was in the forefront of much of the activity during these years. Government action in this field was piecemeal and, to a large extent, public health was a matter for provincial, and especially municipal, authorities. The establishment of the Dominion Department of Health, first proposed by Council in 1905, did not take place until 1921. The emergence of public health policies was slow, and differing provincial realities produced a patchwork state of affairs across the country. The licensing of doctors and nurses, the state regulation of asylums and hospitals, the development of procedures to cope with epidemics, the enactment of sanitary codes for buildings and housing developments, the imposition of clean water and air standards, and the provision of minimum health care for

---

17 *Yearbook*, 1910, p. 34.

children and pregnant women, were all matters where concerted government action took decades to develop. In Canada, at the opening of the twentieth century, the problems of public health were certainly recognized, but the concept of state intervention in such matters only barely accepted.

The Council, at both the national and local levels, worked continuously for the support of community action in public health. Through their own associations and through Council machinery, women laboured for change in such diverse areas as hospital construction, the training of nurses, infant mortality in Montreal, and standards of cleanliness for milk, bread and meat. Their interest was in the provision of services and also in the monitoring of services provided. Many women spent considerable time investigating exactly what was being done, and as Strong-Boag has remarked, "often became semi-professional welfare workers."[18] From 1906 onwards, the Council coordinated its activities through a Standing Committee on Public Health. Frequently, this Committee, through the provision of detailed research papers, helped local councils lobby effectively to prevent cuts in the health budgets of their town councils. This happened, for example, in Toronto in 1914.[19]

On an issue where health and urban planning were linked, namely, the provision of water filtration plants, local council women often spearheaded demands for action. This issue is an excellent illustration of the subtle difference between the work of those within the elected political system and that of women working through local councils. For most men, the issue of urban planning revolved around the question of "utility regulation and ownership," the control of "waterworks, street railways, electric power and the telephone system." [20] For local councils the issue was the immediate reality of disease and death, the question of urban institutional structures being, in their eyes, almost irrelevant to the immediate needs of citizens.

The debate over this issue in Toronto is typical of similar action and debate in Montreal, Ottawa, Winnipeg and Vancouver. In common with most Canadian urban centres in the first decade of the twentieth century, Toronto suffered from periodic typhoid epidemics, and in 1908 the local council began to lobby for a by-law establishing a filtration plant and a proper sewage disposal system. Civic officials heard the delegation from the

---

[18] Strong-Boag, *Parliament of Women*, p. 245.
[19] *Ibid.*, p. 268.
[20] Paul Rutherford, "Tomorrow's Metropolis: The Urban Reform Movement in Canada, 1880–1920," in Gilbert A. Stelter and Alan F.J. Artibise, eds., *The Canadian City: Essays in Urban and Social History*, (Ottawa, 1984), p. 439.

11. Mrs. W.E. Sanford, President 1918–1922

Council but protested that the cost would be prohibitive. Council women suggested that people might prefer to pay rather than to die. At the next municipal elections "Toronto Council women ...mobilized their forces to bring women voters to the polls, and distributed cards bearing information as to the purpose of the proposed filtration bylaw among factory workers."[21] The newly elected City Council promised to built the filtration plant immediately and three years later the work was completed.

Council played an interesting role in the complex issue of immigration. There is no doubt that on the eve of the First World War, the immigrant in Canada was accepted as a necessity but was also seen as a danger for the developing nation. As Reg Whitaker has remarked, "mass immigration spawned the first mass campaigns of nativism and racism."[22] In the first year of the War, the annual report of the Methodists remarked that:

> While many of the non-Anglo-Saxon population are amongst the best of the people from their native lands...it is lamentable that such large numbers have come to Canada during the last decade bringing a laxity of morals, an ignorance, a superstition and an absence of high ideals of personal character or of national life... They may constitute a danger to themselves and a menace to our national life.[23]

Prejudice was shaped by a number of factors, the state of the economy and the origin of the migrant being two important variables. Immigrants from the British Isles, the United States, Germany or Scandinavia were usually well enough received since, in the words of John Herd Thompson, they "satisfied prevailing prejudices about which ethnic groups made suitable building blocks for Canadian society. Others from Southern, Eastern, or Central Europe met animosity; ethnocentric journalists denounced Italians as 'stiletto-carrying dagos' and Ukrainians as 'degenerate Eastern Europeans.' Even a minuscule migration from India, China or Japan aroused virulent nativism."[24]

But while racism and nativism were quite visible in Canadian political and social life in the years before the First World War—and in the years that followed—many in the country worked then, as they do now, to mitigate the

---

[21] Shaw, *Proud Heritage*, p. 43.
[22] *Ibid.*, p. 8.
[23] Annual Report of the Methodist DESS, 1915–16, p.29, cited in Valverde, *The Age of Light*, p. 53.
[24] Thompson, "Ethnic Minorities," p. 3.

impact of prejudice and intolerance. Then, as now, anti-migrant views were founded upon a dual belief in the superiority of the speakers' ethnic and religious heritage, and a frightened contempt for the incoming group. The wish of those expressing such views was the preservation of what were believed to be the right norms for Canadian society, in contrast to the supposed weakening infection of people of different, and lesser, cultures. The main difference between the position of those who, at that time, held the view that migrants would contaminate the essential nature of Canadian culture, and many of those who express such views today, is the fact that Canadian society, as a whole, has moved to accept multiculturalism as a Canadian value. A striking illustration is provided by Winnipeg, at that time the immigrant city of Canada: "the concept of cultural pluralism (or a cultural mosaic)...was not even contemplated...it was the "British" who were 'to provide the recipe and stoke the fire.'"[25]

The women who led Council on the eve of the war were no more, if no less, subject to the infection of racism and nativism than the men who were the country's elected politicians. Both men and women could be found struggling for ways in which to help migrants adjust to the new society and also retain something of their distinct cultural inheritances. Despite the very strong anti-Asian prejudices in Vancouver society, the local council passed a resolutions on June 1, 1914 to ask "the secretaries of the educated Chinese and Japanese societies to co-operate with Council if their Constitution and by-laws permit."[26]

On the whole, however, the reports at both the local and national levels reveal an unselfconscious acceptance of the idea that English Canadian society had already established norms to which newcomers to English-speaking Canada must adhere. In 1913 Mrs. Shortt,[27] the Vice-President for Ontario, spoke to National Council on the issue of "Canadianization." She remarked that:

> One of the greatest problems confronting us as a young nation today,
> is the many types of people who are rapidly coming to us from the
> nations beyond the seas. How shall these peoples of diverse tastes,

---

[25] Alan F.J. Artibise, "Divided City: The immigrant in Winnipeg Society, 1874–1921," in Stelter and Artibise, eds., p. 308.

[26] UBC Archives: Records of the Local Council of Women of Vancouver, Minutes of Council meetings.

[27] She was the wife of the Dominion Archivist, and came to National Council in the first place because of her membership on the Ottawa Local Council as the representative of the Aberdeen Reading Circles.

temperaments and trainings be assimilated and be made desirable citizens? How shall they be taught right views of the housing question?
How shall we teach them the sacredness of the ballot? How shall the
women and children of these incoming peoples be given the high
social and moral ideals which are so dear to all true Canadians? Our
towns and cities in Canada are bristling with problems of this kind,
and surely our Council of Women could not incorporate and emphasize a more important subject than this.[28]

Before either the Council of Women or the country generally, could find, and
articulate, coherent policies for the manifest problems posed by recent immigrants, international events demanded their attention. Like the majority of
Canadians, members of the Council were not overly concerned with the
course of world affairs in 1913 and early 1914. The National Council had
about it a very vague aura of support for international co-operation because
of its affiliation with the International Council of Women. Lady Aberdeen
had resumed the presidency of the latter in 1904, and with only one other
interruption (1920–1922) would hold the office until 1936. The strong links
between the Canadian National Council and Lady Aberdeen were responsible
for much of the Canadian support for the international organization. Lady
Aberdeen followed much the same policy as President of the International
Council as she had in founding the National Council of Women of Canada,
focusing upon what women of widely divergent views could accept, and
delaying discussion of matters, such as birth control, which might permanently alienate some National Councils.[29] In 1914 the International Council
considered that it represented six million women from twenty-three different
countries, Finland and South Africa having joined since 1909.[30]

One of the standing committees of the International Council was that of
International Peace and Arbitration, which began with a membership of a
dozen nations.[31] Through association with the International Council, the
National Council of Women of Canada was linked with a number of other
international women's organizations, such as the International Women's

---

28 "Report of the Provincial Vice-President for Ontario," *Yearbook*, 1913, pp. 33–4, cited in Strong-
   Boag, *Parliament of Women*, p. 247.
29 Strong-Boag, "Peace Making Women: Canada 1919–1939," in Ruth Pierson, ed., *Women and
   Peace: Theoretical, Historical and Practical Perspectives*, (London, 1987), p. 178.
30 Finland joined the International Council in 1909 and was omitted in the count of that year, *Women
   in a Changing World*, pp. 41 and 350.
31 Sandi E. Cooper, "Women's Participation in European Peace Movements: the Struggle to Prevent
   World War I," Pierson, ed., *Women and Peace*, p. 56.

Suffrage Association. In the final analysis, however, the impact of the International Council of Women upon the National Council of Women of Canada was not such as to alter the strong commitment that most of the members of the latter felt for the Imperial connection.

Canada's entry into war in 1914 was sudden and enthusiastic. It was undertaken amid scenes of general enthusiasm and, as in France and England, was envisaged by many as a crusade for civilization. As soon as the news of Britain's declaration of war was received in Canada, the Prime Minister, Sir Robert Borden, summoned Parliament and the country pledged "to put forth every effort and to make every sacrifice necessary to ensure the integrity and maintain the honour of our Empire."[32] On August 5, 1914 the Montreal newspaper *La Patrie* proclaimed "There are no longer French Canadians and English Canadians. Only one race now exists, united by the closest bonds in a common cause."[33] At both the national and local levels, Council partook of this enthusiasm. The Toronto Local Council, for example, set about fund-raising for the war effort within three days of the declaration of Canada's involvement. Within a short space of time $33,000 was raised, the money being set aside "in a vault in the King Edward Hotel," for use as the Executive might direct.[34]

By 1918 over six hundred thousand Canadians had served in the army[35] and nine thousand more in the navy.[36] There was no distinctively Canadian air force in the First World War but 22,812 had joined the British flying services, of whom more than 13,000 were pilots or observers.[37] When the First World War ended on November 11, 1918, there were more than 60,000 Canadians dead and, as Desmond Morton remarked "as many more would return hopelessly mutilated in mind or body."[38] In other words, roughly a third of Canada's young men of military age had seen service between 1914 and 1918 and one in five of these was killed or wounded.[39]

---

[32] *Documents on Canadian External Relations*, I, 37.

[33] Cited in Brown and Cook, *Canada 1896–1921*, p. 250.

[34] *Yearbook*, 1915, p. 89.

[35] See Colonel G.W.L. Nicholson, C.D., *Canadian Expeditionary Force 1914–1919: Official History of the Canadian Army in the First World War*, (Ottawa, 1964), Appendix C, p. 546, it gives final army enlistment as 619,636.

[36] Naval enlistment figures are from Ramsay Cook with John Saywell and John Ricker, *Canada: A Modern Study*, Revised edition, (Toronto, 1977), p. 185.

[37] S.F. Wise, *Canadian Airmen and the First World War: The Official History of the Royal Canadian Air Force*, vol. I, (Toronto, 1980), p. 633.

[38] Morton, *Short History*, p. 157.

[39] The argument for these statistics is in Desmond Morton, *A Military History of Canada*, Revised edition, (Toronto, 1990), Section IV "The Great War," in particular p. 135. Roger Graham estimated that 172,950 were wounded, "Through the First World War," in Careless and Brown, eds., p. 185.

The immediate cost of this effort touched almost all aspects of Canadian life, economic, social, political and cultural, from the length of women's dresses to their right to participate fully in political life. The long-term impact of Canadian participation was a series of profound changes in the assumptions governing political and social action. As Canadian society at large was altered, so too were the programs and policies of the National Council of Women. Both the context in which the Council worked, locally and nationally, and the priorities of programs of action by councils, were inevitably modified.

Some of the changes experienced by society as a whole had no particular or special repercussions on the National Council. The necessary financial and economic organization for the support of the military effort, for example, meant changes to the banking system and higher taxes.[40] The impact on the women of the Council was simply part of the general impact upon society at large. The same observation can be made regarding many other institutions and policy changes, in the industrial and agricultural sectors and in the country's foreign trade.

In contrast, the actual induction of men into military life had immense and particular consequences for Council. Voluntary activity of members intensified and expanded into new fields. Council was deeply involved in the development of social policies aimed at supporting the families and dependents of those who enlisted. Such policies required much greater volunteer effort and a much augmented state role in social programs. Council also had to concern itself with the broadening participation of women in the labour force. It should be born in mind, however, that as Ceta Ramkhalawansingh has pointed out, "World War I did not mark a significant departure from [the] slow rise in female employment, but it did produce a temporary influx into the work force, changes in occupations and some changed attitudes."[41]

Canada's entry into the war obviously meant immediate mobilization, the initial commitment of Parliament being to send a contingent of 25,000 men to the United Kingdom. While many who first enlisted were men without family obligations, and a fair number of them recent immigrants, others were the sole support of relatives, whether widowed mothers or wives and children. As the war continued, more and more men with family obligations

---

[40] A clear exposition of this matter is given in Brown and Cook, *Canada 1896–1921*, chapter 12, "The War Economy," pp. 228–249.

[41] Ceta Ramkhalawansingh, "Women During the Great War," in Janice Acton, Penny Goldsmith and Bonnie Shepard, eds., *Women at Work Ontario 1850–1930*, (Toronto, 1974), p. 261.

joined the forces. It was assumed by government that married men who enlisted would secure their wives' consent for this action. It was also expected that soldiers, where appropriate, would make provision for part of their pay to be forwarded to their dependents. There were other provisions for those left behind: a Canadian Patriotic Fund was immediately established, along the lines of those organized during the Crimean and South African War, to support soldiers' families. By the end of 1914 the fund had collected $6 million and by the end of the war $47 million.[42] In addition, both provincial and federal governments offered varying supplements for the families of enlisted men. But good intentions were often frustrated by an inadequate, if not frequently incompetent, bureaucracy and many women were left close to destitution when their menfolk departed for military service.

Women's volunteer activity for the relief of social distress was very important at this critical time. If the war did not mark a significant departure in the overall pattern of the employment of women, but merely an acceleration of their entry into the paid workforce, it did heighten emphasis on women's volunteer activity in the realm of social services and bring new respect for it. In 1914 there was no coordinated state structure for the provision of social services and the wartime conditions underlined every community need, from care of the poor and destitute, and the mentally and physically sick, to aid for the deserted and the unemployed. While much of the work that women undertook in the field of social welfare between 1914 and 1918 was directly linked to wartime conditions, it was also the logical development of past activity and would lead to the professionalization of large sectors of social welfare once the war was over. The women involved in volunteer social work during these years contributed significantly to shifting Canada away from reliance on private action for the alleviation of public misery to provision of social services through the machinery of the state.

Not only did new associations spring up in 1914; the established associations, many of which were already linked to Council, expanded their membership dramatically. The Canadian Red Cross, which had received its charter from the Canadian government in 1909, expanded both its memberships and the number of its branches, some of which were affiliated with local councils.[43] The I.O.D.E., a very important affiliate of Council at both the

---

[42] Morton, *Military History*, p. 132.

[43] McKenzie Porter, *To All Men: The Story of the Canadian Red Cross*, (Toronto, 1960), p. 36. The Red Cross was not a national affiliate of Council: the *Yearbook, 1919–1920* reports it as being affiliated at the local level with councils in Halifax, Nova Scotia; Kingston, Ontario; New Westminster, British Columbia; Pincher Creek and Ponoka, Alberta; Sarnia and Sault St. Marie, Ontario; Vernon, British Columbia; West Pictou and Yarmouth, Nova Scotia.

national and the local level, grew almost exponentially. In 1914, for example, the Vancouver municipal chapter "had thirteen chapters under it with a total municipal membership of 350; by June 1915, there were twenty-one chapters [of the I.O.D.E] with an enrolment of 800."[44] Further, new organizations, such as the Khaki Leagues, the Patriotic Fund auxiliaries, and the women's Recruiting Leagues were established, and the local chapters of many of them immediately affiliated with local council. Affiliation of auxiliaries of the Patriotic Fund was particularly frequent. This body, almost always in cooperation with the local council if one existed, provided immediate monetary aid to women and general advice on the management of their affairs in the absence of husband, brother or son.[45]

At the municipal level, by 1914, local councils had gained a reputation for being capable of forceful and productive action in civic affairs. They were known for the preparation of clear reports outlining need for future action, and for the effective organization of cooperative effort among many different associations in the face of epidemics or fire. Throughout the war years, there was a great need for this kind of coordinating activity to bring order to volunteer action and, most often, local councils provided the answer. They had to bring together newly founded patriotic associations whose sights were set exclusively on causes explicitly linked to the war, with the older philanthropic associations, whose work for the indigent and the ill was still vital for the proper functioning of Canadian communities. In some cases, local councils foundered because war-related associations absorbed the volunteer energy of a small town. The Local Council of North Bay, Ontario, for example, was established late in 1914 and then went into hibernation for the duration of the hostilities, since local women were not able to sustain an umbrella organization as well as their primary associations.[46]

Generally speaking, however, local councils received wide support during the war and their numbers grew. Two councils had been established in early 1915, both in Ontario: Temiskaming and North Bay.[47] Twenty new branches were established between January 1916 and December 1918,[48]

---

[44] Charles W. Humphries, "Keeping the Home Fires Burning: British Columbia Women and the First World War," paper delivered at the C.H.A.'s annual meeting, Charlottetown, P.E.I., May 1992, p. 16.

[45] Strong-Boag, *Parliament of Women*, p. 323. There has been much debate about whether such advice was unwarranted interference by middle class women or whether it was intelligent counselling by the privileged to those less fortunate.

[46] *Ibid.*, p. 295.

[47] *Yearbook*, 1915, p. 170.

[48] *Yearbook*, 1919–1920, pp. 274–336.

12. Mrs. Laura Jamieson, the first woman magistrate in the British Empire

bringing local council numbers to more than forty. More western than east-
ern councils were established during these years, but Ontario numbered eight
new councils. In 1916 local councils were established in Mcleod, Medicine
Hat, Olds and Red Deer, Alberta; Pembroke, Ontario; and Saskatoon,
Saskatchewan. In 1917 local councils were organized in Pincher Creek and
Ponoka Alberta; Dauphin and Portage La Prairie, Manitoba; St. Catharine's,
St. Thomas, Sault St. Marie, Strathroy and Trenton, Ontario; and Moose Jaw,
Saskatchewan. New councils were established in Galt and Welland Ontario;
Sackville, New Brunswick; and Swift Current, Saskatchewan.

The program of both the National Council and the local councils during
the war years reflected an immediate response to the war as well as continued work on matters of long-term significance. As far as the war effort was
concerned, the work undertaken at the local level fell into four categories:
care for the wives and families of servicemen, and attention to needs of servicemen before they shipped overseas; raising money for all kinds of war-
related causes; the organization of supplies for the Red Cross and the Khaki
League; and what can perhaps best be called the articulate support of
Canada's participation in the war.

In organizing help for the wives and children of servicemen, Council
women were carrying on the tradition of support for home-life, something
which had been a constant thrust of Council action since its inception. The
problems of women and children in poverty were the central concerns of
many organizations, such as the Ladies' Aid societies, the Friends of the
Poor societies, and the Children's Aid Societies, which had been affiliated
with respective local councils for many years. The new situation was that
many women and children were faced with poverty as a result of the men
responding to a government call. As one Vancouverite, Agnes Georgeson,
complained, "...what really is the matter [is] that I ain't getting my money
from the Army the way I ought to....I have got to have money soon or I must
have my husband home to see if he can't get a job, as we are practically
starving. I will be sick myself soon. I can't rest, I am just worried to death
thinking about the whole business."[49] What most of these women faced was
the result, to a very large extent, of bureaucratic confusion over what ought
to be done and what could done for dependents of enlisted men. Charles
Humphries lists example after example of women suddenly bereft of all

[49] Cited in Humphries, "Keeping the Home Fires," p. 5; from National Archives of Canada, vol. 4656,
file 99–88 (subvolume 3): A. Georgeson to Lieut.-Col. J.W. Warden, O.C., 102nd Overseas
Battalion, 17 March 1916.

financial support because of red tape or because their circumstances placed them outside the scope of "regulations." Men who moved from battalion to battalion, for example, might cause their dependents to lose not only the assigned portion of their pay for some months, but also the right to help from the Patriotic Fund. The latter would not subsidize a family unless the man had embarked for overseas.[50] Another example given by Humphries is that of a woman, a Mrs. E.B. Busst, whose husband had deserted her, leaving her with four children. Two of her sons enlisted and assigned her portions of their pay but this was insufficient to keep her and the younger children, especially when she fell ill and could not work. The government denied her a separation allowance because Mrs. Busst could not prove her husband was dead.[51] She was advised to apply to the Patriotic Fund. The supplemental benefits provided by this organization helped to keep many families above the poverty line during the war.[52] However, while most of the aid given by Council came through the older, church-linked, charitable organizations, there was a very close tie between local councils and the Patriotic Fund. This was particularly true in the case of the Montreal[53] and Toronto Councils but, at one point or another, most local councils helped to raise money for the Fund between 1914 and 1918.

The Yearbooks during these years are full of details about the way in which local councils contributed to what was known as "patriotic work." Any local council in a city close to an army camp made efforts to improve life for the soldiers. There were, for example, over 2,000 soldiers stationed in Victoria in 1914 and the local council there worked with the Social Service Commission to provide them with recreation and assembly rooms.[54] There was similar activity in Montreal and Halifax. In 1915, the London local council organized aid for Belgium: $1000 was raised and food and

---

50 *Ibid.*

51 *Ibid.*, p. 6.

52 The author is much indebted to Humphries' paper for an understanding of how the Patriotic Fund worked. He notes that "when the Patriotic Fund was started, it allowed a completely dependent wife $1.00 per day, plus 25c per day for a child between 10 and 15, 15c per day for a child between 5 and 10, and 10c per day for a child under 5. If her husband was a private, she would receive $20.00 per month in separation allowance; and if her husband assigned half of his monthly pay to her, she would receive another $15." *Ibid.*, p. 5, fn. 7.

53 The work of Helen Richmond Reid, who organized Montreal's Patriotic Fund, was renowned for its professional nature. She was Montreal-born, received a B.A. from McGill University in 1899, and then studied abroad in Germany and Switzerland. Queen's University awarded her an LL.D. in 1916 and she was a governing fellow of McGill University for fifteen years. After the war she would be a member of the Canadian government's Repatriation Committee. She was awarded the C.B.E. in 1935.

54 Hastings and Ellenwood, *Blue Bows*, p. 28.

clothing were sent abroad. In that same year Renfrew, Ontario raised $450 to support the initiative of the I.O.D.E. for a hospital ship.[55] Lethbridge raised $1000 for the Patriotic Fund. The local council in Vancouver ensured that all its affiliated societies were involved in supporting Red Cross activities and in 1915 some $25,000 was raised for military hospital aid.[56] Brantford, whose population that year was approximately 25,000, reported an extraordinary effort with the provision of 2167 pairs of socks, 310 Balaclava helmets, 300 scarves and 4999 pairs of wristlets to be sent to soldiers overseas; 498 hospital gowns, 500 dozens of bandages, 132 sheets, 106 pillow slips, 8 dozen towels, 32 dozen linen handkerchiefs, 150 dozen cheesecloth handkerchiefs, 1900 12x16 surgical pads, 3136 9x12 surgical pads, 3732 6x7 surgical pads, 12,000 dozen sponges, 1876 dozen compresses and nine cases of clothing for the Belgian Relief fund as well as 37 cases of canned goods for Belgian soldiers and 1100 Christmas mitts for Belgian babies. A further 365 garments and quilts were assembled for local social services, as well as an odd miscellaneous collection of 2986 coloured and black handkerchiefs, with 1019 pieces of castile soap and 298 silk scarves, whose intended destination the record does not make clear.[57] Saint John, New Brunswick, contributed a shipload of furs for Italian soldiers fighting in the Alps.[58] While these examples are taken from the records for 1915, they are typical of the actions engaged in by local councils throughout the war.

The articulation of patriotic feelings was a regular function of meetings held at both the local and the national levels. Council women were, like most Anglophone Canadians, convinced of the necessity of articulate public support for the war effort. There were pacifists who were members of Council, women such as Dr. Ritchie England, but they were very much in the minority.

This response to the war absorbed a very large amount of energy, but the long-term aims of Council continued to be pursued at both levels. Local councils still paid attention to matters on which they had worked for years: living conditions, particularly those of working girls, the conditions under

---

[55] This was a very popular cause and in fact some $238,000 was collected. The money, however, was used to purchase forty ambulances, which were used by the British, and to help build two naval hospitals in England. See Shaw, *Proud Heritage*, p. 155.

[56] Hastings and Ellenwood, *Blue Bows*, p. 29.

[57] *Yearbook*, 1915, p. 111.

[58] In common with other local councils who responded to this cause, the Saint John Council underlined that the furs were "for practical not decorative purposes." R. Philip Campbell, *1894–1979 Challenging Years: 85 years of the Council of Women in Saint John*, (n.d., n.p.), p. 35. This was a particular project of Lady Aberdeen and free transportation of the fur shipments was provided by the C.P.R. and the Dominion Express Company.

which food was distributed and sold, the functioning of the justice system, and matters of health care. In 1915, all local councils became involved in the issue of city housing as a result of a National Council resolution on this matter. From 1914 onwards, the National Council had a Standing Committee on Household Economics and this body now supported Local Council attempts to regulate local markets, dairies, cold storage for meat and fish and other consumer-oriented matters.[59] As a consequence, local council efforts to obtain regularly inspected abattoirs, reasonably sanitary conditions in bakeries and fish shops as well as some control over milk supplies, were helped by the provision of information from the national level as well as by solidarity of action across provinces.

The watching brief which councils considered it their duty to hold over the actions of police, jails, juvenile courts and reformatories continued. In the western provinces, the appointment of women magistrates who were also Council members was seen as indicating public approval for work by Council in this area. V. Strong-Boag has listed the early appointments made.[60] The first female judge in Canada was Mrs. Alice Jamieson, appointed in Alberta in 1914.[61] She was well-known to Council, having been a participating member at both the local and the national levels. Her appointment was recorded in the *Women's Century*,[62] whose editors commented: it "links up the whole womanhood of Calgary with a leader who is true and just, and whose one and only aim in life is 'service to her country'...she passes up to this highest office yet achieved by woman, with the hearty support and best wishes of 3,000 women behind her of the Council, as well as thousands of others not so connected."[63] She shared her courtroom with Mrs. Frederick Langford, another Council member. In 1916, Edmonton appointed Mrs. Emily Murphy as a police magistrate and in 1917, Saskatchewan selected Ethel MacLachlan as its first judge of the Juvenile Court.[64]

---

[59] *Yearbook*, 1915, 1917; Strong-Boag, *Parliament of Women*, p. 316.
[60] Strong-Boag, *Ibid.*, pp. 319–320.
[61] Biographical information about Mrs. Jamieson is scant. Her husband's initials were R.R. She was President of the Calgary Local Council between 1912 to 1915. She has been over-shadowed by Emily Murphy.
[62] This was the contemporary name for the newsletter of the NCWC. There has almost always been some kind of official publication put out by the head office of the NCWC. Unfortunately, little effort has been made to preserve these sources, and even the runs at the National Archives of Canada are incomplete.
[63] "Work of Calgary Women Well Known," *The News-Telegram*, April 20, 1914, p.15.
[64] None of these women are as widely known as they should be and none has yet been the subject of a scholarly monograph. All faced direct challenges to their authority in their court-rooms. The Alberta government was solidly behind its appointments and the status of that province's female

The war years saw the membership of societies and associations affiliated at the national level increase in much the same way as had the affiliation
of organizations at the local level. The National Union of Women Suffrage
Societies of Canada, soon to be called the National Equal Franchise Union,
joined National Council in 1914. In 1915 the Young Women's Christian
Association became a member at that level. In 1917 the Canadian
Association of Trained Nurses affiliated to National Council, as did the
Ontario Women's Liberal Association, the Queen's University Alumnae
Association and the Saskatchewan Grain Growers, Women's Section. The
Home Economics Societies of Manitoba joined in 1918 as did the Manitoba
Grain Growers' Association, Women's Section, the Ontario Women's
Citizen Association, the United Farm Women of Alberta and the Women's
Institutes of Alberta. Some affiliates kept national membership for only a
short time but even as early as 1915 their participation strained the structure
of Council. In that year, as the corresponding secretary, Mrs. Emily
Cummings,[65] remarked, the Executive had 111 members, being composed of
the representatives of Local Councils, the "Nationally Organized Societies,"
the conveners of the Standing Committees and the officers of the
Association.[66] In reality, the most important people were the elected vice-
presidents, provincially selected vice-presidents and the conveners of the
major committees, perhaps some thirty women. Nevertheless, reform of the
constitution, which had been mooted in 1913, would become more and more
necessary as the years passed. In the meantime, Council functioned in large
measure because women who gave it their time and attention believed in its
worth.

By 1916, any illusion that going to war meant glory without sacrifice
had disappeared. The battles of the Somme had brought 24,029 casualties to
the Canadian forces alone.[67] The politics of Canadian unity were soon to be

---

jurists was settled in 1917, when Mr. Justice Stuart stated in the Supreme Court of Alberta that:
applying the general principle upon which the common law rests, namely that of reason and good
sense... there is...no legal disqualification for holding public office in the government of this country arising from any distinction of sex...R.v. Cyr (1917), 3 W.W.R. 849, cited in Linda Sylva Dranoff,
Women in Canadian Law, (Toronto, 1977), p. 92.

[65] Born the daughter of the Reverend John Shortt on May 11, 1851, she married a journalist,
Willoughby Cummings, in 1871. He died in 1892 and from 1893 to 1903 she was a member of the
editorial staff of the Toronto *Globe.* She then moved to Ottawa, became a civil servant in the
Women's Department of the Annuities Branch of the Department of the Interior. From 1894 to
1918 she was corresponding secretary of the N.C.W.C. She became the first woman to receive an
honorary degree from a Canadian university, being granted a D.C.L. from King's College, Windsor
in 1910.

[66] *Yearbook,* 1915, p. 171.

[67] Nicholson, *Canadian Expeditionary Force,* p. 198.

subjected to severe strain by the scale of recruitment necessary to sustain Canadian troops in the field. The Senate was warned as early as March 1916 that the present system of voluntary recruitment would not be sufficient to replace the losses due to death, wounds and general discharges of men already in the field.[68] Moreover, as the months of battle went by, the requirements of agriculture and industry increased. As Colonel Nicholson has pointed out: "Seventeen months of war had wrought a tremendous change in Canada's economy. The conditions of stagnation in business and unemployment which had existed at the outbreak of the war were being rapidly dissipated..."[69] By summer of 1916 the question of manpower had become urgent, and the government attempted to solve it by more efficient recruitment strategies rather than by coercion.

August 16, 1916 is the date of the first of a series of Orders in Council which set up a National Service Board.[70] This was a civilian organization and it was charged with ensuring that "all available labour [was] utilized to the greatest advantage." Thus, early in 1917 cards were distributed through all Post Offices in Canada, asking men to fill in details about themselves and return the information to the government. The temper of the country can be judged by the extent to which even this measure was seen as controversial. Canadians were not used to such a profound intrusion of government bureaucracy into the choices they made in the disposition of their lives. This was an unparalleled encroachment of bureaucratic action onto their liberty and it was not responded to with enthusiasm. More than a million and a half cards were sent out and some 80% were returned; final analysis of the information by the Board revealed no more than 470,703 military prospects, of which only some 286,976 were not already engaged in an essential occupation.

Council women were as uneasy as other Canadians about any form of direct government coercion for the purpose of military service. There was considerable discussion across the country about what this voluntary registration scheme really meant. To some, it seemed a logical development of the war effort. The Montreal Local Council supported it and early in December 1916, it asked the National Council to back the idea publicly. The National Council Executive consulted local councils about the issue and received seventeen replies: eight in favour, seven opposed and two wishing to register abstention.[71] As a result, National Council deferred the matter "for

---

[68] *Ibid.*, p. 215.
[69] *Ibid.*, p. 219.
[70] What follows is a précis of Nicholson's p. 219.
[71] Strong-Boag, *Parliament of Women*, p. 330.

future consideration." In the meantime, information about prospective recruits had gone out to appropriate local recruiting officers, but the situation continued to deteriorate. The total number of men enlisted in April 1917 was 4671; that same month the Canadian victory at Vimy Ridge cost the Canadian Corps 10,602 casualties in six days. For the Canadian government, the situation of the Allies on the Western Front was such that, both politically and militarily, Canada's contribution had to be maintained.

The argument for compulsory service seemed unanswerable. On May 18, 1917, Prime Minister Sir Robert Borden said in the House of Commons that "the voluntary system will not yield further substantial results." Therefore he announced that "early proposals will be made...to provide, by compulsory military enlistment on a selective basis, such reinforcements as may be necessary to maintain the Canadian Army today..."[72]

With this statement, the "Conscription Crisis" became an explicitly political question in Canada. It was not merely a matter of sustaining the national will to support what was still accepted by Canadians as unarguably right policy. It became a bitterly divisive issue between English and French Canadians,[73] although there were French Canadians who supported conscription and English Canadians who did not. The National Council of Women was certainly split; for example, the President of the Montreal Local Council, Grace Ritchie England[74] was against conscription, while her council was for it. In Edmonton, the local council as a whole was for conscription, but the Executive against it.[75]

The conscription debate was much broader than a mere quarrel between Anglophones and Francophones over the extent and nature of Canada's commitment to the war effort. It laid bare deep Anglo-French dissensions concerning education and language rights in Ontario that had been obvious long before 1914. It led to a general quickening of ethnic and religious antagonisms. Hostility developed between Canadians of British and German extraction, and antagonism between Protestant and Catholic Irish Canadians reached new depths of embitterment. In the midst of the arguments and

[72] Cited in Nicholson, *Canadian Expeditionary Force*, p. 343.
[73] On this see Susan Mann Trofimenkoff, "The Prussians are Next Door: Quebec and World War I," in J.M. Bumsted, ed., *Interpreting Canada's Past*, vol. II, *After Confederation*, (Toronto, 1986), pp. 208–221.
[74] She was born in Montreal, the daughter of W.Ritchie, Q.C. She graduated in 1888, with a B.A. from McGill University in natural science, and married F.R. England, M.D. in 1897. She was a member of the first class of women who graduated from McGill University and the first woman to receive a medical degree in the Province of Quebec. She did graduate work in Vienna.
[75] Strong-Boag, *Parliament of Women*, 380.

debates the National Council of Women met in Winnipeg, between May 31 and June 8, 1917. During these eight days, the strengths, the weaknesses and the essential nature of Council can be seen. The importance to these women of the most urgent political question of the day, the conscription crisis, is apparent, but of equal importance to them were the government proposals for extending the franchise. The commitment of Council to the betterment of community life is as clear as the very diverse views held by different members of Council as to methods of securing the desired improvements. Financially secure, educated mostly through good private schools, very few of them having any university experience, anchored with family obligations but committed to a working public voice in community affairs, these women were no more carbon copies of one another than their male connections and counterparts. Political questions of the time produced debate and dissension in Council just as they did in the federal Parliament.

The annual meeting of 1916 had been cancelled, "owing to the war" and the *Yearbook* was not published that year. In order to comply with the Act of Incorporation, however, the Executive, in all its cumbersomeness, met in Kingston, Ontario on November 16, 1916 and immediately adjourned. Thus the last annual meeting had been in Toronto in 1915, nineteen months earlier. Mrs. F.H. Torrington was still President and her elected Vice-Presidents included Mrs. Willoughby Cummings D.C.L, Professor C.M. Derick M.A., Mrs. F.T. Frost, Mrs. H.P.H. Galloway, Mrs. W.E. Sandford and the past-president, Lady Taylor. The Provincial Vice-Presidents (these titles did not imply the existence of an organization of Provincial Councils before 1919) were Mrs. O.C. Edwards (Alberta); Mrs. C.A. Welsh (British Columbia); Mrs. H.W. Dayton (Manitoba); Mrs. G. Sanford (Ontario); Madame J. Dandurand (Quebec) and Mrs. W.C. Murray (Saskatchewan).

All except Mrs. Torrington were Canadian born. Mrs. Willoughby Cummings, Mrs. O.C. Edwards, Mrs. Sanford and Lady Taylor were widows. Mrs. Willoughby Cummings and Professor Derick were working women, earning their livelihood. Lady Taylor and Mrs. Torrington were people whose husbands' positions placed them very much in the upper ranks of the social elite, and whose major interests were in art, literature and activities stemming from their specific religious affiliations. Together with Mrs. Sanford, sometimes considered the embodiment of "Victorian virtue," these women worked above all for the gradual change of society, reforms which would improve the life of the poor and wretched, but not upset the social hierarchy to which they were accustomed. Professor Derick and Mme. Dandurand were, without doubt, committed to much more radical social reform, as was Mrs. Edwards.[76] She had helped found the Working Girls' Association some thirty years earlier, when she was 26, to provide vocational training for young women. She supported divorce on equal grounds for men and women, prison reform and mother's allowances.

Mrs. R.P. Williams, the President of the Winnipeg Local Council, said in her welcoming remarks that:

> We women of the middle west have a keen sense that our whole position has been altered. The change is difficult to analyze but no woman could have been in public life the last 15 months in Manitoba without realizing that we have come into entirely new days. For ourselves we seem to stand more squarely on our own feet, we have a new sense of responsibility, of opportunities; from others we seem to receive willing recognition of the new plane in which we stand, a welcome is given to us as equals which rings far more true than that which often greeted us in our so-called 'pedestal' state of former days.[77]

Much of her enthusiasm came from the fact that the franchise had been extended to women at the provincial level from the Ottawa river to the Pacific within the past year. Manitoba had adopted the requisite legislation in January, 1916; Saskatchewan in March, 1916; Alberta in April, 1916; and British Columbia in May, 1916. Ontario yielded the right to vote to women in April 1917. It was clear that they would very soon be allowed to vote at the Dominion level.

At the time of the 1917 annual general meetings, however, the question of suffrage was still very much at issue. The National Council of Women of Canada was not, of course, primarily an association dedicated to women's suffrage. Council had endorsed the extension of the vote to women and many, at both the national and local levels, worked hard for enfranchisement. But a good number of Council members considered women's suffrage as only one among many worthwhile causes. Some took the view that the issue ought not to be brought forward in wartime, in case it distracted energy better devoted to the needs of war. Others believed that suffrage was something

[76] Henriette Louise, née Muir: born in Montreal in 1849, died at Fort McLeod, Alberta, November 10, 1931. She was the Chairman of the NCWC's Committee on Laws for the Better Protection of Women and Children for thirty-five years.
[77] *Yearbook*, 1917–18, p. 13.

won, not granted, and at least one Manitoban considered that women in "the eastern provinces" needed more education before they would be able to use the vote wisely.[78] The divisions among women, as to when and to whom the franchise should be extended, had become strikingly clear when, in 1916, Nellie McClung[79] called for the franchise to be limited to British women.[80]

Enfranchisement took place slowly. In those days of late spring, 1917, the Prime Minister, Sir Robert Borden, thought the situation facing the country was sufficiently grave that a coalition government was the sole solution. Sir Wilfrid Laurier, the Leader of the Opposition, refused to join, but many other Liberals in English-speaking Canada accepted the proposition and in October 1917 the Union government was formed. It went to the polls in December, 1917 but before it did so, two new electoral acts were passed. One measure gave votes to soldiers overseas and to their female relatives, mothers, wives, and sisters, at home. This was the Military Voters Act. The other act removed the right to vote from citizens of enemy origin naturalized after 1902. This was the Wartime Elections Act, passed by the House of Commons on September 14, 1917. Thus some women gained the suffrage at the Dominion level in 1917, but in the context of bitter Anglo-French conflict in Canada, and at the cost of legal discrimination between Canadian citizens.

The majority of Council repudiated this idea of partial enfranchisement. While some members of the Executive, including the President, publicly supported the restricted measure, Council as a whole came out firmly in opposition to it. Commentary was particularly sharp in the West. Regina Local Council considered that women's participation in the war effort had earned them the vote.[81] Tension over the issue ended on May 24, 1918, when the final formality of royal assent was given to the extension of the franchise at the Dominion level to "every female person" who "was a British subject, at least twenty-one years of age and possessed of the qualification which

---

[78] Strong-Boag, *Parliament of Women*, p. 327.
[79] Born Nellie Monney in Ontario in 1873 and died in Victoria, British Columbia in 1951. She moved with her family to the west in 1880. She was married on August 24, 1896 to Wesley McClung, the son of a Presbyterian minister. She was elected to the Alberta legislature in 1921, serving as an MLA until 1926. In 1936 she became the first woman member appointed to the Board of Governors of the Canadian Broadcasting Corporation. In 1938 she was one of the Canadian delegates to the League of Nations. She was a writer and speaker of unusual and vivid gifts and was deeply committed to better working conditions for women, prohibition and the extension of political rights for women. She was neither more nor less consistent in pursuit of her aims than are most people in public life.
[80] Strong-Boag, *Parliament of Women*, p. 326.
[81] Papers of the Regina Local Council of Women, Minute Book No. 3, Minutes Sept. 25, 1917.

would entitle a male person to vote in the province in which she resided."[82]

The right to vote in provincial elections in the Maritimes and Quebec was accorded after campaigns which reflected the essentially different political and social climates of those provinces. Cleverdon considered that the suffrage movement in Nova Scotia was basically the result of activities of the Women's Christian Temperance Movement. Nova Scotia accorded women the right to vote and to sit in the provincial legislature in 1918. One of the women who fought for these gains remarked to Cleverdon in 1943: "At the end it came without a struggle in recognition of women's services during the war. Things often work that way I find. You struggle and struggle to no direct effect, and suddenly in a lull the whole thing snaps into place."[83] The campaign in New Brunswick produced more widespread public action; there was a greater volume of petitions and more frequent delegations to the government in Fredericton, many of them mounted by the Local Council in Saint John. The province gave women the right to vote in 1919 but managed to avoid granting them the right to hold office until 1934. The Act to enfranchise women in Prince Edward Island at the provincial level was passed in 1922. Quebec women did not win the battle until 1940.

There was, however, much less formal discussion of the issue of extending the franchise during the National Council annual meeting of 1917, than debate over how women would use the vote. Once accorded this privilege, would women use it any differently than men? Many hoped that they would. Nellie McClung certainly did. When Alberta granted the franchise to women in 1916 she had helped to form a committee of local councils in that province, to discuss how the vote could best be used to "unite women on the issues of home and children."[84] In her Presidential address, Mrs. Torrington addressed this issue. She said:[85]

> But having suffrage, what shall we do to make it [count]...incorporating into our home, municipal and national life, the principles for which the National Council stands? How are we to continue the educational work until every woman realizes her responsibility as a voter and citizen? What is the best plan? Shall Women join themselves to the existing political parties? If not, how best can they

---

[82] Cleverdon, *Woman Suffrage*, p. 136 .
[83] *Ibid.*, p. 176.
[84] *Yearbook*, 1917, pp. 32–4.
[85] *Yearbook*, 1917–1918, p. 17.

make their influence felt in the nomination and election of the best representatives?

She expressed the view of many who hoped that women might do much to mitigate the bitterness of party politics when she went on to declare:

> A sceptre, in the form of a ballot, has been placed in the hands of every woman, not that by her vote and influence she may strengthen the Liberal or Conservative Party, but that in order she may protect the highest interest of her hearth and home, and help to establish the law of righteousness or right living which alone exalteth a nation, and remove the social sins and inequality that are a reproach to any people.[86]

Despite considerable politicking by its members, who showed themselves as divided and partisan in their attitude to the Union government as any comparable group of men, the Executive of the National Council managed to maintain a strict political neutrality. There were calls by some of the affiliated associations, such as the Canadian Women's Press Club, for endorsement of the national government. The editors of the *Women's Century*, very much the official organ of the National Council, headlined the September 1917 issue with the words: *"Women's Century.... stands for a Union Government, Conscription and Winning the War."* The Executive, however, was quick to disavow this as a policy of the Council as a whole.

In fact, while considerable attention has been paid to the importance, in 1917, of the suffrage and conscription issues for Council, an examination of the revised edition of the "Women's Platform," adopted by Council in that year, reveals a very different emphasis.[87] It was a much longer and more sophisticated document than that put forward in 1912. There were six main areas considered to be of major importance for study, work and lobbying activities: the needs of "Woman as Citizen" came fourth, being preceded [in order] by matters of "Public Health," "Employment and Professions for Women" and "Conservation and Thrift." The last two issues listed were "Education and Recreation" and "Immigration and Settlement."

It is in the discussion of resolutions that are contained in this platform that the essence of Council concerns and methods of action are seen at their

---

[86] *Yearbook*, 1917, p. 17.
[87] *Yearbook*, 1917–18, pp. 69–73.

best. Here the steps taken in the long path from charity concerns to state-provided social welfare policies are visible. The topics brought together concerning Public Health were introduced by the affirmation that "it is the duty of the State to provide care and training for those who are either permanently or temporarily unfit for normal life." However much the women who were members of Council considered volunteer charitable work as a religious obligation, and however much time and money they dedicated to providing aid to what they considered "good causes," they were also women educated by experience to see the need for structured, state action. The re-iterated demand in these resolutions for a federal Department of Health and a Child Welfare Department within such a body, is an important stage in the process of transforming charitable action into modern social work.

Similarly, the resolutions concerning the "Employments and Professions for Women" brought together the work of bodies such as the Canadian Association of Nursing Education, the Women's Institutes and other associations working for medical training for women. These directives were introduced with the statement that the National Council of Women "reaffirms its desire that opportunities for [professional and industrial] training should be accessible to all, both boys and girls." It is within this grouping of resolutions that the Council gathered its demands for: "adequate factory inspection (including women inspectors); the regulation of the hours of labour, of holidays, and rates of wages of women and children in industrial establishments."[88]

The rhetoric of debate of past years can sometimes hide the contemporary importance of a subject. Under the title "Conservation and Thrift" Council first advocated the need for proper care of children and for "pensions granted to mothers in cases in which it becomes necessary for the mother of young children to become a wage earner."[89] This proposition was followed by a lengthy resolution asking that the Federal Government pay proper attention to farming and food production and that this attention be aided by:

the public ownership of Cold Storage Plants and Abattoirs, and Government control of the milling industry, together with the nation-

---

[88] *Ibid.,* "Women's Platform," (2) f.

[89] On this see Veronica Strong-Boag,"Wages for Housework: Mothers' Allowances and the Beginnings of Social Security in Canada," *Journal of Canadian Studies/Revue d'études canadiennes,* vol. 14, no. 1, Spring 1979, pp. 24–33.

13. Carrie Derick

alization of coal fields in Canada and the granting to municipalities of the right to operate coal and wood yards.

The motivation behind these last resolutions was in part reaction to wartime conditions, and to fears for the future. Of course, the Council was also motivated by the tradition of pragmatic conservatism which had led to the development of public enterprises in a number of Canadian provinces.[90]

There was nothing quite as radical in the resolutions gathered together under the rubrics of "Woman as Citizen" and "Education and Recreation" and "Immigration and Settlement." The Council called for a public audit of campaign expenses and pointed out that, since recreation was a very necessary part of education, recreational facilities should be monitored by the community. Finally, in the section devoted to "Immigration and Settlement," the principle was stated that attention must be paid to: "The best method of absorbing the foreign immigrant into the national life, while preserving his national gifts."[91]

The problems raised and the questions asked in the "Woman's Platform" were a direct result of the work of the Standing Committees of Council. During the coming year, these bodies would send out information on resolutions, request commentary on them from local councils, and monitor ways in which lobbying for their implementation was being done. Because of the structure of the entire organization, the increasing subtlety and political acumen shown in the development of resolutions reflected not only the skill of the leaders of Council, but also the continuing political education of the 150,000 women it linked together.

This institutional strength would be important for women as Canada strove to meet the challenges of peace and the bitter cost of victory. The war years had brought far-reaching changes for women but much remained to be achieved. Not only was the franchise denied to women at the provincial level from the Ottawa river to the Atlantic, but the right to vote did not automatically mean the right to stand for public office. Women, of course, were not yet admitted as possible candidates for appointment to the Senate. Further, it was clear that the extension of the franchise had been granted not so much because men were convinced that women should have the right to vote, but

---

[90] On the tradition of pragmatic conservatism, particularly the provincial ownership of hydro-electric plants in Ontario, see S.F. Wise, "Ontario Political Culture: A Study in Complexities," in Graham White, ed., *The Government of Ontario*, 3rd edition, (Toronto, Nelson, 1990).

[91] *Yearbook*, 1917, Resolutions, VI (c).

because of the desire of governments that women from a particular sector of the community should be equipped to counter the votes of male elements deemed to be less desirable. Final debate on the full extension of the franchise in Commons and Senate revealed that sexism was alive and well. The comment by the British Columbian Senator, Hon. H.J. Cloran, summed up much of the emotional opposition to votes for women. "I would not," he said, "deprive my wife, or my mother, or my daughter of any right that would bring them comfort, or ease, or emolument. No, I love them too much for that; but I love them more by not exposing them to disagree with me..."[92]

Moreover, the Armistice did not mean that Canada would find social peace in its cities and villages. The cultural and political tensions generated in the last years of the war were heightened by the unrest and discontent of those who had expected the end of hostilities to bring an immediate beginning of prosperity and a new order of social justice. The reorganization of effort from war to a peace-time footing was accompanied by labour strife and political disaffection. In this new age, the National Council would find it had difficulties within its own organization, as well as problems with the implementation of its aims.

---

92 Cited in Cleverdon, *Woman Suffrage*, p. 153, from Canada, *Senate Debates*, 1918, p. 365.

CHAPTER 5

Searching for a New Dispensation
1919–1929

ONE OF THE most difficult and challenging stages in the history of an organization is the period when it passes from the hands of those who established it into the care of those who join at a later stage. So many matters will have been settled among its founders, almost without discussion, because those who brought the association into being were very clear about why they wanted it. Yet if it is to live, a new generation of people must be brought into the executive, and they may be individuals who see the organization as fulfilling needs subtly different from those its founders envisaged. The National Council of Women of Canada, from the outset, was well aware of this. If the discussion of finances has been one staple item at the annual meetings of Council, another has been need to recruit members from the next generation of volunteer women. This problem was particularly acute in the twenties because Council reached its thirtieth anniversary during these years, and those who birthed it and nurtured it were now in their sixties and seventies. In addition, the changing circumstances of the Canadian polity meant that there were many more ways for women to have a public voice than had been the case in the previous generation. While Council was able to effect the necessary generational change in leadership without major disruption, the inevitable modifications in both policy and structure absorbed much of the time and energy of its members.

At the 1918 annual meeting of the National Council of Women of Canada, held in Brantford, Ontario, Harriet Sophia Sanford was elected as President. She had been a member of the National Council since its inception and would serve as its President until 1922. The daughter of Thomas Vaux, who became accountant to the House of Commons, she had been born in Montreal and educated in Quebec. In 1866, at the age of seventeen, she became the second wife of William Eli Sanford. He was an established Hamilton businessman, who became known as the "Wool King of Canada." In 1887 he was appointed to the Senate and he died in 1899.[1] They had four children, two daughters and two sons. One son died in infancy and the second in 1898. Sophia Sanford worked with Council from the outset, joining the Hamilton Local Council in 1893 as the representative of the Wentworth Historical Society. She was elected Hamilton's President in 1894, and served in that capacity for the year. Her main interest in Council related to its links with the International Council of Women and she usually managed to attend the quinquennial meetings of that body, serving as its Treasurer for twenty-six years, from 1904 until 1930.[2] At the 1909 meeting of the International Council of Women she was personally thanked for her work for the Council in India and Japan.[3]

Mrs. Sanford was in her seventieth year when she became President and the difficulties she had to confront were greater than those faced by most of her predecessors. The very growth and success of the organization had diminished its homogeneity, just as the expansion of Canada was presenting its governments with problems of increasing complexity. At its first annual meeting in 1894, the National Council of Canada was a federation of eight local councils and three nationally affiliated associations, in a country with a population of not quite five million. In 1919, the annual meeting of Council brought together representatives of forty-four local councils and nineteen federally or provincially affiliated associations, in a country whose population stood at nearly nine million. Further, while the political situation in 1894 had been fraught with dissension and the rhetoric of debate over policy was harsh and bitter, the context of argument was a general belief in progress. In 1919, the legacy of the First World War had shattered any unthinking optimism about human progress. "Its physical consequences alone," as S.F. Wise

[1] Morgan, *Men and Women*, (1912 edition).
[2] Lady Aberdeen wrote her obituary for the *Globe and Mail*, most of which was published in the *Yearbook*, 1938. Mrs. Sanford died on February 21, 1938.
[3] Aberdeen, ed., *International Council of Women*, p. 79.

14. Miss Caroline C. Carmichael, President 1922–1926

has pointed out, "were enough to slow the onward march of civilization and to destroy that general belief in the inevitability of human progress which had marked much of the philosophy of the nineteenth century."[4] And while the Armistice heralded peace, it also heralded dissension. As Desmond Morton has pointed out, "two contradictory hopes sustained most Canadians during the war years: on the one hand, that they would find a new and finer world; on the other, that they would return to the old one."[5] In the first years of peace Canada was deeply divided over the way in which the post-war world should evolve. There was a wide gulf between labour demands and the response of business, a growing antagonism between farmers and industrialists, and political controversy over the way in which the command economy of the war years should be dismantled. Canada in 1919 was a country almost obsessed by talk of new directions. For women, as Strong-Boag pointed out, this meant that the time had come "to discover just what all the talk of new directions, whether in child care, education, employment, domestic technology, or politics, meant for them in particular."[6]

The changing situation of Council was signalled by the circumstances of the election of its new President. While, as was then customary, Mrs. Sanford was acclaimed for the position, records show that at least one other name was being discussed. The possible alternative was Mrs. Adelaide Plumtre. An Englishwoman, born in 1874, she had come to Canada in 1901 with her husband, the Reverend Henry Pemberton Plumtre. He was appointed rector of St. James Cathedral in Toronto in 1909. One of her major interests was the Red Cross and she served as secretary of the Canadian Red Cross from 1914 to 1920. One of her biographers mentions her "flair for business and executive work"[7] and she had been most influential in the formulation of the "Women's Platform" in 1917. In the eyes of many, Mrs. Plumtre spoke for younger women, and those committed to seeing that the post-war world would be very different from the state of affairs existing before 1914. Mrs. Sanford, on the other hand, stood for "the older, more cautious and conservative element within Council."[8]

The growing complexity of Council business, of which this muted con-

4   Richard A. Preston, Sydney F. Wise and Herman O. Werner, *Men in Arms: A History of Warfare and its Interrelationships With Western Society,* (New York, 1962), p. 273.
5   Morton, *Short History,* p. 158.
6   Veronica Strong-Boag, *The New Day Recalled: the Lives of Girls and Women in English Canada 1919–1939,* (Toronto, 1988), p. 2.
7   *Canadian Who's Who,* 1936, p. 880.
8   Strong-Boag, *Parliament of Women,* p. 337.

tention for the Presidency gives a hint, is further exemplified by discussion over its constitution. Such debate, in itself, was neither unusual nor worrisome. From the earliest days, the structure and functioning of the organization had been a matter of concern to the membership. Issues of procedure and by-laws, as well as proposals for radical reform of the constitution, have surfaced frequently during Council's history. Rarely has there been an annual meeting that did not spend at least one session considering constitutional issues, although it was not a regular practice to create standing committees on the constitution. In part this restraint is due to the ever-present Canadian bias toward regionalism, in part to the normal tensions of Canadian federalism. Both factors have an unavoidable impact upon any nation-wide institution. For example, the increasing disaffection of the western provinces from the federal government, in the years immediately following the Armistice, was responsible in large part for the restiveness between western local councils and the National Council.

But other factors were at work in 1919. The particular exasperation of the Winnipeg Local Council which led, that year, to its withdrawal from affiliation with the National Council for three years, was as much due to an outworn, and therefore inevitably insensitive pattern of National Council action as it was to the normal strains of Canadian politics. After all, the National Council had gone a long way to removing some of the regional dissatisfaction with institutional procedures by formally organizing provincial councils in 1918. These bodies were intended to coordinate the actions of local councils within various provinces, on issues essentially provincial in character. This was an important step in clearing the path to the lobbying of provincial governments and bureaucracy. Previously, a local council wishing to make representations on some issue to its provincial government had to secure the attention and cooperation of the National Council executive for its action. Now, while the National Council still had to be notified of the action contemplated, its support was much more readily forthcoming because it did not have to provide personnel for provincial lobbying efforts. The president and executive of a provincial council could meet with provincial legislators, simply keeping National Council informed of their actions. Moreover, and this would become particularly important for the western provinces, provincial councils were also able to bring into affiliation province-wide associations, which might, or might not, be members of local councils in their province, or might be part of a national association. Finally, the presidents of provincial councils were automatically members of the national executive.

The resolution passed by the Winnipeg Local Council in the fall of 1919 indicates that something more than regional disaffection was at work. The resolution reads as follows:

> Whereas, under the present system of representation in the National Council of Women, it seems impossible to secure either democratic organization or progressive action at a time when both are vital to the women of Canada now enfranchised:
>
> Therefore be it resolved that the Local Council of Women withdraw from affiliation with the National Council until such time as the Constitution of the National Council be adequately revised:
>
> And that this Council continue its work as a Council of women for city and Provincial purposes.[9]

Speaking to the issue, in the Local Council Executive meeting of September 26, 1919, the Winnipeg President, Mrs. McWilliams, gave her view of the annual meeting held in Regina that summer. She remarked on its "disappointing nature, through the fact that important matters purporting to advancement and reconstruction were continually being blocked and voted down, principally by means of proxies, while trivial matters were allowed to take up time and energy to no result, and even in cases where progressive measures were adopted no implement was supplied to see that they were put in operation." In defending the resolution of her Executive to a public meeting of the Winnipeg Local Council, held on October 24, 1919, Mrs. McWilliams stated that:

> it carried no idea of forming a Western Council of Women, nor of trying to destroy the National Council, nor was there any idea of permanent withdrawal from the National Council, rather was it an attempt to show that our women now enfranchised were looking for Education and leadership and had failed to find it in the National Council Convention held last June, but instead were compelled to listen to animated discussions on trivial matters, with no opportunity for the expressions of minds of different centres. The work of several years on the revision of the Constitution was thrown out almost entirely by the abuse of the proxy system, and any other progressive action met the same fate.

---

[9] Winnipeg Council of Women, Executive Meeting, Sept. 26, 1919: f 5, p. 3586, Manitoba Provincial Archives, Winnipeg.

The subject commented upon by presenters of this resolution was broader than that of the procedures used by National Council to transact business at the annual general meetings. It broached upon the usefulness of having a national body at all. In terms of procedure, the particular operation of the proxy system which Winnipeg Council objected to, and through which the Executive of the National Council exercised formidable control over the casting of votes, was reformed within the year. The 1920 annual meeting, held in Saint John, New Brunswick, June 15–24, debated this issue, politely but firmly ensured reform, but concluded with a motion that it was understood that past practice had been a matter of good intentions.[10] The issue would arise again, but debate would never reach the same level of acerbity as in 1919. The more profound criticism in that year contained the charge that National Council did not address effectively the concerns of its membership. This was only partially an issue of Council structure and procedures. It was also, as noted above, a question of the usefulness of such a federation as the National Council purported to be.

Function and form were linked together in the minds of Council's critics, and it has often been difficult for Council presidents to articulate anew the peculiarly broad goals that had led the organization's founders to adopt its particular constitutional structure. The constitution of 1893 had been drawn up, at the request of Lady Aberdeen, by Sir John Bourinot, the Clerk of the House of Commons. It was designed to allow the maximum amount of freedom of action for the membership while giving shape to the federation itself. Politically speaking, the whole was to be more than the sum of its parts, but those parts would always have their distinctive characters recognized. Those who founded Council had turned away from the unifying force of any political ideology, except their belief in the humane treatment of human beings, and from any political agenda, other than their common concern to make their communities more responsive to the problems of everyday life. The constitution was built deliberately so as to enable affiliates to retain their autonomy. The shining vision of the founders was belief in a fundamental human morality, transcending codes of theology, going beyond circumstances of social status and inspired by the conviction that each individual person was of value. They drew on the powerful social ideology of separate spheres for men and women and, as has been pointed out, "on a culture of

---

10 *Yearbook*, 1920, pp. 138–141. The history of the development of the abuse, and its eradication, can be most easily traced by following the development of the "Procedures and Bye-Laws" of the National Council of Women of Canada, in the versions printed in the Annual Reports.

womanhood that celebrated not only the home but the bonds between women."[11] Further, the Golden Rule was so fundamental to the ideas and beliefs of those who founded Council, that Lady Aberdeen never felt the need in her opening remarks to the first annual meeting of 1894, to explain what it was. She took it for granted that all, Catholic, Protestant and Jewish, would know that it was "Do unto others as ye would that they should do unto you." The importance of membership in Council would not lie in a uniformity of policy, but in the discovery of matters of common interest, and in agreement to cooperate for the attainment of successive, selected, limited goals. Intellectually, acceptance of the Golden Rule meant, for the founders of Council, an emphasis on addressing obvious and agreed problems of human suffering without bringing differing political and religious beliefs into conflict.

In order for the National Council to function at all, however, the ideals captured by the text of the constitution had to be translated into rules of procedure and by-laws governing the circumstances of action. The ways in which people became members of Council both strengthened and weakened the coherence of the organization. The single criterion for membership, either individual or of an affiliate, was, and remains, the commitment to the general goal of working for the improvement of society through actions inspired by the "Golden Rule."

These membership rules allowed an extraordinary number of different organizations to affiliate. Grace Ritchie England was commissioned by Council in 1924 to produce a report on the "Machinery and future policy of the National Council of Women." In her Report she pointed out that Council was really made up of two federations. "There are," she wrote, "first the Nationally Organised Societies, and second, the Local Councils in themselves federations of Local Societies...how very different in origin and character are these two component parts of Council."[12] The Canadian pattern differed from that of most national councils in Europe and Latin America: the affiliation of nationally organized societies was less important than the evolution of local councils. Until the early nineteen-nineties, the number of nationally organized societies incorporated in the NCWC was always less than the number of local councils. But the former were both important and powerful, though less numerous, than the local councils. The backing of such organizations as the Canadian Girl Guides and the W.C.T.U. for the

---

[11] Prentice, et al., *Canadian Women*, p. 168.
[12] *Yearbook*, 1925, p. 70.

15. Mrs. J.A. Wilson, President 1926–1931

national level of Council greatly helped Council's lobbying activities. Their support was important not only because of the numerical strength Council could cite as backing for its positions, but also because it meant more women were available for the essential dog-work of lobbying — persuading friends, writing letters, visiting officials, preparing position papers, and organizing meetings designed to provide information and to induce further public pressure. The representatives of these organizations had great influence, through their private and their public action, on the NCWC. Most of the women who attained executive positions in one or another of the nationally organized societies met socially. There was considerable informal discussion about Council issues, comparable to the ordinary social contacts between powerful male politicians.[13] At the same time, the constitution gave each nationally organized and nationally affiliated society six votes, in contrast to the a local council's single vote.

The fact remains that the broad membership of local councils was never reflected by the affiliation of provincially and nationally organized associations with their Council counterparts. In small cities and towns, the strength of a local council was rooted in its ability to bring women together, in a space of their own, to tackle problems which obviously transcended all barriers of creed and class. Very often the local council meeting was the only occasion where women encountered those of differing religious and political beliefs. As the Local Council of Welland, Ontario, reported in 1921:

We started the year 1920 with seven societies, this increased to 11 and now in the beginning of 1921 we have 15 societies, which means that we have the co-operation of nearly every women's society in the city, and by standing thus united and by eliminating all differences of religion, class distinctions and party politics, we can accomplish almost all tasks to which we bind our energies.[14]

It was also, quite as often, the only place where social contact between women was not a function of acquaintanceship between their fathers, husbands or brothers.

The network for community action which local councils built was, and remains, extraordinary. This fact is particularly evident in small population

[13] The private correspondence of the presidents of the NCWC is the best, and almost unexploited, source on this aspect: see NCWC, subject files in MG 28 I25, National Archives of Canada.
[14] *Yearbook*, 1921, p. 250.

centres. In 1919, not quite half (twenty one out of forty-four) of the local councils were in towns of less than 10,000, thirteen of them in places of less than 5,000 inhabitants. The minimum number of affiliates needed to form a local council was three, but the majority of these councils had between eight and ten. While some of the local councils founded in very small towns had only a short life, many endured in spite of the small population base. Ponoka, Alberta, with a population of 1594, which established itself with the Ladies' Aid (Methodist), the Red Cross Society and the Women's Missionary Society, lasted less than ten years. Pincher Creek, Alberta, whose population the 1921 census would report as 888, had eight members in 1919: the Eastern Star, the I.O.D.E., the Ladies' Hospital Auxiliary, the Rebekah Assembly, the Red Cross Society, the St. John's Auxiliary and the St. John's Guild, and the Women's Missionary Society. Again, it was a short-lived local council, disappearing in the mid-twenties. Such local councils really owed their existence to wartime conditions, and the cessation of hostilities meant a redirection of energy in these centres. What is more remarkable is that councils in slightly larger centres, such as Sackville, New Brunswick, whose population was 3265 in 1921 and which grew very little in the following years, endured for almost a generation. This council brought together the I.O.D.E. (Lord Sackville Chapter), the Ladies' Aid, (Methodist Church), the W.C.T.U., the Women's Auxiliary Episcopal Church, and the Women's Civic Council. Swift Current, Saskatchewan, with a population of 3518 in 1921, was unusual in bringing together nineteen affiliates: the Altar Society, the Fortnightly Club, two branches of the I.O.D.E., the Great War Veterans' Auxiliary, the Girls' Aid (Knox), Ladies' Aid (Metropolitan), the Ladies' Betterment League, the Ladies' Curling Club, the Ladies' Guild (St. Stephen), the Rebekah Lodge, the Senior Mission Circle (Metropolitan), the Women's Auxiliary Missionary Society, (St. Stephen), the Women's Hospital Aid, the Women's Missionary Society(Knox), the Women's Missionary Society (Metropolitan), the Women's Musical Club and the Y.W.C.A. For a local council to endure for more than a decade, the population base needs to be approximately 3000, which means at the most, during the years between 1900 and 1939, some five hundred adult women.

There is no doubt that within these small population centres in the early twenties, Council was almost exclusively an organization of Protestants, as were the settlements themselves. In larger centres, however, both Catholic and Jewish associations were often members, although the majority of organizations affiliated were either non-denominational or Protestant. But local councils differed considerably from one another in the actual mix of their membership. Many of their programs were the result of particular local conditions and the impact of the differing personalities of the women who joined. The variation in their character comes through strongly in reports given at the annual meetings. While councils reported dutiful cooperation with directives from National Council and provincial council and the study and discussion of designated issues, they also reported their own special activities. Virden, Manitoba, with a population reported in 1921 as 1361, had six affiliated societies and, among other matters, proudly informed the annual meeting of its work in the 'flu epidemic of the previous winter, the achievement of founding a library with 800 books and its support of the Red Cross. It noted that committees had been struck to consider questions relating to agriculture, health, household economics, education, citizenship and supervised play. Given that Virden probably had less than 400 adult women at this time, it is not surprising that the local council disbanded within a couple of years. But this report remarked that "perhaps the greatest benefit of the Council is the bringing together of the different churches to work in cooperation with other organizations for the general benefit of the community."[15] Even a short period of existence encouraged inter-faith harmony in a very sectarian age. Truro, Nova Scotia, with a population of 7562 in 1921, and ten affiliated societies, emphasized the work of its "Education Committee" and its "Committee on Agriculture." For these councils, connection to the National Council was important because it validated their actions and provided them with information and ideas about the general run of problems they faced.

For the nineteen local councils which existed in towns and cities of between 10,000 and 100,000 inhabitants, National Council was expected to be something more. This viewpoint was particularly common among the councils of the four large metropolitan centres: Hamilton with its population of 114,131, Montreal with 618,506 inhabitants, Toronto with 521,898 inhabitants and Vancouver with 163,220. What emerges is the wish for Council to act as the coordinating voice of women's associations in Canada. It is here that the influence of the nationally organized associations was most apparent. As Dr. England pointed out, the very format of the annual meeting in a country with "our vast extent of territory and our comparatively sparse population" had the consequence that meetings are "largely local in character, and not truly representative in a national sense." Even delegates from the local

---

15 *Yearbook*, 1919, p. 220.

councils who could afford the time and money to attend the NCWC annual meeting would find it difficult to make their influence felt. "The central Provinces and Councils preponderate," Dr. England asserted, "and the more distant have only an occasional opportunity of impressing their difficulties and their view points."[16]

It is therefore evident that, at the national level, the formation of policy demanded the careful balancing of very divergent priorities. Dr. England was well aware that the nationally organized associations were each composed of a membership dedicated to an articulated and explicit common purpose, and that the common purpose of Council was the much less clearly stated wish to work "for the common good." She also understood the way in which local councils had to work with the competing aims of their constituents. But she considered these councils "the very bone and marrow of the National Council." She wrote:

> These Councils depend on their local affiliated societies on the one hand, and on the other, on their affiliation with the National. In order to elicit and maintain the interest of their respective communities, the Councils must attack local problems, and in so doing, very carefully refrain from interfering with the work or arousing the jealousy of other societies, whether affiliated or not. They are also expected to give careful consideration to the more abstract national questions, which their own communities are apt to overlook, or evince slight interest in.[17]

She expressed great dissatisfaction with the current situation of the provincial councils which, by 1925, had been in existence for almost six years. She felt they had not been properly established, either institutionally or financially. She hoped the constitution would be developed so that such councils would "occupy a dignified and influential position in the National Council" and "some direct *interprovincial* contact...[could] be devised, by means of which the different provinces might compare their problems, and suggest or organize concerted action, where such may be thought desirable and practicable."

There was an additional and delicate problem which Dr. England outlined, that of the category "Honorary Officer/Honorary Member." In the

---

16 *Yearbook*, 1925, p. 71.
17 *Ibid.*, p. 71.

early years of Council, women of social standing — wives of federal and provincial party leaders, Governors General and Lieutenant Governors — were frequently elected to an honourary position for life, a position which, in 1925, gave voting rights at annual meetings and the right to stand for elective office "in which event their voting power would be doubled."[18] In some ways, it was an issue of principle rather than a matter of practical politics. There were only eleven honorary officers in 1925: Her Excellency, Lady Byng of Vimy, the wife of the Governor General and the ten wives of the Lieutenant Governors. In that year there were also fifteen honourary members, elected for life.[19] No immediate action was taken on this issue — which has always been governed by the by-laws rather than the constitution — and the practice in any given year has reflected the current wishes of Council.[20]

The National Council came safely through this period of critical appraisal: its past achievements stood it in good stead. It had effectively, and often self-effacingly, coordinated efforts by different, and differing, groups in the field of social welfare, particularly those of public health and conditions of work for women and children. Council's method of action was to gather information, both by collecting the studies of others on particular problems and by initiating its own surveys, and then using the material to press for immediate action at the local level, while suggesting major alterations of government policy and action at the provincial and federal levels. It provided, through its standing committees, a mechanism for disseminating information about the activities of local councils, and it gave local councils organized agendas for study and action. This mechanism also allowed national surveys to be done on very specific issues, such as the way in which problems of city hygiene were being tackled across the Dominion.[21] In 1919 there were, among others, standing committees on the Care of the Mentally Deficient, Education, Laws for the Better Protection of Women and Children, Professions and Employments for Women, Public Health, Supervised Playgrounds, Recreations and Social Centres and Women in

---

18 *Ibid.*
19 Apart from past-presidents of the NCWC, Mrs. F.H. Torrington and Mrs. Harriet Sophia Sanford, these included Mrs. F.T. Frost; Professor C.M. Derick; Mrs. Cummings; Lady Gibson; Agnes M. Machar; Mrs. Samuel Lyle; Mrs. Coad; Mrs. David McLellan; S. R. Crease; Mrs. O.C. Edwards; Mrs. Charles Archibald; Dr. Stowe Gullen; Mrs. Adam Shortt; Mrs. Dignam. Order as in the *Yearbook,* 1925, p. 8.
20 The related categories of individual membership, life memberships, patrons (persons who have been accepted as such at an annual meeting, having given a donation of a sum approved by the membership committee) sustaining memberships, and emeriti members, have also varied according to the changing views of Council. For present practice, see Appendix G.
21 *Yearbook,* 1921, "Reports of the Standing Committee on Housing and Town Planning."

Industry. Almost uniformly, the reports of these committees, delivered at the annual meetings, detailed two particular areas of endeavour: specific problems, identified and coped with on the local level, and the presentation of policies for debate concerning what ought to be done to answer the broad questions of need. In 1920, for example, the Report of the Committee for Laws for the Better Protection of Women and Children, given by Mrs. Henrietta Muir Edwards, touched on the action of a particular local council, Hamilton. That year had seen this council establish a Children's Aid Society. But the Report also summarized the state of legislation across the Dominion, relating to such issues as mothers' pensions, the care of delinquent women and girls, and the civic status of illegitimate children. It concluded with resolutions on subjects ranging from the need to obtain for women the right to homestead and to serve on juries, to a request that adultery be made a crime.[22]

This interweaving of reports of particular, specific localized action with discussion of lobbying activities on policy issues at the appropriate political level had been the hallmark of Council action in the past, and it would continue to be so in the future. Local councils found in this process both support for their own initiatives and the strength that comes from realizing that one is not struggling alone.

From the standpoint of most women involved with Council, the problems of Canada in the twenties were not fundamentally different from those the country had known in the past. The census of 1921 showed that the country had continued its trend towards urbanization. The urban/rural split in that census was so close that analysts have debated whether or not more Canadians lived in the country than in the towns that year. By 1930 it was clear: nearly 53% of the population of 8.8 million lived in towns.[23] Canada was developing as an urban society. For Council women, this demographic trend meant business as usual. Experience within their different associations dedicated to specific intents, merely indicated that needs were escalating. It was the activity of women, though not of Council women alone, that was the driving force behind local support for hospitals and orphanages, the creation and maintenance of playing grounds and parks, and the establishment of hos-

---

[22] *Yearbook*, 1920, pp. 124–129. At this time the law governing homesteading provided that all men, but only widows and women with dependents under the age of twenty-one, had the right to homestead, which gave entitlement, when certain specific conditions were met, to free legal title to lands. The problem continued until the nineteen-thirties, when control of public lands passed from federal to provincial control. See Prentice, et al., *Canadian Women*, pp. 199–200.

[23] Firestone, *Canada's Economic Development*, p. 60.

pices for unmarried mothers and the indigent elderly. It was mostly through the efforts of women that Canadian towns established and maintained museums, libraries and art galleries. Through the structures of Council many women were able to channel their efforts to make Canadian towns livable. They sought to improve the conditions of life by specific municipal reforms, so that town and city life did not necessarily mean slums. Local councils worked for clean water supplies, the maintenance of sewer systems, the provision of proper housing, the inspection of marketing practices affecting bread, meat and milk, and the provision of a modicum of health care free of charge.

The established pattern of Council action had allowed local council women to bring concerted and uniform pressure to bear on municipalities across Canada on specific matters, such as the provision of antiseptic conditions for abattoirs. The coordination by Council of broader policies on social issues, such as the work done to present, and then lobby for, the ideas contained in the "Women's Platform," provided members with a way to make their views and ideas known. This was a successful policy. In 1917 membership of Council had been reported as "more than 150,000."[24] In her Presidential address in 1923, Miss Carmichael reported membership at 400,000.[25] The accurate tally of any federated organization is a matter of debate but, however approximate these figures are, they are indications of development.

The organization found its major support among urban women, particularly women in Ontario towns. The local councils of major cities throughout the Dominion played a significant role in developing the policies of the National Council. Representatives of the Local Councils of Victoria, Vancouver, Calgary, Saskatoon, Winnipeg, Montreal and Halifax had a profound steering effect on the organization, as did the Provincial Presidents, once they were created. Nevertheless, the membership of local councils in the national body fluctuated between thirty-five and fifty, and local councils from Ontario usually accounted for fifteen to twenty members. Given the distribution of Canada's population this is not unexpected. But the absence of member councils from the province of Quebec — save for Montreal and, intermittently, Quebec City — meant that Ontario carried the greatest weight.

There is considerable debate over whether the Council, as a national

---

[24] *Yearbook*, 1917, p. 19, "Report of the Corresponding Secretary."
[25] *Yearbook*, 1923, p. 17.

16. Mrs. Irene Parlby

force, was in decline during the twenties. It was clear that the rising membership had come about through an increase in affiliates to particular local
councils, rather than an overall increase in the number of such councils. The
decade witnessed an almost exact balance between the number of councils
that disbanded and those that were founded. Between 1919 and 1929, twelve
local councils came to an end: in Olds, Pincher Creek, Ponoka and Red Deer
(Alberta), Vernon (British Columbia), Virden (Manitoba), Chapleau, Galt,
Guelph, Ingersoll, Strathroy and Temiskaming (Ontario). During these same
years, eleven councils were founded: Chilliwack and Nanaimo (British
Columbia), Georgetown, North Bay, Owen Sound, Smith Falls and Stratford
(Ontario), Moncton (New Brunswick), North Sydney and Westville (Nova
Scotia) and Quebec City (Quebec).[26]

The most serious blow to Council, during the twenties, was the change
in the affiliation of societies at the National level. All the western farming
associations which had had membership at this level withdrew: the Manitoba
Grain Growers' Association, the Saskatchewan Grain Growers' Association
and the United Farm Women of Alberta. In some ways, the action taken by
the women in these associations was explicable, since they held full rights in
the men's farming organizations in these areas, where there was a "disposition among the Farmers to leave to the women a chief voice in framing
demands for legislation on subjects dealing with education, health, home
life, etc."[27] But the withdrawal of the Women's Institutes of Alberta, the
Women's Institutes of Manitoba, the Women's Institutes of Ontario and the
Ontario Women's Citizens' Association was less easy to accept. To a certain
extent, it was a rural/urban split, and the support the National Council gave
to the Canadian Manufacturers' Association on the issue of buying goods
bearing the label "Made in Canada" was, in the eyes of many, a political act.
A particularly contentious resolution, adopted in 1919 by the National
Council, directing that Ottawa be requested to "restrict exports of national
resources," fuelled the discontent of farm women. They interpreted it as "an
Ultimatum from the National Council of Women to the Agricultural people
of this dominion to go out of Business."[28] However the uncoupling of affilia-

26 This information comes from a comparison of the listing of presidents of local councils in the
   1919–1920 and the 1929 *Yearbooks*. It differs slightly from the listing given by Strong-Boag in
   Parliament of Women, (Appendix VI). The brief lives of some local councils were not recorded in
   the National Council records.
27 *Canadian Annual Review of Public Affairs*,(1920), 773, cited in Strong-Boag: *Parliament of Women*,
   p. 392.
28 "Back to the Dark Ages," *The Grain Growers' Guide*, (Oct. 29,1919), 42, cited in Strong-Boag,
   Parliament of Women, p. 391.

tion at the national level did not mean the cessation of all interaction at the local level. Indeed, some farm women argued that local council was their "only contact with urban women."[29] In 1929 local branches of the Women's Institute still remained in affiliation with the Local Councils in McLeod and Medicine Hat, Alberta; Chilliwack and Victoria, British Columbia; Portage La Prairie, Manitoba; Hamilton and Kingston, Ontario.

Other associations that terminated their contact with the National Council during the twenties were the Canadian Suffrage Association, the Canadian Women's Press Club, the Homemakers' Club and the Independent Order of Foresters. The withdrawal of some associations was not necessarily due to anything the National Council might, or might not, have done, but rather to the particular situation of the affiliate itself. Some, such as the Single Tax Association of Ontario simply disappeared. Some found their aims and activities subsumed by other associations, and were absorbed by a more vigorous body: this was true of the Peace and Arbitration Association, most of whose members moved into societies directly supporting the League of Nations. Some associations found they lacked the strength to continue to run their own affairs and support the Council: this was true of the Order of Allied Mothers in Sacrifice.

While a number of associations withdrew, others joined. In these years, the National Council acquired five affiliates, of which the Salvation Army, in 1923, and the Hadassah Organization in 1929, were the most significant. The others were the Canadian Social Hygiene Council, the Girls' Friendly Society and the National Girls' Work Board. It was clear, however, by the end of the decade, that the National Council's ambition to speak for all Canadian women could not be realized.

Much of the policy of the National Council in the twenties and thirties primarily reflected the ideas and beliefs of mature, small "c" conservative, women across Canada, and was fashioned, in large measure, in accordance with the views of urban Ontario. Those who made the Council work were women linked, either by marriage or career, to the business and professional world. For the most part, they had served their apprenticeship in a particular association before being named as a representative to the local council. The overwhelming majority were married and their lives were shaped by the necessities of family life. To a considerable extent they were women whose children were beyond infancy. Only when this stage was passed did they

---

[29] *The Woman Worker*, Feb. 1928, cited in Joan Sangster, *Dreams of Equality: Women on the Canadian Left, 1920–1950*, (Toronto, 1989), p. 44.

have time to give, not only to an association dedicated to a particular goal, but also to the additional work involved in Council membership. While Council attracted the patronage of upper class women in the major metropolitan centres, the grind of committee work, at both the local and national levels was done by women whose economic circumstances were comfortable rather than affluent.[30] It must also be born in mind that at the local council level, the activities also involved, through the membership of the Protestant church auxiliaries, many women whose circumstances were very modest.

The first months of peace had witnessed unprecedented labour unrest in Canada. The Winnipeg General Strike of 1919 was only the most obvious and most massive demonstration of discontent, in a year of strikes. "More than 420 [strikes] were fought, far exceeding the number of conflicts in any previous year."[31] The role that was played by the Winnipeg Local Council in the strike has come to stand, for some, as firm proof of the essentially right-wing nature of the National Council as a whole.[32] On May 15, 1919 some 500 telephone operators in Winnipeg left their jobs, the first of more than 22,000 workers to stop work. The Local Council of Women called on them to submit their grievances for arbitration, and when this was turned down, offered the Mayor of Winnipeg cooperation in containing the strike. It is unclear from reports, both of the unions involved and of Winnipeg Local Council, whether any Council members actually replaced the strikers. It is also difficult to judge how important the action of the Local Council was, given the complex nature of the strike.[33]

It would be wrong to argue from this single event in Winnipeg that the Council, at both the local and the national level, was merely an organization of middle class women defending their privileges. The reality is more complex. In 1917 the Council had defeated by only 26 votes — the count was 137 to 111 — a motion to have union labels on all National Council of Women of Canada publications.[34] In 1918 the Committee to report on

30 Strong-Boag has pointed out that, as far as women are concerned, terms such as "working class" and " middle class" are "a guide to the status and power of women's families" rather than to the standing within a community of the woman herself, *New Day*, p. 3.
31 Bryan D. Palmer, *Working Class Experience: Rethinking the History of Canadian Labour, 1800–1991*, 2nd edition (Toronto, 1992), p. 200.
32 The history of the Winnipeg General Strike has been recounted time and again, but see G.S. Kealey, "1919: the Canadian Labour Revolt," *Labour/Le Travail*, 13 (Spring, 1984), pp. 11–44; Mary Horodski, "Women and the Winnipeg General Strike of 1919," *Manitoba History*, 11 (Spring, 1986), pp. 28–37.
33 See Donald Avery, "The Radical Alien and the Winnipeg General Strike of 1919," in Bumsted, ed., *Interpreting Canada's Past*, vol. II, *After Confederation*, pp. 222–239.
34 *Yearbook*, 1917, pp. 46–7.

"Trades and Labour Unions in Relation to Women and Children" made it clear that industrial workers had a perfect right to struggle for a living wage and better working conditions.[35] In 1919, the convenor of the Committee on Industrial Unrest, Constance Hamilton, reported that the Committee believed that "the present industrial system is the cause of great injustice," and that "poverty and hardship are not necessary evils" but could be removed by a process of "levelling up, so that the privileges now enjoyed by the few, may be available to all."[36]

Further, other strikes, in different places and at different times, produced different reactions from local councils. The bitter struggles of Cape Breton miners led to action in New Brunswick. The St. John Local Council organized a "Tag Day" for the "Families of the Miners in Cape Breton, suffering sorely in consequence of the coal-miners' strike" and raised thirteen hundred dollars.[37] Sackville's Local Council reported that "in response to the crying need of the miners on strike in Cape Breton we shipped to them nineteen cartons of groceries, two tubs of butter and other food supplies."[38] Committed to a position which reflected no overt ideological engagement, the National Council rarely took courses of action which could be interpreted as the consequence of formal and rigid political principles.

Even arguments about moral issues, which might be expected to produce a firm Council policy, were rarely pursued to the bitter end. For example, Council managed to keep the W.C.T.U. as a member, even though its own support of prohibition was never more than lukewarm. Basically, of course, membership was about cooperation between people of different views for the protection of community projects. It is not possible to generalize from the conduct of the Local Council of Winnipeg at the time of the General Strike to any valid conclusion about the political stance of the general membership of the NCWC, particularly since the Winnipeg Local Council actions were not supported at the national level. The history of Council is not the history of an anti-labour organization. The main goal of most members was the immediate alleviation of need, as can be clearly seen from the reports, year by year, of actions such as that of the Local Council of Macleod, Alberta, in 1926, who purchased spectacles for "a young girl who was unable to attend school."[39] This gesture hardly has the characteristics of a

---

35 *Yearbook,* 1918, p. 112.
36 *Yearbook,* 1919, p. 99.
37 *Yearbook,* 1926, p. 48.
38 *Ibid.,* p. 133.
39 *Ibid.,* p. 127.

community project, but it is something that springs naturally from the philanthropic aims of the volunteer organizations that were the prime interest of most members of Council.

It is not surprising that, in 1919, the particular strengths of the new President, Mrs. Sanford, were a solace to much of the membership. It is easy to criticize her as representative of the "autocratic interests in Canada."[40] She was a member of a wealthy elite, and had friends in high places both nationally and internationally. Her personality, however, was the opposite of autocratic: she was soft-voiced and tactful, and her charm was often remarked upon as an important factor in her role as Treasurer for the International Council of Women. During her four years as President she travelled Canada tirelessly, preaching the value of discussion and consultation among those working in their communities. In their reports to the National Council, in the minutes of their Executives, local councils testify to the sense of renewal her visits brought. It is due to a large extent to her peace-making activities that Winnipeg petitioned for re-admittance to Council in 1922.

Mrs. Sanford, however, was not just a conciliator, important though that role was for the leader of the National Council in 1919. Both Mrs. Sanford and Miss Caroline E. Carmichael,[41] who became President of the National Council in 1923, were closely involved in the International Council. The very controversy surrounding the links between the National Council of Women of Canada and the International Council of Women provided Mrs. Sanford with a powerful cause for action on something other than domestic issues. While there was considerable anti-German feeling in Canada in the immediate post-war years, there was also a strong wish for the establishment of an enduring peace. Mrs. Sanford was helped by the fact that Lady Aberdeen, the much cherished first President of the Canadian National Council of Women, was once more elected President of the International Council in 1920. Lady Aberdeen rebuked, in strong language, those members of the National Council of Women who wished to withdraw that body

---

[40] This was not so much a personal criticism as one aimed by its writer at the leadership of the National Council in general. What particularly provoked that person's ire was the institution of annual and life time patrons of the Council, something she considered "a retail business in titles." "The National Council," in *The Grain Growers' Guide*, (June 5, 1918) cited in Strong-Boag, *Parliament of Women*, p. 337.

[41] Born in New Glasgow, Nova Scotia, she died in 1942. She worked for more than twenty years through the New Glasgow Local Council and the Provincial Council of Nova Scotia. Her affiliation with Council was through the Missionary Society for the Presbyterian Church in the Maritime Provinces. She was appointed by the Canadian government as an official representative to the Factory Inspection Section of the International Labour Division of the League of Nations, Geneva, 1924. She was awarded the C.B.E. and a Doctorate of Civil Laws by Dalhousie University.

from affiliation with the International Council. She wrote:

> Do you really wish the I.C.W. to be utterly paralysed and useless at
> this time of the world's great need, that this great federation of orga-
> nized women's societies should confess itself unable to call its mem-
> bers together to confer how best they can take up again their work of
> healing and good will?[42]

The meeting of the International Council at Christiania (later Oslo),
Norway, in September 1920 was attended by four Canadian delegates, Mrs.
Sanford, Miss C.E. Carmichael, Miss Matheson, and Mrs. Ninian Smillie. It
was reported on at length, when Council held its annual meeting in Calgary,
from June 13–17, 1921. In giving her report, Carmichael took the opportunity to explain what the International Council was about.[43] In her eyes, the
gathering at Christiania represented the views of 20,000,000 women. Miss
Carmichael remarked upon the issue of membership, noting that during the
war:

> Some members of our Canadian Council felt strongly, that unless
> connection was cut with the enemy countries, Canada should discon-
> nect herself with the I.C.W. but the saner view taken was, that as all
> nationalities were on equal footing, no one Council could expel
> another, and patience and the cessation of action was the course to
> pursue.

The main issues discussed, at this Sixth Quinquennial meeting of the
International Council, related to a woman's rights as a citizen, especially the
right to retain her own nationality after marriage; famine relief; the question
of education for women, and the general issue of health. Miss Carmichael
emphasized in her concluding remarks the call made to the delegates of the
National Councils of Women for united efforts toward peace. She reported
the words of Frau von Frith of Austria, which came close to those of the
British heroine, Nurse Edith Cavell. Before being shot as a spy, Nurse Cavell
had said: "Patriotism is not enough! I must have no hate in my heart for anyone." Frau von Frith said, commenting on the common suffering of mothers,
"I could have no hatred in my heart for anyone."[44]

---

[42] Aberdeen to Cummings, December 19, 1919; cited in Strong-Boag, "Peace," p. 179.
[43] *Yearbook,* 1920, p. 63.
[44] *Yearbook,* 1921, p. 77.

From this meeting onwards, throughout the nineteen twenties and thirties, the NCWC showed a strong and continuing interest in the activities of the International Council and in working for international harmony. Reports from particular committees linked to the ICW were regularly presented at annual meetings of the National Council, and in 1923 the Council became a corporate member of the Canadian League of Nations Society. Moreover, in the following decades, a number of NCWC members were selected by the federal government to represent Canada at international gatherings, including sessions of the League of Nations. In 1922, Dr. Ritchie England was appointed to the Pan-American Conference of Women as an official Canadian delegate.[45] In 1923, President Carmichael was appointed as the Canadian representative to the Factory Inspection Section of the International Labour Division of the League. In 1927, Mary Dignam, whose work for the "Art and Culture" committees of Council had been outstanding, was appointed to be Canada's delegate to the Popular Arts Congress, called by the League of Nations to meet that year in Prague.[46]

The attention paid to international concerns did not diminish the attention of Council members to domestic issues. In particular, Council examined the critical question raised by the Winnipeg Local Council: of what real use is the National Council? It addressed this question by action through its committees rather than through philosophical debate. One of the major issues, during the years in which Mrs. Sanford was in office, arose from the need felt by women in general — and particularly the women whose organizations were building blocks of the National Council — to decide what impact their right to vote should have on their continued support for collective actions in private, volunteer associations. There were many, both men and women, who believed that women were, inherently, more compassionate, more generous, more capable of a right ordering of political principles from humane and moral motives than men. Consequently, they could be expected to vote on political issues in accordance solely with the most altruistic vision of public needs. Women would hold the balance of power in political life, removed from the sordid strife of political expediency, patronage and the general ruck of party politics. If this were indeed so, the best arena for women's activity would now be the mainstream political life of the country. Many people however, both men and women, were convinced not only of the essential sameness of the political nature of men and women, but also of the contin-

[45] Strong-Boag, "Peace," p. 179.
[46] Strong-Boag, *Parliament of Women*, p. 388.

ued existence of discrimination against women, and a continual need to do battle against it. They did not look for immediate change in the political process as a result of female suffrage and, at the same time, they did not expect the traditional bias against equal rights for women to disappear because certain political disabilities had been removed. The consequences of women's changed political rights remained an issue for Council throughout the twenties, both in debates on the way in which women ought to act politically, and in the on-going consideration of the need to eradicate sexual discrimination, exemplified by the fight for the right for women to be senators.

Council's response to this situation was to demonstrate its own immediate usefulness as a clearing house of ideas, and a spur to action. These impulses are seen in the reports of the Standing Committee on Citizenship. It was chaired for many years by Dr. Augusta Stowe Gullen, the daughter of Dr. Emily Howard Stowe. She was as forthright as her mother, and as committed to justice for women. In common with all those who chaired this Committee during the twenties, she made it her business to find out what the sub-committees were doing at the local level and prodded many into activity. In presenting her report at the meeting in Regina in 1919, she laid out what, in her view, needed attention if women were to use the franchise effectively. She started by outlining a program that was as much about social reform as it was about citizenship. Only four out of its twelve points dealt with matters such as the establishment of discussion groups on constitutional issues and debates over whether "Party politics [is] essential to national life."[47] The remaining eight were concerned with the age of consent for marriage, the mother's rights as guardian of her children, the employment of children under 14, the need to "establish the maxim that equal labour demands equal pay," the need to establish an eight-hour day, the need for a minimum wage bill, for healthy working conditions, for a revision of property acts, especially those which were established on the premise that women were the property of males, and equality of treatment under marriage and divorce laws for men and women.

Dr. Stowe Gullen reported that, in corresponding with the Citizenship Councils at the local level, she found that the influenza epidemic of the past winter (1918–19) had hampered the registration of women voters, and the participation of council members in municipal elections, either as candidates or as electors. These difficulties were often attributed to the role of the mar-

---

[47] *Yearbook*, 1919–1920, p. 116.

ried woman as mother and family nurse, and the demands on that same woman as a source of labour for community action in times of epidemic. But, however faltering and incoherent this report might seem, it had the result that local councils devoted substantial attention to municipal politics in general, and to women's role in municipal politics in particular. It was an affirmation of one of the major roles that Council had played since its inception: that of a training school for women, educating them in the ways Canadian political life functioned. As the years went by, Council members distinguished more clearly between process and program, between how things should be done and what things ought to be done. At all times and at all levels, however, Council meetings allowed women to discuss the workings of institutions and the pros and cons of particular policies.

Throughout the twenties, reports of the Standing Committee on Citizenship, as well as information scattered through annual reports of local and provincial councils to the National Council, showed the attention paid by members to municipal politics. The non-partisan creed of Council meant, as Veronica Strong-Boag has pointed out, that the emphasis throughout these years was on "political education rather than political activism."[48] There were three major areas in which local councils worked: the dissemination of information about how local and provincial governments operated, and the registration of women voters; the presentation of women as candidates, sometimes for election to the municipal council itself, but more often for positions on boards of education and on boards of health; and the involvement of women in the process of elections. For example, the Citizenship Committee report in 1920 noted that the Local Council of Port Arthur organized its members to act as scrutineers and poll clerks in both the provincial and municipal elections; achieved the election of two women to the Board of Education; and raised the question of revisions to the Municipal Act, to allow women property owners the same voting rights as men.[49] Hamilton was listed as having "gained the co-operation of the city newspapers in a series of articles on the importance of the women's vote." Swift Current achieved the addition of "a large number of women" to the voters list, and secured the re-election of two women to the Board of Education as well as the appointment of "their nominee" to the Board of Health. Kingston had the President of the Local Council elected to the Board Health, something which

---

[48] Strong-Boag, *Parliament of Women*, p. 383.
[49] *Yearbook*, 1920, p. 52.

(as Dr. Gullen noted in her report), ensured close contact "with the active Social Work in the Community" and had given "a new sense of responsibility and of power to the Local Council of Women."[50] The year 1920 also saw Toronto, Brandon, Halifax and Regina report vigorous activity on the part of their sub-committees on citizenship.

Throughout the twenties local councils signalled their successes in having women appointed to a broad range of municipal boards and committees, and in making the press carry full accounts of municipal meetings. They reported frustration, in considerable detail, at their experience of finding that women willing to stand for election at the municipal level had been omitted from the requisite electoral lists.[51] Strong interest in the local political scene did not exclude continued attention to women's political rights at the provincial and federal level. There was continuing emphasis on discussion of the "Women's Platform" at annual meetings. In particular, the 1920 meeting drew up a short list of political aims under this heading, dividing them into federal and provincial categories. It was a less coherent document than the 1917 "Platform," mingling demands for specific action with other requests for general moral behaviour. Politicians at both levels of government, for example, were asked to aim for equal moral standards in public and private life, and the abolition of patronage. They were also asked specifically to work for the publication of amounts contributed to party funds and the open nomination of political candidates. They were requested to support political equality for men and women, and to practice thrift in the administration of public and private affairs.[52] Under the heading of social standards were resolutions concerning the need for uniform marriage laws and equality of cause for divorce, as well as the removal of all financial barriers to divorce. This section also contained resolutions asking that the age of consent (for marriage) be raised to eighteen, and that the sale of intoxicants be prohibited. Finally, in the section addressed to federal politicians under the title "Industrial Standards," the "Women's Platform" endorsed the principle of collective bargaining, called for the implementation of "Equal Pay for work of equal value in quantity and quality" and asked that the "basis of employment [was] to be physical and mental fitness without regard to sex."

Most of the resolutions addressed to those elected at the provincial level were more specific. Requests were for a Child Welfare Section in all

---

50 *Ibid.*, p. 53.
51 As in Toronto, *Yearbook*, 1921, p. 120.
52 The details are given in the *Yearbook*, 1920, pp. 62–63.

Departments of Health, at both the provincial and the municipal levels; the segregation and care of the feeble-minded; the prohibition of the sale of intoxicants; the equality rights for women with respect to guardianship of children; the legal recognition of a woman's share in her husband's property and income during her life; medical inspection of all schools, with dental clinics where this was possible; the physical training of boys and girls in all schools; and equality of training without regard to sex in all technical areas. A number of resolutions were clear in intent but vague in scope. Adequate mother's pensions were called for, with no suggestion as to what this might mean. Similarly, adequate salaries for teachers were proposed, without analysis of pay scales. Free and compulsory education in all provinces was advocated, but its duration and content went undefined.

While one might regret the lack of introductory argument for these resolutions, and their rather haphazard presentation, with no indications of relative priority, they nonetheless testify to the essentially feminist nature of the National Council. They show that members of Council believed that discrimination against women was to be fought in the political arena, in the educational sphere and in the work-place. Hazy they might be on details, with a tendency to propose ideals for policy rather than specific programs of action; nevertheless, Council members were clear enough on the principles underlying the whole range of women's rights, from equal partnership in marriage and divorce to equal rights for education and employment.

The presidency of Council changed hands in 1922, at the annual meeting held that year in Port Arthur and Fort William (West Algoma), from June 19 to June 28. In the two terms served by Mrs. Sanford, Council had begun to come to terms with the new and changing demands of Canada in the post-war world. Under the presidency of Miss C.E. Carmichael, which would also last for two terms, the process of establishing the long-term strategy of Council was continued. While her interest in international matters was the subject of her first presidential address, given at the annual meeting held in Halifax, Nova Scotia, June 20–27, 1923, much of Miss Carmichael's time was spent on addressing specific tactical issues. These included contacts between the NCWC and the federal government; organization of the agendas of Council committees; the connections of the National Council with those national organized associations, such as the I.O.D.E., which were its affiliates; and last, but by no means least, the communication network between standing committees and the local councils.

It was Miss Carmichael who managed to institute formal meetings between members of the Executive of the NCWC and members of the federal

Cabinet, including the Prime Minister. Her knowledge of the political workings of Ottawa, gained from observing her father's life as a senator, led her to
an understanding of the best way to lobby for the Council. The report of the
corresponding secretary for 1924 noted that a delegation from Council,
including the president, Mrs. Edwards, Mrs. Smillie, Mrs. Carpenter, Mrs.
Wilson, Mrs. Cummings and Miss Hart, was attended on the government side
by the Prime Minister (Mackenzie King), the Minister of Justice (Sir Lomer
Gouin) and the Minister of Health (Henri S. Béland). This first "official"
meeting developed over ensuing decades into formal presentations of
Council's program to the Prime Minister and senior federal Cabinet ministers.
There is no doubt that in these early years, National Council presidents were
always able to make their views known to government through their social
connections. It is also clear that the opening of a semi-formal channel of communication between a non-governmental agency such as the NCWC and the
federal government was due, to a very large extent, to the social status of
women on the Executive of National Council. But however much class privilege helped to secure this form of access, the result was the presentation of
Council policies directly to members of government.

At the same time, Council reorganized its Parliamentary Committee. This
was largely the result of work by the Ottawa Local Council.[53] Their efforts
made it possible to monitor systematically the lobbying activities of National
Council with the federal government. The fate of Council resolutions,
despatched to Ministers and M.P.s, was tracked, requests for information were
traced, government responses were tabulated, and the Council was able to follow government reaction to its requests.

These initiatives in lobbying procedures were accompanied by a growing
sophistication among Council members as to what they wished to accomplish.
The very web binding the affiliates of Council together allowed an uncritical
gathering of resolutions to be placed before the annual meetings and could, in
turn, result in a veritable hodge-podge of resolutions to be taken further by the
Executive. During the second half of the twenties, the NCWC began exercis-
ing stricter control over priorities for action. The report of the first meeting, in
1924, of members of the Executive with members of the federal Cabinet, listed a broad spectrum of topics discussed, and presented them as having been
dealt with in no particular order. The reports reads in part as follows:

... a request for an amendment to the British North America Act, so

---

[53] *Yearbook,* 1924, p. 47.

that a woman might be appointed to the Senate. Another [request] would make women equal to men in divorce. A pure bedding law was urged, as also that the importation of junk filling for mattresses be prohibited. That the venereal diseases grant to the social Hygiene Council be not reduced, and a request for representation on the Dominion Health Committee; that the government allow the manufacture and sale of oleomargarine; for personal naturalization of married women; that wife desertion be made an extraditable offence; that the Homestead act be so amended as to extend its privileges to women on the same terms as is now open to men; that in connection with divorce a wife's domicile be where she resides...[54]

Three years later, in 1927, when the next meeting took place, the NCWC presented a much more organized agenda. This meeting was attended by the Honourable Ernest Lapointe, Minister of Justice, standing in for Prime Minister Mackenzie King, and ten other ministers. Eleven resolutions were presented, two of them (Nos. 1 and 2) dealing with Soldiers' Insurance Schemes and the Soldiers' Pensions Act; two of them dealing with the representation of women on international bodies, a woman lawyer on the International Committee for the Codification of International Law, and the appointment of a woman to the Art Congress to be held in Prague, 1928 (Nos. 3–8); the fourth resolution being a request for the appointment of a woman to the Senate, No. 5 dealt with the question of international laws governing trafficking in women; the sixth concerned raising the age of consent to marriage; number seven dealt with the tax on works of art dutiable in Canada; number nine with the protection of persons without nationality; number ten with necessary amendments to the Criminal Code to protect women and children, and the last dealt with needed amendments to the Naturalization Act, to provide that a woman's national status would be considered independent of her husband's.

This narrowing and focusing of the agenda of the NCWC as a whole was also reflected in the work of its committees, both standing and ad hoc. Reports given at annual meetings became more tightly written, and the variation in Canadian experience was better presented. From 1924 onwards, the reports published in the *Yearbook* very often give a synopsis of the present situation of the issue under discussion, rather than a simple account of

---

[54] *Ibid.*, pp. 21–2.

actions taken. For example, in that year Henrietta Muir Edwards, the Convenor of the Standing Committee on "Laws concerning Women and Children," presented an overview of past Council requests, including their few successes, such as the appointment of the first woman to jury duty in Vernon, British Columbia, November 8, 1923.[55] She summarized the legal status of women and children across Canada at that time, listed the lobbying efforts made by Council, and made suggestions as to what ought to be done next. In this and in an interim report from the "Special Committee on the Property Relations of Husband and Wife," which she also presented, clear and accurate information on legal rights of women and children is given. When one considers that this information would reach a minimum of 400,000 women, one can understand something of the educational value of NCWC work in an age before television and radio.

Another important example is the Special Report on Maternal Care, given by Mrs. Adelaide M. Plumtre at the annual meeting, held in Toronto, May 30–June 6, 1928. Mrs. Plumtre surveyed all sources of information used in the report and highlighted the areas of particular concern for the country. While infant mortality had decreased, in 1928 "Pregnancy [stood] second in causes of death of all women between 15 and 50 in Canada, being exceeded only by tuberculosis."[56] The report went on to note that in Toronto the rate of mortality due to this cause was steadily rising. "In 1925 it was 6.3 per thousand living births; in 1926 it was 7.2; in 1927 it had risen to 7.7..."[57] Mrs. Plumtre concluded her report by observing, with some acerbity, that the death rate in rural Canada was 4.3 per thousand living births, and that "we might conclude that the life of the mother is safer in the country, where there are few, if any, opportunities of obtaining skilled medical and nursing care..." if it were not for the fact that Saskatchewan had the fewest medical resources and the worst statistics of maternal death.

The increasingly professional character of Council activities was further enhanced by repeated public formulation of clear statements about what Council was, and how it operated. In her second presidential address, given at the annual meeting of Council, held in Toronto, October 9–15, 1924, Miss Carmichael remarked that "sometimes one hears murmurs as to the N.C.W.C. having fulfilled its mission." She went on to observe:

---

[55] *Ibid.*, p. 76.
[56] *Yearbook*, 1928, p. 112.
[57] *Ibid.*

> The women actively engaged in the work of this organization are not of that sort, who can afford to spend their energies on a lost or finished cause. So let us for a very few minutes...examine ourselves as an organization. First of all let us emphasize the fact that we are <u>not</u> a society composed of individuals, but an organization or affiliation of societies; that we are <u>not</u> at all responsible for the individual beliefs or the principles of any one of our component parts; that our broad principle is the Golden Rule; that our object is to act together for a common purpose, national or local, and that our Executive is composed of the heads of all of our affiliated associations.[58]

She placed great emphasis on the fact that the National Council was *"not* an independent society working as rivals to the W.C.T.U., the I.O.D.E. Nurses' Associations, Missionary societies, Y.W.C.A, etc., etc., but [was] these very societies banded together with their officers as [the] executive."[59]

In her farewell address, in 1926, Miss Carmichael deplored the fact that, during her term in office, "we cannot report growth in accession of nationally organised societies nor even in local councils."[60] From the mid-nineteen twenties the organization was often criticized, both by its own members and by others, for its inability to sweep into its fold all women's societies and associations in the country, or to achieve a quick growth in local councils, similar to the expansion during World War One. This criticism reflects disappointment at the loss of a vision rather than an appreciation of the actual position of Council. There is no doubt that the organization both lost associations, such as the Women Grain Growers' Association and the Women's Press Club, and failed to attract many of the newer professional women's organizations. But it recruited other groups such as the National Parks Federation in 1927.

Thus despite some losses throughout the twenties Council slowly grew. Its membership was 400,000 in 1923, and after the affiliation of Hadassah in 1929 reached more than half a million. That affiliation in itself says something about the NCWC's stand against narrow sectarianism. While certain local councils, such as Montreal and Toronto, had always included some Jewish organizations, the twenties saw the growing recruitment of Jewish organizations into a number of local councils. In 1924, Halifax had recruited

---

58   *Yearbook,* 1924, p. 37.
59   *Ibid.,* p. 38.
60   *Yearbook,* 1926, p. 32.

the Hebrew Ladies' Aid, Dauphin (Manitoba), the Jewish Ladies, Calgary, the Hebrew Ladies' Aid. Further Jewish affiliations with other local councils followed.

By the end of Miss Carmichael's presidency it had become apparent that the Canadian political system would accommodate the women's vote in much the same way it had accommodated working men's votes a generation earlier. Dreams of a "Women's Party" faded, the recruitment of women into existing political parties, especially those of the left, absorbed exertions that might otherwise have been channelled via the Council. While female political candidates were to remain few in number — for many many years — there was a development of "women's auxiliaries" within political parties, and women's participation in union activity increased. As years went by women were increasingly drawn into a wide variety of public activities, even though their status was most often that of assistant rather than principal actor.

The Council came to represent a particular sector of Canadian women, bound together by a willingness to spend energy, time and money on a wide variety of volunteer, community activities, rather than by an immediate political agenda. Its continuing strength came from its validation of the lives many women led. Its agenda emphasized women as people, but it was an emphasis that was founded on acceptance that family life was the normal experience of women. Given that, in 1931, 82.7% of women had married by the age of 44,[61] the emphasis might be conservative but it is hardly to be argued with. The conditions of family life represented a state of affairs that Council members assumed, rightly, to be of great and continuing consequence to women. The philosophy of the Council was not radical, but the organization continuously fought for the rights of women as wives and mothers, and supported changes in marriage and divorce laws to such an extent that Catholic societies have hesitated, and still hesitate, to seek affiliation.

Miss Carmichael's sense of disappointment came from hopes and ambitions unfulfilled, rather than an assessment of what Council was actually achieving. The stabilization of a considerable membership was paralleled during her presidency by Council's growing effectiveness as a lobbyist at the provincial and federal levels, on particular issues, selected with increasing care, that concerned women and the family. This would be helped during the

61 Dominion Bureau of Statistics, 1956. Analytical Report: Marital Status. Table XV, cited in, *Women at Work*, p. 294.

coming years by the establishment of a national office in 1928 and the launching of a Foundation fund in that year. The necessity of a properly funded head office had become obvious, as had the need to find some money for the travelling expenses of officers attending the annual meetings. Mrs. F. Etherington, at that time President of the Kingston Local Council, raised the question at the 1926 annual meeting in Vancouver. She herself contributed the initial seed-money with an immediate donation of $10,000 and headed a committee to explore ways and means of establishing the fund.[62] At the annual meeting of 1928, held in Toronto from May 30–June 6, the ground-work for its development was properly established.[63] The aim was to build a capital fund of $100,000, the interest on which would assist the establish-ment and maintenance of a head office in Ottawa; contribute to the general expenses of the National Council; and help to defray the travelling expenses of local council delegates to the annual meeting.[64] By 1930, the income from the fund, a capital investment of about $54,000, was $3,200, and its exis-tence was of crucial importance for the continued functioning of the NCWC during the thirties.[65] It proved to be a successful enterprise and has remained so to this day.

Mrs. J.A. Wilson succeeded Miss Carmichael as President in 1926. She was born Henrietta Tuzo in British Columbia, had been educated in England, and was both an explorer and a mountain climber. Mount Tuzo, a peak in the Canadian Rockies 10,685 feet above sea-level, was named in her honour. She had been President of Ottawa Local Council. She served two terms, and was therefore in office in the first desperate months of the Depression. In her opening speech, delivered at the 34th annual meeting of Council, held at Stratford, Ontario, from October 4–7, 1927, she asked bluntly, "Why do not Canadians avail themselves of their advantages and really know both their official languages?"[66] She went on to remark that the issue of language teaching had already been raised at the annual meeting held in 1920 and that, in her view, "Council should now urge that French be taught in the public schools under each province." She went on to express the wish to have a major address on a topic of importance delivered by an acknowledged expert

---

62 Mrs A. Turner Bone, Mrs. F. Etherington, Mrs. Edgar D. Hardy, *Necessity of Establishing This Fund, Founding of Fund- June, 1926 Brief History of Succeeding Years To Date* (Internal evidence would place date of publication in 1956), n.d.,n.p.
63 *Yearbook*, 1928, p. 27.
64 *Yearbook*, 1938, p. 69.
65 For the development and continuing importance of this fund, see Appendix B.
66 *Yearbook*, 1926, p. 32.

at every annual meeting, and to emphasize her faith in the League of Nations as the harbinger of peace. In her conclusion she encouraged the Council to understand how much work needed to be undertaken for the betterment of society, remarking that, "really only the most obvious pieces of work have been done and these are not complete." It is not surprising that the first mention of NCWC support for Quebec suffrage comes during her presidency.[67]

Much of the time and energy of Mrs. Wilson's first two years as President were devoted to the I.C.W., whose last Quinquennial meeting had been held in 1925. That event had been followed by the meeting of the standing committees of the International Council in Geneva in 1927. Mrs. Wilson's second presidential address to the thirty-fifth annual meeting pointed out the extent to which the convenors of the Canadian standing committees were linked with their international counterparts. She remarked forthrightly: "we know the League of Nations exists, and vaguely we don't like war, but not so many are banded together to make that public opinion which would make it impossible."[68]

While the annual meeting was held in Toronto in the early spring of 1928, from May 30 to June 6, before any intimation of the coming Depression, the Corresponding Secretary, Lydia M. Parsons, opened her report with a summary of an address given by the President of the Trade and Labour Congress to the Executive of Council in February. The points on which Lydia Parsons reported concentrated concerned the scope of the problem of unemployment as a national and international condition, rather than just a local issue; the impact on Canadian unemployment of immigration and tariff policies; and the fact that municipalities have "less than any other authority to do with causes of unemployment, yet [it is] frequently upon them that the full burden falls."[69] The conclusions she reported stressed that the first necessity was to "organize local relief so as to remove to the utmost the taint of charity and thus prevent the demoralization of the recipient." Her final statement was, ironically, that "unemployment is a question that needs attention in good times as well as bad and is worthy of the best consideration of every Canadian." At the next annual meeting, the Council would be faced with the need to consider the extent to which these ideas would govern their reaction to the economic misery into which the country had begun to plunge.

---

[67] *Yearbook,* 1928, p. 61.
[68] *Ibid.,* p. 24.
[69] *Ibid.,* p. 29.

CHAPTER 6

Confronting the Depression
1929–1939

THE THIRTY-SIXTH annual meeting of the National Council of the Women of Canada was held in Saskatoon, from May 27 to June 1, 1929. It was the last meeting of Council before the Depression. The presidential address, by Henrietta Wilson, would be the last such speech for ten years, containing no mention of the overall economic problems of Canada. Just as the First World War had wrought change throughout Canadian society, so would the Depression. In his classic short study, *Politics of Chaos*,[1] Blair Neatby wrote that "the impact of the Depression differed by region, by community and even by family."[2] He pointed out that for some families in the slums of Montreal and North Winnipeg welfare payments had been their only income for a decade, whereas others were not significantly affected. "But even these fortunate people," Neatby went on to say, "did not escape unscathed. It was impossible to live in Canada without absorbing the depression mentality. No matter how secure a person might be there were always relatives or friends whose plight brought home the reality of the depression."[3]

In the spring of 1929, for Council, as for the country as a whole, the arrival of grave economic problems was still a cloud on the horizon "no bigger than a man's hand." Thompson and Seager have written: "The Great Depression took Canadians by surprise...In their annual reports to share-holders in January, 1929, Bank presidents searched for superlatives to

---

[1] H. Blair Neatby, *Politics of Chaos: Canada in the Thirties*, (Toronto, 1972).
[2] *Ibid.*, p. 21.
[3] *Ibid.*, p. 22.

praise the economy."[4] It was not until later that summer that the unmistakable signals of trouble appeared. Then it became clear that "wheat prices had declined from their highs of 1927, and the price and demand for newsprint had begun to slip."[5] It should be no surprise that the agenda for the Council meeting of spring 1929, and the tone in which the issues raised were discussed, showed no greater foresight concerning the problems that would face the organization in the "Dirty Thirties."

Nevertheless, issues were raised at that meeting which in the coming years would become matters of nationwide discussion. The health of women and children, the place of married women in the workforce, the continued need to ensure women rights of full citizenship, were all subjects of full-length reports and extensive debate at the 1929 meeting. The long-term interest of Council in such areas as education, culture, and town planning were also addressed, as well as the continuing desire of Council members to make the operations of Council both efficient and democratic.

The work which Adelaide Plumptre had begun as convenor of the Special Committee on Maternal Care in Canada continued. Under her direction, a questionnaire was prepared with the aim of stimulating discussion of the state of care for mothers at the three crucial periods in their lives: the pre-natal months, the actual time of confinement, and the post-natal period. The questionnaire opened with a short introduction covering what a pregnant woman needed to know about diet and exercise; particular symptoms that should be reported to a doctor; the need for help during birth and the type of post-natal care that should be given. The questions themselves ranged over every subject: what medical personnel, doctors, nurses, midwives, were available in a given region, what the community had in terms of clinics and education centres for pregnant women, and the extent to which lack of proper care was due to financial need. With the help of the Canadian Medical Association and the federal Department of Health, some 8000 forms were printed and distributed.[6] In 1930, the final report of her Committee appeared, its main finding being that the Canadian rate of mortality in childbirth was unacceptably high. In 1929, it was 5.7 per 1000 living births, as against 4.5 in England, Wales, Germany and New Zealand, and 2.5 in Scandinavia, France and the Netherlands.[7] The report recommended that much more pub-

---

4   John Herd Thompson and Allen Seager, *Canada 1922-1939: Decades of Discord*, (Toronto, 1985), p. 193.
5   *Ibid.*, p. 193.
6   *Yearbook*, 1929, pp. 124-129, including the actual questionnaire, pp. 127-129; 1930, pp. 122-129.
7   *Yearbook*, 1930, p. 123.

lic education be provided concerning the accepted norms of pre-, intra- and post-natal care. It also raised an issue which would be debated until the present day, concerning the usefulness and professional recognition of midwives.

It was obvious from this report, as it had been from the report prepared by Charlotte Whitton on Child Welfare in 1929, that the success of any National Council initiative depended on the level of enthusiasm of the local councils for action in this area. Adelaide Plumptre noted that "if every Local Council had sent in as admirable a report as that received from Hamilton, and if all federated Associations had reported as fully as the Women's Institutes of Alberta, the committee would have had a much more exhaustive report to lay before Council."[8] In her first report as convenor of the Standing Committee on Child Welfare, Charlotte Whitton[9] noted that eleven local councils had appointed Child Welfare convenors since the formation of the national Committee: "Toronto, Hamilton, Vancouver, New Westminster, Winnipeg, Saskatoon, Moose Jaw, Edmonton, Dauphin, Niagara Falls, and Renfrew."[10] Charlotte Whitton expressed the hope that the other forty-one local councils would do so in the near future. As she said, these figures meant that Child Welfare Convenors existed in less than 20% of the local councils.[11] Some convenors conveyed their exasperation with a poor response from local councils with irony, but Charlotte Whitton delivered herself of a long reproach.

> Obviously it is somewhat discouraging and impractical to attempt to align this tremendous potential power of the Local Councils in any Child Welfare Programme of general applicability nationally unless some arrangements can be made within the Council for correlation of local effort to the national program....your convenor's first and most urgent plea...that you will appoint local convenors immediately in justice to national plans and in justice to those Councils that have

---

8   *Ibid.*, p. 127.
9   Social worker, politician and feminist, Charlotte Whitton was born in Renfrew, Ontario on March 8, 1896 and died in Ottawa on January 25, 1975. She was a brilliant student and received her M.A. from Queen's University in 1918. This was not a graduate degree but an honour awarded to outstanding students who achieved "full honours in two subjects and a double first." Her first job was with the Social Service Council of Canada in Toronto, and she would spend the rest of her life engaged directly in social welfare work or in working for social welfare politically. She was elected to Ottawa's municipal council in 1950 and became Canada's first woman mayor in 1951. She was re-elected mayor in 1952, 1954, 1960 and 1962.
10 Whitton's order: probably by date at which such action was taken, *Yearbook*, 1929, p. 65.
11 *Ibid.*, p. 63.

already taken action.

The work which Charlotte Whitton hoped would be undertaken, was, firstly, the general monitoring of child welfare; secondly, the lobbying necessary to persuade Canada to adhere to the International Child Labour Conventions. "It is urged," she wrote, "that...every Council should make a special effort through local members of the Legislatures and provincial councils to bring their respective provinces into line."[12] Thirdly, she urged Council to give priority to studying the juvenile immigration problem, this being the continuing paid immigration of British orphans to Canada. Fourthly, she listed the problem of recreation for children, including the need to supervise distribution of motion pictures. Finally, she listed the problems of neglect as the "most complex and most numerous" of all the problems facing the child welfare workers.

Whitton resigned as chair of the Child Welfare Committee in 1932 and the direction of its activities altered as the Depression continued. It became less interested in the discussion of theories and surveys, and acted much more as a general clearing house for reports from local councils on the economic problems of children. Barbara Blackstock, who succeeded Charlotte Whitton, reported in 1933 that local convenors were "acting successfully as coordinating agencies in the specific interests of the child" but that "almost universally it has been necessary for the Child Welfare committees to adjust their local programmes to the general economic situation."[13] By 1935 her reports made it clear that the main work at the local level was relief. Form and quantity might vary from one local council to another, but the main activity was aid to the needy. For example, Regina's Child Welfare Committee was responsible for the milk fund in that city, which in that year supplied 6000 quarts of milk to needy children.[14] In the East, Sackville's committee "endeavoured to see that children of families on relief are suitably clothed for school." In Toronto, the committee spent much of its efforts on the creation of a Maternal Welfare service to provide general aid to indigent mothers. Truro's report, from a small local council of eleven federated societies, captures the broad spectrum of needs that had to be met: it related that the Council had "served hot lunches to undernourished school children and milk to preschool children in their homes—also with help of service clubs

---

[12] *Ibid.,* p. 67.
[13] *Yearbook,* 1933, p. 64.
[14] *Yearbook,* 1935, p. 74.

providing clothes and bedding for those in need."

The impact of the Depression on the development of the Child Welfare Committee was symptomatic of its impact on Council as a whole: the agendas established before 1929 were visibly modified by the immediate demands of communities in distress. Nevertheless, the impact was modification and reorganization rather than radical transformation. The Standing Committees on Economics and on Trades and Professions were already, in 1929, discussing such issues as married women's right to work, hours of work and control of part-time working conditions. It was clear that the employment of married women was already a subject for debate. Jennie S. Hill, the convenor of the Economics Committee, reported that it was her experience "to be assured that the employment of married women is a real grievance to many young women."[15] Some women asserted that such practices were the direct cause of "a number of girls going astray." However, Jennie Hill urged Council members to consider "a woman's right to judge for herself just how she shall make best use of her time." By 1935, her report was emphasising the work of local council women in the general provision of relief. The Hamilton Local Council was particularly involved in this activity. It supervised not only the city relief fund but also the fund contributed by its seventy-four affiliated associations. Such activities resulted in the pooling of efforts of associations as diverse as the Veterans of France, the Council of Jewish women, the two chapters of the I.O.D.E., the nine chapters of the W.C.T.U., the Wesley United Ladies' Aid, the Council of Social Service of the Church of England and the nine branches of the Women's Institutes.[16] Other local councils reported through the Economics Committee their attempts to help with both the day-to-day problems of living in poverty, and the provision of employment opportunities. Kingston announced the establishment of cooking classes, with such successful results that it was proposed to ask the Technical School to establish, with Council help, a permanent cooking course.[17] New Westminster reported that it was organizing direct relief for women in the form of food, shelter and clothing, and Winnipeg's report was so detailed that the suggestion was made that it be issued as a pamphlet and sent to all local councils as a model for action.[18]

It was not only the agenda of the Standing Committee on Economics that

---

[15] *Yearbook*, 1929, p. 75.
[16] *Yearbook*, 1935, p. 192.
[17] *Ibid.*, p. 84.
[18] *Yearbook*, 1925, p. 85.

responded to contemporary urgencies; the Committee on Trades and
Professions was similarly affected. Again, the alteration was one of emphasis
rather than basic change. In 1929, Lydia M. Parsons devoted much of her
report to an analysis that had been made by Toronto Local Council of the reasons why 300 women, employed as stenographers and secretaries, were
working.[19] At this time knowledge about what women actually did, as
opposed to what it was expected women should do, was slim. This survey
related that 79% of the women were living with their husbands and of these
54% reported that their husbands had steady employment. Thus, contrary to
common belief at the time, this category of employment was the preserve of
married rather than single women. Further, 57% of the women surveyed had
children. Question 4 asked whether the respondent was "working to support
herself?", and question 5 asked whether she was working to "take care of
some emergency outlay?" In answer to question 4, 35% said they were working to support themselves, 8% that they were working in order to live more
comfortably, another 8% had taken employment in order to support a mother,
2% in order to meet liabilities, and 13% to assist in the education of children.
Four percent said they were working partly to support themselves and the
remaining 28% said that self-support was not their objective. There is no correlation given between these answers and those to question 5, regarding
which 33% said they were working to take care of some emergency outlay,
and 4% specifically not working for an emergency. Eight percent were working to make payments on the home, 4% in order to buy a home, and 1% to
save the home they had. Eight percent said that some type of financial difficulty, a husband's reverse in business for example, was the reason they
worked. There were 27% who worked because of doctor's bills, or some
other medical need, 6% who cited their husband's insufficient wage, and 1%
who said that it took two pay envelopes to support four children. Other
responses cited the seasonal nature of their husband's occupation (1%), aged
parents (2%), the need to provide a fund for old age (5%); 9% of respondents
said they earned more than their husbands. When asked how long they
intended to work, 52% replied either "indefinitely," "always" or "as long as
able." The same percentage reported that they did their own housework after
hours, and 4% had husbands who helped with the housework. There were
35% who said that they had someone to take care of the home, and 7% who
lived with their parents; 15% were in lodgings. This report provides a snap-

---

[19] *Yearbook*, 1929, pp. 108-111.

shot of a single group of employed women, rather than a comprehensive survey of a major category of women. It demonstrates Council's general interest in documenting the broad scope of women's experience, rather than a policy on social issues. Nevertheless, the solid information it provided contributed to the basic knowledge which members of Council needed to form their own opinions about women in society.

Such detailed material had considerable value in later years when, as the 1935 report of Eva T. McKivor for the Committee on Trades and Professions clearly showed, the question of married women working had become a matter of considerable controversy. The debate, at this time, was not about why they worked but whether they ought to be encouraged to do so. Toronto Local Council, while deploring "the tendency on the part of employers to ignore applications received from women beyond middle age," also urged that "married women should not be employed unless their cases are exceptional." The Montreal Council agreed with Toronto, and the Local Council in Kitchener urged that firms "should hire a single girl in preference to a married woman during these times of unemployment."[20] Hamilton Council, on the other hand, quoted the resolution adopted by the International Council of Women in Washington in 1925, urging National Councils "to do all in their power to suppress any tendency to limit the work of married women."

The right of married women to work, however, was of less importance in both 1929 and 1935 than the question of minimum wages, maximum hours and conditions of work. In 1929, the report of the Committee on Trades and Professions merely listed the hours of labour that were legal: British Columbia and Manitoba had fixed a nine-hour day, Ontario, New Brunswick and Quebec a ten-hour day. Saskatchewan had a 48-hour week as a limit but no regulation about hours per day. Nova Scotia had no regulations at all.[21] In 1935, the report from the same Committee dealt, first and foremost, with the general question of unemployment. The Ottawa Local Council commented on the "increasing number of unemployable women past middle age."[22] Regina, in contrast, remarked on the increase of unemployment among young women. Winnipeg referred to exploitation of women in domestic service and noted that "the wages of domestic workers are as low as $3.50 per month. The unemployed girls, who were interviewed, stated that, unless they received a wage of at least $10.00 per month, they preferred the relief, which

---

20 *Yearbook,* 1935, p. 133.
21 *Yearbook,* 1929, p. 111.
22 *Yearbook,* 1935, p. 134.

paid the equivalent of $14.00 per month and [permitted] them to earn $5.00 per month in addition." By 1935, however, the issue of women and work extended beyond the terms of reference of any single Standing Committee of Council and became a major concern of the organization as a whole.

As critically important as the right of women to work outside the home, both in 1929 and in 1935, was their right to participate fully in the political life of the country. The 1929 report of the Standing Committee on the Laws Concerning Women and Children was presented that year by Henrietta Muir Edwards. She was one of five women involved in the appeal from the Supreme Court of Canada to His Majesty's Privy Council in England on the question as to whether women were to be considered "Persons" under the terms of the British North America Act, and therefore eligible for appointment to the Senate of Canada. The others were Judge Emily Murphy,[23] Mrs. Nellie McClung, Irene Parlby,[24] and Mrs. Louise McKinney.[25] Much of Mrs. Edwards' report was taken up with the state of legislation governing pension act provisions and the complicated circumstances surrounding the granting of divorce across the country. However, she also presented a précis of the argument as to whether the word "persons," in the light of the British North America Act, was applicable to both men and women. She traced the efforts of the National Council, from the petition which it had sent in 1919 to the Federal government, requesting the appointment of women to the Senate, through the Council's subsequent lobbying during the twenties. She concluded by stating in full the argument on this issue that had been made before the Supreme Court.[26]

---

[23] Née Ferguson, born at Cookstown, Ontario, March 1868, died at Edmonton, Alberta, 27 October 1933. She was the daughter of a prominent Ontario lawyer and she married an Anglican minister, moving West with her family in 1903. She combined an active family life with a successful writing career. She worked through a number of women's organizations, including the Canadian Women's Press Club. She became the first woman magistrate in the British Empire in 1916, when she was appointed as police magistrate for Edmonton. Her interest in the rights of women received a particular impetus when a lawyer challenged her on her first day on the bench by asserting that she was not a person in the eyes of the law.

[24] Née Marryat. Born in London, England, 9 January 1868 and died at Red Deer, Alberta, July 1965. She moved to Canada with her family when she was thirteen. An early supporter of the United Farmers of Alberta, she was elected President of its Women's Auxiliary in 1916. In the 1921 provincial election she won the Lacombe riding and held it for fourteen years. She was one of the Canadian delegates to the League of Nations in 1930.

[25] Née Crummy. Born at Frankville, Ontario, September 22 1868; died at Claresholm, Alberta, July 10, 1931. She was the sixth of ten children and attended Normal School in Ottawa. She was one of the organizers of the Women's Christian Temperance Movement, serving as the Dominion Vice-president from 1908 until 1930. She married in 1896 and moved to Alberta in 1903. She was elected in the 1917 Alberta election as an independent member for Claresholm and served for four years. She was named a Commissioner for the first General Council of the United Church of Canada and was the only woman to sign the Basis of Union.

[26] Yearbook, 1929, pp. 85-6.

In the following year, 1930, Mrs. Edwards had the joy of beginning her report to Council with the words: "It is with much pleasure that I present the Law Report for 1929–1930, for in it you will hear of...the decision of the Privy Council" in favour of the petitioners. She pointed out that "the rejoicing all through Canada over [this]....was not so much that it opened the door of the Canadian Senate to women, as it was that it recognized the personal entity of women, her separate individuality as a person."[27] She went on to remark that the victory was "due first to the National Council of Women, second to the Federal Government, third to a committee of five Alberta women, who were the harvesters to go forth to reap where others had sown."

It is clear that for many who worked with Council, one of its most important benefits was the access it provided to government. As in the case of most non-professional associations, the contacts with bureaucrats and politicians depended both on the circumstances of the time, and on the particular people involved. During the thirties the strength of Council grew, at both the national and provincial levels, but its development reflected the complex nature of the decade, involving a balance of gains and losses. Alberta displayed the most dramatic shifts in its type of political action and its membership. On January 13, 1930 the Executive Committee of the Alberta Council met with the Premier and his cabinet. In much the same way as the National Council had done when making representations to the federal cabinet, the Alberta Provincial Council quickly learned to arrange its agenda. Within a year, the list of resolutions presented to the Premier and cabinet had been reduced to eleven, and were grouped together by subject: the first three dealt with matters of schooling, particularly the health of children; the fourth raised again the issue of the rights of women to homestead; the fifth was concerned with the issue of punishment in schools; the sixth with government control of firearms; the seventh with question of standards for stage entertainment; the eighth with the recognition of the value of a wife's labour in the home; the ninth with the need to amend the Jury Act, so that women could serve; the tenth with the need to amend the Mother's Allowance Act and lastly, the eleventh was a repetition of the request for penalties for false registration as man and wife.[28] These meetings continued until 1935, in which year the Provincial Council disbanded. It may be noted that the local councils of Calgary, Edmonton and Medicine Hat remained reasonably healthy.

Calgary Local Council shrank from a membership of 47 in 1930 to 27 in

---

27 *Yearbook*, 1930, p. 81.
28 *Yearbook*, 1931, pp. 55-56.

1938; Edmonton went from 32 to 19; Medicine Hat from 17 to 11. The local councils of Macleod and Lethbridge paid their dues for the last time in 1933. Nevertheless, the remaining Alberta local councils were robust enough to attract a broad spectrum of affiliates. Calgary in 1938 included, along with the W.C.T.U. and the Ladies' Aid of Central United Church, the Business and Professional Women's Club, the Calgary section of Jewish women, the Hadassah Chapter of Jewish Women, the Unemployed Women's Association, the Women's section of the Dominion Labor Party, the Women's Labor League and the women's section Ukrainian Labor-Temple. Edmonton included not only the Women's institutes and the W.C.T.U. but also the Women's Liberal Club, the Women's C.C.F. Club, the Women's Auxiliary to the International Typographical Union and the Women's Conservative Association.[29]

While there were declines elsewhere, nothing matched Alberta's experience. British Columbia saw growth, not only in the number of affiliations to large councils but also in the number of councils within the Province. Vancouver Local Council expanded from 72 to 76, Victoria from 44 to 47, New Westminster from 21 to 29. North Vancouver had established its Local Council in 1930 and Kamloops did so in 1933. Moreover, the Executive of the Provincial Council met in 1935, 1937 and 1939 with the Premier of British Columbia and his cabinet. The meetings were particularly concerned with the issues of Mothers' Pensions, Juvenile Delinquency Laws, State Health Insurance plans and Old Age Pensions.[30] Similarly, Council activities were strengthened in Saskatchewan during these years. The annual meetings of Provincial Council with the Premier and cabinet began in 1932 and carried on throughout the decade. The main issues brought forward concerned the appointment of women to various public bodies, such as the Board of Tubercular Sanatoria, general issues of education, and questions relating to divorce laws. While affiliates of the Saskatoon Local Council fell from 45 to 32, those of Regina rose from 41 to 47. Swift Current had one net loss, falling to 14, and as did Moose Jaw, which had 21 affiliates in 1938.

In Manitoba the Provincial Council was less obviously important as a lobbyist, but the local councils themselves flourished. The expansion of Dauphin between 1930 and 1939 is interesting because, while it lost the Girl Guides and the I.O.D.E., it attracted the Teachers' Federation, the Business and Professional Women's Club, the Graduate Nurses' Association, and both

---

[29] *Yearbook*, 1938, pp. 198-199.
[30] Hastings and Ellenwood, *Blue Bows*, p. 49.

17. Mrs. M. Winnifred Kydd, President 1931–1936

the W.M.S. and the Y.W.M.S. of the United Church. Winnipeg increased the number of its affiliates from 56 to 61, bringing in as members the Federation of French Canadian Women, the Jewish Women (National Council), the Liberal Women's Association, the Polish Gymnastic Society, the Society of French Canadian Women in Manitoba, the Ukrainian Women's Club and the Women's Conservative Club. Of course, the raw numbers of affiliations at both the national and the local level of Council give only a very broad idea of the history of either as a collective. Many volunteer organizations have very brief lives, so that in one year a poetry society may exist and in the next it may have died, to be reincarnated as a drama group in the year after that. Further, those associations with more stable profiles often had their freedom of action restricted by policies of their parent organizations. The affiliation of associations of Catholic Women with Council always depended on the attitude of the local bishop. He might, or might not, accept the reality of Council's dedication to freedom of belief for its members, after observing, in particular, the work of Council for the rights of divorced women. Thus, Montreal Local Council numbered the Catholic Daughters of America as a member during the thirties, and occasionally during these years the Catholic Women's League. Halifax was almost always able to report Catholic affiliates, as was London, but Winnipeg, Hamilton and Toronto rarely, if ever, managed to do so.

The change in the profile of local councils is as interesting as their change in size. For example, the arrival, during the thirties, of the representatives of the women's auxiliaries of the major political parties as members, must be taken into account if Council's political role is to be understood. Again, the appearance of representatives of particular ethnic communities at local council meetings signals a broadening of the membership base.

The Local Council of Montreal, the only one in the Province of Quebec, increased the number of its affiliates from forty-nine to sixty-one, and the pattern in New Brunswick and Nova Scotia was similar. Halifax increased its affiliates from forty-three to sixty-four, and the number of local councils in Nova Scotia increased by one: Stellarton, established in 1931. Saint John, New Brunswick, increased its membership from thirty-two to thirty-five, but the number of affiliates linked to the Moncton Local Council fell from twenty-four to fifteen. Neither the Maritime councils, nor that of Montreal, drew in political organizations during the thirties. While both New Brunswick and Nova Scotia organized Provincial Councils, neither really found their feet until the end of the decade.

If Alberta recorded the most obvious decline, growth was most significant in Ontario where, in 1936, the Provincial Council announced that it had "19 Local Councils, 562 affiliated societies, 6 provincially federated societies, making a total membership of 450,000."[31] This was almost equal to the national strength of Council in the early twenties. Ontario had seen six local councils fold: Brampton, Chatham, North Bay, Pembroke, Renfrew and Trenton. But it had also witnessed the creation of five new councils: York in 1930, Kitchener and Weston, both in 1932, Windsor in 1934, Goderich in 1937. While Ottawa's affiliates had declined from one hundred and two to ninety-three, and Hamilton's from seventy-seven to fifty-six, London's membership had grown from twenty-nine to forty-five, picking up the Women's Liberal Club, the Women's Liberal Association and the Women's Conservative Association. Toronto too increased the number of its affiliates to seventy-two.

Further, the Ontario Provincial Council had developed its structure during this decade, organizing both an Executive and standing committees. It had been in existence since 1919, in which year the first meeting was chaired on November 13, 1919 by Dr. Stowe Gullen. During the Depression years it increased its affiliates. In 1933 a "large and representative delegation waited upon the [Ontario] Government,"[32] to discuss, among other matters, questions of family law, education, the need for an eight-hour day in both shops and factories, the need for hospital care for those of moderate means, as well as other aspects of health care. At a further meeting in that year, between some members of the cabinet and the Council Executive, the Attorney General remarked that "in looking over my records I have been amazed to find how much of the legislation petitioned for by the Provincial Council of Women in past years, is now on the statute books."[33]

While continuing to draw strength from the local and provincial councils the National Council, during the thirties, gained a number of new affiliates. In 1929, fifteen associations were linked to it: the Canadian Branch of the King's Daughters; the Canadian Girl Guides; the Canadian Nurses' Association; the Canadian Social Hygiene Council (which became the Health League of Canada in 1936); the Canadian Women's Christian Temperance Union; the Girls' Friendly Society in Canada; the Hadassah Organization; the Imperial Order of the Daughters of the Empire; the Medical Alumnae of the University of Toronto; the National Council of the Young Women's Christian

---

31 *Yearbook,* 1936, p. 61.
32 *Yearbook,* 1933, p. 53.
33 *Yearbook,* 1934, p. 68.

Association; the National Girls' Work Board; the Queen's University Alumnae Association; the Salvation Army in Canada; the Victorian Order of Nurses and the Women's Art Association of Canada (which changed first to the Lyceum Club and then, in 1931, to the Women's Art Association of Canada). In 1931 the Canadian Federation of Business and Professional Women's Clubs affiliated. In 1937 the Women's Missionary Society of the United Church of Canada joined at the National level, as did the Canadian Division of the National Council of Jewish women in 1938. The Canadian Dominion Council of the Mother's Union, the Ukrainian Women's Association of Canada and the Women's League of Health and Beauty all joined in 1939. It is difficult to estimate accurately the number of Canadian women who were connected in some fashion to Council in 1939, but given Ontario's claim to have some 450,000 members, the large number of affiliate memberships in Halifax, Montreal, Winnipeg, Vancouver and Victoria, and the estimated membership of the national associations, a reasonable guess would be in the neighbourhood of three quarters of a million.

Throughout the decade, the National Council improved its lobbying tactics. This owed little to the ability of the President and Executive to meet with the current Prime Minister and cabinet. In fact, National Council was much less successful than Ontario and Saskatchewan in meeting with the government of the day during the thirties. Only one such encounter was arranged in these years, with Prime Minister R.B. Bennett in December 1933. What was achieved, however, was the effective organization of the Parliamentary Committee of Council, and of the Head Office itself. It has already been mentioned that at the close of the previous decade, the Parliamentary Committee had begun to organize its work, so that the list of resolutions, passed at an annual meeting, was recorded, and their despatch to the relevant ministry, as well as the response received, was noted. This pattern of action had become clearly established by 1934. Council followed up issues by correspondence when necessary, noting when a reply of the minister was inadequate. The Head Office also kept track of who was seeing whom about what, so that delegations to ministers about particular concerns did not get in one another's way. The organization of the office led to an extraordinary amount of correspondence. In 1935, for the first time, the Corresponding Secretary reported to the annual meeting, held that year from June 10 to 14 in Toronto, some statistics on the work of the Head Office. During a period of eight months, 5807 pieces of correspondence were dealt with by the Corresponding Secretary and one employee.[34] This tally omits

---

[34] *Yearbook*, 1935, p. 37.

the constant social contact between Council members and the power-brokers of society, the conferences attended, speeches listened to and given, entertainment received and reciprocated. For women working through Council, the private sphere of acquaintanceship was an acceptable arena for the discussion of their volunteer activities. The fine art of private, social pressure for public action was second nature to many of those women who served on the executives of Council at whatever level.

In the foregoing outline of the history of the National Council of Women of Canada during the thirties, the emphasis has been on the adaptation of Council's past practices to events. In considering the overall direction of Council throughout the Depression, one is struck by the way in which it reflected both traditional concerns of the organization and the new directions of society. During the last years of Mrs. J.A. Wilson's leadership, and throughout the Presidency of Miss M. Winnifred Kydd, (that is until 1936), a great deal of attention was paid to Council's links to the International Council of Women. Henrietta Wilson had been instrumental in the organization of the League of Nations Societies in Canada in the 1920's.[35] In 1929 she had concluded her presidential address with an appreciation of the work of the International Council, remarking that it was now "needed more than ever," given the state of international affairs.[36] At the eighth quinquennial meeting of the I.C.W., held in Vienna, May 26 to June 7 1930, there were 34 Canadian women present, either as delegates, alternates or visitors.[37] In 1931, the year that Miss Kydd was elected President of the National Council, Canada had four women holding office in the I.C.W., Mrs. W.E. Sanford, an Honourary Vice-President, Mrs. C.H. Thorburn, Mrs. J.S. Dignam, and Winnifred Kydd herself, who was the Vice-Convenor of the Standing Committee on Migration. That year twelve Canadians were members of other standing committees of the International Council.

Winnifred Kydd was a close friend of Lady Aberdeen and affectionately signed letters to her "The Ginger Kitten."[38] Her education had been at McGill University and at Bryn Mawr.[39] She came into Council through Montreal,

[35] See, in particular, her Report in *Yearbook*, 1926, pp. 54-57.
[36] *Yearbook*, 1929, p. 23.
[37] *Yearbook*, 1930, p. 27.
[38] Winnifred Kydd to Lady Aberdeen, from Queen's University, June 8, 1937, NAC MG 1245, vol.20, box 52, file 305.
[39] Precise dates for Miss Kydd's biography are hard to come by as she was very reticent about such details. She was appointed Dean of Women at Queen's University in 1934, a position she held until 1940. She was Chief Commissioner for the Girl Guides 1942-49. It is understood that she settled in Scotland before the end of the forties.

having been President of that local council from 1929 to 1931. She soon
established a reputation in the field of the international activities of Council.
In 1929, she attended the International Conference of Rural Women's
Organizations, which was sponsored by the International Council of Women,
and took place at the same time as the meeting of the Executive and Standing
Committees of the latter in London, April 29 to May 8. She was present at
the quinquennial meeting of the I.C.W. in 1930, as the official delegate of the
Canadian National Council. She was appointed by the Canadian government
as a delegate to the Disarmament Conference in Geneva in 1932, and, on her
return, her tour of local councils stimulated interest in disarmament and government control of the manufacture of arms.[40] Partly as a result of her
unavoidable absence, and partly because "present conditions" would prevent
a reasonable attendance,[41] the 1932 annual meeting was replaced with a
Statutory Executive meeting held in Ottawa on June 28. In 1933, the
President attended the Executive meeting of the International Council in
Stockholm. In 1934, she was appointed Dean of Women at Queen's
University, a post she held until 1940. In 1936, the last year of her presiden-
cy, she attended the meetings of the International Council in Calcutta.

Given the bitter international rivalries that shook the world in the thirties,
there was something of value in the continuing and traditional involvement
of the National Council of Women of Canada with the International Council
of Women. It provided both a channel for the contribution of Canadian
women to the international scene, and a source of information to many local
councils about women's global concerns. From the outset, the International
Council of Women was directly linked to the League of Nations and, later
on, would be granted advisory status by the United Nations. Membership of
the National Council in the International Council of Women brought many
local councils to an interest in the League of Nations which might otherwise
not have been apparent.

In sum, there were three major benefits that accorded to the National
Council through the I.C.W.: information about the general status of women
and children across the world; information about the strategies various countries were using to fight sex discrimination; and participation in the general
international effort to achieve better understanding among peoples. If much
of the knowledge gained merely served to emphasize the magnitude of the
problems faced, it also made clear the need for continued effort. In many

---

[40] *Yearbook,* 1933, Report of Corresponding Secretary, p. 34.
[41] *Yearbook,* 1932, p. 26.

ways, the I.C.W. reinforced action already begun within Canada. Lydia Parsons' report from the I.C.W. Standing Committee on Trades and Professions in 1930, for example, highlighted the worldwide divergence between the wages of women and men, noting that reports from sixteen countries showed that "many, if not most employers, seem to act on the premise that a woman should earn considerably less than a man."[42] Such reports clearly stated that the removal of legislative disability did not inevitably mean social change. Denmark, it was noted, had "in 1919, passed legislation for equal pay for equal work, but it does not seem to have helped, as there has been a tendency to attack and question on [sic] the quality of women's [sic] work, to keep her [sic] out of desired positions."[43]

Requests from the International Council for information about the experience of Canadian women very often led to discussion and action at the national level. In 1936, for example, Eva T. McKivor, the Convenor of the Trades and Professions Standing Committee, remarked that the responses received "to a questionnaire sent out to Local Councils in order to gather information for the I.C.W. Council" revealed a great deal about the status of older, unemployed woman. "All Councils," it was observed "agreed that some special help be given to these women."[44] Similarly, other Standing Committees, such as that concerned with Laws regarding Women and Children, and the Committee on Child Welfare, brought Canadian attention to problems because the international body demanded information. Finally, it should not be overlooked that the International Council meetings brought Canadians into close touch with other international organizations working for women's rights, such as the International Alliance of Women for Suffrage and Equal Citizenship.

Though Winnifred Kydd was deeply involved on the international scene during her presidency, the growing hardships of the Depression forced Council to devote the greater part of its energies to domestic issues. As Ramsay Cook has written: "What seemed 'temporary' in 1930 had become unremitting by 1935. What made the crisis in Canada so desperate was that both industrial and agricultural sectors of the economy were hit; first by the decline in investment and demand, and second by the shrinkage of markets and the ravages of nature."[45] "By the summer of 1930," Cook goes on, "more

---

42 *Yearbook*, 1930, p. 112.
43 *Ibid.*, p. 113.
44 *Yearbook*, 1936, p. 120.
45 Cook, "Triumph and Trials," p. 443.

than 390,000 workers were reported jobless." To borrow the words of another account, "the number of unemployed was 116,000 in 1929, 826,000 in 1933 and more than 522,000 in 1938. Translated into percentages of the non-agricultural labour force, these figures mean that under 5 per cent of Canadians were unemployed in 1929, 27 percent (or more) in 1933, and 16 percent in 1938."[46]

What did these figures mean for women? And what part did the NCWC play in alleviating the distress?

Any assessment of women's experience during the Depression has to take into account not only Neatby's caveat, cited earlier, regarding the uneven impact of the disaster, but also the dual nature of women's experience, as it unfolded in the lives of those employed directly in paid labour, and those whose work was recompensed through the wages of another. The overall decline in annual per capita income in these years is the common framework for both kinds of experience, but there were great differences in the particular circumstances of individual lives. The wife and mother in a single-income family, with the male breadwinner "out of work," had one set of problems to confront. The young girl come to Saskatoon or Regina to work for money, for herself and her parents, had to face another set. Ramsay Cook has looked at the overall picture in terms of income. "Between 1928 and 1933 annual per capita income in Canada declined by 48%," he observes and goes on to break down the figures into regional patterns. "Saskatchewan led with a drop of 72 percent, from $471 to $247; Alberta followed with a 61 percent fall, Manitoba 49 percent and B.C. 47 percent. Ontario, where the highest per capita incomes were enjoyed, declined by 44 percent, with Prince Edward Island, Quebec, New Brunswick and Nova Scotia always at the lower end of the scale, falling between 49 percent and 36 percent."[47]

It has been estimated that in 1931 women working for pay made up 19.4 percent of the workforce, some 666,859 in 1931.[48] This number fails to include all sorts of women's employment: part-time workers, seasonal workers, women who worked in family businesses as bookkeepers, and particularly, women on the farms. Nevertheless, the figure does provide an indication of the importance for many women of work remunerated by wages. A breakdown of this figure into participation rates by age, shows that women between 14–35 were most often found in paid occupations. In 1931, girls

[46] Robert Bothwell, Ian Drummond, John English, *Canada 1900-1945*, (Toronto, 1987), p. 248.
[47] Cook, "Triumph and Trials," p. 444.
[48] Leary, ed., *Historical Statistics*, Series D107-122, 2nd edition.

aged 14–19 made up 26.5% of the female labour force; women aged 20–24 accounted for 47.4% and those between the ages of 24 and 30, 24.4%.[49] Further, as V. Strong-Boag has pointed out, women were heavily concentrated in only six of the twenty-five categories of employment recognized by the census-takers: textiles and clothing, retail and wholesale trade, education, health and welfare services, food and lodging, and personal and recreational services—73.20 percent in 1931 and 71.98 per cent in 1941.[50] This "ghettoization" of women restricted the available opportunities for work when unemployment struck particular occupations. Across the country office work vacancies fell dramatically in 1930: by 36% in Montreal, 48% in Ottawa, 40% in Toronto, 48% per cent in Hamilton, 52% in Winnipeg, 52.5% in Regina, 54% in Edmonton, 57.8% in Calgary, 60.2% in Vancouver and 32% in Victoria.[51] The women who lost these jobs found few alternative avenues of employment open.

Whether the Depression hit working women harder than men is debatable. Certainly prejudice against working women, and especially working married women, grew apace in the thirties, and there is much evidence to show that "male workers were undercutting women's wages and supplanting them in several industries."[52] For both men and women, hard won employment benefits disappeared as the surplus of labour became apparent. Working conditions deteriorated, wage cuts were common, hours of work increased. The priority given by all levels of government to aiding married men and families, made it much harder for single women to obtain relief.[53] Older women who were separated, widowed or divorced were particularly vulnerable, both to exploitation in the job market and to destitution through unemployment.

Reaction by Council to the particular situation of working women during the Depression took three forms: the traditional lobbying of all three levels of government for the enforcement of laws governing the working conditions for women and children; particular support for working women during local crises; and the organization of direct relief for unemployed women and girls. Throughout the decade, Council continued to press for reasonable working conditions for women, including the right of married women to work. The influence of the International Council of Women probably helped to keep the

49 *Ibid.*
50 Strong-Boag, *New Day*, p. 51.
51 *Yearbook*, 1930, p. 110.
52 Prentice, et al., *Canadian Women*, p. 234.
53 *Ibid.*, p. 236.

National Council in line, but the unwavering stand of the Hamilton Local Council on this matter at annual meetings was crucial. By 1935, almost every local council was calling for the rigorous enforcement of the Minimum Wage Act and its extension to all classes of workers and industries. Views differed among the local councils about the seriousness of the economic situation, partly because of regional variation, and partly because of the composition of particular local councils. However, there was general agreement with the views of Ottawa Local Council in 1937 that "workers should increase their knowledge regarding the laws that give them protection."[54] Nor is there any doubt that many councils shared the bitterness underlying the report presented in 1937, by the Regina Local Council to the Standing Committee on Trades and Professions, which stated that "the lowering of the Minimum rate of wage, and the increasing number of hours per week, plainly shows the value placed on women's work."[55]

The most dramatic example of direct aid for working women from a local council during the Depression was that of the Toronto Local Council, which endeavoured "to better conditions for women in the textile industry."[56] During the 1934 strike in Eaton's dressmaking department, called by workers belonging to the International Ladies' Garment Workers Union, members of the Toronto Local Council "raised funds for the strikers, lobbied government officials to force a settlement and even joined the picket line."[57] Moreover, when the strike failed, the local council provided funds to help some of the strikers to set up their own cooperative dressmaking shop.[58]

Apart from the action taken by the relevant Standing Committees at the national level, particularly the Committees on Laws regarding Women and Children, and on Trades and Professions, the predominant form of Council help to working women at this time was through aid at the local level to the unemployed. One local council after another reported, year by year, the attempts made to cope with the situation in their community. Many councils established what were, in fact, unemployment agencies for women. New Westminster set up a "permanent bureau for Unemployed Women with a woman in charge."[59] In Hamilton in 1931, the local council opened an office

---

[54] *Yearbook,* 1937, p. 109.
[55] *Ibid.,* pp. 109-111.
[56] *Yearbook,* 1934, p. 162.
[57] Prentice, et al., *Canadian Women,* p. 239.
[58] Ruth Frager, "Uncloaking Vested Interests: Class, Ethnicity and Gender in the Jewish Labour Movement of Toronto, 1900-1919," (Ph.D. Thesis, York University, 1986), pp. 289-91, 357.
[59] *Yearbook,* 1931, p. 142.

18. Mrs. George O. Spencer, President 1936–1941

where women could appeal for work and relief, and followed this up in 1932 with a special committee to distribute relief to unemployed women. In 1931, Edmonton, Kingston and St. Catharine's established a register of unemployed women. Moose Jaw reported that it used the local council itself as an employment bureau and the Ottawa Local Council stated that it was paying-particular attention to unemployed business women. Vancouver's "Scheme of work" for women and Victoria's "Women's Work Room" were attempts to give women additional avenues through which to find work with local council help. St. Catharine's, Toronto and Winnipeg all announced that they worked with the established municipal relief agencies. There has been some criticism of these actions as being merely the provision of servants for middle and upper class women. Some unemployed women who had previously worked in industrial or secretarial occupations may very well have entered domestic service by this route. However, the pattern of women's employment was not significantly altered. In 1931, the census of Canada reported 227,000 women as being engaged in "personal service," or 34.3% of women in the labour force. The comparable figures for 1941 were 288,000, or 34.7%.[60]

It very quickly becomes difficult to separate out the efforts of councils on behalf of working women from those made for women within families and the generality of relief work. Either directly, or through the work of their affiliates, local councils were a central part of the machinery of relief. For example, many of them were the organizing and distribution points for clothing, something of which all those struck by the Depression sooner or later found themselves in need. In 1933, for example, Ottawa's mayor requested that the Local Council of Women take over the collection, repairing, purchasing and distribution of clothing to approximately 4000 families.[61] Moncton in 1935 reported having gathered and mended, purchased and/or made 4499 articles of clothing for distribution.[62]

Food, clothing, shelter and health needs were the demands that local councils tried valiantly to meet. While few people died from outright starvation, the struggle to obtain sufficient food was a widespread source of anxiety. Local councils not only helped with the gathering and distribution of produce, but also undertook special projects. Milk for pre-schoolers, lunches for children of school age, and food delivered directly to expectant mothers were common activities of councils. Brampton, in 1933, purchased fruit and

---

60   Census of Canada, 1931 cited in Thompson and Seager, Canada 1922-1939, p. 348.
61   Yearbook, 1934, p. 138.
62   Yearbook, 1936, p. 154.

sugar and arranged for women to can fruit for their own consumption. Many councils also followed the example of Toronto which, throughout the Depression, canned fruit and vegetables for distribution through welfare agencies, producing in 1933 alone 20,000 jars.[63] It was the Montreal Local Council that was most enterprising in terms of health needs. It established its Medical Relief Fund, to pay for prescription drugs, in 1933.[64]

Perhaps the sole enterprise undertaken by the National Council which aimed at a particular segment of the Canadian population during the Depression, instead of the alleviation of suffering in general, was its coordination of local council work for the "Comfort Fund." This fund was set up in June 1933, following a resolution passed at the annual meeting that year. The year before, in 1932, labour camps had been established for the "single, homeless, unemployed" men and "for the next five years these camps contained an average of twenty thousand men."[65] The National Council resolution read, in part, as follows: "Resolved that, in compliance with a request re peace service of assistance of Comforts in unemployment camps, The National Council of Women of Canada take the necessary steps to inaugurate a Fund ... to sponsor the supplying of Comforts..."[66] Money was raised and everything from blankets to books, cards, games, newspapers, and magazines was collected, or bought, and despatched. Within the year, twenty-nine of the forty-eight local councils, listed in the 1934 *Yearbook*, had contributed to this enterprise in one way or another.

By 1935, it was clear that the fortunes of the federal Conservative government were in decline, as the Depression showed no real sign of ending. The Prime Minister, R.B. Bennett, went to the country with a program of reform measures: there were proposals for "unemployment insurance, minimum wages and maximum hours of work, and new fair trade practices legislation."[67] He was roundly defeated by Mackenzie King and the Liberal Party. King's government did not immediately initiate a stream of new policies. But the advice of the National Employment Commission, which it established in 1936, was slowly, if reluctantly, accepted. A new fiscal policy was established with the budget of 1938 when, "for the first time a government [in Canada] consciously decided to spend money to counteract a low in the business cycle."[68] The 1939 budget continued on the same path with increased

---

63   *Yearbook*, 1933, p. 150.
64   *Ibid.*, p. 132.
65   Neatby, *Politics*, p. 34.
66   *Yearbook*, 1934, p. 122.
67   Cook, "Triumph and Trials," p. 452.
68   Neatby, *Politics*, p. 85.

federal monies for relief and for spending on public works. While it would take a war to bring prosperity to Canada, by the summer of 1939 the country had begun to emerge from the Depression.

In large part because of the election, the National Council, in 1935, produced a summary of the 24 resolutions which it had been presenting to the government since 1927.[69] They included requests for the appointment of women, not only to international bodies dealing with issues relating to women but, as an immediate measure, to "all advisory committees or commissions" involved in relief activities. Several resolutions dealt with the right of women to retain their own nationality upon marrying or, if their status was that of *femme sole*, to apply for naturalization. Vancouver Council was credited with authoring the resolution requiring that equal attention be paid to the "problems of unemployed women as well as unemployed men." It was requested that it be compulsory for women to be appointed to juries in criminal cases involving women and children. Other resolutions asked for laws against prostitution, and, in particular, against men profiting from prostitution, to be strengthened; for adultery to be made a crime; for punishment for crimes against morals and those against property to be brought into some kind of balance. It was asked that divorces be registered. The need for the active promotion of physical health, especially for children, was the subject of several resolutions, as was the need to regulate the production of films especially for children. A series of resolutions dealt with the need to control firearms and arms manufacturing in general. Finally there were resolutions requesting that proper care be taken of Canadian World War memorials, that the protection of migratory birds be strengthened, and that the conservation of parkland be seriously considered.

Mrs. George O. Spencer was elected as President of Council at the annual meeting held in Halifax, Nova Scotia from June 8 to June 12, 1936. She had been born to John and Hannah Nugent in Moncton, New Brunswick on August 17, 1885, and married her husband on July 10, 1911. At times she worked as a freelance radio commentator. In her first speech as President, at the 1937 annual meeting held in Ottawa from May 28–29, she described local councils as "the community round table." Her most innovative action on becoming President was the organization of a "Study Programme," which would list the main topics that local councils ought to consider during the coming year. The agenda for 1937–1938 listed the questions of venereal dis-

---

69   *Yearbook*, 1935, pp. 215-218.

ease and of general public health; international peace; liquor control; housing and slum clearance; migration; women in industry and the professions; and matters relating to the cultural side of Canadian life, including adult education and leisure time.

In 1938, at the 45th annual meeting, held in Vancouver from May 23 to May 28, a recorded address by Lady Aberdeen was broadcast to the gathering.[70] It was, above all, an expression of faith in the idea of the Council, an expression of confidence in the ability of the movement to help "bind up wounds and repair the broken." Mrs. Spencer's address also stressed both faith in the future of the NCWC, and the record of the orderly growth of Council over the past forty-five years.[71] The continuing shadow of the Depression darkened many of the reports given, both by local councils and the conveners of the standing committees. From Chilliwack, British Columbia to New Glasgow, Nova Scotia, councils reported the relief of distress brought by money and goods.[72] Eva T. Burwash, the convenor of the Committee on Trades and Professions wrote:

Each year our educational centres turn out hundreds of boys and girls filled with the enthusiasm of youth to meet a world which supplies them with no avenue to a successful future.[73]

Her report included a survey showing which provinces had legislated minimum wage provisions for women, whether these provisions were being implemented, and whether this legislation made a positive difference to women. Edmonton Local Council, for example, pointed out that "in beauty parlours, operators hesitate to give their wage rates to those investigating."[74] Winnipeg too found that girls were unwilling to testify about their wages, and Calgary remarked that most legislation did not apply to domestics or farm workers. Eva Burwash stated bluntly that the problem of older unemployed women awaited action and that, "the government has undertaken no project to give women work."[75]

At the 1939 annual meeting, held at McMaster University in Hamilton,

---

[70] *Yearbook*, 1938, pp. 27-28.
[71] *Ibid*, p. 29.
[72] *Ibid.*, pp. 163-182. For example, New Glasgow noted that during the year a great deal of milk was supplied to the under-nourished and Thrift Bags for worn clothing were distributed.
[73] *Ibid.*, p. 148.
[74] *Ibid.*, p. 152.
[75] *Ibid.*

from May 30 to June 3, the proceedings were much influenced by recollections of Lady Aberdeen, who had died on April 18 that year, at the age of 82. Mrs. F.H. Torrington, who had herself been President of the Council from 1911 to 1918, recalled her impression of Lady Aberdeen at the inaugural meeting of October 26, 1893.[76] She described her as the inspiration for women who "courageously entered fields of service hitherto barred to women, and led the difficult way to improving conditions in Canada, especially for women and children." This emphasis upon the community service role of the National Council of Women was repeated by the authors of *Canadian Women: A History* when they wrote that "by the outbreak of World War II, National Council members had reason to feel their work had helped to achieve considerable improvement in the quality of life for Canadian women. The care of the old and the sick had improved, women had benefitted from mothers' allowances, infant mortality and tuberculosis rates had declined, new urban parks served children's recreational needs, and in some regions innovative education programs had been put in place."[77]

Certainly, the National Council of Women of Canada had, by 1939, played a significant role in the development of social services in Canada. The movement from private charity to government funded programs as the foundation of community social assistance, had advanced considerably during the first forty-six years of Council's existence. The form of that advance had been greatly influenced by Council action. Through both the local and the national organizations, Council brought pressure to bear on municipalities, on provincial governments, and on the federal governments to aid effectively in the provision of community services for those in need. Often women worked through Council to relieve distress directly, and then campaigned for the civic authorities to take over the work they had begun. This was particularly true in the area of health care for infants, dental and optical care for children, and the general care of the indigent, the aged, and the infirm. Further, Council helped the professionalization of social services through its support of social welfare education programs, and of women's entry into these programs at university level.

But even though such efforts dominated the activities of Council during the thirties, to categorize them is to state only a part of the organization's significance for many Canadian women. It soon became an instrument which

---

[76] *Yearbook*, 1939, p. 31.
[77] Prentice, et al., *Canadian Women*, p. 267.

gave Canadian women an opportunity for a public life. The criticism that it was, above all, an organization of middle and upper class English-Canadian women misses the point. It was *the* organization of middle and upper class English-Canadian women. It was a clear and effective alternative to the established institutions of Canadian life, at that time pre-eminently the domain of Canadian men, for women who wished to have a public voice. Council was, above all, an organization aimed at exerting influence on many different issues. Its unique strength during the interwar period was its capacity for channelling the political wishes of many differing volunteer organizations run by women, into one formidable and effective body. The fight for the vote had, after all, been precisely that: a fight. Opponents did not fade away merely because a battle had been lost. There remained in Canada, as in the rest of the western world, a very strong belief in the inferiority of women. It pervaded social structure and convention as a prevailing wind of negation, something that could stunt, warp, and diminish women's lives. Throughout these years, Canada placed legal disabilities on the lives of its female citizens, and Canadian society reinforced disparities in opportunities for men and women. The public places of power within the country — political parties and parliamentary institutions, boardrooms and management positions, universities and the majority of the governing bodies of the institutions of religion, the judiciary, the military, the press — were all male-dominated. The tenor of public opinion was such that women, even when granted legal rights to participate fully in the public life of society, had to counter widespread criticism of such action. For a woman whose life was centred within a family, and whose economic status was that of a dependent, working through the volunteer associations that made up Council, and then through Council itself, often provided her with a non-controversial and effective avenue for a public role.

It is an error to define those women who worked through Council by their affiliation with Council alone. First and foremost, Council members were people with diverse wants and needs, diverse beliefs, diverse circumstances. They chose to spend time, energy and money through associations and societies that attracted them. So far, the cultural activities of Council have been neglected. But, besides providing a market place of ideas and action for women interested primarily in social welfare activities, Council also drew the support of women whose interests were in writing, art, music and the theatre. From the outset, Council had a Standing Committee on Arts and Culture. Furthermore, the existence of Council meant that there was a nationwide knowledge of what was happening in a particular area of endeavour. In 1933, Mary Dignam, who had been the convenor of the Arts and Letters Committee since the early twenties, remarked, at the opening of her report, that "Canadian literature was fast assuming not only National but International importance."[78] She went on to particularize local council work from coast to coast, emphasizing the support of local libraries, the organization of craft shows, as well as the presentation of music and drama festivals. Reading clubs were reported active, art and science lectures described as well attended. Calgary and Kitchener related how they had raised money for scholarships for attendance at art schools. Edmonton, Moose Jaw, Winnipeg, Saskatoon, Toronto, Montreal and Halifax were reported as having presented the work of Canadian musicians, authors and artists. In 1936, the then convenor of the Committee, Elizabeth S. Nutt, reported a wide variety of cultural activity undertaken by local councils:[79] Brampton had organized a story hour in the public library, and throughout the year some 248 children attended; Brantford organized the performance of an operetta; Dauphin set up a scholarship fund for high school students; Halifax gave support to the College of Art; Kingston helped in the celebration of Bach and Handel anniversaries and Montreal Local Council arranged concerts through these years; Vancouver supported its Elgar choir, and Truro put on an exhibition of the paintings and drawings of the kindergarten classes. This potpourri of activity is no more than a bare indication of the interest that local councils displayed in the provision of concerts and educational activities, in arranging art exhibitions and establishing libraries. It serves to underline the fact that a highly significant value of Council was its role as a recognized centre of culture and public life for middle and upper class women in Canada.

The Council was the creation of Canadian women whose life's efforts built, in their daily actions, much of the context of Canadian society. Council did not take the place of mainstream political and social action for Canadian women as a whole; its members were not only active in public life through their association which linked them to Council, but also through other collectives. The definition which the organization provided to its members was much more diffuse than that obtained through other affiliations in their lives, whether of church or politics. What it did provide, however, was an effective means of cooperative public action for women on very specific goals in an atmosphere that minimized ideological differences. What Council meant was the strength of the group: of women, and the gathering of information, by

---

78 *Yearbook*, 1933, p. 56.
79 *Yearbook*, 1936, p. 67.

women. It represented women in action.

As the thirties ended, Council could count among its affiliates, at the national level, the Canadian Association of Business and Professional Women's Clubs, and two of the most important Jewish women's organizations: the Canadian Division of the National Council of Jewish Women and the Hadassah Organization of Canada. At the local level councils had, by 1939, been joined by the women's auxiliaries of the Liberal and Conservative parties and, occasionally, the auxiliary of the C.C.F. While the central support of Council was to be found in the many Protestant volunteer organizations, it frequently also encompassed Catholic and Jewish associations at the local level. While it was overwhelmingly linked to Canadians of British heritage, it also slowly recruited those of other backgrounds. Its executive officers were drawn mostly from the well-to-do, but the majority of its membership were women of moderate means. And while the agenda was established at the national level, its most important activities were rooted in the various regions of Canada. Council was not only a "community round table," but above all a meeting place for women which actively encouraged them to speak out.

By the eve of the Second World War, the Council had become a part of Canadian culture. In the forties, as in the thirties, it would serve as a very valuable forum for a great many Canadian women.

CHAPTER 7

War and Aftermath
1940–1950

ALTHOUGH CANADA, along with the rest of the industrialized world, was preoccupied with the Depression during the thirties, the pitch-and-toss of international affairs was also a matter of concern to many. Generally, interest in global issues was much greater in Canada after the First World War than before. That carnage had led Canadians, in common with much of the rest of the western world, to seek ways to prevent another such conflict. The resulting attention to international affairs was enhanced by the techniques of rapid communication that evolved in the twenties and thirties. Newspapers, thanks to effective exploitation of radio, cable and telephone links, brought the problems of the rest of the world home to the people of this country. While there was much sympathy for a policy of isolationism, especially within the federal government, many Canadians were strong supporters of the League of Nations and, in 1921, branches of the League of Nations Society were established in Canada.

There were close links between this body and the National Council of Women of Canada, both through cross-membership and through joint actions. As always, individuals used whatever means were to hand to further their ideas, their hopes and their ambitions and a number of women were prominent members of both organizations, among them Charlotte Whitton, Nellie McClung and Canada's first woman senator, Cairine Reay Wilson.[1] Senator Wilson was President of the League of Nations Society of Canada from 1936 to 1942. By 1926 forty-two of the fifty-six local councils in

---

[1] Née Mackay, born in Montreal, 4 February 1885, died at Ottawa, 4 March 1962.

Canada had established League of Nation Committees,[2] and these committees worked in close cooperation with the local branches of the League of Nations Society. Throughout the twenties and thirties, local councils organized study sessions, sponsored lectures and established speaking contests in support of the League. The interest that Winnifred Kydd showed in international affairs during her presidency of Council was an important factor in encouraging these efforts. Added to the support of Senator Wilson, the backing of the Council for the League of Nations Society helped it to become the voice for women's work for peace in Canada.[3]

In addition, the tie between the National Council of Women of Canada and International Council of Women was strong. It was given a particular energy through the affection in which Lady Aberdeen was held by Canadian members of the International Council, but it was principally built upon Canadian representation on the international body, including the Executive, and upon contacts made at the quinquennial (after 1930, triennial) meetings. Canada was almost always represented with the full complement of ten delegates at the International Council meetings, no matter where they were held. At the time of the eleventh meeting, which took place in Edinburgh in 1938 and brought together 200 representatives of thirty-six National Councils,[4] two Canadians were members of the International Council's Executive, Mrs. C.H. Thorburn and Winnifred Kydd. The resolutions presented at the International Council meetings were always discussed at the annual meetings of the National Council of Canada, as were the very full reports that the Canadian delegates brought back.

The International Council had held its first triennial meeting in Paris in 1934. The previous year, the Executive Council had met in Stockholm and had expressed its sorrow and concern at the demise of the German National Council of Women. This Council had been one of the very earliest national councils, having been established in 1895 and affiliated to the International Council in 1897. The Paris meeting was informed of the reasons why the Council disbanded. At the time of Hitler's accession to power, there were fifty national affiliates of the German National Council of Women. In May 1933, the German National Council had been asked to swear unconditional loyalty to Hitler; to recognize that women had special tasks in life that

---

2   Strong-Boag, "Peace," p. 176.
3   Prentice, et al., *Canadian Women*, p. 286.
4   Twenty-two were in Europe, six in the Americas, four in Asia and two in Australia. Anon, *Women in a Changing World*, p. 72.

restricted their spheres of activity to the home and the provision of social welfare; to exclude women of Jewish origin from the board of officers of the German National Council, as well as from the boards of all affiliated associations, including those of local councils; to accept the appointment of Nazi women to leading positions within the organization. The National Council of Germany refused to comply with any of these demands and immediately disbanded.[5] The whole issue was reported to the Canadian Council at its annual meeting in 1934.[6]

The growing barbarism in Europe was brought home to the Canadian Council still more vividly through the report given in 1939 by one of its affiliates, the Canadian Division of the Council of Jewish Women. The Report noted that "in Montreal, Winnipeg and Vancouver the [Jewish] Council has been the organization handling refugees in transit through Canada on their way to Australia or the Orient. Almost every week has seen parties ranking in size from twenty to a hundred arriving by steamers at the Eastern Ports, being looked after in Montreal and provided with home hospitality and food and necessities for the long train journey ahead. They were met again in Winnipeg, again given provisions to last them until they reached Vancouver...The Vancouver women, in co-operation with the B'nai B'rith ...saw to their every comfort until they embarked on the steamers carrying them across the Pacific."[7] The Report also recorded that the "project for refugee children is still being retarded by the attitude of the Canadian government. After admitting five children, further applications have been refused."

Increased knowledge about the dangers abroad in the world did not necessarily translate into support for any political stance or a willingness to undertake effective action. Even after the declaration of war on September 10, 1939 many Canadians found little to disagree with in their Prime Minister's outburst, during negotiations over the Commonwealth Air Training Plan, that "This is not our war."[8] By the spring of 1940, however, Canadian attitudes had altered and the country was committed to full participation in the struggle.

In 1939 Canada was a country with a population of 11,506,655,[9] which was "less than a quarter of the population of the United Kingdom and only

---

5   *Ibid.,* pp. 64-5, and p. 214.
6   *Yearbook,* 1934, p. 139.
7   *Yearbook,* 1939, p. 187.
8   Morton, *Military History,* p. 180.
9   Leary, ed., *Historical Statistics,* Table, Series A2-14.

about a twelfth of that of the United States."[10] As Donald Creighton remarked, "everybody agreed, either proudly or regretfully, that Canada, unlike the United States, had not become a "melting pot."[11] There were distinctive cultural divisions, not only between aboriginal peoples and those who came later, and between those of French and English heritage, but also between many of the "New Canadians" and those already established in the country. The origins of the later immigrants included the Ukraine, Poland, Scandinavia, Holland and Central Europe in general, as well as Asia. A very large measure of imagination and will was needed to mould this heterogeneous population into a coherent society; and to bring such a country united into, and through, the Second World War within a generation would require very great political skill.

The instant enthusiasm which had greeted the declaration of war in 1914 was not repeated in 1939. The bitter fact was that the country was facing armed conflict for the second time in a generation, and, moreover, many of its people were still experiencing the effects of the Depression. There was little innocent optimism about humanity's future in 1939. Even those who wholeheartedly supported Canada's entry into war, did so with a calculated response. As far as the National Council was concerned, Canada was fighting on the side of right in a just war. A special meeting of a sub-committee of the Executive had taken place in September, 1939 and resolved that, "... the National Council of women of Canada have placed themselves at the disposal of the Government for service in any way which they may be used, [and] the National Council of Women of Canada urge their Local Councils and Nationally Organized Societies in federation to continue the regular line of work undertaken in their communities in order that the normal trend of life may proceed quietly and efficiently...in doing war work, Local Councils be urged to co-operate with recognized organizations already specializing in war work, rather than to set up new projects of their own."[12]

This note of "as far as possible, business as usual" was struck even more firmly with the resolutions which the President of Council, Mrs. Spencer, delivered in person to several members of Mackenzie King's Cabinet.[13] There were four resolutions and all four were concerned with the status of women. They requested His Majesty's government: "1. To give the proper

---

[10] Donald Creighton, *The Forked Road: Canada 1939-1957*, (Toronto, 1976), p. 17.
[11] *Ibid.*
[12] *Yearbook*, 1940, p. 36.
[13] *Ibid.*, p. 35.

status of Canadian Army Medical Corps to your women doctors. 2...to name a woman to the Censor Board... 3. to name a woman to the Wartime Prices and Trade Board... 4...that [to the recently created National Film Board] be added at least one outstanding woman, and that the President of the National Council of Women be consulted concerning this appointment." Throughout the war years, to an extent unknown and unimaginable during the First World War, Council would lobby for the government to call upon "well-trained, highly qualified and well known women who could make a valuable and definite contribution to the various Government Departments and Boards on which women should have representatives in this time of emergency."[14]

Of course Council activities at all levels — national, provincial and local — went far beyond these resolutions. Council agendas reflected the deep concern of their members with the general question of women's participation in the war effort, both within civilian life and the Armed Services, and the equally deep commitment to nurturing the social fabric of their communities. The voluntary organizations of women, within and without Council, moved to coordinate women's efforts well before the government established the Women's Voluntary Services Division of the Department of National War Services, in late 1941. At the forty-seventh annual meeting, which was held at the Royal York Hotel in Toronto, June 12–13, 1940, support was given to the proposal of Senator Iva Fallis[15] for the organization of a "Voluntary Registration of Canadian Women" in order that future demands for the "women power" of Canada would be easily and effectively met.[16] This project led to the development of a number of local committees, affiliated in various ways to local councils,[17] and in 1941 to a direct recommendation by the National Council that all local councils "set up a Volunteer Bureau" which would work not only for immediate wartime needs but also for "peacetime

---

14 The Council also suggested that the person named be the President of the Canadian Women's Press Club. Partial text of a resolution sent to the Dominion Government, January 1941, *Yearbook*, 1941, p. 30.

15 She was born Iva Campbell Doyle at Castleton, Ontario, 23 June 1883. She taught school for five years before her marriage in 1909, and then moved to Saskatchewan to farm with her husband. They returned to Peterborough in 1923 and Fallis became very active in the federal and the Ontario Conservative party organizations. In 1930 she toured the country from the Atlantic to Alberta in support of R.B. Bennett. As a reward for her services, he appointed her to the Senate, the first Conservative woman so named and the second woman appointed to that body. She died in Peterborough, 7 March 1956. J.K. Johnson, ed., *The Canadian Directory of Parliament*, (Ottawa, N.A.C., 1968), p. 196.

16 *Yearbook*, 1940, p. 37.

17 In particular, for efforts in Winnipeg and throughout Ontario, see Ruth Roach Pierson, *"They're Still Women After All": The Second World War and Canadian Womanhood*, (Toronto, 1986), pp. 35-36.

adjustments."[18] This preparatory organization laid the groundwork for the way women would cope, as they had done during the First World War, not only with the continuing problems of everyday life, but also with the need to cooperate with government plans for placing the economy on a wartime footing and, especially after 1942, for bringing an increasing proportion of women into the paid labour force, both civilian and military.

This recognition in the early years of the conflict of the need for post-war planning was shared by government. It reflected both a belief in victory and a determination that, when peace came, Canadians would build a society in which the social and economic disasters of the Depression could never happen again.

Women's volunteer work between 1939 and 1945 was as essential as it had been during the First World War, but Canada in 1939 was a much more structured society than it had been in 1914. There were subtle and important differences, in the type of volunteer work demanded, from that which had characterized the earlier conflict. There was no direct equivalent, for example, of the Patriotic Fund, but the support of women for the government's economic policies was of crucial importance. This was recognized when, in 1943, at the Fiftieth Anniversary meeting of Council, the then Minister of Finance, J.L. Ilsley praised Canadian women for the economic assistance they had given to the war effort.[19] Their support for Victory bonds was decisive. The National Council not only spoke, often and emphatically, of how necessary it was to place money in "War Savings Certificates"[20] but moved much of its own monies, including part of the Foundation Fund, into government bonds.[21] In 1945 the Council had $75,000.00 invested in this way.[22] As well, throughout the war, many local councils raised funds through salvage operations, such as the gathering, sorting and baling of newspapers and rags, to buy bonds.[23]

The Second World War imposed more severe strains upon domestic consumption than had the First, and the responsibility for coping with government policies in this area lay squarely on the shoulders of the 2,285,370 women who reported their occupation as housewife.[24] Again, as in the First

18 Yearbook, 1941, p. 59.
19 Yearbook, 1943, pp. 53-56.
20 See, for instance, Yearbook, 1941, p. 31.
21 Yearbook, 1942, p. 30-31.
22 Abridged Report, 1945, p. 32.
23 For example, Brantford, Yearbook, 1941, p. 130.
24 Genevieve Auger, Raymond Lamothe, De la poêle à frire à la ligne de feu: la vie quotidienne des québécoises pendant la guerre '30-'45, (Montreal, 1981), p. 53.

World War, women planted, harvested and preserved vegetables and fruit; made clothes and then mended and patched them; coped with dilapidated household furnishings and made do with whatever domestic equipment — stoves, sewing machines, washing machines, ice-boxes and refrigerators — lay to hand. During the Second World War, however, women pressed hard for effective government support for their activities. In particular, the National Council was concerned about proper nutrition. It made a request to government in 1941 for the appointment of a "specially trained nutritionist" to the federal Department of Health, as well as "a Nutritionist in each province" so that instruction on food values and proper meals would reach every home.[25] Throughout the war years, at all levels of Council, there was concern about proper nutrition, and local councils set up courses on diet and combined them with cooking classes. At the same time, any information booklets which one local council found useful were quickly sent on to other councils for distribution. Lobbying for government action on the need for an appointment in this field continued, and in 1945 the convenor of the Public Health Committee reported that "seven of the nine Provinces have a Graduate Home Economist appointed to the Departments of Health and a good many cities also have trained Nutritionists in their Health Departments."[26]

The existence of the Wartime Prices and Trade Board, which had been established almost immediately after the declaration of war in 1939, created for Canadian housewives an environment different from the inflation and shortages the First World War had imposed. The Board was set up to monitor production quotas and maximum prices for many consumer goods to prevent rising employment and increased wages from triggering an inflationary spiral. Its operations occasioned considerable Council activity. In the first place, much lobbying was undertaken to secure the appointment of women members to the Board and its various committees. Mrs. R.W. Lang acted as liaison officer between the National Council and the Consumer Branch of the Board. One of the latter's most important functions was the publication and circulation of the *Consumer News*. It was distributed throughout the country for the purpose of explaining the reasons behind rationing, prices and shortages, and was of major importance in making women aware that their housekeeping difficulties were part of a general Canadian problem. Secondly, it

---

[25] *Yearbook*, 1941, p. 39.
[26] *Abridged Report*, 1945, p. 102.

was through the price-monitoring activities undertaken by local councils, in common with other volunteer organizations, that the policies established by the Board worked. It has been estimated that the "fourteen regional committees coordinated the efforts of over 101,000 liaison officers supplied by women's voluntary organizations."[27] Thirdly, in 1947, as a direct result of wartime experience, the National Council of Women took the lead in establishing the Canadian Association of Consumers.

In both wars volunteers sought to provide a variety of services and comforts for members of the armed forces. The major difference, of course, was that in the Second World War, from the time of the establishment of the Canadian Women's Auxiliary Air Force — by Order-in-Council of July 2, 1941 — servicewomen's needs also had to be met.[28] The annual reports of local councils on work done in this field show the wide range of activities that were undertaken. A cursory survey of what was done during 1941, for example, shows the local councils gathering and sending off books and magazines to military centres; running hospitality centres and canteens; and making up parcels to be sent to those serving abroad. In 1942 the National Council established a committee with particular responsibility for looking at the needs of "Members of National Defence Services and their dependents." In 1944, the report of this committee noted, among other matters, that the A.W.A. house in Montreal had provided "25,000 beds and 62,766 meals for women in the service."[29] Books, magazines, cards, mittens and scarves and other comforts, were routinely gathered and packed, to be sent, by this date, not only to military centres but also to prisoner-of-war camps. Ditty bags were sent to the Navy League, cigarettes gathered to be sent to clearing stations in Italy. Halifax and Saint John Councils worked particularly hard to provide home hospitality for sailors as well as supporting the hostels which had been established in those ports.[30] Further, in common with many other local councils, that of Port Arthur, Ontario, began to lobby for improved pensions for service personnel and better discharge payments.

The most visible work of Council, however, was linked to the shift of the country from the Depression to the wartime economy, and the consequent increase in the employment of women in the paid labour force. Estimates

27 Prentice, et al., *Canadian Women*, p. 297.
28 An Order-in-Council of August 13, 1941 established the Canadian Women's Army Corps, and the Women's Royal Canadian Naval Service was established by Order-in-Council of July 31, 1942.
29 *Abridged Report*, 1944, p. 103.
30 *Ibid.*, p. 104.

vary, but the unemployment rate in 1939 is usually given as 11%.[31] By mid–1942 the pool of surplus labour had been drained through the demands of the armed forces and wartime industries. Unemployment between 1943 and 1945 has been estimated at under 2% of the labour force.[32] It was during these years that women entered paid employment in much greater numbers than previously. By 1945, more than "43,000 women had enlisted in the armed forces: 21,000 in the Women's Army Corps, 16,000 in the Women's Division of the Air Force and 6600 in the Women's Naval Service. In addition some 2500 joined the Nursing Service and 38 women doctors signed up for medical duty."[33] Further, the number of women in munitions work in Ontario and Quebec reached 44,000 by July 1, 1944 and women in the aircraft industry numbered 33,000.[34] In sum, it was estimated that in 1939 the number of women in the paid labour force had been 600,000; by the end of the war that number had more than doubled, exceeding 1,200,000.[35] To put it another way, "in 1944, at the peak of wartime employment, one third of all women over the age of 15 were in the paid labour force."[36] This figure, as Ruth Roach Pierson has pointed out, did not "include part-time workers or the 800,000 women working on farms."[37]

The National Council, at all levels, expressed two major concerns over the growing participation of women in paid labour outside the home. Consistent with its traditions, it treated the conditions of employment offered to women and rates of pay and benefits, as matters for immediate attention. By 1943, approximately 255,000 women were working in factories linked to wartime needs.[38] During the war years, the reports from local councils, collected together by Lottie O'Boyle, who was convenor at that time for the Standing Committee on "Trades and Professions for Women," had three main themes: the presence of women in new positions and occupations; the increase in the number of women in paid employment, and their working conditions; and the need to defend a women's right to enter any occupational field for which she was qualified.

---

[31] Firestone, *Canada's Economic Development*, p. 58, gives the lowest estimate: 523,000 out of a labour force of 4,607,000. Ruth Roach Pierson considers that 900,000 were unemployed, of which an estimated 20% were women. Pierson, *Still Women*, p. 9.

[32] Bothwell, et al., *Canada 1900-1945*, p. 352.

[33] Prentice, et al., *Canadian Women*, p. 303. The total number of Canadians who served in the armed forces is usually given as a million.

[34] *Ibid.*, p. 300.

[35] Pierson, *Still Women*, p. 61, fn. 189·

[36] Prentice, et al., *Canadian Women*, p. 311.

[37] Pierson, *Still Women*, p. 9.

[38] Prentice, et al., *Canadian Women*, p. 298.

The 1941 *Yearbook* strongly emphasized the growth in employment of women, the increase in their wages, and the widening of the choice of occupations. Calgary, for example, remarked that "the women's employment office shows an extra large number of placements, with a 3% or 4% increase in wages"; Fort William reported that "800 girls are demonstrating that a woman can drive rivets and weld steel and duraluminum [sic] as well as a man, that they are just as efficient as men."[39] Ottawa Local Council noted the changing nature of women's employment, mentioning that "a small number of women scientists is engaged in Ottawa, chemists, tool designers, nutrition experts and two appointed economic advisers."[40] It was Montreal, however, that observed what was, for that city, the most striking advance. In the province of Quebec women had only been accorded the right to vote in provincial elections, and in some municipal elections in 1940. Montreal Council reported in 1941 that "for the first time in the history of the province, three women were appointed [sic] to Montreal City Council: Miss Elizabeth Monk, a lawyer; Miss Kathleen Fisher, and Mrs. Théodule Bruneau."

It was also at the 1941 annual meeting, held in May just before the government established the women's branches of the armed forces, that the National Council took its stand on the issue of women's place in the military. To a very large extent, the women who entered the Canadian armed forces were seen by the military as support, rather than as operational personnel, and as replacements for men rather than as recruits in their own right. In 1942, when shortage of manpower — in the literal sense — led to a concerted attempt to recruit women for the armed forces, both pay and benefit provisions were discriminatory. As Ruth Roach Pierson has observed, at the very beginning "of the formation of the women's services, basic pay for all ranks was set at two-thirds that of men holding equivalent rank." Moreover, dependent allowances were not paid for the relatives of women, "be they husbands, mothers, fathers, sisters or brothers."[41] Apparently, the needs of dependent children of service women were even more inconceivable to the military mind than husbands who needed the financial aid of their wives.

The first resolution on this issue to be discussed by the Council organization was that brought forward by Ontario Provincial Council. It was debated and carried at the forty-eighth annual meeting, held in Winnipeg from May

39 *Yearbook,* 1941, p. 121.
40 *Ibid.,* p. 122.
41 Pierson, *Still Women,* pp. 113-14.

20 to May 23, 1941. The resolution read as follows:

> That whereas many women in Canada are undergoing expert training with a view to serving in the defence of their country; we, the Ontario Provincial Council of Women would ask that the National Council of Women approach the Government to urge that, if and when these women are needed for active service and are mobilized, they may be admitted to the military forces on an equal standing with men doing similar work.[42]

The following year a very specific motion was brought forward by the New Westminster Local Council to the forty-ninth annual meeting of Council, held at the Windsor Hotel, Montreal, May 26–29, 1942. This motion noted that "male recruits enlisted in the services — Army and (or) Air Force of Canada receive on enlistment regular soldier's pay of $1.30 per day; Female recruits enlisted in the services receive on enlistment 90 cents per day..." The motion went on to say that since "information from the Department of National Defence declares recruits to C.W.A.C (Canadian Women's Army Corps) and to the R.C.A.F. (Women's Division) will be called upon to relieve men in the Canadian Army and (or) Air Force for active service, Be it resolved that female recruits to C.W.A.C. and (or) R.C.A.F. (Women's Division) receive the same pay as male recruits..."[43] Over the next months resolutions such as these were repeatedly presented to National Council, and repeatedly endorsed.

Mrs. Edgar Drury Hardy had replaced Mrs. George Edgar Spencer as President of the National Council in 1942. She was American-born and had been educated at Mount Holyoke. After her marriage, she and her husband, a businessman, moved to Canada and became Canadian citizens.[44] Mrs. Hardy campaigned vigorously for the views of Council on conditions for women in the Canadian forces. She organized meetings between members of the National Executive and federal members of Parliament, and she herself wrote to and called upon government members, including the Prime Minister.[45] The response of the Department of National Defence to the resolution of the

---

[42] *Yearbook,* 1941, p. 44.

[43] *Yearbook,* 1942, p. 48.

[44] Information about Mrs. Hardy is sketchy, in that dates of birth, education and naturalization are not recorded in press biographies and obituaries.

[45] "National Council of Women of Canada," vol. 84, Prime Minister of Canada, Correspondence: National Archives of Canada, MG 28, 125.

Council was slow and conceded only part of what was requested. It was more than eighteen months later, on July 24, 1943, that the Minister of National Defence, Colonel J.L. Ralston, announced in the House of Commons that "the basic pay of women in the forces was to be raised to 80 per cent of that paid to men in the same rank."[46] Other changes were made to married women's pay rates and to the rates for women training for the same occupations as men. However, the changes did not mean equality of treatment for men and women: the discrepancy between rates of pay had merely been reduced (from 33 1/3 per cent to 20%) and while dependent allowances could now be paid to mothers, fathers and siblings of women in the service, no allowances were given for dependent husbands and children.[47] The National Council continued to work for complete equality, but this would not be achieved until the women's forces were reconstituted after the war.

During 1942 the most vexatious problem, both for the country as a whole and the National Council in particular, was the issue of conscription. Mackenzie King, the Prime Minister, had hoped to avoid the bitter dissension which the issue had caused during the 1914–18 war through "the all-party agreement, at the war's outset, that voluntary enlistment was the best policy."[48] The need for greater mobilization of recruits than this policy furnished, however, became increasingly clear, and the issue was made the more sharp by the entry of the United States into the war after Pearl Harbor. Mackenzie King sought to defuse the issue by holding a national plebiscite but the result was what he had feared most. Across the nation the "yes" forces won by 2,945,514 to 1,643,006,[49] but, in Ramsay Cook's words, "In English Canada the forces supporting an affirmative vote were overwhelming. Among French-speaking Canadians...opposition was even more powerful...As he looked at the returns, [Mackenzie King] wrote in his diary: "I thought of Durham's report on the state of Quebec, when he arrived there after the Rebellion of 1837–8, and said he found two nations warring in the bosom of a single state. That would be the case in Canada, as applied to Canada as a whole, unless the whole question of conscription from now on is approached with the utmost care."[50] The government moved very slowly and did not actually institute conscription until the last months of the war.

The Council rode out the 1942 debate over conscription with the help of

---

46 Pierson, *Still Women*, p. 116.
47 *Ibid.*
48 Cook, "Triumphs and Trials," p. 460.
49 Bothwell, et al., *Canada 1900-1945*, p. 325.
50 Cook, "Triumphs and Trials," p. 460-62.

Mrs. Hardy's strong leadership. On April 9, 1942, as President of Council, she had received a letter from Norman McLarty, at that time the Secretary of State, asking her to make all members aware of the necessity of voting on April 9, 1942 on the question of whether "they are in favour of releasing the government from any obligation arising out of any past commitments restricting the methods of raising men for military service."[51] Mrs. Hardy sent a general letter of comment to all members of Council on April 10, 1942, in which she wrote "whether we approve or not of the action of the Dominion government, the plebiscite has now been taken out of party politics." She went on to remark that "with a recognition of this, we believe that an affirmative vote on the plebiscite will strengthen our war effort... The last war gave women the franchise. It behooves each one of us now to exercise our prerogative, thereby standing strongly behind every effort to increase Canada's position and strengthen the cause of the United Nations."[52] Once the plebiscite results were known, Mrs. Hardy made every effort to make her own personal view understood. In a letter she sent to the *Financial Post*, May 4, 1942, she wrote: "The loyalty of Quebec to Canada is unquestionable. The large percentage of her sons who have enlisted voluntarily for overseas attest to this fact. I personally feel that loyal Canadians now should make every constructive effort to strengthen Canadian unity."

1943 marked the fiftieth anniversary of the National Council of Women of Canada and the annual meeting was held in Toronto at the Royal York Hotel, from June 16 to June 19. It was an occasion on which to look back and celebrate achievements, to take stock of Council's aims and purposes in the context of present imperatives, and to set out a plan for the future. Miss Beatrice Barber presented a "Brief history of fifty years of The National Council of Women of Canada." It was pithy and to the point, noting:

for fifty years the National Council of Women of Canada has provided a common platform and means of co-operation for all who work for the promotion of its aims — to serve the highest good of the family and the state. It is non-sectarian and non-political and its activities are carried on through twenty-two standing committees, special committees (appointed as the need arises), Provincial Councils, forty-eight Local Councils, twenty-one Nationally Organized Societies and over one hundred local organizations.[53]

---

51 "National Council/ Subject File: vol. 80, f 12," N.A.C.
52 *Ibid.*
53 *Abridged Report,* 1943, p. 36.

The main activities of the Council were summarized as having:

covered the collection of data on all phases of Education, paid labour
for women and children, the proper conservation and uses of nutri-
tional foods, the registration of, whenever necessary, the improvement of health conditions dealing not only with women but with
child welfare, housing and slum clearance and with the assimilation
of immigrants into the life of Canada and [having] worked for years
for control of venereal disease. Many changes in the criminal code
have been made as a result of our constant pressure on the government. To the credit of the members of the Organization and especially of five outstanding Canadian women in a successful appeal was to
the Privy Council of Great Britain in 1929, whereby women were
declared "persons" as described in the British North America Act
and therefore eligible to sit in the Senate of Canada.[54]

Most of the twenty-two standing committees traced their roots to the
very early years of Council's existence. The titles under which they worked
had in some cases altered but the agendas for discussion and action remained
very much the same. Over the years, however, Council had paid a great deal
of attention to ensuring that its committee structure was as well adapted as
possible to the changing scope of Council interests. Besides this, the growing
sophistication of Council, the way in which its members learnt effectively
and quickly to follow procedures which would render action more efficient
and productive, was reflected in fairly frequent reorganizations of its developing bureaucracy and committee structure. Thus by 1943, the concerns
addressed in 1899 through the Committee for the "Custodial Care of Feeble-
minded Women" and the "Care of the Aged Poor" had been entrusted to the
"Committee for Public Health" and the "Committee for Child and Family
Welfare." The 1899 Committee on "Laws for the Better Protection of
Women and Children" was still in existence in 1943, but issues handled in
early years by the Committee on the "Length of working hours for Women
and Children" were now on the agenda of the "Committee for Trades and
Professions." The full slate of standing committees in 1943 included Cinema
and Printed Matter; Citizenship; Housing and Town Planning; National
Resources and Industries; Economics and Taxation; Arts and Letters;

---

[54] *Ibid.*, p. 37.

19. Mrs. Edgar Drury Hardy, President 1941–1946

Education; National Recreation; Finance; Child and Family Welfare; Public Health; Mental Hygiene; Laws concerning Women and Children; League of Nations; Moral Standards; Migration; Publication and Publicity; Members of Defence Services and their Dependents; and Trades and Professions. Special committees included the Committee on the Constitution; the Parliamentary Committee; the Foundation Fund Committee; and the Canadian National Committee on Refugees.

There was never complete certainty as to what subjects ought to be on the agenda of any particular committee. The structure of Council meant that matters could be reported, and presented for discussion, in at least three ways: through the annual report of each local council, through the reports of committees — Standing, Special and ad hoc — and through the annual reports of the associations and societies affiliated at the national level. Issues could also be raised through the reports of the president, the provincial vice-presidents — where such existed — and through correspondence. Examples may be given of the way concerns were routed through the structure. While there was, as noted above, a Committee on Members of the Defence Services and their Dependents, it was to the Committee on National Recreation that many local councils sent information about provisions that had been made for men and women on leave. New Westminster Local Council reported to that committee on the opening of "Westminster House," a recreation centre for men in the services, and Regina related its particular efforts for women in uniform passing through the city. The usual agenda of this committee dealt with parks, libraries and children's playgrounds.[55] Other local councils reported their work for servicemen and women in their annual reports. That is where Kitchener's sponsorship of the Corvette H.M.C.S. "Kitchener" is recorded. In it one can read that the Local Council forwarded "61 turtle neck heavy sweaters; 61 prs. woolen mitts; 61 aero caps; 122 prs. socks; quantity of soap; 61 prs seamen's boots stocking- which go over the knees; 61 scarves, donated by the Kitchener Red Cross; 61 leather jerkins, made and donated by the Ladies Aux. Scots Fusiliers; at least 200 books and magazines, 240 chocolate bars, and odd games and cigarettes."[56]

As for the Committee concerning "Members of National Defence Services and their Dependents," its 1942 report records that West Algoma

---

[55] The reports of some local councils were still primarily concerned with these activities. Fort William reported the provision of "three open air rinks with heated accommodations ...for young skaters;" and Halifax mentioned that the playgrounds of that city were kept open on Sunday afternoons. *Yearbook,* 1943, pp.115-16.

[56] *Yearbook,* 1943, p. 142.

(Port Arthur and Fort William) was already agitating to ensure that the care of servicemen and their families at the war's conclusion would be the best possible; that Toronto was organized to do sewing and mending "for men in Camps"; that Kingston had sent playing cards to Toc H in the Orkneys, and that in Montreal "contributions of knitted goods, books and magazines by thousands [had been] made to I.O.D.E. and Soldiers Wives League."[57] One sometimes has the impression that local council divided their work, as far as reporting is concerned, in such a way as to have something to say to each Standing Committee of National Council, instead of grouping activities by rational categories.

However disorganized the reporting system of Council might have been, there is no doubt that the activity of those women working with and through the structures of Council at the time of its fiftieth anniversary, had an important impact upon every aspect of the fabric of Canadian life, from social issues to cultural ventures.

This is a convenient point at which to review the membership of the Council. In 1943, the twenty-one nationally organized societies federated with Council at the national level were: the Canadian Branch of the King's Daughters and Sons; the Canadian Dietetic Association; Canadian Division of the National Council of Jewish Women; the Canadian Dominion Council of the Mother's Union; Canadian Federation of Business and Professional Women's Clubs; Canadian Girl Guides' Association; Canadian Women's Temperance Union; Dominion Women's Association of the United Church of Canada; the Hadassah Organization of Canada; Health League of Canada; Imperial Order of the Daughters of the Empire; Lyceum Club and Women's Art Association of Canada; Medical Alumnae, University of Toronto; National Council of the Y.W.C.A.; the National Girls' Work Board of the Religious Educational Council of Canada; Queen's University Alumnae Association; Salvation Army in Canada; Silver Cross Women of the British Empire; Ukrainian Women's Association of Canada; Victorian Order of Nurses; and the Women's Missionary Society of the United Church of Canada. The main thrust of all of these organizations was social welfare, health and cultural activity. Statistics of membership are not easily compiled, but the majority of the organizations had forty to fifty branches throughout Canada, with membership in a branch running from thirty to more than a hundred. In 1943, the Business and Professional Women's Clubs reported

57 *Ibid.*, pp. 122-23.

forty affiliates; King's Daughters and Sons reported eighty-eight Circles; and the Women's Missionary Society of the United Church of Canada reported 1018 War Service Units.

In 1943, the local councils, with the number of their affiliates given in brackets, were: Brantford (35); Calgary (24); Chatham, Ontario (17); Chilliwack (7); Dauphin (8); Edmonton (7); Georgetown (6); Halifax (57); Hamilton (41); Kamloops (8); Kingston (33); Kitchener (20); London (47); Medicine Hat (7); Moncton (17); Montreal (57); Moose Jaw (15); Nanaimo (7); New Glasgow (21); New Westminster (32); Niagara Falls (30); North Shore B.C. (13); Ottawa (86); Owen Sound (19); Peterborough (60); Portage La Prairie (7); Regina (33); St. Catharines (21); St. John (36); St. Thomas (23); Sackville (7); Smith's Falls (8); Stellarton (8); Swift Current (13); Toronto (66); Truro (14); Vancouver (65); Victoria (43); West Algoma (54); Weston (18); West Pictou (11); Westville (12); Windsor (38); Winnipeg (70); Yarmouth (26).[58] Overall, the Council reports and documentation must have reached close to three quarters of a million women.

The impact on public opinion of such a formidable association of women's interest groups was fully recognized by the federal government, when it turned to the National Council for help with the problem of "rumours" and recruitment of women into the armed services. As Ruth Roach Pierson has shown, there were two major attitudes which hindered recruitment of women: opinions as to whether employment in the armed services was compatible with "femininity," and questions about whether "really nice girls" would engage in such a thing.[59] There is no doubt where Council stood on the first issue: in its opinion, femininity was part of what women were, not something that was engendered by occupation. There was more debate about the second issue, and during the fiftieth annual meeting Brigadier-General James Mess spoke to the assembled women on June 18, 1943. He said that the idea that service in the armed forces was a danger to the moral life of young women was false. "We have traced rumours up hill and down dale and found nothing to them," he said, "and we want your help in stamping out these rumours."[60] The senior officers of the women's divisions of the armed forces had written letters to Council reinforcing the Brigadier-General's plea and that afternoon Council passed the resolution stating that "the National Council of Women of Canada desires to express

[58] *Ibid.*, p. 4.
[59] Pierson, *Still Women*, pp. 129-87.
[60] *Yearbook*, 1943, p. 61.

admiration for, and confidence in, the women of all ranks in the Women's Divisions of the Armed services of Canada, and will support in every way the further recruiting of women for all branches of the services." It is, however, typical of the spirit of the National Council during these years that this resolution was followed immediately by another, to the effect that the National Council "re-affirm their request that the Dominion Government provide allowances for the dependents of women in the armed forces."[61]

One of the most important events at the 1943 meeting was presentation of the Council's "Program for Post-War Planning." This document had been put together by a Special Committee of Council on Reconstruction and it was circulated throughout the organization, becoming, over the following months, an item on the agenda for most local councils.[62] A wide variety of issues was addressed, and requests for consideration of proposals ranged from very idealistic proposals to the concrete and practical. After a preamble expressing support for the Atlantic Charter and the idea of the United Nations, the first section dealt with "International Collaboration." The Council was in favour of five proposals: "1. Some limitation of national sovereignty; 2. The maintenance of collective security by an international police force; 3. An international court of justice; 4. A strengthened International Labour Organization; and 5. Financial and economic control, within the framework of the international organization, to provide for fair treatment between nations in trade relationships, including access to raw materials."

Section II dealt with "National Unity" and asked for continued consideration of the Rowell-Sirois Report on Dominion-Provincial Relations, as well as "unceasing efforts to promote better understanding between...French-speaking and English-speaking peoples." The eight topics selected in Section III, which dealt with "Social and economic planning," covered the steps needed for an orderly shift of the economy from a wartime to a peacetime footing. Among the provisions called for to assist members of the armed forces returning to civil life, were the right to "reinstatement in former employment," the provision of "educational opportunities for professional training, vocational training or re-training," and land settlement schemes. Section IV was dedicated to "National Health and Nutrition" and called for "Dominion leadership...in making provision for an adequate program of health, nutrition and child welfare for Canada." Not only was a request made for "strengthened and improved health services," including "adequate hospi-

---

61 *Ibid.,* pp. 61-62.
62 *Ibid.,* pp. 78-84.

tal accommodation for tubercular...and mentally defective patients...clinics for child welfare, heart diseases, venereal diseases, cancer, tuberculosis and mental disorder," but also for "a government plan of compulsory health insurance for those in low-income groups" and "free care for those not included in a governmental insurance plan, who are unable to pay."

Section V, dealing with "Education," began with the demand to raise the standard of compulsory school attendance. It is not clear whether this meant the raising of the school leaving age, or the control of truancy. It was linked with the request that all secondary education be free, "including vocational education," and that "the government" become involved in providing university scholarships. Council also suggested that national standards for the professional qualification of teachers be developed, and that there be an extension of facilities for adult education. This section concluded with a request for the "establishment of a Dominion Bureau of Education, available to all interested, as a centre for research, information and consultative service."

Sections VI and VII were short and perhaps the most radical parts of the proposed program. They were very different, in that the first comprised concrete suggestions while the second submitted idealistic propositions. Section VI was headed "The Social Insurances" and listed three matters for legislation:

1. An extension of benefits under the Unemployment Insurance Act;
2. The establishment of a national plan of contributory old-age pensions;
3. The establishment of a national plan of compulsory health insurance...

Section VII was entitled "Labour Matters" and also contained three recommendations. The first asked for "Increasing voluntary co-operation between employers and employees with consequent improvement in the whole field of labour relations." The second was a request for "sympathy and support for labour in its efforts to secure better working conditions through collective bargaining." The final proposal was for the "development of a more effective working relationship between Dominion and provincial governments to make possible implementation of the conventions and recommendations adopted by conferences of the International Labour Organization..."

Section VIII dealt with housing, its basis a request for "comprehensive and co-ordinated Housing" for the country as a whole. This proposal was in direct response to the impact of wartime demands for raw materials upon the housing industry. Housing construction peaked during the war years in 1941, and fell sharply thereafter. In addition, dwellings that were built were concentrated in places where the government placed wartime industries and military encampments. As has been pointed out, "the result, outside most large Canadian cities, was a series of 'federal villages,' instantly recognizable because the houses were built in a few standard designs which recurred without variation from coast to coast."[63] By 1943 it was obvious Canada was facing a housing shortage and that when peace came building programs would need both support and supervision.

Section IX was concerned with "Immigration". In the recommendation of this section Council struggled to come to terms with its own bias in favour of traditional migrants from north-western Europe. It proclaimed its belief that an immigration policy "should be carried out without regard to race or creed," but it also announced that this should be done "with recognition that the problem of Oriental immigration will require special attention." While suggesting that a quota system might be considered, the Council also stated that "Canada should now do its part in offering a new homeland to some of the people abroad who, without number, have been cruelly uprooted by war." In the coming years, women working with Council would attempt to implement the fourth clause in this section. This asserted that "Canadians should welcome all immigrants and help to assimilate them into the life of the country." The text went on to say that "in this endeavour various organizations have played a part in the past, and they and others should stand ready to do more now and in the future."

Section X called for the recognition of the national significance of the fitness and health of the population and asked for provincial and municipal initiatives in this area.

The title of Section XI was "Women in the Post-War World" and was a clear and succinct statement of Council aims for women. There were seven requests presented. They read as follows:

1. A greater share (for women) in the responsibilities of government through election to local, provincial and Dominion governing bodies, and representation on administration boards;
2. Appointment of well-qualified women on bodies concerned with peace terms and post-war reconstruction;
3. Gradual demobilization after the war of women employed in war industries;

---

[63] Bothwell. et al., *Canada 1900-1945*, p. 376.

4. Resistance to a policy of shutting women out of employment in industries and occupations they entered during the war;
5. Adoption of the principle of equal pay for equal work;
6. Opposition to discrimination against women in various lines of employment and against the employment of married women;
7. The right of women to retain or acquire citizenship without regard to their marital status.

The program ended with an expression of belief in the need for Canadians to approach the problems of the post-war world with an emphasis on "the brotherhood of man," on the need to attempt to eradicate poverty and with a reaffirmation of faith in democracy. If one puts to one side the feminist flavour encapsulated in the last section of this program, it is very little different from the plans for reconstruction the Liberal government had been developing since 1940. Donald Creighton has called the emergence of such policies "the coming of the planners."[64] Commenting on the emergence of the family allowance program, Creighton wrote that it was "only the most conspicuous of a series of projects which made up the Liberal post-war plan for Canada. They were intended both to honour the obligations of the past and to grasp the opportunities of the future: and they were so numerous, complex, and ambitious that they required the reorganization of the Cabinet and the creation of several new departments of government."[65]

Personal testimony of Mitchell Sharp, who joined the Department of Finance in 1942, has emphasized the extent to which there was an absolute determination among civil servants to pursue policies that would make any repetition of the Depression impossible. Never again should Canadians have to witness the degradation imposed upon the unemployed by an uncoordinated welfare system, the wreck of human lives produced by inadequate health services, the cutting back of talent because of a lack of educational opportunities. In sum, for Mitchell Sharp, there existed a widespread conviction among many of the political and bureaucratic elites, that the country suffered more through a lack of means whereby community could exercise responsibility for the lives of its individual members, than because of a belief on the part of its citizens that self-help was the best response to adversity.[66] In other words, Canadian elites did not believe that poverty was the visible judgment

---

[64] Creighton, *Forked Road*, Chapter 5, p. 88.
[65] *Ibid.*, pp. 88-9.
[66] Speech before the History Society, Carleton University, October 1992.

of God on sinners; instead, they believed their polity had lacked the institutional means to translate private philanthropy into public succour.

It is a fact that at the time of the fiftieth anniversary of the Council, the King government, and especially its principal industrial minister C.D. Howe, was considering the Marsh Report. This was the work of Leonard Marsh, a McGill University professor of sociology. It argued for "the adoption of a comprehensive system of social insurance for health, income and old age, and a massive program of public works."[67] But consideration does not mean acceptance, and neither King nor Howe were whole-heartedly in favour of the all-embracing social reconstruction advocated by Marsh. Nevertheless there were many, both politicians and civil servants, who did work for a clear vision of state-supported social justice, although even the first steps towards the translation of that vision into reality would take a considerable time.

In sum, the main proposals of the reconstruction program of the National Council can be seen as supporting much of the more enlightened social planning of the forties. However, the explicitly feminist parts of the program found no echo whatsoever, within or without government circles. In her presidential address Mrs. Hardy remarked that "we hear often, generally from men, the remark that "after the war women will go back to the kitchen." She went on to say, "Probably the reason for our aroused indignation is that we are in effect being told what we *are* to do before we have been given the chance to express what we intend to do." She went on to confront point-blank the question: "Will those women who have proved beyond any doubt their ability to learn skilled jobs and have taken their place in industry beside men wish to continue or will they be satisfied to go back into the home?" Mrs. Hardy affirmed bluntly that "one of the policies, not only of the National Council of Women of Canada but of the International Council of Women, has always been the recognition of women's rights to seek a career or position, not because of her sex, but because of the contribution she is able to make. Therefore women holding executive positions or positions of trust should not be asked to step aside provided their ability merits the same recognition as that of men." "Women," she concluded, "will not be satisfied to be idle when peace comes."[68] For her, part of the solution to a general problem would be the realization that "because of the independence young women have found in taking war jobs and the satisfaction of having their own pay envelopes, men will have to understand that there must be a com-

---

[67] Morton, *Short History*, p. 205.
[68] *Yearbook*, 1943, pp. 40-44.

plete readjustment in the post war period...The wife, who has had her war job, will have to be recognized as a partner with an equal right to her part of the pay cheque in lieu of the pay she received when while working."

This note of independence and conviction on the subject of women's rights was present throughout the Council deliberations of 1943. It was struck in the reports of convenors and of the local councils. Lottie O'Boyle, the convenor of the Committee on Trades and Professions for Women wrote: "We gladly note the recent appointments of a woman judge, a coroner, an aeronautical engineer, an astronomer, a consul, house surgeons, nutritionists, industrial inspector and radio broadcaster..."[69] She went on to say that the post-war period would present challenging problems of fitting and refitting women for their readjustment "in the industrial and commercial world, the election of more women to responsible positions of leadership, the strengthening of cultural influences..." Mrs. A. Johnson, of the Calgary Local Council wrote that "the fact that women are proving so efficient in men's jobs may perhaps overcome a great deal of prejudice that obtains against equality of sex...The war may bring recognition of the housewife as a wage earner, and, in industry and commerce, approximation of equal pay for equal work."Miss Mildred Pickering of Hamilton noted that Canadian women had undertaken everything asked of them: "Trundling wheelbarrows, operating steam hoists, shovelling slag, lifting rails, cutting pulp, carpentering and structuring ships (one woman being a supervisor of ships hulls) are a few of the occupations."[70] This attitude was spelt out again in the report of the "Business and Professional Women's Clubs," whose national secretary remarked that "While giving much attention to War Services the Canadian Federation has not overlooked the principal for which it organized — the advancement of women in public life."[71]

The fifty-first annual meeting was held at Port Arthur, June 12–16, 1944.[72] Mrs. Hardy emphasized again the positive role of women in society. She noted that "Canadian women control one half of the vote for Government representative [sic]; women are beneficiaries of over 95% of all insurance; women are 85% of the consumer class; women own one half of

---

[69] *Ibid.*, p. 124.
[70] *Ibid.*, p. 125.
[71] *Ibid.*, p. 167.
[72] Beatrice Barber, the corresponding secretary summed up the office work undertaken over the past year: typed letters mailed 1,113; circular letters 5,206; mimeographing and mailing letters received from National Convenors, abstract of Minutes of Sub-Executive and Executive, copies of resolutions, together making an approximate total of 9,175 pages of mimeographing for 1943-4. *Yearbook*, 1944, p. 20.

the bonds which finance Canada's Government and industries; women have the chief interest in education; women are responsible for family health; women dominate church functions; women actually operate most of the charities. So we have not only the power but the justification for making our contribution to the plans for peace."[73] Once more the Council reaffirmed its belief "in the freedom of every women, to choose where and at what she will work." The resolution in question went on to state that the National Council "deplore[s] the tendency, among women or wherever it may occur, to discriminate against the employment of married women."[74] Once more the varied occupations of women formed the basis of the report from the Committee on Trades and Professions. Miss Jessie Redmond of Fort William noted the employment of women as jig-borers and carbide-tip cutters in the Canadian Car factories. The Regina report, given by Mrs. Roy Campbell, recommended the regulation of wages, hours and general conditions of work.

It was at this meeting that the idea was put forward, and planning undertaken, for a meeting of fifty national associations of women to be held in Toronto, on February 1 and 2, 1945.[75] The Council had twenty-two nationally organized societies in federation that year, and it is unclear from the surviving records whether there were forty-nine other associations invited, or just twenty-eight. The wife of the Governor General, Princess Alice, Countess of Athlone, lent her backing to the plan and the meeting took place at the Royal York Hotel. It is obvious from the minutes that Mrs. Hardy was the driving force of the gathering, and that the National Council of Women represented by far the most open views on women's role in society. The traditional role of women as centred in the home was strongly emphasized by those who spoke in the name of the Women's Auxiliary of the Anglican Church, the Women's Missionary Society of the United Church, and the Commissioner of the Girl Guides. However, the representatives of the Y.W.C.A. and the Canadian Brotherhood of Railway Employees, Mrs. Ryland New and Mrs. Jones, supported resolutions on "the equal right of wives to benefits under social insurance."[76]

---

[73] *Ibid.*, p. 32.

[74] *Ibid.*, p. 47.

[75] The reports and planning of this conference are in NCWC files, vol. 86, file 1, N.A.C. Much of the original material seems to have been mislaid. No list of those invited has been preserved but internal evidence suggests that some or all of the following were present: Canadian Dietetic Association, Cercle des Fermières, Canadian Home Economics Association, Federated Women's Institutes of Canada, and the women's auxiliary organizations of both the main Protestant denominations and the major political parties.

[76] "Findings of Conference of National Women's Organizations in Canada," Feb. 1-2, 1945: NCWC files: vol. 86, file 1, N.A.C.

This conference seems to have had as much impact upon Canadian society as a whole as a ripple of wind over a lake. There was no follow-up, such as the presentation of general resolutions to government bodies, and it did not initiate a series of such meetings. As far as Council was concerned, and in particular Mrs. Hardy — who remained president until 1946 — the event confirmed their belief that the National Council of Women of Canada was one of the truly great women's organizations. This was the note struck both at the fifty-second annual meeting held in Sackville, New Brunswick, June 21–27, 1945 and the fifty-third meeting held in Niagara Falls, June 3–7, 1946.

Mrs. Hardy concluded her presidency in 1946, having been awarded the O.B.E. in 1944 for her volunteer work. She was succeeded by Mrs. R. J. Marshall. The new president had been born Blanche Edy in London, Ontario, January 31, 1886. She received her B.A. in science and English from McMaster University, where she met her future husband, Robert J. Marshall, an engineer. They had four children. She was President of the Toronto Local Council from 1938 to 1940 and of the Ontario Provincial Council of Women from 1942 to 1946.[77] In 1949 she received an honorary doctorate of laws from McMaster University. Her association with voluntary work was through the Federation of University Women and Zonta international. The most important and successful year of her presidency was, perhaps, 1947. This year saw the establishment of the Canadian Association of Consumers, largely because of the work of Council and Canadian attendance at the first full meeting of the International Council of Women since 1938.

At the conclusion of the 1945 annual meeting in Sackville, New Brunswick, Mrs. R.W. Lang prepared a questionnaire, to be circulated among all local councils, on the kind of information women wanted about goods they bought. In 1946, at the Niagara Falls annual meeting, she introduced the replies to her questionnaire by noting that the need for a consumer's association had arisen because of changes in the technology of daily living. Her examples dealt with the need to know the composition of ready-made clothes, the components of home cleaners, the ingredients in packaged foods. Analysis of responses led her to propose the establishment of a research bureau to investigate what actually did go into products offered for sale, and to set up a channel of communication between this bureau and the general public. Women wanted to be sure the standards set by government through

[77] Information from an unsigned, undated biography held by the NCWC head office.

20. Mrs. R. J. Marshall, President 1946–1951

the Wartime Prices and Trade Board would be kept and, in fact, that such work would be expanded. In sum, women had clearly indicated, through the network of local councils, that they wanted a bureau which would be free to make product investigations, to consider what sorts of goods ought to be investigated, and design labelling which would inform the buyer of the grade of food] products, (e.g. 1,2,3 instead of the currently used designations: Fancy, Choice, etc.). Women wanted to be informed, when they bought textiles, what the thread count was, what shrinkage could be expected, and whether the material was colour-fast and waterproof, water-repellent or only water-resistant.[78] The replies given to the questionnaire were reinforced by particular resolutions of local councils. Edmonton, for example, wanted standardization of the sizes of children's clothing and the marking of shoe size by a readily understandable method. Winnipeg sent in a further request to the national office, on November 7, 1946, asking that the standardization of food containers be considered.

As a result of these initiatives the Council passed a resolution on June 5, 1946 requesting the federal government to continue the Standards Division as a Branch of the Department of Trade and Commerce and to call a conference to discuss the formation of a Consumers' Council.[79] The government did nothing. It was on Mrs. Marshall's initiative that the presidents of some fifty-six national organizations of women met on September 29 and 30, 1947, together with women who had chaired the regional advisory committees of the Wartime Prices and Trade Board, women from the major French-speaking organizations, and representatives of the Women's Institutes.[80] This was the meeting that established the Canadian Association of Consumers as an entirely voluntary, non-sectarian and non-partisan association, independent of both government and business. In its inception and development, it was an organization imagined and organized by women, and its policies and procedures were determined by women. Mrs. Marshall became its first president with Mrs. W.R. Lang acting as the liaison officer between the new organization and the NCWC.[81] Within a year this body had "achieved such aims as ceiling prices on butter and lard...the lifting of the embargo on certain vegetables, removal of sales tax on some essential foods and articles of clothing, informative labelling, and fixed standards."[82]

[78] "Report re: questionnaire," W.R. Lang, 3 May 1946 in NCWC, MG 28 I 25, N.A.C.
[79] Yearbook, 1946, p. 38.
[80] Yearbook, 1948, p. 104.
[81] Shaw, Proud Heritage, p. 91.
[82] Ibid., p. 92.

1947 was also the year of the fourth triennial meeting of the International Council of Women, in Philadelphia. The state of the post-war world was clearly a matter of concern for the Canadian Council, which had spent a large part of the 1946 annual meeting discussing resolutions of the "Inter-Continental Conference," a gathering held in May 1946, in New York, as a necessary planning step for the Philadelphia meeting. There were two hundred delegates there, twenty-five of them from Canada. Four-fifths of the latter were directly linked to Council, either as convenors of council committees, provincial presidents of council, or presidents affiliated at the national level. Among the rest, there were two women reported as attending who had no affiliation to any group, Senator Cairine Wilson and Hanka Romanchych; Madame H.E. Vautelet was named as representing French Canadian women; Mrs. Alfred Watt as representing the Associated Country Women of the World; and Dr. Olive Russell, the Executive Assistant to the Director-General of the Rehabilitation Department of Veterans' Affairs was there in her official capacity.[83]

Five areas of concern were reported and plans made to lobby national governments for action in each case. The problems discussed encompassed starvation; homelessness; denial of human rights; nationalism; and economic barriers between states. These became the major items on the agenda of the International Council meeting. At the Fiftieth Anniversary meeting of the International Council of Women, which had taken place in Edinburgh, July 11–21, 1938, it was estimated that the gathering represented "forty million women in thirty-six countries."[84] The number of Councils at the Philadelphia meeting had fallen to twenty-four: twelve councils in Europe had disappeared, those of the Baltic Countries and Bulgaria, Yugoslavia, Portugal, Hungary, Poland, Czechoslovakia and Romania. Madame Plaminkova, the President of the Czechoslovakian National Council, had been imprisoned and executed by the Nazis, Princess Cantacuzene, President of the Romanian Council had died in confinement. Rosa Manus, President of the Netherlands National Council and Mrs. Siemienska, President of Poland's Council, had both died in concentration camps.[85]

The Philadelphia meeting could not have taken place had it not been generously funded by the National Council of the United States, which covered the majority of the travel expenses of the women from Europe. The work

---

83 *Yearbook*, 1946, p. 50.
84 *Yearbook*, 1939, pp. 142-55.
85 Anon., *Women in a Changing World*, p. 78.

done took three forms: firstly, restatement of the aims of the Council; secondly, reorganization of its bureaucracy; and thirdly, definition of the nature
of its relationship to the United Nations. The restatement of the aims of the
International Council of Women was simple. The movement existed in order
"to unite women of the whole world without distinction of race, nationality,
faith or class...in order to promote the welfare of the individual, the family
and humanity."[86] Baroness Boll, who concluded her Presidency of the
International Council at this meeting, and had spent much of her term as a
prisoner of the Germans, told the delegates that "the education of women
who have not yet reached your standard is your responsibility. As long as
somewhere in the world woman is still treated as a slave, the rights we have
fought for may be called in question and the emancipation of women is but a
word. The position of women anywhere affects their position everywhere."[87]

The reorganization of the bureaucracy of the I.C.W. was also a fairly
simple matter, involving the establishment of a secretariat in Zurich, under
the presidency of Madame Jeanne Eder-Schwartzer, herself of Swiss nationality. The complicated task was the initiation of formal linkage of the
International Council with the United Nations and its major agencies. The
decisions arrived at would have consequences, later on, for women who
worked through the Canadian Council. The International Council was given,
and retains, "consultative status — Category 2," a status that was raised to
Category I in 1969. It therefore has the right to be represented on United
Nations agencies such as UNESCO (United Nations Education, Scientific
and Cultural Organization), FAO (Food and Agricultural Organization), ILO
(International Labour Organization), WHO (World Health Organization),
UNEP (United Nations Environmental Program), UNIDO (United Nations
Industrial Development Organization), UNCTAD (United Nations
Conference on Trade and Development), UNDP (United Nations
Development Program) and all the economic commissions of the United
Nations. Furthermore, the International Council has almost always had the
right to send delegates to major United Nations Conferences. More important
still is that it is entitled to suggest women for United Nation's committee
work, and to ensure that the ideas of the International Council committees

---

[86] *Ibid.*, p. 82.
[87] Baroness Boll had been born in Ghent in 1877 and studied in Paris in the nineties. In 1898 she
      married an industrialist, whose position enabled her to concentrate on her volunteer activities.
      These were centred upon health questions. She spent a considerable part of the First World War
      imprisoned by the Germans because of her links to the peace movement and her work for prison-
      ers-of-war. *Ibid.*, p. 83 and p. 110.

become part of the working papers of similar United Nations bodies. As will be seen, ideas have emerged from the grass roots work of local councils in Canada to be used as the basis for possible United Nations resolutions on the rights of women and children in debates of the sixties and seventies.

As Canada began to confront the aftermath of war, the women who worked through Council turned their attention back to the community work needed within their own towns and villages. This orientation did not mean, however, that national and international issues were abandoned, but signifies instead a change of emphasis. In some ways, the forties were an uncomplicated era for women, priorities being set by the requirements of the war effort and the initial stages of demobilization. Even so, ideas expressed during these years provided the foundation for the generation that would work towards a revolution in the position of women in Canada — the generation born in the forties, and reaching its full maturity in the seventies and eighties.

CHAPTER 8

Reorganization and Continuity
1950 – 1960

TO SELECT A particular year, or even a decade, as the time when a major shift occurs in the orientation of a long-lasting and eclectic body, such as the National Council of Women of Canada, is to ask for an argument. The probability of dispute is especially high in the case of Council, an association which has always prided itself on maintaining the ideals and traditions of its founders. Was there really a fundamental change, if the association itself did not explicitly articulate it? Even if one can point to a significant alteration over time, is it really accurate to suggest that it can be seen as beginning with a particular event, at this time, rather than with that event at that time? Despite the difficulties an attempt of this kind must be made from time to time, because long-lasting institutions do alter over time, if only to survive, and the pattern of alteration is an important part of their historical development.

There is in fact no doubt that the Council changed significantly some time during the third quarter century of its existence. After all, Council was, and remains, an integral part of Canadian society and Canada altered significantly between 1943 and 1967. The immediate post-war years witnessed fundamental changes in the ordering of Canadian society. As Desmond Morton has remarked, "it was the combination of social reform and free enterprise that allowed Mackenzie King his narrow election victory on June 11, 1945. By the end of the month, family allowance cheques had reached most Canadian mothers....Means-tested old-age pensions and provincially funded allowances for the blind and for abandoned mothers helped to create a welfare state that was utterly unprecedented for Canada."[1] Morton went on

---

[1] Desmond Morton, "Strains of Affluence," in Craig Brown ed., *The Illustrated History of Canada*, (Toronto, 1987), p. 470.

to conclude that "without really admitting the fact, post-war Canada had evolved into a social democracy."[2] Since the Council itself was the product of women's volunteer work in associations largely dedicated to social service, the arrival of a state-organized system of social welfare was bound to change the aims and methods of many Council members.

Further, the effects of these profound changes in the context of volunteer social welfare work were deepened by a demographic transformation of Canada. Immigration was important but natural increase accounted for the greater part of the country's population growth after 1940. The population of Canada was 11,507,000 in 1941; 14,009,000 in 1951; 16,081,000 in 1956; 18,238,000 in 1961 and reached 20,015,000 in 1966.[3] Between 1946 and 1959, the fertility rate of young Canadian women climbed steadily, and that of older Canadian women at a comparable rate fell.[4] In 1956, nearly one half of all live births consisted of third or later children.[5] While this baby boom was taking place, immigration to Canada revived sharply; 13% of the newcomers were refugees, and between the end of 1946 and the end of 1958 Canada absorbed 223,299 such people, "chiefly Czechs, Germans, Jews, Hungarians, Poles, Ukrainians, Russians and Yugoslavians."[6] In total, net migration brought roughly 1,336,000 people to Canada between 1951 and 1966.[7] The population growth swung the urban/rural balance of Canadian life irrevocably in favour of the cities. In 1951 the census counted 7,941,222 urban dwellers and 6,068,207 rural Canadians. In 1966 there were 12,625,848 inhabitants in the cities and 7,389,096 people living in the countryside.[8]

At first sight, the emergence of a state-structured welfare net and an increase of nearly 25% in population within sixteen years, did not seem to produce any radical alteration in Canadian priorities, or in those of Council. Yet in 1966 the country, while superficially much the same as in 1951, was in the process of confronting, in the words of the preliminary report of the Royal Commission on Bilingualism and Biculturalism, "without being fully conscious of it...the greatest crisis in its history."[9] The very nature of

2   *Ibid.*, p. 471.
3   Leary, ed., *Historical Statistics*, Tables A78–93.
4   Robert Bothwell, Ian Drummond, and John English, *Canada Since 1945*, (Toronto, 1989), pp. 10–11.
5   Prentice, et al., *Canadian Women*, p. 311.
6   Bothwell, et al., *Canada Since 1945*, p. 13.
7   Leary, ed., *Historical Statistics*, Series A339–349, "Changes in population through natural increase and migration...."
8   *Ibid.*, Series A67–69.
9   Morton, "Affluence," p. 496.

Canadian nationhood was being called into question. In that same year, Council had joined with other, non-affiliated associations of women in calling for the establishment of a Royal Commission on the Status of Women, a Commission which would contribute to a transformation, already in the making, of views about women's place in Canadian society and, so far as the Council was concerned, to radical change in its influence and power.

For both Canada and the Council, the political trends which were to lead to ongoing and passionate debates about the shape and nature of Canadian federalism in the seventies and eighties were only part of the forces shaping a path of fundamental change in the fifties and sixties. By 1967 there were not only more people in Canada, but a greater number of them whose ethnic heritage was neither British nor French. For example, the arrival of Italians and Greeks, Ukrainians and Poles had, by 1961, transformed Toronto. In 1939 the city had been as firmly British in its ethnicity as any in England; in 1961, Protestants had become a minority within its limits.[10] While Ontario and Quebec continued to hold the majority of the Canadian population, Alberta and British Columbia had significantly increased in size.[11] In contrast, Quebec's proportion of the total population of the country shrank. During the fifties, the prosperity of the country masked the extent to which these changes demanded a new political vision.

Similarly, a most significant alteration in Canadian society and one which, then as now, is only imperfectly understood, was the changing nature of women's participation in the paid labour force. Much emphasis has been laid by historians on the fall in women's participation in the paid labour force immediately after the war. The authors of *Canadian Women: A History* remark that "in 1944, at the peak of wartime employment, one third of all women over the age of 15 were in the paid labour force. Two years later, only one quarter were working for pay. Only in 1967 did women's participation rate surpass the 1944 level."[12] But, as they themselves note, an argument can be made that the decline in the period immediately following the war appears to have been caused less by the withdrawal of women from the workforce than by the lower participation rate of younger women entering paid work.

As well, the overall percentages of women's participation rate in the

---

10 *Ibid.*, p. 483.
11 The growth for these provinces between 1951 and 1966 was, for Alberta, 939,501 to 1,463,203; for British Columbia, 1,165,210 to 1,873,674. Ontario increased its population from 4,597,542 to 6,960,870 and Quebec from 4,055,681 to 5,780,845. Leary, ed., *Historical Statistics*, Series A1.
12 Prentice, et al., *Canadian Women*, p. 311.

labour force, and the percentage share of women in the paid labour force both rose steadily, decade by decade. In other words, more women worked outside the home, and their importance to the labour force also grew. In 1941, just over 20% of women worked, making up 18.5% of the labour force; in 1951, 24% of women worked, making up 22% of the labour force; in 1961, 29.5% of women worked, making up 27.3% of the labour force and in 1971, the corresponding figures were 39.9% and 34.6%.[13] Moreover, as is pointed out in *Canadian Women*, the proportion of married women among paid female workers continued to rise. "In 1941 only slightly more than 10 percent of all employed women were married; during the war the estimated proportion was from 25 to 35 per cent. By 1961 nearly half of all female workers were married."[14]

It remains true, of course, that throughout these decades the majority of married women still worked exclusively in the home, and were outside the paid labour force. But the sea-change had begun and the remaining decades of the twentieth century saw an uninterrupted growth in the participation of women in the public work world. By 1991, 45% of the labour force was female and 60% of women worked.[15] This new balance produced deep divisions among women. Working-class women, that is to say women who work with their hands, are paid wages instead of salaries, do not employ other people and, as the wives and daughters of men similarly situated, have a very different perspective on paid work from that of women engaged in prestige occupations, as salaried employees or as self-employed professionals.[16] There has often been a considerable lack of understanding, by some feminists, of women who prefer their homes to poorly paid, repetitive and boring office and factory work. This uncomprehending attitude has also been displayed towards women who, given the choice, have preferred not to undertake paid labour, even if the work offered has been both highly remunerative and interesting. After 1950, the political and ideological divisions, which had always existed among women no less than among men, gradually became much more obvious and important. As a new wave of feminism gathered strength in the nineteen fifties, these divisions grew within women's volunteer associations and would critically affect the future of Council.

---

[13] Pat Armstrong and Hugh Armstrong,"Women's Work in the Labour Force," in Arlene Tigar McClaren, ed., *Gender and Society Creating a Canadian Women's Sociology*, (Toronto, 1988), Table I: p. 276.
[14] Prentice, et al., *Canadian Women*, p. 312.
[15] *Globe and Mail*, March 3, 1993.
[16] On this, see Elizabeth Roberts, *Women's Work 1840-1940*, (London, 1988).

In the years leading up to the Diamond Jubilee of Council, celebrated at the annual meeting held in Winnipeg from June 15 to June 19, 1953, the transformations were almost imperceptible. The Presidency of Mrs. R. J. Marshall concluded with no major change of direction. In her 1950 address, Mrs. Marshall had said that "Council...still stands pre-eminently for the cause of women, for representation on public bodies, for equality of pay and opportunity, for women's contribution to the public good."[17] The twenty-six resolutions forwarded to the Executive were, to a very large extent, concerned with topics that had been the essence of Council work over the decades: town planning; the rights and responsibilities of Canadian citizens; the need for sufficient nursing personnel, and therefore, the need to pay attention to the training of nurses; the proper treatment of veterans; the need to tackle alcoholism; the protection of Canadian natural resources; the improvement of the penal system; and education. These topics had been constant themes of Council meetings, as had the substance of the concluding resolution, dealing with proposals to improve the "continuing function, increased efficiency and expansion of the Council."[18]

There were four resolutions, however, which pointed to future directions; one of them was tabled, and three were carried. The proposal of the Toronto Local Council to have "the Bill of Rights incorporated in the Canadian Constitution so that human rights and fundamental freedoms may be ensured to all Canadians" was tabled, being sent out to all local councils for discussion. The three resolutions that were carried were brought forward by the Committee of Officers of Council. They all concerned the rights of Canadian Indians. The first (no. 6 of the resolutions presented at this annual meeting), read as follows:

> Whereas all races, with the exception of Canadian Indians, are entitled to vote in Federal elections;
>
> whereas no reason exists for this discrimination against the aboriginal inhabitants of Canada who, by their outstanding service in two Great Wars and by their many cultural and economic contributions to the general life of the community, have demonstrated their ability to take their proper place in the government of the country in accordance with democratic principles;
>
> Be it resolved that this Council urges that when the Dominion

---

17 *Yearbook*, 1950, p. 12.
18 *Ibid.*, pp. 21–32.

Elections Act is amended, the Canadian Indians be given the right to vote in the manner as citizens of other racial origins.[19]

The second resolution asked that "Indians be granted old age and blind pensions in the same manner as citizens of other racial origin." The third requested that "Indians be given a more direct voice in the conduct of Indian education." There was no immediate follow-up to these resolutions that year, beyond the fact that they were brought forward, along with the other resolutions directed to the federal government, at the meeting of the Council Executive with the Prime Minister and members of the cabinet.[20] But issues relating to the status of Indian peoples was a new preoccupation for Council, and one that it would continue to address in the coming years.

In her last presidential address, at the fifty-eighth annual meeting, held in Montreal, September 24-29, 1951, Mrs. Marshall commented on lobbying techniques involving the presentation of resolutions at meetings with the federal cabinet. While she admitted that many resolutions "have been repeated from year to year" she felt that there had been a fair level of success, especially in matters pertaining to amendments to the penal code and to questions of health care. In particular, she attributed to Council lobbying the right "to apply the Federal grant not only to hospitals but to nurses' residences, thus ensuring accommodation for a larger number of nurses in training." During the fifties and sixties, the Prime Minister of the day and a number of Cabinet Ministers met annually with Council, no matter which party was in power. The success of these meetings depended on the extent to which the Council President, and those members of her Executive chosen to accompany her, were properly prepared for the meeting, and on the degree of seriousness with which the government members took the delegation. In January, 1953, for example, Mrs. Marshall brought forward resolutions concerning, among other issues, the succession rights of women, women's pension rights, the control of gambling, the need for some censorship of children's reading material, and the supervision of convicted sexual offenders. In his diary Lester Pearson recorded the meeting as follows:

Today at 12:00 o'clock the cabinet, or part of them (some of my male colleagues must have been frightened), received a delegation

---

[19] *Ibid.*, p. 24. Indians were granted the vote in federal elections in 1960.
[20] *Yearbook*, 1951, p. 19.

from the National Council of Women, who wished to present resolutions to the Government. They were a strange bag — I mean the resolutions, not the ladies — notably particularly for the relatively inconsequential things that some of them dealt with, while a lot of important developments or possible developments, were ignored. There was nothing about peace, the United Nations, or international affairs, but something on race track betting and sex offenses. The P.M. was at his best with the ladies and by the end of the hour they were practically on his neck.[21]

The delegation from the Council were insufficiently focused to make a major impression on their audience, and those meeting them had little sensitivity to the fundamental importance of resolutions on the discrimination against women present in Canadian property laws or relating to children's vulnerability to sexual predators. Later meetings in the decade were more successful as the Council become more focused and the government more aware of the importance of the organization's core concerns.

Indeed, after 1952, members of Council were regularly appointed as representatives to government bodies. Council members had been nominated for such appointments in the past, and had often been named to different posts, but the relationship became much more formal in 1952. That year, Mrs. Turner Bone, who had succeeded Mrs. Marshall as President in 1951, was a member for Council of the National Advisory Committee on Manpower, the Physical Fitness Awards Committee and the National Advisory Council on Vocational Training. Similarly, Mrs. G.D. Finlayson, a member of the Ottawa Local Council and a national vice-president, was a member of the National Employment Committee.[22]

This close relationship with the federal government sometimes disturbed relationships among Council members. In the fall of 1951, Mrs. Marshall went to Paris as a Canadian delegate to the General Assembly of the United Nations. There were newspaper reports that the Ontario delegates to the 1951 annual meeting in Montreal alleged that this "free ride to Paris, all expenses paid, for Mrs. Marshall is the government's reward for her management of the annual meeting."[23] The Ontario delegates remarked that they had wanted a full discussion of the possibility of price control but had been ruled out of

---

21 Pearson Diary, January 27, 1953. NAC, MG 26 N8, v. 5, cited John English, *The Life of Lester B. Pearson*, (Toronto, 1993), vol.II, p. 73.
22 *Yearbook*, 1953, p. 2.
23 Newspaper clipping: no identifying information in NCWC files, MG I25, vol. 91, #11, NAC.

order by Mrs. Marshall. The issue was presented by Mrs. W.R. Lang, the liaison officer between the Council and the Canadian Association of Consumers, whose report argued that the time had not yet come for a renewal of price control. Mrs. Lang pointed out that price controls are only workable for a limited length of time and in times of real emergency. For the time being, she and the Consumers' Association counselled a "wait-and-see" attitude."[24]

Some of the Ontario delegates, however, charged that the Montreal annual meeting was "so dominated by friends of the government that it might well have been a Liberal party meeting." Lester B. Pearson, then Minister for External Affairs, asserted that Mrs. Marshall was named a delegate to Paris "because we feel a sense of obligation to the National Council of Women of Canada for the work it has done." Mrs. Hardy, Council President from 1941 to 1946, issued a statement that read in part as follows:

> From 1931 to the present, presidents of the National Council of Women have each been singled out for recognition by appointments to important government boards. The members of Council should never lose sight of the fact that our great organisation is non-political and is so recognized by the Dominion government.

She added:

> From the appointment of Miss Winnifred Kydd as the only woman delegate to the Disarmament Conference,1932, by a Conservative government, to the appointment of Mrs. Marshall, the government, recognizing the influence and leadership of Council, made these appointments to represent Canadian women as a whole and in no sense have these appointments been political.[25]

This unedifying squabble died away under the cool hand of Mrs. Turner Bone, the incoming President, but it was an indication that the political neutrality of Council might be harder to preserve in the future than it had been in the past, as many of the women who gave time and energy to volunteer work also became involved in mainstream political party work.

Mrs. Turner Bone had been born in Toronto to Alfred Price and his wife. Mr. Price started to work with the C.P.R. when he was thirteen and remained

---

[24] *Yearbook*, 1951, p. 114.
[25] *Ibid.*

with the company all his life. He rose to a the position of general manager.[26] His daughter, Enid Margaret, attended schools in many different parts of Canada before enrolling at McGill University. There she studied with Stephen Leacock, who was very dubious about admitting women to university. However, his half-hearted acceptance of her idea that she study what happened to the women in factories after the conclusion of the war in 1918 enabled her to write the M.A. thesis which was later published under the title "Change in the Industrial Occupations of Women in Montreal, 1914–18."

In 1922 Enid Margaret Price married Allan Turner Bone, a construction engineer whom she met at McGill University, and the young couple travelled extensively before the family settled in Montreal.[27] Her work for the Council began through her service to the Local Council of Montreal, and her children remember their house being strewn with pamphlets entitled "Pourquoi Maman ne peut pas voter?" and their mother talking endlessly on the telephone, in both English and French, about the need for action on immediate issues of the day.

In her address to the Winnipeg meeting in 1953, Mrs. Turner Bone emphasized the "increasing awareness of the Government of Canada of the stature and importance of the N.C.W.C," as evidenced by the continuing appointment of Council women to government bodies.[28] That year there were fifty-one local councils, six Provincial Councils — British Columbia, Manitoba, New Brunswick, Nova Scotia, Ontario and Saskatchewan — and twenty-two nationally organized societies affiliated.[29] Since 1945, Councils had appeared, or reappeared, in Brandon, 1952; Fredericton, 1946; Kelowna, 1950; Mission City, 1949; and Orillia, 1953. There were 160 different societies affiliated at either the local or provincial level. Some existed only in a particular town, such as the Auxiliaries for the Police Association in Peterborough, and were therefore only linked to the particular local council. Others were societies with a number of branches which were only linked to a limited number of local councils. For example, the Women's Auxiliaries of the Locomotive Engineers and Firemen were members of the Local Councils of Brandon, Medicine Hat and West Algoma, but not of councils elsewhere. Other union-linked memberships which were only associated with one town included the Auxiliary of the Railway Conductors in Medicine Hat, the

---

26 The author is indebted to Elizabeth McEwen, Mrs. Turner Bone's daughter, for the biographical details about her parents' life.
27 Anon. notes, NCWC papers: MG28 I25, vol. 94, #14, NAC.
28 *Yearbook*, 1953, p. 36.
29 *Ibid.*, p. 26.

Auxiliary of the United Mineworkers of America in Nanaimo, and the International Woodworkers of America in Vancouver. Significant membership of associations at the local council level included the University Women's clubs, participating in twenty-two local councils; the V.O.N., in twenty-four local councils. The Women's Institutes belonged to twenty Local Councils, from Kamloops, British Columbia to Yarmouth, Nova Scotia, and also to the Manitoba Provincial Council.

The backbone of Council, however, was the support of Protestant women, all councils having women from one or more of the following churches: Anglican, Adventist, Baptist, Presbyterian, Unitarian and United. What is important about the Protestant core of Council, however, is that it did not produce a monolithic religious body composed solely of like-minded believers. The organization really did maintain a welcome for women of all creeds and beliefs. It is true that there was an interesting variation in the membership pattern of the women's organizations of the Catholic church. The Catholic Women's League joined the local councils in the Maritimes and in the West but not in Ontario or Quebec.[30] They were an important source of strength in these provinces but Council stands on divorce, on planned parenthood — and later, on abortion — caused some members of the Catholic hierarchy to doubt the organization's claims to ideological neutrality and forbid Catholic organizations to join. The Ottawa Local Council solved this problem by inviting the Catholic organizations to affiliate through individual members, who could not vote and therefore would not be required to comment on policies involving a possible conflict with Church doctrine.[31] In the western provinces the women's auxiliaries of the Ukrainian churches joined Council.

Jewish membership was also widespread. In 1953, the B'nai B'rith Women were members of the Councils of Montreal, Ottawa, Halifax, Hamilton and Windsor, the Hebrew Benevolent Society Sisterhood were members of the Councils of Niagara Falls, Ottawa, Regina and Yarmouth while Hadassah was a member of eighteen local councils. The National Council of Jewish Women held membership in twelve councils, all of them in large cities: Calgary, Edmonton, Hamilton, Kingston, London, Montreal, Ottawa, Regina, Saskatoon, Toronto, Vancouver and Winnipeg.

As well as religious associations, all three political parties were linked to

---

[30] See Appendix for listing for 1953, *Ibid.*, pp. 150–154.
[31] First Annual Report of the Local Council of Ottawa, 1894–5 in the Bronson Family Papers: NAC.

21. Mrs. Allan Turner Bone, President 1951–1956

a number of Councils. The C.C.F. guild was a member of ten local councils in the western provinces, as well as the Saskatchewan Provincial Council and the Councils of Brantford, London and Windsor. The Women's Liberal Club Association was a member of nineteen local councils. The Women's Progressive Conservative Association was a member of twenty-four local councils and also a member of the Ontario Provincial Council.

Apart from the groups listed above, the W.C.T.U. provided the largest membership in 1953, with affiliation at the local level to thirty-five councils and also to the Provincial Councils of Saskatchewan and British Columbia. Again, given the strength of this support, it is interesting that Council did not adopt prohibition as a cause. Health workers were almost equally enthusiastic supporters, the Hospital Aid Auxiliaries' Associations held membership in thirty-one local councils and in the Manitoba Provincial Association; the Nurses' Association and Registered Nurses were linked with twenty-eight local councils as well as with the Provincial Councils of Saskatchewan and Nova Scotia. Both the Business and Professional Women's Clubs and the I.O.D.E had membership in twenty-seven local councils.

In its sixtieth year of operation, the diverse membership of Council was as difficult to organize as it had always been. It was the particular mix of membership at the local council level that gave the organization its strong identity, but it also produced, and it still produces, friction. No local council was a carbon-copy of any other and the membership of large councils, such as Vancouver and Toronto, varied as much as did that of the smaller ones, such as Chilliwack and Fredericton. Much of the Diamond Jubilee meeting was taken up with discussing possible revisions to the constitution and by-laws, particularly the latter. From 1951 to 1953 the national office had carried out a survey of the membership regarding their wishes in this matter, and proposals for reform were accordingly presented by the Executive at the Winnipeg meeting.

Certain changes, dealing with the number, terms of reference and functioning of Standing Committees were immediately adopted. One of the best reforms can already be seen in the Yearbook for 1953 — published immediately after the meeting — where the previous list of twenty Standing Committees and six ad hoc Committees has been reorganized into one of twelve Standing Committees, six Administrative Standing Committees and three "Special Committees." The twelve Standing committees established were Arts and Letters; Economics; Education; Films; Health; Housing; International Affairs; Laws; Migration and Citizenship; Radio and Television; Social Welfare; and Trades and Professions. Further, short and clear terms of reference are to be found, printed under the name of each Standing Committee, and it was made clear that "these terms of reference are applicable to Local Committees also."[32]

Proposals for other reforms were limited, because the essential finding of the survey had been the number of organizational problems described in detail, which its members felt were urgent, rather than suggestions for solving those problems. But there were, in these proposals for reform, two indications of a new path for Council; one related to substance and one to style. Under the heading for substance, a number of suggestions displayed strong evidence of grass roots discontent. For example, it was proposed there should be more opportunities for meeting between the provincial president and the national president, and greater attention to the interpretation, by local councils to their affiliates, of the work of the National Council. Further, the actual concept of a national office with an executive secretary was brought forward for debate, and the suggestion made that the work at that level could be carried on by a full-time volunteer. This, be it noted, was in a year when mimeographed sheets despatched from the office numbered 58,000 and the volume of outgoing correspondence had risen to 16,071![33]

There was also considerable dissatisfaction expressed over the relationship between local and Provincial Councils, especially in Ontario. There the Provincial Council wanted a much tighter control over local councils than had been the case in the past, arguing that "Local Council reports, correspondence and finances should be passed through the Provincial Councils to the National and vice versa."[34] The Provincial Council of Ontario considered that lack of clear organization was a major weakness of the Council movement. It asserted that the work of the Provincial Councils, which dealt with many matters of importance to women at the level of the provincial governments, was not recognized. Neither the question of the status of Provincial Councils within the Council structure, nor problems of Provincial Council funding, had ever been addressed in such a way as to recognize the contribution made by this level of Council organization. There was no resolution on the Ontario suggestions, partly because local councils fought against the territorial ambitions of their Provincial bodies. The annual meeting sensibly decided to postpone action on these and other matters of constitutional change.

---

[32] See Appendix.
[33] *Yearbook*, 1953, p. 22.
[34] Vivien R. Kerr, *A Flame of Compassion: A History of The Provincial Council of Women of Ontario*, (Toronto, 1967), p. 59.

Dissatisfaction of local councils with the leadership at the national level was not new, but there was a sharpness of tone in the debate in 1953 that was only blunted by the exercise of considerable skill by the President.

So far, the indication of the change of style foreshadowed, in some ways, a much greater predicament for Council than debates about institutional structures. The rhetoric of argument in 1953 was far more practical and less philosophical than it had been in the past. "The Master problem" of Council was defined, at this meeting, as the need "to achieve unity of purpose, understanding and achievement in an organization made up of three types of federated associations."[35] Mrs. Turner Bone in her Presidential address, spoke of "our objective of uniting women in Council more closely together to accomplish worthwhile aims" and she remarked that "we hold high our motto which is a command, DO unto others as ye would that they do unto you."[36]

One can argue that, in view of the increasingly secular temper of Canadian life, her words went as far as was then socially acceptable to present the philosophical basis for Council. Moreover, there was a strong hint of the need to guard against "loose living and slackening of moral standards," not only in the presidential address, but also in the reports of some standing committees, and the resolutions presented to the meeting as a whole. The Committee on Moral Standards, for example suggested that the coming year should see local councils discuss

1. Control of liquor advertising.
2. Watching the trend of television and its effect on children. Constructive ideas to be encouraged.
3. General support of committees keeping the movies clean, danger of salacious literature, control of heavy drinking, especially among teen-agers, and the use of drugs and the evils of betting.
4. Efforts to improve racial relations.
5. The elevation of home life and confirming of religious ideals.[37]

However, only eight of the fifty-one local councils sent reports to this committee. Although all Committee convenors complained, regularly, of the lack of response from local councils — the Citizenship convenor asked bitterly in this year: "WHY do women accept local Chairmanships if they do

---

35 *Yearbook*, 1953, p. 46.
36 *Ibid.*, pp. 38–9.
37 *Ibid.*, p. 100.

not assume the responsibilities connected with the Office?"[38]— this response rate was well below the average. Most convenors gathered between twenty and thirty annual reports from local councils.

The lack of response to the Committee on Moral Standards may have been due in part to the change in the emphasis of this particular committee. In the past, it had concerned itself with the need to provide active support for alcoholics, for the children of women in the sex industry, and alternative reading materials to replace magazines and books deemed obscene. Such resolutions were not brought forward in 1953. In the future, the agenda of this committee would become the concern of the Standing Committees on Education, Films, Radio and Television and Social Welfare.

In the early fifties, though there was no obvious change in the general tenor of proceedings at the annual meetings, it is possible to detect a diminishing emphasis on the philosophy of Council. The rhetoric of debate was shifting away from community service to the political needs of women. Nevertheless, the immediate aims of Council, as outlined by Mrs. Turner Bone in her address in 1953, were in harmony with past Council goals. They were: "1. Services for children, 2. Current needs of new Canadians, 3. Problems of older workers, 4. Services for the older folk." Furthermore, resolutions brought forward by the major standing Committees that year continued the tradition of working for women's rights in marriage, for the care of the sick and the indigent, and for the recognition of women through appointment to public positions. One such resolution protested Ontario's action over the Dower Act in 1952, which had abolished the rights of a woman separated from her husband to one third interest in his property. It asked for Council action to request this be reversed "until legal recognition is gained of a wife's right to a fair share of the estate built up jointly by husband and wife in marriage."[39] Among the other resolutions one pointed out that requiring blind persons to submit to a means test was an indignity that neither stimulated the blind to contribute to their own support nor helped those in real need; another asked the federal government to name a women to the Civil Service Commission and to recognize outstanding Canadian women by appointing them to the Senate. As well, Council continued to combat discrimination against women in the paid labour force and the Executive was asked to thank government for establishing the Woman's Bureau in the Department of

---

[38] *Ibid.,* p. 76.
[39] *Ibid.,* p. 54.

Labour. It was hoped the new Bureau would provide solid information on the particular problems that faced women in paid employment. Marian Royce was appointed its first Director in 1954.

At the sixty-first annual meeting, which took place in Fredericton, June 25–July 1, 1954, Mrs. Turner Bone remarked on her visit, during the past year, to the nine local councils of British Columbia. Before she retired from office in 1956, she would visit every single local council, ending with visits to Orillia, Windsor, Hamilton and Brantford.[40] This pastoral care meant a great deal to the local membership, and formed an integral part of the great effort by Mrs. Turner Bone throughout her presidency to improve relations among varying components of Council. One of the most effective moves to this end was the organization, at the annual general meetings, of separate sessions where representatives of the various levels of Council could meet with their peers. Thus the presidents of the nationally affiliated societies were brought together, as were the presidents of the Provincial Councils and the presidents of the local councils. This led to the establishment of a Constitution Committee in 1956, as a Standing Administrative Committee, with terms of reference stating that it was:

1. To be responsible that newly made amendments are written into the Constitution and By-Laws and that Federated Associations are advised of them.
2. To give rulings as required through the year, and at meetings of the Council.
3. To receive and review, proposed changes in Provincial and Local Council Constitution (sic) and advise N.C.W. [41]

Mrs. Turner Bone's administrative talent was also applied to financial organization. Membership dues were expected to cover general expenses related to organizing the annual meeting, running the national office and the President's execution of her duties. Additional monies were available from the Foundation Fund, and these were, in principle, to cover half the expenses of delegates to the annual meeting, and any shortfall in the resources necessary for the operation of Council at the national level. The Foundation Fund had always been run by a special committee. In 1956, however, Council also

---

[40] *Yearbook,* 1955, p. 34.
[41] *Yearbook,* 1956, p. 17.

established a Finance Committee as an Administrative Standing Committee with the following terms of reference:

1. To study the finances of N.C.W. in relation to its program of activities and to the finances of its federated societies.
2. To consider and make recommendations on measures for raising funds which will establish and keep the finances of N.C.W. on a satisfactory basis.
3. To set up a close liaison with the Treasurer and the Chairman of the Foundation Fund, so that facts relevant to the progress of the current money raising projects may be available to the Finance Committee.[42]

Mrs. Turner Bone's final gifts to Council were administrative committees dealing with publicity and with the relationship between the National Council and the International Council of Women, also established in 1956.[43] The latter committee was particularly important because Canada was to host the triennial meeting of the I.C.W. in Montreal in 1957.

Although it took time and energy to oversee these changes in the institutional structure and to pay visits to local councils, Mrs. Turner Bone also found the stamina to carry on with normal activities of a Council president, including meeting with the Prime Minister and selected members of the Cabinet,[44] and with the Presidents of the nationally affiliated associations. She also accepted speaking engagements to explain the work of Council, attended meetings dealing with the I.C.W., and put together both a survey of the recent achievements of Council and a plan for the coming year's activity, presented at each annual meeting. In 1954, her presidential address emphasized the need to encourage "more women to enter public life" and "...women to enter voluntary work." As well, she wished Council "to examine the effect of an employed mother on the children and home life."[45]

Sessions on all three topics were organized at the 1945 annual meeting. The session on working mothers reported to the full meeting of Council that,

---

[42] *Ibid.*, p. 17.
[43] For terms of reference, see Appendix D.
[44] For the meeting of December 11, 1953, see *Yearbook*, 1954, p. 20. In 1954, the meeting was with the Acting Prime Minister, C.D. Howe and eleven cabinet ministers, *Yearbook*, 1955, p. 33; and in 1955 the meeting was again with the Prime Minister and eleven members of the cabinet, *Yearbook*, 1956, p. 111.
[45] *Yearbook*, 1954, p. 29.

after considering both the good and the ill effects, "the services of working mothers are an essential part of our society." "It was felt," the report noted, "that the right of every woman to express herself as she wishes should be protected; that we have no right, either by law or by planning, to determine the career of a woman, whether married or single."[46] In conclusion it was emphasized that:

the first and basic thing is to break down the prejudice which exists against working women outside the home and to educate the communities regarding the social problems which may be created, and this with a view to solving these problems. More father and mother co-operation in planning the care of home and children. Adjustment by industry of working hours to meet the needs of mothers. Establishment of day nurseries and nursery schools in housing developments and in industry and by support of Government. More and better supervised recreation facilities and playgrounds opened all year round. More child guidance clinics and guidance officers in schools.

Local councils were urged to discuss these issues over the coming year and to present suggestions about "how social legislation may be brought about to put these suggestions into effect."

It was particularly appropriate that the issue of working mothers was the subject of general discussion at this meeting, given the unanimous approval of a resolution brought forward by the Toronto Local Council. This resolution came with a lengthy preamble, pointing out that "the women of the Province of Ontario, spearheaded by a group of members of the Business and Professional Women's clubs, which Clubs are affiliated with the Council of Women at local, provincial and national levels, were successful in having Bill No. 120, 'An Act to ensure Fair Remuneration to Female Employees' passed by the Ontario Legislature in 1951. It went on to note that in a recent debate in Parliament on Bill No. 2, a measure to require equal pay for equal work within federal areas of jurisdiction, Milton F. Gregg, V.C., the federal Minister of Labour stated: "I feel it is ...significant that the National Council of Women, in making their recommendations to the government, did not mention this matter." The resolution itself was simple: the National Council

---

[46] *Ibid.*, p. 47.

of Women of Canada was urged to make representations to the government of Canada that "legislation be enacted to provide equal remuneration for men and women workers for work of equal value."[47]

The Council was appalled at the lapse of its traditional, explicit support for equal pay for equal work, something which had been an integral part of its resolutions from the time of its foundation. Senator Muriel Fergusson[48] was present at this annual meeting as a representative of the Business and Professional Women and she urged Council to support the campaign of that association for equal pay. Council was particularly shaken by the fact that such support had not been included in its explicit lobbying work for ten years. As a result, it unanimously approved the resolution and girded itself for action. Within two years, Milton Gregg, still Minister of Labour, introduced government legislation to implement equal pay "to cover over 70,000 women working under federal jurisdiction." He admitted that his action was "largely taken because of the pressure exerted by the National Council of Women, including [his] own wife and the Business and Professional Women's Clubs."[49]

At the same time as action was taken at the national level, Provincial Councils put pressure on their respective legislatures. In 1956, Manitoba and Nova Scotia were both able to report that their approaches had led to promises to enact similar legislation to ensure "Equal pay for equal work."[50] The report from Halifax emphasized that the legislation in that province "would be a result of the culmination of the persistent and continuous efforts of the Women's Council and the Federation of Business and Professional Women's Clubs throughout the province."[51]

The annual meeting of 1955, the sixty-second, was held in Saskatoon, from May 16 to May 20. It is clear from reports Provincial Councils brought forward this year, that these bodies were playing a more assertive role in the

---

47 *Ibid.,* p. 39.
48 She was born on May 26, 1899 in Shediac, New Brunswick, the daughter of James McQueen and Julia Jackson. She graduated from Mount Allison with a B.A. in 1921 and then read law in her father's law office, passing the New Brunswick bar exams in 1925. She married Aubry S. Fergusson, also a lawyer, in the fall of 1926, and they settled in Grand Falls, N.B. When her husband became ill in 1936 she returned to the practice of law and assumed several of his responsibilities: judge of the Probate Court; clerk of the County Court; clerk of the Circuit Court and town solicitor of Grand Falls. These positions were ratified on Mr. Fergusson's death in 1942. She was elected the first woman alderman of Fredericton in 1950, having moved to that city in 1947. In 1953, Prime Minister St. Laurent appointed her to the Senate.
49 Prentice, et al., *Canadian Women*, p. 333.
50 *Yearbook*, 1956, p. 137 and p. 143.
51 *Ibid.,* p. 155.

political life of their provinces. All Provincial Councils reported with pride the extent to which provincial governments had appointed Council members on government boards. Saskatchewan Council members, for example, were named to the Saskatchewan Audio-visual Board, the Advisory Committee on Curriculum Planning, the Health Institute, the Saskatchewan Physical Fitness Committee and the Education Week Committee. While some Provincial Councils were more successful than others in arranging meetings with provincial premiers, all of them were becoming sophisticated in their lobbying efforts, following up letters to ministers with telephone calls and further correspondence. British Columbia's Provincial Council with Mrs. R.H. Armstrong as its president, had had a successful year. The meeting with Premier W.A.C Bennett and his cabinet, February 24–25, 1954 had been an occasion for continuing the campaign of the British Columbian Council, which had begun in 1951, to "amend the Municipal Election Act to place the municipal franchise on the same basis as the provincial and federal Acts." In their view "the denial of civil and municipal vote to women, and to a lesser extent a number of men, who are Canadian citizens and are qualified as to residence, is a denial of specific liberty and the natural right of citizenship."[52] The first success in this undertaking was achieved with the granting of the municipal franchise to the spouses of landowners that year. Saskatchewan's Council, now in its 39th year, was involved in organizing a province-wide survey of the treatment of women in provincial jails. Here it may be noted that the Saskatoon Local Council, in particular, was interested in the "ill treatment of Indian women."[53] Manitoba Provincial Council, founded six years previously, was similarly interested in the lives of Indian and Metis women.

The Ontario Provincial Council showed particular appreciation for the visits of Mrs. Turner Bone and her argument that, within a province, local councils must use the Provincial Council, if they wished their views to be taken seriously. Her remark that "if Council is to represent the voice of Ontario women, that voice must be heard with strength at the proper time" was quoted, with approval, by the Provincial council.[54] The particular concern of Ontario in 1955 was, however, the question of employment. This province steadily brought forward questions relating to the labour market throughout the nineteen fifties. In 1951, the Council had asked for considera-

52 Hastings and Ellenwood, *Blue Bows*, p. 65.
53 Mrs. Marguerite Harrison and Mrs. Marian Beck, *The Provincial Council of Women of Saskatchewan: Provincial Council History 1919–1984*, (Regina, 1984), p. 40.
54 Kerr, *Flame*, p. 65.

22. Mrs. Rex Eaton, President 1956–1959

tion of a revision of the Minimum Wage Act, in order to have the minimum raised, and in 1952 it brought forward the issue of compulsory retirement as something to be discussed and reconsidered, with the recommendation that men and women should have the same compulsory retirement age and that "if any variance is to be made as to the age limit it should be in favour of the women as they possess a longer life expectancy."[55] The slight recession caused by the aftermath of the Korean War led to an actual decrease in employment in Canada in 1954.[56] While this concerned the Provincial Council of Ontario, there were matters of wider import which it wished the National Council to consider, particularly the question of "buying Canadian products when they are equal in quality and value to competitive products."

New Brunswick's Provincial Council expressed astonishment at the volume of correspondence that had been conducted out over the past year, some 400 letters having been received and answered. For both the New Brunswick and the Nova Scotia Councils the subjects which the National Council had suggested were of prime importance, and time and attention were given to a recruitment drive for Council, as well as the question of women's right to be considered for jury duty, and the general issue of what women's role should be in public life.

In the mid-fifties, no Provincial Council existed in either Alberta or Quebec, but the Montreal Local Council acted very much as if it represented the province as a whole. Montreal reported, through the Standing Committee on Laws, that it had not only presented a brief to the Quebec Government on proposed revisions to the Civil Code, but had ensured that the majority of its 116 affiliates had separately endorsed its stand.[57] The five main points covered in the Council resolution were:

1. A wife separate as to property [i.e. possessed of property not the gift of her husband] should be given the right to deal with immovable property.
2. The legal capacity of married women should be fully recognized.
3. Both mother and father should be given equal rights in respect to their children.
4. The age at which marriage may be contracted should be raised to

---

55 *Ibid.*, p. 88.
56 Bothwell, et al., *Canada Since 1945*, p. 15.
57 *Yearbook*, 1956, p. 140, The Montreal Council of Women, *Sixty-first Yearbook and Annual Report, 1954–5*, pp.14–29.

18 for a boy and 16 for a girl.

5. Provision should be made for couples married outside the province to draw up a valid marriage contract on becoming resident in Quebec.

Both in 1955 and at the sixty-third annual meeting, held in Kingston, from June 8–15, 1956, the new committee structure established in 1953 resulted in some very clear reports. There was continuing confusion, however, about the reference of particular problems to specific committees, and much variation in the numbers of reports sent to any particular standing committee in any given year. The essence of local council's role was, and is, their concern for all aspects of their own community life. The agenda of these bodies was set as much by what was happening in their respective communities through the year, as by requests from National Council to study particular problems. Thus, at any given time, the work of one or another of the standing committees would be of particular importance for some local councils but of less interest to others. The average number of reports received by any standing committee was twenty. Further, some standing committees were predominately organizations for the exchange of information and reports on activities; others were centres for the development of resolutions. The convenors of the committees represented the breadth of local council affiliations, so that all parts of Canada had a spokesperson within this particular sector of the institutional structure of Council.

To take an example: the Arts and Letters Committee, except when there was a Royal Commission in operation (such as the Massey Commission, which demanded a general response on Canadian culture from Council members) worked to encourage local activities. They exchanged information on where Canadian artists, like Lois Marshall, were performing in a given year, and what could be done to encourage municipalities to pay attention to aesthetics. It almost always received more than twenty-five reports. Chaired in 1955–56 by Miss Beatrice Brigden of Winnipeg, it reported in both years on actions taken to ensure that work of local artists was exhibited, that concerts and theatrical performances were supported, and that libraries and auditoriums were maintained. Similarly, the Committee on Economics and Taxation was a source of information for local councils as to government policies in this area. In 1955–56 it was chaired by Mrs. F.E. Underhill of London, Ontario, and had begun to take an interest in environmental conservation.[58]

---

[58] *Yearbook*, 1956, p. 117.

The Committee on Education, a newly established Standing Committee, chaired by Mrs. Jean D. Newman of Toronto, spent much of the year organizing its agenda for ongoing study of three distinct issues: the education of particularly gifted children, the education of children with mental handicaps, and the problems of educating for old age. All three themes would become matters for Council resolutions during the following ten years.

Mrs. Al Caldwell of Saskatoon chaired the Committee on Films and Printed Matter. Two major issues brought forward by members to this committee were, firstly, the need to rank films so parents could exercise intelligent supervision of their children's viewing and, secondly, the need to find some method of distinguishing comic books meant for children from those published for adults. Similarly the Committee on Radio and Television, chaired in 1955 by Mrs. Wendell Colpitts of Moncton, was concerned with the sorts of entertainment children would watch. It also participated in the preparation of a Council brief to the recently appointed Royal Commission on Broadcasting (the Fowler Commission) which would report in 1958. Both these Committees pursued the Council interest in censorship, particularly through study of the following questions: when should public interest demand a limit to the principle of free speech? could public morality be best served by a system of categorization rather than one of prohibition? to what extent could proliferation of good material inhibit the propagation of bad?

Dr. Marguerite Bailey of Toronto chaired the Committee on Health in 1955–56. The fluoridation of water was discussed during these years, and approval expressed for initiatives in this area. Moncton Council, in company with a number of other councils, brought up the need to ensure uniform standards across the country for the compulsory pasteurization of milk; for the chlorination of all community water supplies; for regular physical examinations of all food handlers; and the compulsory inspection of all meat intended for sale.[59] Local councils were concerned with the health of mental patients in their communities, now that mood-altering drugs enabled many to leave institutions. Concerns forwarded to this Committee were often similar to those sent to Lt. Col. Annie Fairhurst, from Toronto, who chaired the Committee on Social Welfare. This body gathered information about a wide variety of topics, from housing projects for older people (North Shore Local Council) through the conditions of jails (Montreal Local Council) to the provision of playgrounds for children (Kingston Local Council).[60]

---

[59] *Ibid.*, p. 128.
[60] *Ibid.*, pp. 151–54.

Mrs. R.G. Gilbride of Montreal chaired the Committee on Housing, another new standing committee. The major issues on its agenda were slum clearance in Montreal and Toronto, the need to lobby for low-cost housing, especially for senior citizens, and the question of rental housing.[61] The Committee on International Affairs was also chaired by a Montrealer, Mrs. Saul Hayes. Like the Committee on Economics and Taxation, this Committee was above all concerned with information. Organizations such as the United Nations International Children's Emergency Fund and the World Health Organization were the subject of lectures presented by the local councils.

Miss Gwendolyn Shand, of Halifax, chaired the Committee on Laws. She announced that the Committee as a whole was working on a survey of the legal and social status of women in Canada, but emphasized that general work on pressing issues would continue. The rights of widows, the rights of deserted wives, the question of women's obligation to accept jury duty (at this time women were excused simply on their request), as well as the treatment of sex offenders, were all matters discussed by this Committee. Saskatoon reported their interest in the Prince Albert's Women's Jail, particularly in the "Indian Female prisoners"...who were "found to be of average to high intelligence with little formal education."[62] A companion committee to the Committee on Laws was that dealing with Trades and Professions, chaired in 1955–56 by Miss Lorraine Johnson of Vancouver. It had been an active committee since the beginnings of Council. In the fifties it was particularly interested in "facilities available for the training of the older woman for employment."[63] Frequently this committee gathered the reports of women elected to political office, and in ensuing years would actively pursue the issues of equal pay for equal work, and equal opportunity for women.

In this decade, the Standing Committee on Migration and Citizenship, chaired by Mrs J.R. Hoag of Regina, became the centre for Council work concerning Indian rights. In 1956 it asked all local councils to "study the Indian situation in their own area."[64] That year reports on this issue were fragmentary. Chatham Council reported that "Indian children from the Moravian reservation attend Ridgetown public school" and they were being encouraged to continue to high school. Edmonton announced that the next year would see a concentrated effort to understand the Indian question.

---

[61] *Ibid.*, pp. 131–34.
[62] *Ibid.*, p. 142.
[63] *Ibid.*, p. 154.
[64] *Ibid.*, p. 144.

Fredericton reported that a "great deal of time" was spent working individually "with various members of the Indian population with very encouraging results." Serious and organized work was begun by Council on this issue in 1956, partly as a result of a major address delivered at the annual meeting by Ann Shipley, M.P.[65] on the "Indian Problem." She emphasized the need for "a new policy of education" and considered that Indian children would be "better in ordinary public day schools, rather than in residential and segregated schools."[66]

Taken as a whole, the fields of interest of the standing committees encompassed the full range of problems facing Canadian citizens. The shifting nature of their concerns, and of the types and forms of resolutions they brought forward to the annual general meetings, reflects the changing realities of Canadian society. Never uniformly organized, and never united and consistent on all issues, the standing committees did manage to assemble a mosaic of views of a significant proportion of Canadian women concerning the ways they wanted their society to function.

The administrative standing committees in 1955 included, in addition to those already mentioned, a Parliamentary Committee, whose business it was to ensure effective lobbying of the federal government was pursued; a Resolutions Committee, which had been established to ensure that motions brought to the annual general meeting were properly presented; and a Public Relations Committee, concerned with publicity in general and the production of a newsletter and the Yearbook.

Mrs. Turner Bone ended her presidency in 1956, and she could be well content with what had been achieved during her years in office. She left Council in a strong position to welcome the International Council of Women for its Fifteenth Meeting (Seventh Triennial) in Montreal in 1957. Mrs. Rex (Fraudena Gilroy) Eaton was the incoming President. She was Nova Scotia born but spent much of her adult life in British Columbia. In the commemorative speech given when she was awarded an honourary Doctorate of Laws by the University of British Columbia, October 24, 1958, it was noted that:

---

[65] She was born to William Dennis Killins and Mary Ann Lamont at Lawrence Station, Ontario, April 8, 1899. She joined the federal civil service, in the Department of Finance, in 1915. In June 1925 she married Dr. Manly A. Shipley and they had two daughters and one son. Mrs. Shipley became reeve of Teck Township, Ontario in 1943, a position she held until 1952. She won the riding of Temiskaming for the Liberals in 1953 and served in the House of Commons until 1957. She was Canada's representative on the United Nations Commission on the Status of Women in 1957. Gwynneth Evans, *Women in Federal Politics: A Bio-Bibliography/ Les femmes au federal: une bio-bibliographie,* (Ottawa, 1975), pp. 39-40.

[66] *Yearbook,* 1956, p. 68.

23. Mrs. G.D. Finlayson, President 1959–1961

the quality of her service has been demonstrated and recognized in the fields of industrial and labour relations, in prison reform, in Civil Liberties, in the development of the profession of Nursing, in the advancement of the work of the United Nations, as Associate Director of the National Selective Service during the war (for which she received an O.B.E.) and today as re-elected President of the National Council of Women.[67]

Before her election in 1956, Mrs. Eaton had been both a Local Council President — in Vancouver — and also President of the British Columbian Provincial Council, holding the latter office from 1951 to 1953.

She served as President until 1959, and her term was marked by the continuation of traditional policies: the functioning of Council was still a preoccupation, but lobbying for the public support of women in paid employment, and the general needs of women and children were the major concerns during this period. From many points of view there was no obvious signal for Council to change its ways. The election of John Diefenbaker as Prime Minister of Canada, on June 21, 1957, brought to an end the long period of Liberal rule. But although the new Prime Minster was a passionate advocate of a "new vision," it was a vision of an expansion of the Canada in which he had grown up, not the creation of a new polity, based on the changing mix of Canadian citizenry. It was a vision focused upon Canada's northern heritage, in terms of Diefenbaker's understanding of Canadian history, rather than on the Canada now taking shape. It centred upon what a revived Canadian-British Commonwealth connection might produce, rather than upon the realization that Britain itself had accepted the inevitable and become a post-colonial power. From the viewpoint of Council, the policies put forward by the federal government between 1957 and 1963 did not stimulate either vigorous support or major opposition.

Perhaps the most significant Council action during these years was its continued attention to issues concerning the Indians of Canada. Among the resolutions passed at the annual meeting in Montreal, June 3–4, 1957, was one dealing at length with the status of Indians as Canadian citizens. The Council suggested that Indians, individually or collectively, be given the right to appeal, from any ministerial decision or any Governor in Council Decision, to "A Judge of the Supreme court of the Province where the Indian

---

[67] *Yearbook,* 1958, p. 9.

or band of Indians is located"; that unless an Indian so desired, his/her status as a treaty Indian was to be considered immutable; and that the Federal Government set about establishing a comprehensive training system for Indian youth.[68]

That year Mrs. Eaton noted prophetically, in her presidential address, that she considered that the "status of the native Indian will be a long term interest."[69] This would be due in part to the increase in Canada's native populations between 1951 and 1981. After decades of decline both Inuit and the native Indian population had begun to grow. "In 1951 there were 9,733 Inuit and 155,874 native Indians — only 1.2 per cent of Canada's population. In 1981 there were 23,200 Inuit and 293,000 status and non-status Indians...[a] demographic resurgence that was both sign and cause of renewed self-confidence and assertiveness among native peoples."[70] Whatever might have been thought earlier of the possibility of the "Indian question" being solved by the gradual disappearance of an Indian population, the new demographic shift now faced Canada with a set of questions respecting those who had first lived in the land. Council seems to have sensed the change in the situation considerably earlier than most sectors of Canadian society.

In 1958, the question of Indian voting rights was made the main issue for actions by the Migration and Citizenship Committee, which reported the results of three years of study and evaluation. The report made by the Chairman, Mrs. J.R. Hoag, was explicit. "[The Indian] is a displaced person in the very real sense of the word without the assistance so readily available to this category from foreign lands," she wrote and she went to say that "the Indian Act is a paternal document...We believe that when the act is fully revised it must be with the full participation and cooperation of the Indian." She concluded, "we believe that the granting of the vote could be the instrument to accelerate and facilitate the event."[71]

At the Council held in Wasagaming, Manitoba, June 11–16, 1959, Council extended its interest in the First Peoples of Canada to include those in the far north, and passed a resolution with the following preamble:

> Whereas the Canadian far North suddenly has become subject to revolutionary changes with promise of large economic developments in the near future; and

---

[68] *Yearbook*, 1957, p. 67.
[69] *Ibid.*, p. 53.
[70] Bothwell, et al. *Canada Since 1945*, p. 14.
[71] *Yearbook*, 1958, pp. 100–101.

Whereas present federal policies, as administered through various government departments have shown sincere concern in assisting
the Eskimo people in the midst of such changes as affect their living,
though such assistance has been within the limits of inadequate funds
and facilities:

asked for increased government funding for counselling generally and education health projects in the Far North so that all Eskimos alike would:

advance their political, educational and economic status, as well as
[be protected in] their physical, social and moral welfare.[72]

In the penal domain, Council expressed its views on capital punishment.
In 1958, at the annual meeting held in Vancouver, June 6-11, it adopted its
first resolution on this subject. Its decision was to study the issue and consider whether the Council should "assume responsibility of leadership in rec-
ommending the abolition of capital punishment."[73] A similar resolution was
passed every year for the next three years, and the preambles to each made it
clear that Council considered capital punishment to be both barbaric and
ineffective. However, in 1961, the Council defeated a motion to request government to abolish the death penalty, and the issue was dropped as a regular
agenda item.[74] However, an execution in 1962 was the last in Canada, and
capital punishment — except under the provisions of the National Defence
Act, for cowardice, desertion and unlawful surrender, and spying for the
enemy — was abolished in 1976.

Mrs. G.D. Finlayson was elected President to succeed Mrs. Rex Eaton at
the annual meeting in 1959 but, unfortunately, illness and death cut short her
term of office. She served a full year but most of the second year of her term
was filled by Mrs. C.W. Argue as Acting President. In the obituary published
by the *Globe and Mail* on March 30, 1961 it was remarked that Mrs.
Finlayson was the first woman to be appointed by the federal government as
a qualified expert in matters of insurance. Indeed, she was the first to be
employed by the Unemployment Insurance Commission as an actuary.[75]
Born in Nova Scotia in 1891, she had been educated at Dalhousie University,

---

72 *Yearbook*, 1959, pp. 72–3.
73 *Yearbook*, 1958, p. 66.
74 *Yearbook*, 1961, pp. 23–24.
75 *In Memoriam: Yearbook*, 1961, p. 39.

where one her professors recommended that, when applying for a position, she use her initials rather than her Christian name of Ishbel on the application. She married Dr. G.D. Finlayson. Her introduction to Council came through the affiliation of the University Women's Club of Ottawa to that local council and through her activities in the United Church. She was elected to the Ottawa School Board, and served a term as its Chairman.

At the annual meeting of Council in Niagara Falls, May 30–June 3, 1960, Mrs. Finlayson presented her vision of Council, underlining Lady Aberdeen's call to work for "the promotion of unity, the prevention of waste, the production of force for the improvement of society."[76] Those gathered to hear her speak represented a Council that had passed through the fifties with little obvious change. Any estimation of membership is open to dispute, but the reporting structure of Council meant its work was well-known, from reports given to its national affiliates and to the local councils.[77] One of the nationally organized societies affiliated to Council had withdrawn: the Canadian Home Reading Union in 1953. But the Canadian Federation of University Women had joined in 1952, and in 1956 the Health League of Canada affiliated at the national level. In 1957, the National Council of the Hospital Auxiliaries of Canada, always a strong support in the local councils, also affiliated at the national level. In 1960, the national affiliated societies numbered twenty-two.

Alberta resurrected its Provincial Council in 1957, and a new local council was established at Red Deer in 1959. In all, at the conclusion of Mrs. G.D. Finlayson's first year in office, there were fifty-seven local councils, several of them recently established. In 1950, there had been fifty-one local councils and so more had been established than had foundered. British Columbia, in particular, had expanded its local councils considerably during this decade, although it lost Alberni Valley. Vernon and District refounded itself in 1958, Abbotsford came into being in 1959, with five federated groups; Burnaby had twenty-three federations and Comox, a smaller organization. Trail and White Rock and District were organized in 1960. In Ontario, Port Colborne was established in 1959.

Mrs. Finlayson was particularly interested in the ways Council could

---

[76] *Yearbook*, 1960, p. 37.

[77] Working with a variety of membership statistics, such as the report that the membership of the Canadian Nurses' Association in 1961, was 59,664; the Dominion Council of the Women's Association of the United Church of Canada reported 218,735 members and the Salvation Army considered that it had a membership of 15,503, I would estimate the membership of the National Council of Women of Canada was well over a million in 1960. This estimate allows for cross-membership.

strengthen the work of nationally affiliated societies. She hoped to make the presence of Council a real force on federal Boards where it was represented. In 1961 it had representatives on four major government boards: the National Advisory Council on Vocational Training; the National Employment Committee; the National Housing Design Committee; and the Canadian National Commission for UNESCO. The Council also sent representatives to four national associations: the Canadian Conference on Education; the Canadian Association of Consumers; the United Nations Society of Canada; and the Conference of Eskimos.[78] Partly through Mrs. Finlayson's efforts Council was, within a year, also officially represented at the Conference of Non-Governmental Organizations accredited to the United Nations; the Canadian Conference on Children; the Canadian Association for Adult Education; the Canadian Highway Safety Council; the Canadian Centenary Council; the Canadian Welfare Council; the Canadian Committee for the Control of Radiation Hazards; the Canadian Mental Health Association and the Freedom From Hunger Committee.[79] All in all, as Council mourned its President's death at the Annual meeting held in Windsor, June 5th-9th, 1961 there was ample reason for satisfaction with the history of the past decade. The Council had maintained its overall membership, organized its structure and pursued, successfully, a number of public issues. It had been granted an interview each year with the Prime Minister and a number of members of the cabinet.

In 1961 the National Council of Women appeared to have established itself as an enduring and significant part of Canadian society, without doubt the leading voice for women's organizations in Canada. In 1957 it had seen the publication of a commissioned history of its first sixty-four years, written by Rosa L. Shaw. She was a journalist, the first women's news editor of the *Montreal Gazette*, and had acted as editor of consumer publications for the Wartime Prices and Trade Board. The work *Proud Heritage*, was written as a thematic treatment of the many areas of Council interest, and is a clear and valuable record of many Council activities. Council could look back on those sixty-four years with great pride, but the coming decades would offer severe challenges to its position as the major voice for women's concerns.

---

[78] *Yearbook*, 1960, p. 6.
[79] *Yearbook*, 1961, pp. 80–87.

CHAPTER 9

Towards the Royal Commission
1960–1969

IN MANY WAYS the major characteristic of the nineteen fifties, for Canadians as well as for much of the rest of the western world, was adaptation to the needs of peace, even though serious and frightening tensions continued to dominate international affairs. In a world dominated by the politics of the Cold War, the threat of a nuclear holocaust cast an ominous shadow. Canada had retained significant military forces in the post-war era, making the country a useful player in a divided world. Canadian foreign policy was, of course, centred well within the limits of the Western alliance but it was pursued with the aim of encouraging the United States to consider world opinion on matters such as the nuclear test ban treaty of 1963.

As far as Council was concerned, international affairs meant first and foremost support for the United Nations; secondly, working for nuclear disarmament; thirdly, maintaining the links between itself and the International Council of Women. The records of various committees dealing with the United Nations show how much Council encouraged knowledge of, and support for, that body and its agencies. In the matter of nuclear disarmament the policy of Council had been determined at its annual meeting in 1951. The Local Council of North Shore had in that year brought forward a resolution condemning the use of napalm in Korea. It withdrew this motion in favour of the resolution passed by the International Council of Women at its thirteenth Council meeting, held in Athens earlier that year.[1] In this resolution, the I.C.W. had called upon all its members to support the authority of the

---

[1] *Yearbook*, 1951, p. 34.

United Nations and to press their governments to accept effective international control of all weapons of mass destruction.[2] Over the next three
decades, local councils brought forward a series of resolutions, all asking for
the control or abandonment of nuclear weapons.

It is, however, through its links with the I.C.W. that Council really developed and exercised an international presence. During her brief term in office,
Mrs. Finlayson represented Canada at the sixteenth meeting of the I.C.W.,
held in Istanbul in 1960. She prepared a report on the occasion for the 1961
meeting of the Canadian Council, which was delivered after her death, as the
President's address, by the Acting President, Mrs. C.W. Argue. The point
which Mrs. Finlayson chose to stress was the role of councils, whether local,
provincial, national or international, in allowing women to have a voice in
public affairs. In particular, she noted the extent to which membership of
Council gave women training for public life, something which the structure
of politics in many countries prevented.[3] This perspective was unusual but it
was one which had particular relevance as membership of the I.C.W.
expanded. In 1938, there had been thirty-six Councils affiliated at the international level, of which twenty-two were in Europe, six in America, four in
Asia, two in Africa and two in Australia.[4] In 1963, at the time of the seventeenth I.C.W. meeting (ninth triennial) there were forty-nine members: thirteen from Europe, ten from America, twelve from Asia, twelve from Africa
and two from Australia. Thirty-one of these Councils had been founded since
1950.[5]

This seventeenth meeting was also the seventy-fifth anniversary of the
founding of the International Council. It was held in June 1963, in
Washington, D.C., the city where both it and the United States National
Council had been founded. Its theme was "Inheritance from the past, responsibility for the future." Mrs. Saul Hayes [Beatrice] led the Canadian delegation. She had been elected as President of the Canadian Council, succeeding
Mrs. Finlayson, at the annual meeting in Windsor two years earlier. She was
the third President Montreal gave to the national organization, the others
being Winnifred Kydd (President of the Montreal Council, 1929–1931) and
Mrs. A. Turner Bone, (President of the Montreal Council, 1945–1948). She
was the daughter of Harry and Fanny Rosenbaum. She graduated from

---

2   Anon., *Women in a Changing World*, p. 88.
3   *Yearbook*, 1961, pp. 36-38.
4   Anon., *Women in a Changing World*, p. 105.
5   *Ibid.*, p. 105 and Appendix 11, p. 350.

McGill with a B.A. in 1932. She married Saul Hayes on September 2, 1934. Her work for the Jewish Vocational Service of Montreal and the Montreal Co-ordinating Council on New Immigrants brought her to that city's local council and she had served as its President from 1957 to 1960.

Mrs. Hayes and her companions came to Washington directly from the seventieth meeting of the Canadian Council, held at the Banff School of Fine Arts, June 10–13, 1963. In her speech to that general meeting, Mrs. Hayes remarked on the recently published work *The Silent Spring*, by Rachel Carson.[6] She suggested that Council pay "major attention" to the issues of air and water pollution and conduct a study of the Carson thesis.[7] In Washington, the President of the National Council of the United States introduced the writer herself, who gave one of the banquet speeches. Rachel Carson told the I.C.W. delegates "of the urgency of directing the attention of responsible opinion in their own countries to the need for safeguards to ensure only the judicious and appropriate use of these valuable technological aids to progress, otherwise so potentially destructive to humanity."[8]

As well as a common interest in the ecology, the Canadian Council and the I.C.W. had similar concerns in other areas: the continuing battle for equal status for women, both in law and in practice; family planning; race relations; and the fundamental question as to whether voluntary organizations still had a significant role to play in the rapidly changing world of the sixties. Mrs. Lefaucheux, who was the retiring I.C.W. President at this meeting,[9] asked whether the time had gone by for effective action by the I.C.W. She answered the question for herself by underlining two points, the first being the usefulness of a freely constituted, non-governmental agency that could bring together women of different countries, some of whom were pursuing

---

[6] Rachel Carson, *The Silent Spring*, (New York, 1962).

[7] *Yearbook*, 1963, p. 34.

[8] Anon., *Women in a Changing World*, p. 112.

[9] Marie-Hélène Lefaucheux was ICW President from 1957-63. She had been born Marie-Hélène Postel Vinay in Paris in 1904. While she had started her education in musical studies she became one of the first women students admitted to the École des Sciences Politiques, where she met her husband Pierre Lefaucheux, an engineer and lawyer. During the German occupation she and her husband were members of the Résistance and he was arrested by the Gestapo and sent to Buchenwald. She was awarded the Croix de Guerre and the Rosette de la Résistance. After the war her husband became the President and General Manager of the newly nationalized Renault works and she was nominated Deputy of the Aisne Department in the First Constituent Assembly (1945). She was the Vice-President of the Paris Municipal Council and from 1946-48, a member of the French Senate. A member of the French delegation to the First General Assembly of the United Nations in 1946, she represented her country on a number of different commissions, including the Status of Women Commission, of which she was President from 1947 to 1951. She became president of the National Council of Women of France in 1954. She was tragically killed in an aircraft accident when flying from Mexico to New York, February 25, 1964, Anon., *Women in a Changing World*, pp. 124-25.

conflicting policies. Her second point was that the significant reputation gained already by the I.C.W. ensured that its advice was sought, and occasionally followed, by both national and international bodies. Such influence for women ought not to be lightly discarded. At the concluding banquet, Mrs. Katie Louchheim, the American Deputy Assistant Secretary of State for Public Affairs recalled how "the voluntary contributions of women have changed the faces of their communities, urged reforms which could have waited for the passage of law and fought long and hard for laws that made such reforms permanent."[10]

In preparation for the celebrations of its Jubilee meeting, the I.C.W. had asked the National Councils to send in brief summaries of their history.[11] These were published as part of the official history, commissioned in 1960, of the first seventy-five years of the I.C.W. What is worth noting is the extent to which National Councils differed from one another, each one reflecting its own particular culture and society, and displaying wide variations in institutional structure and programs of action. From this documentation, it is clear that the Canadian Council was one of the most effectively organized and that its net of local councils gave it an unusual strength. Canada's Council was, of course, second only to that of the United States in age.

The encouragement Mrs. Hayes must have gained from discovering how similar the work and aspirations of the I.C.W. and Canadian Council were, would stand her in good stead when she returned to Canada. There she faced something she had already remarked upon at the Banff meeting: the urgent problems of Canadian domestic politics. In the 1958 federal election, John G. Diefenbaker had received the largest majority ever recorded, 208 seats out of a house of 265. The next federal election, June 18, 1962 left him with 118 seats and on April 8, 1963, his following was further reduced to ninety-five seats. Lester Pearson and the Liberal Party, which in the spring election of 1963 had received 129 seats, with 41% of the popular vote, formed a minority government. Desmond Morton has commented that "Canadians who voted Liberal in 1963 expected to restore the tranquil prosperous era that John Diefenbaker had interrupted. The prosperity had already returned; the tranquillity would not."[12]

There is considerable agreement among historians that the sixties was a

---

10   *Ibid.,* p. 116.
11   *Ibid.,* Appendix 12, "ICW questionnaire addressed to National Councils concerning their history," Paris, 1960, p. 351.
12   Morton, "Affluence," p. 416.

crucial period of change in Canadian history, even if there is still much dis-agreement as to how far it came unheralded. For the authors of *Canada Since 1945* it was clear that "Canada had outgrown its old political garments, and it had to try out new ones or refashion the old. Internal growth had strained the fabric of Confederation and, by the mid-sixties, few thought simple readjust-ments would ease the strain."[13] For many, the particular strain came from "the re-emergence of a militant French-Canadian nationalism."[14] As far as Mrs. Hayes was concerned, there was no doubt that the issue of Anglo-French relations was "the principal political item" to be tackled and Council had to address the very serious problems raised.[15] She urged all members of Council to give bilingualism and biculturalism their most urgent attention.

The Royal Commission on Bilingualism and Biculturalism was estab-lished on July 22, 1963. In late 1963, the Council established a committee to gather the ideas of its membership on the issues before the Royal Commission and write a brief for presentation. At the annual general meeting of Council, held at McMaster University, Hamilton, June 1–4, 1964, Mrs. Hayes emphasized how important a matter this was. It was not merely her own point of view. The Chairman of the Standing Committee on Education, Mrs. B.W. Walker of Swift Current, Saskatchewan, reported that bilingualism was the most discussed topic among local councils and that there was "wide-spread agreement" that Canadians should be bilingual.[16] In her presidential address, Mrs. Hayes analyzed the problems facing Canada as:

decentralization of government functions versus continuing central-ization; co-operative federalism; economic control of our resources by external interests abetted by the seeming disinclination by Canadians to invest in risk capital ventures; the influence of automa-tion on employment; the social-political-economic implications of Lord Durham's concept of "two nations warring in the bosom of a single state."

She went on to say that there was a current witticism to the effect that in English Canada "optimists are learning French and the pessimists are learn-ing American." She considered "there is some germ of truth in this if we con-

13 Bothwell et al., *Canada Since 1945*, p. 255.
14 Laurier L. Lapierre, "The 1960s," in J.M.S. Careless and R. Craig Brown, eds., *The Canadians 1867-1967*, (Toronto, 1968), pp. 344-45.
15 *Yearbook*, 1963, pp. 34-5.
16 *Yearbook*, 1964, p. 49.

sider that only by accepting **le fait français** as basic to Canadian political life and recognizing that a separatist Quebec could lead to annexation to the United States, can we legitimately discuss present-day Canada."[17]

The views gathered up by Council for submission to the Bilingualism and Biculturalism Commission were as diverse as those presented by any other heterogeneous group of Canadians. This surprised no one, especially Mrs. Hayes, who remarked that "Council is, by and large, a reflection of the moods, ideas and philosophies that compose the entire nation." There was, however, a matter where Council was united and about which it complained strenuously to the federal authorities, namely the "phraseology of the Order in Council which established the Commission." "I reiterate," Mrs. Hayes said to the members,

> that your Officers complained of those sections which gave statutory recognition to the term "race" which seems to contemplate a future constitution for Canada in terms of a bi-racial nation instead of an English-speaking and a French-speaking country...

She went on to stress that:

> Even [Winston Churchill] writing about the people from that 'tight little isle' did not propose writing a history of the English race but of people who spoke the same language.[18]

While the complex questions of the constitutional and political future of Canada represented a central issue for discussion and debate at Council meetings at this time, it was by no means Council's sole area of concern. The organization continued to pay attention to a broad spectrum of interests. Some of these were problems that had preoccupied members of Council for years, such as women's employment and the needs of the family; others were issues brought forward by the national level of Council, such as the state of the environment; and still others were issues raised by one or more local councils, such as problems of organization and general membership, education, and the content of radio and television programs.

Even within the limits of traditional Council activities, there were signs that some of the priorities of Council members were evolving. Regina Local

---

[17] *Ibid.,* p. 37.
[18] *Ibid.,* p. 38.

Council, for example, had discovered by 1959 that there was no longer any need "to administer the milk fund due to assistance available to needy families and closed out a phase of work instituted in 1921."[19] Other Councils slowly followed suit. The social net Canada had been building for more than twenty years meant that poverty, and its relief, took a new shape in the sixties. Want and misery had not disappeared. This point was put to a meeting of the Provincial Council of British Columbia in 1960 by William Dixon, then head of the School of Social Work at the University of British Columbia. That Council had organized a day-long seminar on "The Role of Volunteer Agencies Today" and Professor Dixon underlined the danger for volunteers of the idea that "the ultimate in social advance" had already been accomplished.[20] What seemed obvious, however, was that new ways and types of volunteer social action were necessary, although sometimes a careful analysis of the records shows that much of the alteration, at this time, was cosmetic rather than fundamental. Direct charity, in the form of contributions of money, clothes and patronage, from the fortunate to the needy had obviously decreased as state-supported welfare programs became commonplace. But much Council work continued unabated and relatively unaltered.

For example, the report given by Mrs. C.W. Mellish, for the Standing Committee on Health in 1963 seems, at first reading, to present very different issues from those outlined by her predecessors. In earlier decades, the reports of this Committee had focused upon the need for good dental care for children, the need for hospital care for chronically ill adults, and the work of members of Council as volunteer visitors and care-givers. The report by Mrs. Mellish summarized the actions of Council members in this field in 1963 as:

> Reports to members on the work of the health authorities; Speakers at meetings on health subjects; Members working as volunteers in clinics, health centres for children, pre-natal clinics, the penny round up of the C.M.A.; Distributing information on nutrition door to door for the local health authority; Representation on hospital boards; Collecting for voluntary associations such as the Cancer Society and the March of Dimes.[21]

---

19 Mrs. Thacker and Mrs. Cruikshank, *History of the Provincial Council of Women of Saskatchewan 1919-1954*, (n.d.,n.p.), p. 47.
20 Hastings and Ellenwood, *Blue Bows*, p. 73.
21 *Yearbook*, 1963, p. 53.

Mrs. Mellish saw future work of the Committee as concentrating on the examination of "Environmental health," defined as studying matters of "air pollution, water pollution, pesticides, food and drugs," but she also listed the investigation of "child and adolescent health" and the provision of "rehabilitation, hospital-home care; personal care homes; custodial care for the chronically ill" and "housekeeper services" as matters for Council study. There might be a difference of emphasis between the role of the volunteer as commentator on the delivery of social services, rather than as the provider of direct aid, but it was an adaptation of role and by no means a complete change.

Similarly, the report of Miss Clara M. McAuley, of Moncton, for the Standing Committee on Trades and Professions of Women told of problems that were much the same as those in past reports of this committee. At the outset of the decade, the then Chairman had reported on the survey made in 1959–1960, on a number of issues needing study: the impact of Equal Pay Legislation; the issue of Fair Employment; the need to review the whole gamut of discriminatory practices in hiring relating to race, colour, religion, national origin, sex and age.[22] Three years later Brandon Local Council urged an increase in the minimum wage; the Local Councils of Niagara Falls, Saskatoon and Winnipeg argued for the introduction of new training programs; New Westminster advocated refresher courses for the older women re-entering the work force; Moncton drew attention to the fact that married women in the labour force needed better day-care nurseries and Hamilton brought forward the problems of the part-time woman worker.[23]

Further, while major contemporary developments, such as the constitutional debate, demanded Council's time and energy, work also continued, at all levels, on problems which had been brought forward in earlier years. British Columbia's Provincial Council not only continued its study of the issue of Indian status, begun in the late nineteen fifties, but continued to prod other councils to do likewise. In 1963, it had made this subject its major project, maintaining that:

Canadian Indians are fenced in by laws designed to protect them and there is little chance of first class citizenship for them unless the laws are changed. Too long the government has taken a paternalistic attitude toward the Indian; now when change is desperately needed the

[22] *Yearbook*, 1960, p. 96.
[23] *Yearbook*, 1963, p. 62.

24. Mrs. Saul Hayes, President 1961–1964

Indian is unable to carry it on his own. Without better education the
Indian faces staggering cultural, social and political problems.[24]

In cooperation with the University of British Columbia's Extension
Department, study sessions were organized by local councils in their communities which brought together their own members, their local Indian neigh-
bours and academics. In 1964, Jules D'Astous also addressed the
semi-annual Provincial Council meeting, held in Victoria February 17–19, on
the "The role of the Provincial Government in Indian Affairs." Council
recorded with approval his statement that:

> Progress in solving problems of the native Indian in Canada will be
> in direct ratio to public's and government's realization of Indian par-
> ticipation, and the basis of equality and opportunity with other citi-
> zens must not be contingent on the Indians surrendering their
> heritage, culture, reserves or special rights that have been conferred
> on them as first citizens of Canada unless the Indians so desire.[25]

Throughout the presidency of Mrs. Hayes, local councils continued to
work, as they always had, on their own local interests. Typical of such action,
though perhaps more dramatic than many, was the work of the Calgary Local
Council in the matter of the CPR's proposal to build a new set of railway
tracks along the south bank of the Bow as part of the City-CPR Downtown
Redevelopment Plan.[26] The matter came to general notice on the eve of
municipal elections in April 1963. The Local Council of Women of Calgary
backed Ruth Gorman,[27] their Convenor of Laws at that time, in a fight to
ensure that the proposal for a park along the river, for which the Local
Council of Women of Calgary had lobbied for a decade, would not be abandoned. A qualified lawyer, although she had never practiced, Ruth Gorman

---

24 Hastings and Ellenwood, *Blue Bows*, p. 76.
25 *Ibid.*, p. 77.
26 In what follows I have relied a great deal on Marjorie Norris, *Leaven of Ladies: A History of the Local Council of Women of Calgary*, Chapter VI, "The Greening of the South Bank." The work will be published in 1994.
27 The daughter of one of the city's prominent lawyers, Col. M.B. Peacock, Ruth was born in Calgary, 14 February 1914. Her mother was Fleda Pattyson. Her father allowed her to train as a lawyer but forbade her to practice as "she didn't need the money." She married John C. Gorman in 1940 and they had one daughter. She has spent her life as free legal counsellor for many causes and, in par-ticular, has rendered this service to the Alberta Cree. She was honoured with title of Queen Mother of Cree and Princess of the Stony Indian Tribe of Alberta. She received the Order of Canada in 1968.

coordinated and led the action of the local council. On May 23, 1963 a special meeting of the Calgary City Council approved plans brought forward by the CPR. It soon became clear that the preservation of parkland had a very low priority in these plans. The Local Council of Women organized a major lobby group to investigate what, precisely, the deal involved, and discovered that it not only meant no greenbelt for Calgary but considerable expense for the Calgary tax-payer and extraordinary concessions to the CPR. Through a great deal of hard work by Council, and with help from other interested groups, the whole issue was brought before the Alberta legislature on March 3, 1964.[28] By the end of month, the CPR project was abandoned.

The type of interest displayed by local councils in municipal development was encouraged when the Standing Committee on Housing added to its title the words "and Community Planning" in 1961. This meant the Standing Committee now assumed a broad mandate to encourage local councils to investigate and comment on what their cities planned for development, and to lobby their municipalities when appropriate. In 1964, for example, Owen Sound's Council became active in the maintenance of parkland near Bay Shore. That year the Local Councils of Halifax, Peterborough and Windsor each invited their respective City Planning Directors to address a Council meeting and Edmonton, Portage La Prairie, Regina, Saint John and Windsor all served notice to their local authorities that they were interested in commenting on the development proposals under consideration.[29]

The support of cultural activities was another area where activity at the local council level was traditional, effective and essential for the quality of life in many communities. The reports of the Standing Committee on Arts and Letters continued to recount, throughout the sixties, an extraordinary amount of activity. In 1963, for example, the then Chairman Miss Elizabeth Long of Winnipeg, listed local council initiatives in everything from fund-raising for the support of young musicians through scholarships, to the organization of concerts and drama festivals, from the presentation of art exhibitions and craft-fairs to campaigns for the preservation of historic buildings, and the collection of books for libraries.

At the annual meeting held at McMaster University, Hamilton, in 1964 Mrs. H.H. Steen was elected President. She had been born in Victoria, twice widowed and was in her 71st year. She noted in her first presidential address that she had been part of the annual meetings of National Council, in one

---

[28] *The Albertan,* March 7, 1964, p. 1.
[29] *Yearbook,* 1964, p. 61.

capacity or another, since 1954. She was very clear about the effectiveness of Council, remarking on one occasion:

> This is the image of Council, that we speak for so many thousands when we take a resolution to government. I have followed resolutions from the local level right through the national and seen them implemented. This is no myth! Women together in council can affect both national and provincial laws.[30]

In her address to the seventy-second annual meeting, May 30-June 3, 1965, Mrs. Steen focused upon the issue which would come to dominate Council activity for the rest of the decade: the status of women. She made three points: firstly, that many volunteer organizations were experiencing great difficulty in attracting new workers; secondly, that women made up nearly one-third of the total labour force and that half of these were married women; thirdly, that there were scarcely any fields of employment that did not include women. She went on to say, however, that "relatively few [women] in Canada achieve top positions of responsibility." She noted that:

> Out of some sixty Ambassadors and High Commissioners, heading up Canadian offices abroad, there is only one woman. There is no woman deputy minister or assistant deputy minister in Canada; one Civil Service Commissioner enjoys a rank equivalent to a deputy minister. No woman has ever become a University President, though Dr. Phyllis Ross of Vancouver is Chancellor and Chairman of the Board of Governors at the University of British Columbia and is the first woman to receive such an appointment in Canada.[31]

Her concerns were underlined by that year's report from the Committee on Trades and Professions. Its chairman, Clara McAuley, noted that the theme chosen for study over the past year, 1964–5, had been "Woman Workers in a Changing World" and she pointed out that while different councils worked in different ways there was no variation "**in the conclusions reached** [Bold type in original]." She summarized these as being the need for:

---

30 Reported as having been said in Hamilton, Hastings and Ellenwood, *Blue Bows*, p. 77.
31 *Yearbook*, 1965, p. 35.

revision of acts re equal pay for women with men for comparable work; readily available, up-to-date information for women on employment — part and full-time; counselling and guidance for both young and older women in deciding the type of employment to seek, and the training, if necessary, to take.

She continued by saying that, in order "to successfully cope with the needs of the expanding industrial life women, themselves, must determine a programme whereby opportunity for full development of their potentials may be realized." It was for this reason, she went on,

members of the Trades and Professions committees across Canada have supported all community services that promote such opportunity, and have carried out surveys on such matters as need for establishing certain training courses; day care nursery facilities; counselling and guidance available for youth and older women; facilities for readily available information particularly in connection with employment.[32]

The report concluded with the suggestion that it might be advisable for the Council to request the government to establish a commission to investigate these matters.

Within a year, it was clear that this idea had been taken up by women's groups throughout Canada and a strong demand had developed for a Royal Commission. There were a number of reasons for this. Firstly, the American Commission on the Status of Women, which had been set up by President John Kennedy, had made an impact on English Canadian national associations. Its report had been published early in 1965,[33] and further encouraged women like Doris Anderson,[34] then editor of *Chatelaine*, and Laura Sabia,[35] President of the Canadian Federation of University Women, both long-time committed feminists, to bring together Canadian women's organizations,

---

[32] *Ibid.*, p. 59.

[33] Margaret Mead and Francis Bagley Kaplan, eds., *American Women: The Report of the President's Commission on the Status of Women and Other Publications of the Commission*, (New York, 1965).

[34] She was born in Calgary on November 10, 1925. She attended the University of Alberta and received her B.A. in 1945. She married and was the mother of three sons.

[35] Whether for political reasons or because of a desire for privacy, Laura Sabia is not in *Canadian Who's Who*. Her extraordinary activity for the women's movement deserves the widest possible recognition.

including the National Council, to discuss matters of common concern. As a result, early in 1966, the Committee on Equality for Women was born, which brought together thirty-two organizations, including representation from the National Council of Women of Canada and from most of its national affiliates.

Given the climate of opinion in Canada at the time, even this coalition, though led with energy and passion by Laura Sabia, might not have been successful. What ensured its victory was the support of Francophone women. In 1966, the Fédération des Femmes du Québec (FFQ) was organized by Thérèse Casgrain.[36] This was an umbrella group very much like the Council of Women. Unlike most earlier women's organizations in Quebec, it had no religious ties. The existence of this province-wide movement allowed Laura Sabia, and her supporters, to bridge the traditional divide between Quebec feminists and those in the rest of Canada. She herself was "fully bi-lingual and clearly interested in the new Quebec women's movement."[37] To a very large extent it was to the warmth of her personal invitation that led the FFQ to join the Committee for the Equality of Women. Monique Bégin[38] has pointed out that, given tensions in the country in the aftermath of the Bilingualism and Biculturalism Commission, which had presented an interim report in 1965, it was clear "a royal commission demanded by English-speaking women only was politically impossible."[39] Thus the presence of French-Canadian women as delegates to the Prime Minister requesting the establishment of the Royal Commission, was of crucial importance. Although the FFQ as an association was not present, its first President, Réjane Laberge-Colas was.[40] Other members of the delegation were Laura

---

[36] Née Forget, in Montreal, July 10, 1896; died there November 2, 1981. Born to a wealthy family, she married Pierre-François Casgrain, Liberal lawyer and politician and raised four children. A founding member of the Quebec Provincial Franchise Committee in 1921, she campaigned ceaselessly for women's rights. During the Second World War she was one of the two presidents of the Women's Surveillance Committee for the Wartime Prices and Trade Board. After 1946 she became the provincial leader of the CCF, 1951-57.

[37] Monique Bégin: "The Royal Commission on the Status of Women in Canada: Twenty Years Later," in Constance Backhouse and David H. Flaherty, Challenging Times: The Women's Movement in Canada and the United States, (Montreal, 1992), p. 26.

[38] Born in Rome, 1 March 1936 to Lucien and Marie-Louise Bégin. She was educated in Montreal; M.A. in Sociology, University of Montreal; Executive Secretary and Director of Research, Royal Commission on the Status of Women; first Quebec woman elected to federal parliament, as a Liberal, 1972; Minister of National Revenue, 1976; Minister of National Health and Welfare, 1977-79, 1980-84; Joint Chair of Women's Studies, Carleton University and University of Ottawa, 1986-1990; Dean, Faculty of Health Services, University of Ottawa since 1991.

[39] Bégin, "Royal Commission," p. 23.

[40] Born in Montreal, 23 October 1923 to Dr. Louis and Isabelle (Lefebvre) Laberge: LL.L. University of Montreal, 1951; married Judge Emile Colas, 25 October 1958; three children. In 1969, she became the first woman judge in a Canadian superior court, being appointed to the Quebec Superior Court that year.

Sabia, Margaret Hyndman for the Canadian Federation of Business and Professional Women's Clubs, Julia Schwart for the National Council of Jewish Women and Margaret MacLellan for the National Council of Women. They were accompanied by some sixty observers.[41] There was also general support for the idea from women in all three political parties.

Even with the presence of French-Canadian women at this meeting, the battle was not yet won. Few men in government had any idea of the approaching storm many have come to call the "second wave of feminism." There was no comprehension among the bureaucrats or politicians that women had any real complaints about their status in society, or were even able to articulate such dissatisfactions as they might imagine they had. Simone de Beauvoir's important work, *The Second Sex* had been available in English since 1953, but in 1965 the Prime Minister of the day, Lester Pearson could still turn down Pauline Jewett[42] for cabinet appointment because Judy LaMarsh was already a Minister. It never occurred to him that women really were ordinary human beings and that there could be more than one woman in cabinet.[43] Betty Friedan's brilliant and angry book, *The Feminine Mystique*, published in 1963, had documented the poisoned choice presented to many North American women: either emotional strength or intellectual prowess, either the private world of the home or a public life. Few men believed that the vision of suburbia purveyed by advertisers and journalists was not only a false picture of women's lives, but also one which many rejected. The Honourable Judy LaMarsh, who had succeeded Ellen Fairclough[44] as the sec-

---

[41] On this stage of the Royal Commission see Cerise Morris "'Determination and Thoroughness': The Movement for the Royal Commission on the Status of Women in Canada," *Atlantis* 5. 2 (Spring, 1980), pp. 1-21.

[42] Born St. Catharines, Ontario, 11 December 1922; died Ottawa 1992; Educated at Queen's, Radcliffe, Harvard and Oxford she was a Professor of Political Science (1955-71) and Head of the Institute of Canadian Studies (1971-74) at Carleton University before becoming President of Simon Fraser University 1974-78; she was the first woman to head a major co-educational university in Canada. Jewett was a Liberal M.P. from 1963-65. She moved to the New Democratic party and in the general elections of 1979, 1980 and 1984, was elected M.P. for New Westminster. She was appointed Chancellor of Carleton University in 1990.

[43] See, *Memoirs of a Bird in a Gilded Cage*, (Toronto, 1969), p. 292. Judy Verlyn LaMarsh was born at Chatham Ontario, December 20, 1924 and died in Toronto on October 27, 1980. She was the Liberal M.P. for Niagara Falls, 1960-68. Under her aegis as Minister of Health and Welfare, 1963-65, the Canada Pensions Plan was implemented and Canada's medicare system designed. As Secretary of State, 1965-68, she brought in the Broadcasting Act and presided over the Centennial Year celebrations.

[44] Born on January 28, 1905 in Hamilton, Ontario, she was the daughter of Norman Ellsworth Cook and Nellie Bell Louks. She studied accounting extramurally and opened her own firm in 1935. She married Gordon Fairclough in January 1931 and they had one son. In 1946 Mrs. Fairclough began a five-year term on the Hamilton City Council. She won the by-election in Hamilton West in May 1950 for the Progressive Conservative Party. She was subsequently elected in 1953, 1957,1958 and

ond solitary woman in the cabinet, testified that during her period as Minister, any attempt to secure the appointment of women to public boards was a bitter and thankless task. She very much doubted, she wrote in her autobiography, whether at the time of the establishment of the Royal Commission, "any of the twenty-nine male members of Cabinet or the thirty or forty senior public servants" who advised on appointments even remembered that women existed.[45]

Before the Commission was finally established, those who requested it had to increase their pressure. Laura Sabia proved adept at gaining press attention and by mid-winter, 1967, victory was achieved. LaMarsh later recorded in her memoirs that "without the remarkable organization of Mrs. Laura Sabia" the Commission would never have been set up.[46] But it was, indeed, established by a minute of the Private Council on February 16, 1967.

Mrs. Florence Bird, news commentator and one of the first women in Canada to be a respected political journalist, was appointed as its chairman. Born in Philadelphia, January 15, 1908 she had been educated at Bryn Mawr. In 1930, she came to Canada with her husband, John Bird. In her work she used the pen name "Anne Francis" and published her autobiography using that name as its title. Mrs. Bird was the first woman to be appointed to head a royal commission in Canada. Six other commissioners were appointed, one of whom, the political scientist Donald Gordon, resigned after eight months. He was replaced and the permanent members were: Jacques Henripin,[47] John Humphrey,[48] Lola Mary Lange,[49] Jeanne Lapointe,[50] Elizabeth Muriel Gregory MacGill,[51] Mrs. Robert Ogilvie.[52]

The task of the Royal Commission was set out clearly enough in the

---

1962. In June 1957, Prime Minister Diefenbaker appointed her to be Secretary of State and from 1958 to 1962 she was Minister of Citizenship and Immigration. She was the first woman to hold a federal cabinet position in Canada.

[45] LaMarsh, *Memoirs*, p. 293.

[46] *Ibid.*, p. 302.

[47] Born in Lachine, Quebec, 1929, a demographer, then head of the Department of Demography at McGill.

[48] Born Hampton, New Brunswick, 1905; he had been a professor of law and had represented Canada for twenty years on the United Nations Human Rights Commission.

[49] Born in Edmonton, Alberta, 1922; she had long experience with the Alberta Farm Women's Union.

[50] Born in 1915 at Chicoutimi; a professor of French Literature at Laval University, she had been a member of Quebec's Parent Commission on Education.

[51] Born in Vancouver in 1905; she was the first woman in Canada to become an aeronautical engineer; she was also President of the Canadian Federation of Business and Professional Women's Clubs and a long-time supporter of the National Council of Women of Canada.

[52] Born in Halifax, Nova Scotia in 1919; she was admitted to the New Brunswick Branch of the Canadian Bar Association in 1964 and had been appointed Deputy Judge of the Juvenile Court there in 1965.

Privy Council minute. It was to "inquire into and report upon the status of women in Canada, and to recommend what steps might be taken by the Federal Government to ensure for women equal opportunities with men in aspects of Canadian society..." In particular the Commissioners were directed to inquire into and report on:

1. Laws and practices under federal jurisdiction concerning the political rights of women;
2. The present and potential role of women in the Canadian labour force, including the special problems of married women in employment;
3. Measures that might be taken under federal jurisdiction to permit better use of the skills and education of women;
4. Federal labour laws and regulations in their application to women;
5. Laws, practices and policies concerning the employment and promotion of women in the federal civil service;
6. Federal taxation pertaining to women;
7. Marriage and divorce;
8. The position of women under the Criminal Law;
9. Immigration and citizenship laws: policies and practice with respect to women;
   and such other matters in relation to the status of women in Canada as may appear to the Commissioners to be relevant.[53]

As the Commissioners themselves later complained, the subjects covered in these directives "were so extensive and diverse that they could have been the subject matter for separate Royal Commissions."[54]

From the moment the announcement was made in the House of Commons that this Commission would be established, some two weeks before the publication of the Privy Council minute, there was considerable public reaction. The press was sceptical, TV and radio commentators were less than enthusiastic and, to Florence Bird herself, the general consensus seemed to be that it was a "political gimmick to allow women to let off

---

[53] *Report of the Royal Commission on the Status of Women in Canada*, (hereinafter called *Report...Royal Commission*), (Information Canada, 1970), pp. vii-viii.
[54] *Ibid.*, p. ix.

steam" and that the final report "would be pigeonholed and forgotten."[55] The opening months of the Commission were difficult, as a secretariat had to be assembled and working quarters found. By the beginning of 1969, however, these problems had been overcome and a momentum achieved. The Commissioners proceeded to work by organizing research programs on a variety of topics, by meeting themselves 178 times over a period of nearly four years, by requesting and receiving briefs from individuals and organizations, and by setting up thirty-seven days of public hearings. As the authors of *Canadian Women* have pointed out, "there were no native minority, native, leftist or even younger women in the group,"[56] but the hard work of the Commissioners elicited the views of these people and they received 468 briefs and about 2000 letters of opinion. The whole Commission went to fourteen cities in the ten provinces. The Chairman and Lola Lange, accompanied by the Executive Secretary, Monique Bégin, also held hearings in Whitehorse and Yellowknife. In all, some 880 witnesses appeared before the Commission. Finally, in 1970, their report was released; it was signed by six Commissioners with a minority report by John Humphrey appended. There were 167 recommendations.

Royal Commissions in Canada have, as might be expected, varied considerably both in their immediate and long-term effects. The very best of them have managed to give Canadians an understanding of the issue being studied, a comprehension of what real problems have to be faced and some concrete suggestions about possible action to improve matters. Undoubtedly one of the most important results of the Royal Commission on the Status of Women was the education of both public and government about the reality of women's lives and the real nature of prejudice against women. A comparison of editorials in one newspaper, the *Ottawa Journal*, provides a vivid illustration. On February 4, 1967 this paper printed an editorial which read in part as follows:

> the reaction of Canadian men to news that a Royal Commission on women's rights has been appointed is what one would expect of a tough, hard-working, straight-talking male: fear. Everyone knows what Royal Commissions are like at their worst. Everyone knows what women are like at their worst. Put the two of them together — well we could end up with the longest established permanent Royal

---

[55] Florence Bird, *Anne Francis: An Autobiography*, (Clarke Irwin, 1974), p. 8.
[56] *Ibid.*, p. 149.

Commission in history. Somebody once said that individually women are something, but together they're something else... What makes these girls think any Canadian man in his right mind would sit on such a commission...?

The same newspaper commented on not quite four years later, December 8, 1970:

There is much to approve in the content, in the calm, deliberate tone and lucid exposition of facts and opinion in the Report of the Royal Commission on the Status of Women. The report is a masterpiece of condensation, so crammed with information and so sweeping in scope that the length of time required to bring it forth is now almost understandable. Moreover, women's Lib and all, it has not been overtaken by events; the report is almost agonizingly relevant... The report is too complex to be either uncritically praised or damned... The systematic and thorough searching out of inequities experienced by women in the work force, in education under the law and yes, in the family is the most useful part of the commission's work. The documentation of discrimination is irrefutable, whether deliberate or an unthinking perpetuation of male prejudice.

The impact of the public hearings was at the root of this alteration in perception. In spite of outright prejudice and veiled hostilities, the coverage by the mass media was good. As Florence Bird has written: "The briefs by large organizations pointed out clearly the areas of discrimination and the hardships experienced by many women because they were women." She went on: "There was strong emotional appeal in some of the submissions by Indian women, by sole support mothers and elderly widows, most of them poor."[57] Describing this aspect of the Commission's work, Florence Bird wrote:

Sometimes the commission hearings took place in the auditorium of a shopping centre or in a gymnasium, sometimes in hotels, so that we could reach people living in different parts of a city. Usually there was an audience of from two to five hundred people, most of them women. On a number of occasions, women travelled as far as three

---

[57] *Ibid.*, p. 299.

hundred miles by automobile from small towns which we could not visit in order to bring us their opinions...

There was a significant sameness about the kind of people who came to the hearings day by day, city after city. Most of them were women in their forties and fifties. Many spoke from harsh experience, having come up against discrimination and prejudice at work, where they found that equal pay legislation did not give them the same pay as men even when they did work of comparative value and responsibility. Many were housewives who found themselves bored, dissatisfied, and depressed, sitting in mechanized homes, no longer needed by their children, with thirty-five years of potentially active and useful life ahead of them.[58]

Monique Bégin has also testified to the impact on the Commissioners of those who came to present their ideas. She has written:

As a young woman discovering Canada through other women, I found the experience of the public hearings — and of the whole commission for that matter — one of the most memorable of my life. What I discovered month, after month, week after week, is how universal women's experiences were: this would be a lesson for life. Women in rural areas of Canada, women living and working in cities, native or immigrant women, young students as well as older women, francophone and anglophone women, all said the same things. They spoke of their aspirations and their lack of opportunities, the prejudices and the stereotypes, the need to change marriages and families to attain real and equal partnership. They spoke of the children they cared for. They stressed how the current political, economic and social structures of Canada were an insult to their dignity as women...[59]

In sum, the hearings of the Royal Commission were part of the stream of change which came to be known as the women's liberation movement. A great deal of the energy of the movement came, initially, from the decision of women involved in left-wing politics to speak about their own situation.[60]

---

58 *Ibid.*, p. 274.
59 Bégin, "Royal Commission," p. 33.
60 Prentice, et al., *Canadian Women*, gives a good synopsis of this, pp. 352-366; but see also Myrna

Women at universities, both students and faculty, took up the challenge, looking at what they experienced and the structures which society imposed upon them, to define their place within it. The issue of birth control, and later abortion, affected all women, cutting across class lines and political and religious divisions. The Royal Commission listened to briefs that were, on the whole, presented by the middle-aged, but it inspired younger women to organize themselves into discussion groups, such as the Women's Liberation Group at the University of Toronto and the Feminine Action League at Simon Fraser University, which went on to plan immediate political action. The establishment of the Royal Commission helped legitimize the demand by all women that their experiences be considered as valid and important as those of men.

During these years, 1967–1970, the Council, of course, encouraged members to submit briefs to the Royal Commission and to attend hearings. It also presented its own brief. Not unexpectedly, its main points dealt with the particular needs of women regarding:

> employment, taxation, divorce, domicile, women under criminal law, women offenders, rights of Indian women, the United Nations Conventions concerned with women, not yet ratified by Canada.[61]

This brief was submitted in March 1968, and in October that year the President and three other members of Council's Executive appeared before the Commission to answer questions. Reporting to the annual meeting of 1969, Margaret E. MacLellan — who had been the chairman of the Committee that had prepared Council's brief — remarked that they had been "encouraged by the number of Briefs which urged the implementation of reforms which National Council has been presenting for years." To take heart from this fact, instead of bewailing the lack of success that had attended past efforts, was to display great fortitude in the face of continued opposition. This attitude, however, is to be found all over the world among women who are members of Council. In the preface to the history of the Council of Women of Victoria, Australia, titled *Champions of the Impossible*,[62] the then President of that Council remarked, "the title of this history might equally

Kostash, Melinda McCracken, Valerie Miner, Erna Paris and Heather Robinson, *Her Own Woman: Profiles of Ten Canadian Women*, (Toronto, 1975).

[61] *Yearbook*, 1969, p. 39.
[62] Adele Norris, *Champions of the Impossible: A History of the National Council of Women of Victoria, 1902-1977*, (Melbourne, 1978).

well be 'Baffled, to fight better,' as an indication of the way in which the National Council of Women seeks the realization of an objective until the impossible becomes the possible and the possible, the reality."

Even though the business of the Royal Commission on the Status of Women was central to concerns of the National Council, its existence during a period of nearly four years did not bring to a halt the Council's normal round of activity, including continued pressure for the implementation of resolutions which formed part of its brief to Commission. At the seventy-third annual meeting, held in Saint John, June 6–9, 1966, the President, Mrs. H.H. Steen, reported for the Parliamentary Committee. She noted that it had met with the Prime Minister and members of the cabinet on January 31, 1966. The resolutions which the delegation particularly emphasized in this meeting concerned the need for a Royal Commission on Divorce, and for an amendment to the Criminal Code to allow public health and welfare agencies to disseminate information regarding birth control.[63] Similarly, in 1967, the Parliamentary Committee reported that the meeting held on January 30 had been courteous and encouraging. The government suggested that several of the issues raised would be dealt with in the coming report of the Royal Commission on the Status of Women, but agreed to respond to Council resolutions on a number of questions: among others, those concerning the care of the mentally ill under the Federal Hospital Insurance Scheme and the status of services for T.B. patients.

It can be seen, therefore, that Council, at the annual meetings of 1966 and of 1967 — the latter held in Montreal from June 4 to June 9 — was continuing its traditional path. Highlights from reports of the Social Welfare Committee, given by Kathleen C. Morrisey, show that welfare projects undertaken ranged from "the giving of Christmas dinners to 'poor'[64] families" (elsewhere, Chilliwack reported that 200 such meals had been delivered) to the study of such major community concerns as the needs of the emotionally disturbed child; the battered child syndrome; adequate housing facilities, including foster home care and day centres for older persons, as well as a study in depth on night work for women in industry."[65] Study of the battered child syndrome resulted in a committee request to have Council move a resolution for an amendment to the law making it mandatory on all persons, especially doctors and hospital personnel, to report all cases of sus-

---

63 *Yearbook*, 1966, p. 58.
64 *Quotation marks in original..*
65 *Yearbook*, 1966, p. 52.

25. Mrs. M. F. Steen, President 1964–1967

pected child abuse to child welfare authorities and to require prompt investigation of such reports.

Many reports brought forward in both years, however, related in some way to the celebrations of Canada's Centennial. One of the projects Council was engaged in was the establishment of the Lady Aberdeen Library collection at the University of Waterloo.[66] The idea had first been mooted at the Executive meeting of February 2–3, 1960, when a special Lady Aberdeen Library Committee was set up, chaired by Elizabeth Long.[67] In 1967 a considerable quantity of material, including some 2000 books and a number of cartons of primary sources would be shipped to the University, and a grant of $2000 was raised by Council to help it establish proper quarters for this gift. The donation provided the basis for the establishment, at the University of Waterloo, of a rare book and archive collection devoted specifically to women's history. In her comments on the work undertaken by Council members to create the original gift, Elizabeth Long noted their intention to form a research collection containing material not easily found elsewhere. She envisaged that material would be obtained, through inter-library loan, by "researchers anywhere, through university and public libraries." She went on to underline an issue which demands attention to this day. She observed that:

In searching for library material, you will agree we all have learned much. First and foremost of our discoveries is the general lack of literary sophistication among relatives and friends of Canadian women of note. They neither realize they have a public duty to save all letters and papers related to such a woman's career and also her private life — nor do they know that it never is their duty to sort out and decide which paper should be saved. The reason for this is that customs and ideas vary with the years and no one can foresee how future generations will view the life and achievements of the past. Other countries realize the value of saving all such material as it stands and until such action is general in Canada, we cannot hope for a large body of valuable and entertaining books on our prominent women.[68]

She had seen clearly something which has not, unfortunately, altered

66 Ibid., p. 32.
67 Yearbook, 1960, p. 33.
68 Yearbook, 1966, p. 59.

within this generation: the lives and the work of women tend to be invisible, not only to contemporary society but also, far too often, to the historian. Unless the documentation of women's lives becomes a priority, they will continue to feel that gaining recognition for their experience and achievements, and making society conscious that women are the necessary partners of men, is a task like that imposed on Sisyphus: eternally rolling a stone uphill only to see it tumble once more to the foot.

This 1967 Council meeting — the seventy-fourth — was the last of Mrs. Steen's presidency. One of its minor themes was the health of Council as an organization. There was no doubt it had a large membership. Although Kelowna, British Columbia, had ceased to function, as had Weston, Ontario, and Mission, B.C. the year before, St. John's, Newfoundland had joined. The "Extension Committee," founded in 1962 to look after membership matters, also reported the possibility of organizing more local councils in Quebec, and of founding at least one on Prince Edward Island. The affiliation of associations at the national level was also satisfactory: while the Canadian Nurses' Association had withdrawn in 1966, the Pioneer Women's Organization had joined the next year. But the Constitution Committee, an Administrative Standing Committee, was concerned about the relationships between the three Council levels — local, provincial, national — and had presented new by-laws for consideration over the coming months. The reforms instituted by Mrs. Turner Bone had worked well for more than a decade: the 1967 meeting signalled the need for yet another discussion of Council's constitution.

Mrs. H.H. Steen was succeeded by another Westerner: Mrs. S. M. Milne of Manitoba. She had been born Eleanor Mary Lamont in Winnipeg, where she had married and had four daughters. Her education included attendance at the Success Business College. Her work for the Elizabeth Fry Society and the Anglican Church brought her, firstly, to the Winnipeg Local Council and then to the Manitoba Provincial Council of Women. In her first address to Council, at the seventy-fifth annual general meeting, held in Edmonton, June 2–7, 1968, Mrs. Milne outlined her view of the Council's present situation. She was cautiously optimistic, but considered that once again attention had to be given to the pace of modern change. She remarked that "what was once regarded as an essential function may no longer be so, and any procedures which have ceased to have any real purpose can at once become wasteful, pointless and frustrating." She ended, however, by mentioning that, both at the local and the national levels, there had been expressions of interest from potential new affiliates.

In many ways this seventy-fifth meeting of Council was indeed optimistic. Many of the reports centred upon what had been done to celebrate the Centennial and Mrs. Robert Creighton, who gave the report for the Standing Committee on Arts and Letters, opened by saying:

> The result of Centennial Year has proven to have a lasting effect on the promotion of the arts in Canada. A great upsurge in travelling art collections, concerts, both professional and amateur, interest in museums, libraries and archives has been recorded. It is with great pleasure to note that Council has taken a keen interest in supporting all phases of arts in the community and it is hoped that this support will continue.[69]

The reports of Provincial Councils reiterated this theme. There was a general detailing of centennial projects, from the portrait in oils, commissioned by the Alberta Provincial Council, of Miss Roberta Adams, the first of two women elected to the Alberta Legislature, to the writing of the history of Ontario's Provincial Council of Women.

The report of the Parliamentary Committee was presented by Mrs. Milne. Its members had met with Prime Minister Lester Pearson and three of his cabinet ministers on February 1, 1968. The form Mrs. Milne used to report was more detailed than was customary. She listed the main issues presented and indicated government responses. In response to the request that the Income Tax Act be revised to provide better conditions for women, the Committee was informed that a White Paper would be introduced on this issue in the near future; on the matter of the "establishment of rehabilitation centres for children who are victims of war..," the Committee was informed that the Department of External Affairs was considering the foundation of a centre for this purpose by October 1968. Council's proposal that the Canadian Bill of Rights be revised was met with the answer that the government realized the Bill's inadequacies, and a federal-provincial conference would probably be held on the matter soon; on the needs of the Indian peoples, especially regarding land claims, the response was that "a new Indian Act would be introduced into Parliament very soon"; with regard to the proper labelling of hazardous materials, the answer was that the Department of Consumer Affairs would welcome suggestions; finally, on municipal issues, especially the need for urban renewal projects, the response was given that this would require municipal initiatives.[70]

---

[69] *Yearbook*, 1968, p. 45.
[70] *Ibid.*, p. 65.

Another issue of legislative concern was brought by the Committee on Migration and Citizenship. The chairman, Mrs. R. Hawrish, had sent out a survey on the proposed Bill on Hate Propaganda. The results were extraordinarily inconclusive and Council reacted by abandoning the issue as a topic for action.[71] A strong possibility of legislative action was indicated in the report presented by Mrs. M.W. Menzies, Chairman of the Economics Committee. She began by noting that one of the projects undertaken in the past year had been the preparation of a comprehensive brief, brought together by the Manitoba Volunteer Committee, for the Royal Commission on the Status of Women. It was partly as a result of this work that the main focus of the Economics Committee during the past year had been "to try and assess the position of married women within Canada's taxation system." The result of this study was,

> to question the economic subservience of women in marriage in Canada, to recommend the rejection of the family unit for taxation purposes unless and until there is prior legislation creating a true economic partnership in marriage, and finally to suggest that the whole concept of taxation as it is applied to married women ought to be reexamined with a view to establishing some quid pro quo within the system which would take into account the contribution being made by women to the state on an unpaid basis through rearing the next generation.[72]

Mrs. Menzies would pursue this theme as long as she chaired the committee.

---

71   42 questionnaires were despatched and 15 returned, by the following member organizations: the provincial Council of Manitoba (20 federated societies) and Saskatchewan (15 federated societies); the Local Councils (number of federated societies given in brackets) of Edmonton (34), Halifax (70), Kingston (40), Moncton (25), Montreal (109), Ottawa (77), St. Catharines (25), Saint John (31), Saskatoon (52), Swift Current (19), Vernon and District (18), Windsor (56), Fredericton and Area (27). The results were tabulated- *Yearbook*, 1968, p. 53, as follows:

1 Is hate propaganda a problem?
  Yes - 7   No - 8
2 Can legislation solve the problem?
  Yes - 6   No - 8   Uncertain - 1
3 Should legislation be civil or criminal?
  Criminal - 10   Civil - 3   Uncertain - 1
4 Can hate propaganda be dealt with outside the courts?
  Yes - 8   No - 5   Uncertain - 2
5 Can the problem be solved by focussing publicity on hate mongers?
  Yes - 6   No - 6   Uncertain - 3

72 *Yearbook*, 1968, p. 46.

It was, however, the report given by Mrs. H.P.D. Van Ginkel, the Chairman of the Resolutions Committee, that augered the possibility of radical new paths for Council. She opened by saying that "No outsider reads the NCWC constitution which says that we are devoted to bettering conditions of the family and the state. But everyone can read the newspaper reports of our briefs presented to the government..." "In other words," she went on, "what NCWC stands for finds its expression in the annual crop of resolutions."[73] She considered it inevitable that the "affiliated societies send to NCWC the particular issues which happen to bother them at that moment." The net result, however, was a collection of complaints and requests for action at a very petty level. In Mrs. Van Ginkel's view, "[For] a national organization devoted to improving national conditions [it seemed] that a more general and total view should be taken of the national condition and as a consequence, priorities should be assigned for action." She warned that unless its members were careful the NCWC might well become predominantly a platform for the woes of middle-income women. She called upon those attending the annual general meeting to "remember that those of us assembled here are already privileged...However much penny-pinching and extra work at home were involved we should remember that for many women it would be completely impossible."

Her recipe for renewal started with the proposition:

In the realm of inequities and social difficulties perhaps we should consider first the plight of the low income groups; the woman who must support children and perhaps older dependents, and cannot, for lack of skills command a reasonable wage. Income tax deductions do not help her at all. She cannot provide a decent home for her family and she cannot hire someone of quality to care for her children even if all her income is untaxed.

She went on:

Let us consider the thousands of children who live in a miserable environment, inadequately clothed and nourished, who suffer an enormous handicap — physically, emotionally, intellectually. Welfare does not help — or only to a limited degree. Active programmes of child care are needed for them.

---

[73] *Ibid.*, p. 66.

26. Mrs. S. M. Milne, President 1967–1970

She then turned to the problem of pollution and what she called "the ghastly environment of our cities, which are being constructed and extended not only without amenity but without efficiency." In conclusion, she addressed the question that was close to the heart of many volunteer organizations affiliated to Council at one level or another. She asked the Council to

> consider the basic inhumanity of our services. For example, emergency services where in the case of accident, in most communities, the interests of hospitals, officials and commercial enterprises have greater priority than the needs of the victims. Or the question of compensation for those who are injured in the course of playing a role as good citizen or even as innocent bystander.

Mrs. Van Ginkel had a fine perception of the need not only for vision but for practical organization. She was entering her last year as Chairman of the Resolutions Committee and her final report, given at the seventy-sixth annual meeting, held in London, Ontario, in 1969, outlined a series of propositions for the better ordering of Council work. They were supported by a small sub-committee which had helped to frame them. Basically, it was proposed that: convenors of standing committees should be prepared to undertake a considerable amount of work; they should be required to research and thoroughly check the material submitted to them and provide missing factual information in the brief to be presented to an annual meeting; they should consider that they held a watching brief in their area of concern and should submit a report on the status of past resolutions put forward by Council to the next annual meeting. Finally, the convenor of the Resolutions Committee at the national level should collate all the reports of all standing committees, dealing specifically with resolutions rather than surveys or other matters, and present at the annual meeting a progress report on each resolution adopted in previous years.[74]

This general attention to the functioning of Council led to changes in the way in which the Parliamentary Committee operated. It had, for a number of years, had a report incorporated into the *Yearbook*, entitled "NCWC Reader of Hansard on Resolution Material," the first one having been presented in 1969 by Mrs. W.A. Riddell. Twenty-one topic headings, from Family Planning and Birth Control to Indian Affairs, were used to catalogue, in no

---

[74] *Yearbook*, 1969, pp. 30-32.

particular order, items that had been part of Parliament's business during the past year and about which Council had, at some time or another, made a presentation to Government.[75] However, the annual meeting of the Parliamentary Committee and the Prime Minister remained unchanged in character, except that it was Prime Minister Trudeau and nine members of his cabinet who met the Council President and her companions on January 27, 1969.

This Prime Minister was much more forthcoming about his opinions of women in general, and the National Council of Women of Canada in particular, than any of his predecessors. Trudeau opened the meeting by "speaking in general about the position of women in society and the long distance still to progress in the whole area of women's rights."[76] He stated, reported Mrs. Milne,

> in unequivocal terms that in a properly balanced society there would be adequate use of woman power. He commented upon the use of the creative skills of women in other countries and mentioned particularly the large number of women in the medical profession in Russia. He stated that in an age where skill is more important than muscle there is more scope for the talents of women.

"Society," he said, "must be shaken to its senses."

Mr. Trudeau conveyed his appreciation of Council support for government policies and the concern of his government about what remained to be done, with respect both to the status of women and to the condition of society as a whole. He acknowledged the leadership which Council demonstrated and "expressed the hope that Council would make certain the population as a whole is made aware of policies where its approval has been signified." Finally, the Prime Minister said that "he would like to make it illegal and unconstitutional to discriminate on the grounds of sex."

In discussing specific measures advocated by Council, the Prime Minister said that he and the Justice Minister, Mr. Turner, were actively considering the appointment of women judges and appointments of women to government boards. The Finance Minister, Mr. Benson, said that although the notion of the family unit had been incorporated into part of the Carter Commission Report, the concept was not really an integral part of Canadian

---

75 *Ibid.*, pp. 33-36.
76 *Ibid.*, p. 28.

policy. Agriculture Minister Olson said matters of air and pollution were being considered by his department, along with the problem of soil pollution. With reference to the new omnibus bill, it was reported that Mr. Turner "assured Council that health, per se, includes mental health." Council had a long term commitment to ensure that mental illness was recognized as an aspect of sickness in general. With respect to abortion decisions, the Bill left this issue for medical determination. The Prime Minister's final word was to suggest that upon "the next presentation of matters of concern to Councils of Women the manner take the form of a dialogue rather than a brief."[77]

The final annual meeting for Mrs. Milne as President of Council, before the election of a third Westerner in succession, Mrs. Hnatyshyn, to that office, was held in her home city of Winnipeg, from June 1 to June 3, 1970. It took place before the tabling of the final Report of the Royal Commission on the Status of Women, on December 7, 1970. In many ways it was a meeting over-shadowed by this event. Certainly many government departments had replied to Council's queries, over the past year, by saying that nothing could be done until the report had been submitted. But for the Council President, the challenge contained in the 1969 report of Mrs. Van Ginkel posed an essential problem for the organization. In her final address, Mrs. Milne remarked that "thoughtful women are worried about Council's public image — the uncertainties which prevail in pursuing an active role in social involvement." As far as she was concerned, "in the short term span the emphasis must be placed on planning rather than problem solving."[78]

This wish to pursue strategy rather than policy is understandable, when one considers the vigour of public debate over the status of women at the end of the sixties. Council had flourished because of an intelligent refusal to commit itself and its members to any policy without lengthy debate. It had always moved slowly, so that temporary fashions would not lead it into premature statements of philosophy that would alienate a significant proportion of its membership. Council business was an affair not of majority decision making but of agreements reached. Its most effective actions had always developed out of a process of educating its membership about particular issues, through information and discussion, followed by resolutions representing a very broad consensus. As the sixties drew to a close, however, the position of women within society became a factor of importance in a very broad range of political issues. Treading the path of institutional revision, as

---

[77] *Ibid.*, p. 29.
[78] *Yearbook*, 1970, p. 25.

proposed by Mrs. Milne, rather than that of program and policy renewal, would expose Council to a serious risk of loosing its place as the major arbitrator and mediator of women's volunteer activities.

On the other hand, while one of the strengths of Council had always been its search for harmony, another had been its willingness to listen to new suggestions and ideas. At least two of the reports presented in 1970 outlined new goals for action and new policy proposals for study. Mrs. M.W. Menzies, still chairing the Standing Committee on Economics, stated clearly and bluntly, that "the economic weakness of women will not be overcome by better pay for women, more and better employment opportunities, improved counselling and education, or even the opening of more day nurseries, important and essential as all these features may be."[79] "The fundamental issue to be dealt with," her report stated, "is woman's role in the family and the family role in society." She was encouraged by the fact that the Economic Council of Canada, in its most recent report "had begun to discuss the family as an economic unity taking a first step into bringing the family to the economic framework of society," but she believed that "the central and crucial issue of the economic contribution made by women in the home has yet to be recognized and discussed."

Mrs. Menzies presented Council with a framework in which to discuss their ideas about the value of women, as human beings, as wives and mothers, and as thinking members of society. This forthrightness was also to be found in the report of Mrs. J.R. Hoag for the Committee on Housing and Community Planning. She did not have the philosophical bent of Mrs. Menzies but exemplified the practical tradition of members of Council, of people who had a responsibility for the conditions of daily life in their communities. She urged her correspondents to pay attention to municipal matters and asked: "As a council do you know what your city is planning before it becomes an actuality?"[80]

On the whole, however, Council members waited for the Report of the Royal Commission on the Status of Women with some trepidation, asking themselves to what extent its recommendations would make Council redundant. The fact that the position of women in society had always been one of the many issues concerning Council, though frequently the most important issue, tended to be forgotten. And, as the seventies would show, if some obstacles melted away, there were plenty of other matters needing action, and

[79] *Ibid.*, p. 35.
[80] *Ibid.*, p. 39.

the new President, Mrs. Hnatyshyn, would have no lack of problems to bring
to Council's attention.

CHAPTER 10

Reaction and Resolution
1970–1980

THIS BOOK IS being written less than a generation after the seventies. The passage of time has not yet worked its magic, allowing judgments between the ephemeral and the enduring to be made with some confidence. Even labelling the seventies is not easy. As the authors of *Canada Since 1945* remarked: "the seventies neither roared nor soared nor were dirty...for Canadians, change came quickly yet not in a regular pattern."[1] They go on to point out:

> nearly all the social indicators that Canadians traditionally used to measure the stability of their society seemed to reflect instability in the 1970s. The abortion rate rose from 8.3 per 100 live births in 1971 to 17.4 in 1978...suicides increased from 2,559 in 1971 to 3,317 in 1977...murder convictions from 342 to 624.[2]

These historians also note that rape convictions rose from "1,019 in 1969 to 1,886 in 1977 to 2,550 in 1983." They found this progression particularly disturbing. Their interpretation of this statistic exemplifies the difficulty of interpreting the decade as whole, before the perspective of history has really been established. Many feminist historians would question whether this rise in rape convictions meant a more violent society, one more angry with women, or a society that was, at long last, considering rape to be as serious as other forms of physical assault. They would also wish to comment on the

---

[1] Bothwell, et al., *Canada Since 1945*, revised edition, p. 407.
[2] *Ibid.*, p. 409.

amendments to the Criminal Code concerning rape, many the direct result of work by the Provincial Council of Women of Manitoba.

Whatever adjective is finally used as a shorthand title for the seventies, there can be little argument it was the decade when a major change began in the demographic structure of the family, a trend which continued throughout the eighties. One of the most important aspects of this change was the increased frequency of divorce.[3] In 1961 there were 6,980 divorces. The divorce law was revised in 1968 and between 1971 and 1974 divorces rose from 20,658 to 45,019.[4] From 1980 to 1985, "for every 100 unions created, 33 were dissolved by divorce. This proportion reached 50% in 1987 and then decreased to about 40%."[5]

This change in marriage stability was accompanied by two other important changes in family structure, both of which can be traced to the seventies and continued to develop during the eighties. In both cases the phenomenon had become sufficiently obvious during the seventies for it to become a matter of statistical investigation in the eighties. The first development was the growth of the single parent family, usually headed by a woman. In 1981 16% of families were headed by a single parent and in 1991 the figure was 20%.[6] The second is the growth of common-law unions. This is particularly striking: from 1981 to 1991 the increase was 103.6%. To put it another way, in 1981 the number of families in Canada was 6,324,975 of which 356,610 were common-law unions; in 1991, there were 7,356,165 families, of which 725,950 were common law unions.[7]

In sum, the pattern of marriage began to change dramatically in the seventies, and it was a change accompanied by three other shifts within Canadian society. Firstly, there was the continuing rise in the participation of women in the labour force. In 1971, women made up 35% of the labour force; in 1991, they comprised 45%. To put it another way, 40% of women worked for money in 1971, and in 1991 this figure had grown to 60%. Within a decade, the participation rate of women in the labour force rose from 39.9% to 52.9%, (the comparable figures for men being 76.4% and 79.4% respectively).[8] While the participation rate, of married women during these years rose only by 9.2%,

3 Jean Dumas and Yolande Lavoie, *Report on the Demographic Situation in Canada 1992: Current Demographic Analysis*, (Ottawa, November 1992), pp. 1-3.
4 Bothwell, et al., *Canada Since 1945*, p. 407.
5 Dumas and Lavoie, *Demographic Situation*, p. 41.
6 *Ibid.*, p. 28.
7 *Ibid.*, p. 27.
8 Jacques-André Boulet and Laval Lavallée, *The Changing Economic Status of Women: A Study prepared for the Economic Council of Canada*, (Ottawa, 1984), p. 7.

that of married women with preschool children rose 20.6%, and the rate for women with children aged 6–15, 19.0%.[9] The second major change was a fluctuating economic climate in Canada during the seventies, both across the country and from year to year. While Canada's growth continued it had became less smooth and less general. Productivity growth remained at 2.5% per year on the average until 1975, but the last five years of the decade saw very slow development.[10] Further, during these years growth was concentrated in the West, which emerged as a powerful industrial and business region. Within a generation the rural share of the prairie population had been cut in two;[11] Winnipeg, Regina and Saskatoon more than doubled in population between 1970 and 1980. Alberta oil, Saskatchewan potash and Manitoba nickel mines brought new prosperity and imposed new political pressures on the federal system. At the same time, it became obvious that the economy was less than buoyant in the Maritimes. A third social factor was that tensions between Quebec and the rest of Canada intensified and sharpened all political problems, such as the need to establish an effective economic policy in an international climate, or the need to ensure that the social net established in the sixties really functioned.

But more to the purpose than demographic change, economic difficulties and the tensions of ethnic politics during this decade was the change in the status of women. It did not bring an end to discrimination against women in Canada, nor did it convince all citizens that such discrimination was a bad thing. It was, however, a visible and measurable change in the importance attached to the role women played in every aspect of Canadian public life, political, social and cultural, a change in the way women viewed their role. The decade would end with many women bitterly aware that the battle for equality involved not only the struggle against obvious economic and political discrimination, but also called to eradicate very deep-rooted emotional beliefs on the part of both sexes concerning the "proper place" of women in society; even so, the change was real. It was partly brought about by implementation of a number of recommendations of the Royal Commission on the Status of Women. The federal authorities picked and chose among these recommendations, but by 1974, of the 122 that fell within the federal jurisdiction, 42 (34.4%) had been implemented in full; 37 (30.3%) had been partially implemented, leaving 43 [35.3%] to be carried out.[12]

---

9 *Ibid.*, p. 8.
10 Bothwell, et al., *Canada Since 1945*, revised edition, p. 15.
11 Morton, "Affluence," p. 524.
12 Advisory Council on the Status of Women, *What's Been Done?*, (Information Canada, 1974), p. 34.

Other causes of this change in women's roles and their perception of them, were the appointment of women to positions of importance within government, their entry into political life at all three levels, municipal, provincial and federal, and the increase in the number of women in the professions. Senator Muriel Fergusson became the first woman appointed as Speaker of the Senate, Pauline McGibbon was the first woman to be Lieutenant Governor of Ontario.[13] During the decade, the proportion of university teachers who were women increased from 16.7% to 24.6%; of women physicians and surgeons, from 10.1% to 17.1%; of lawyers and notaries from 4.8% to 15.1%.[14] The first women were accepted by the R.C.M.P. in 1974 and in the following year the first ten women began training with the Ontario Provincial Police.[15]

Perhaps the most important stimulus to change was the emergence of new feminist activity, as a result of raised expectations for women, as much by the process as by the recommendations of the Royal Commission. This phenomenon took two forms. One was the establishment of groups such as the National Action Committee on the Status of Women, dedicated to securing a political response to women's needs. The second was a broad intellectual examination of women's position in society, in the course of which many women began to demand not only equal treatment within the present organization of the country, but a rethinking of what a society might be that was truly free of discrimination against women.

As the decade went on, it became very clear that Council had to respond not only to the normal ebb and flow of Canadian life, but also to these new currents of feminist action and theory. This new demand became apparent during a decade which had opened with Council already observing the first indications of a decline in membership. In 1968, there were fifty-four local councils in existence, representing 1505 affiliates.[16] That same year there were also twenty-one nationally organized associations in affiliation at the national level.[17] By 1970 there were four fewer local councils, though the affiliates had increased slightly to 1533. However, Portage La Prairie, Prince Albert, Sackville, Stellarton, Trail, Yarmouth and Yorkton had been dis-

13 Pauline McGibbon was born to Alfred William and Ethel Selina Mills in Sarnia, Ontario on October 20, 1910. She studied modern history at the University of Toronto, graduating in 1933. She married Donald Walker McGibbon, January 26, 1935. Her c.v. is a roll call of volunteer activity.
14 Armstrong and Armstrong, "Women's Work," p. 293.
15 Minster of Supply and Services Canada, *Towards Equality for Women*, (Ottawa, 1979), p. 7.
16 *Yearbook*, 1968, p. 108.
17 *Ibid.*, pp. 12-14.

solved and while local councils had come into being at Charlottetown, Oshawa and District, and Sudbury; two of the three, Charlottetown and Sudbury, would have very brief lives. The number of nationally organized societies in affiliation in 1970 remained almost unaltered, except that the Canadian Dietetic Association had disappeared.[18] By 1981, there were only thirty-seven local councils, with a total of 921 affiliations.[19] There were, however, twenty-three nationally organized societies in federation.[20] While most of these had already been members in 1968, the seventies were a time of considerable coming and going in this category of membership. All in all, the Council survived the decade, but the tabling of the Report of the Royal Commission placed a heavy obligation on Council members to show dedication and flexibility.

The Royal Commission on the Status of Women had been established through the pressure of educated, literate, women who believed that action within existing structures of the state could produce major social changes. Cerise Morris has pointed out that by establishing the Commission, the federal government:

> clearly, and at one point in time, accepted and thus legitimized the social problem definition of the status of women...the creation of this new social problem definition provided a conceptual framework and beginning vocabulary for the development and articulation of feminist analysis and ideology which was to come.[21]

In other words, the very establishment of the Commission altered the way in which the Canadian polity considered the status of women. In appointing the Commissioners, the Prime Minister and his cabinet accepted the proposition that the place of women in Canadian life was as much a reflection of government policies and social constructs, as much a matter of belief and political will, as of some fundamental characteristic of human nature.

In organizing the context of their work, the Commissioners had little to turn to in the way of a body of Canadian feminist theory. In 1967, the majority of such writings lay in the future.[22] Twenty years later, Monique Bégin

---

[18] By dissolution.

[19] *Yearbook*, 1981, p. 124.

[20] *Ibid.*, pp. 12-13.

[21] Morris, "Determination," p. 19.

[22] The publication dates of the works which became international classics in this field fall in early seventies: e.g. Eva Figes, *Patriarchal Attitudes*, (London, 1970); Germaine Greer, *The Female*

defined the overall ideology of the Commissioners as being that of "liberal and pragmatic feminists."[23] Those who signed the majority report agreed to work from the general premise that for women "there should be equality of opportunity to share the responsibilities to society as well as its privileges and prerogatives."[24] Further, the Commission adopted four principles:

first, that women should be free to choose whether or not to take employment outside their homes...

second...that the care of children is a responsibility to be shared by the mother, the father and society...

third...that society has a responsibility for women because of pregnancy and child-birth, and special treatment related to maternity will always be necessary...

fourth...in certain areas women will for an interim period require special treatment to overcome the adverse effects of discriminatory practices.

These general propositions were the intellectual framework for Commissioners as they considered the briefs submitted to them, information garnered in the public hearings, and the research reports which were prepared.

Their final report contained 167 recommendations grouped into ten sections: women in the Canadian economy; women in education; women and the family; taxation and child-care allowances; poverty; participation of women in public life; immigration and citizenship; criminal law and women offenders; and finally, a plan for action. There is a very familiar ring to these headings. At any given time in the life of National Council, one can find a Standing Committee to pair with each. There is also considerable similarity between the traditional presentation by Council of its resolutions for change, and the way in which the recommendations of the Commission were set out. In both cases, background information was meticulously researched and clearly documented.

Eunuch, (London, 1970); Kate Millet, *Sexual Politics,* (London, 1971); Sheila Rowbotham, *Women, Resistance and Revolution,* (London, 1972). Canadian works also began to appear in the early seventies: e.g. Marylee Stephenson, ed., *Women in Canada,* (Toronto, 1973).

23 Monique Bégin, "Royal Commission," p. 29.
24 *Report...Royal Commission,* p. xii.

In many respects it was as a source of information that the report had its greatest value. Here at least a considerable body of raw material already existed. The Commissioners, in fact, would have been greatly handicapped without the work undertaken previously by the Women's Bureau of the Department of Labour. Since the creation of the Bureau in 1954, the women who headed it, Marion Royce, Jessica Findlay and Sylva Gelber, had firmly inserted "a pragmatic feminist viewpoint in the business of the state."[25] The last named had been appointed to the Bureau in 1968, after serving in the Department of National Health and Welfare since 1950.[26] Her statement, in 1969, that perhaps the time had come for housewives to "insist on a value...being placed on the unpaid domestic services which they provide,"[27] is indicative of the attitude of the Bureau. The statistics this agency had been collecting and publishing were now brought together, highlighted, and commented upon. The inequality of men and women in the labour force was delineated for all to see. For example:

1. Although a million women entered the labour force in the ten-year period between 1961 and 1971, the percentage of women in management only rose from 3.7 to 3.9 per cent.

2. In 1973 there were only five women in a House of Commons of 264 seats.

3. A recent study made by the Department of Labour in four cities showed that in each of ten occupations women's average weekly salary rates were less than those of men for similarly described work...in Halifax, the average weekly salary rate for women material record clerks was $71 compared with $106 for men. In Toronto it was $86 compared with $106 for men.

---

[25] Bégin, "Royal Commission," p. 27.
[26] Sylva Gelber was born in Toronto, December 4, 1910, the daughter of Louis and Sara Gelber. Educated at Havergal and Columbia University, she went to Palestine in 1932, where she worked in the Social Work Bureau from 1932 to 1937, in the Hadassah Medical Organization from 1937-42, and in the Government of Palestine, Department of Labour from 1942-48. She was made a member of the Order of Canada.
[27] Cited in Linda Silver Dranoff, *Women in Canadian Life Law*, (Toronto, 1977), p. 79. See also Sylva M. Gelber, "The Labour Force; the G.N.P.; and Unpaid Housekeeping Services," published in *Women's Bureau '70*, Department of Labour, (Ottawa, 1971).

4. This inequality in pay rates goes right on up to the top...The
   Commission found that women professors receive an average of
   $2,226 a year less than men with the same or lower academic
   degrees.[28]

If the Commission had merely brought this sort of information to general
notice and made it easily available it would have achieved a great deal. But,
of course, it achieved much more.

Even if some of its recommendations, such as those dealing with child-
care provisions and state responsibility for the family, seem utopian today,
most of them could be supported by a large part of the Canadian public. The
Commission's intention was not so much to challenge the life style of
Canadian people as to consider the extent to which women were able to participate in it. In accepting that their main task was to recommend ways in
which more women could really participate within the contemporary
Canadian community, the Commissioners, all white men and women of a
certain age, seemed automatically, and perhaps inevitably, to have concluded
that the view of Canada as a polity of "peace, order and good government"
was already in being.

In some ways, the report gained a great deal from this approach and generally, it was a most reasonable strategy. After all there was, and is, a great
deal of health and strength in the political and social institutions of Canada.
Further, there was at least some willingness in elite circles to change the situation of women, as had been demonstrated not only by the creation of the
Commission but by reactions to its work. The day after the Report of the
Royal Commission was tabled in the House of Commons, the leading editorial in the *Montreal Star* remarked that the most significant thing about its
arrival was:

the extent to which social attitudes in Canada have changed during
the three-and-a-half years in which the report was in preparation.
The appointment of the royal commission...was regarded by many
commentators as a form of mild eccentricity whose chief value
would be as a harmless outlet for the energies of the handful of club
women who really cared about such things. Now, only a few years
later, women's liberation is one of the hot issues of the day...[29]

---

[28] Bird, *Anne Francis*, p. 289.
[29] Cited in *ibid.*, p. 301.

27. Mrs. Helen (John) Hnatyshyn, President 1970–1973

As Anthony Westell, then columnist for the *Toronto Star*, wrote, "they [the recommendations] are reasonable answers to real problems which can no longer be ignored, and governments and public opinion are ready for reform."[30]

Many of the recommendations, like the headings under which they were listed, and the way in which they were presented, were akin to resolutions for change brought forward by the National Council over the years. Whether the issue related to volunteer work within society or to the need to enforce equal pay for equal work legislation, it had usually been addressed by Council at some time. For example, the Council's strong support, particularly since 1954, for equal pay for equal work found a satisfactory embodiment in recommendations 5 to 11 of the Commission.

However, now that the report had been tabled the question of its implementation had to be dealt with. Here the work of Council was two-sided: firstly, it set out to ensure that the contents of the report were known and thoroughly discussed; secondly, it organized pressure for the implementation of recommendations its members supported. At the June meeting in 1970, in advance of the report's publication, Council made an application to the Department of the Secretary of State for a grant to assist the publication and nationwide circulation of a Study Guide. Not only was funding granted but a Steering Committee was formed, with Miss S.M. Steadman representing the NCWC, which met during June, July and August "to organize details for a concise publication to be edited in accordance with Commission security regulations."[31] Entitled *What's In It?*, the publication was ready for distribution as soon as the Prime Minister released the report. While it had been prepared for Council purposes, bodies to which it was circulated included trade unions, the Public Service Alliance, the Canadian Union of Public Employees, the Canadian Labour Congress, the Business and Professional Women's Clubs, the I.O.D.E., the Women's Institutes, the Catholic Women's League, the Vanier Institute, as well as most educational organizations and the Federal and Provincial Women's Bureaus. Within two years, 10,000 copies of *What's In It?* had been sold.[32]

Having helped to provide an analysis of the report, in accordance with Council policy, Miss Steadman recommended that over the next year (1971–72) every local council be encouraged to organize study groups, spe-

---

30   February 8, 1970; cited in *ibid.*, p. 302.
31   *Yearbook*, 1971, p. 98.
32   *Yearbook*, 1972, p. 64.

cial meetings, planned discussions and seminars, so that resolutions concerning major recommendations in the report could be prepared and forwarded to government. Council also established a "Status of Women Committee," to follow up on government action being taken, and on particular steps toward implementation which local councils and nationally affiliated organizations wished to have taken.

So, as was to be expected, the Report of the Royal Commission on the Status of Women was a topic of major interest at the seventy-eighth annual meeting of Council, which was held in Halifax from May 31 to June 2, 1971. But, as was to be equally expected, it was not the sole issue of importance. The meeting was the first at which Mrs. Helen Hnatyshyn presided. She had a long history of involvement in Council, having been President of the Provincial Council of Saskatchewan from 1965–1967. During these years the Saskatchewan Council became deeply involved in the problems of the aged and the chronically ill. Mrs. Hnatyshyn opened her presidential address by remarking that "the Report of the Royal Commission on the Status of Women would provide every Council with 167 instant issues and could be the basis for uniting and involving women on the community level."[33] She went on to stress long-term, traditional Council issues: the need to work within established guidelines regarding Council procedures; the work of the convenors of standing committees and, by implication, a wide variety of Council concerns; and the position of Council as "an established channel of communication between governments and the people," an interaction she saw as "participatory democracy in action."[34] She also mentioned an aspect of Council that was becoming a staple item of discussion at its annual meetings, namely, the fluctuating level of membership, as observed in the local councils.

New procedural guidelines had been the subject of a three-year study, but resulting proposals envisaged no major overhaul. Instead emphasis was laid on the need for Council to carry out established procedures: the organization should remember to act as a Council at all levels, and endeavour to make its bureaucracy as slim and efficient as possible.[35] The work of the committee Chairs, praised by Mrs. Hnatyshyn, was displayed effectively through the reports of standing committees. For example, the report given by Kathleen Morrisey, who chaired the Standing Committee on Health, emphasized the need to respond to the Royal Commission on the Non-Pharmaceutical Use of

---

[33] *Yearbook*, 1971, p. 36.
[34] *Ibid.*
[35] *Ibid.*, p. 30.

Drugs (the LeDain Commission), an issue that was taken up again in the report of the Standing Committee on Social Welfare. That report, given by J.E. Butler, also stressed the problem of the "retarded child as a burden to the family" and the need to provide some kind of help for an average family having to cope with such a stroke of fate.[36]

The most important action taken by this annual meeting was, undoubtedly, the vote on the resolution concerning abortion. Throughout the seventy-eight years of its existence, the National Council had struggled to bring together women to work for the betterment of family and society, without demanding that agreement be given to any particular creed, political or philosophical. The issue of abortion tested this principle to the limit, for it demanded true adherence to the principle of individual freedom of conscience. The resolution presented was simple. It read as follows:[37]

Whereas, Abortion is a matter of personal rather than public morality and

Whereas Abortion should be considered a medical not a legal procedure; therefore

Resolved, That the National Council of Women of Canada request the Government of Canada to remove the sections pertaining to abortion from the Criminal Code of Canada.

It passed with the vote in favour being 103 for, with 13 against and 70 abstentions. The Salvation Army, in particular, asked for its negative vote to be recorded.[38]

There is no doubt this stand had an impact on the membership in the Council, but the picture is very complicated. In 1971, the number of local councils was fifty, bringing together approximately 1400 affiliations,[39] and the number of nationally organized associations had dropped to 18 from 20 in 1970. While the Anglican Church Women joined, the Canadian Federation of University Women and the Lyceum Women's Art Association withdrew.[40] In 1972 the number of local councils was forty-nine, comprising

[36] *Ibid.*, pp. 48, 56.
[37] *Ibid.*, p. 97.
[38] *Ibid.*, p. 31.
[39] *Ibid.*, p. 93. Neither Regina nor Halifax reported their affiliate numbers this year, and the number used has been that of 1970.
[40] *Yearbook*, 1971, pp. 12-14.

1370 affiliates,[41] and the number of nationally organized associations remained the same, but the W.C.T.U had ended its affiliation at this level, while the Canadian Association in Support of Native People had joined.[42]

To present this issue another way, the year after the pro-choice resolution had been adopted by Council, the majority of local councils showed no significant alteration in the number of their affiliates. Thirty councils either maintained a steady membership or lost or gained no more than three affiliations in 1971–72: Brantford, Burnaby, Calgary, Charlottetown, Chatham, Chilliwack, Comox, Dawson Creek, Georgetown, London, Moncton, Montreal, Nanaimo, New Glasgow, New Westminster, North and West Vancouver, Orillia, Ottawa, Peterborough, Regina, Red Deer, St. Catharines, St. John's, Saint John, Saskatoon, Swift Current, Truro, West Pictou, Westville, White Rock and District. Eleven councils showed a noticeable drop: Brandon fell from 36 to 22; Edmonton from 33 to 28; Fort St. John from 20 to 15; Hamilton from 46 to 40; Moose Jaw from 24 to 17; Niagara Falls from 27 to 22; Peterborough from 25 to 22; Vancouver from 59 to 55; Victoria from 21 to 16; Windsor from 56 to 49; Winnipeg from 76 to 69. Six councils recorded a dramatic drop: Halifax, from 67 to 40; Kingston, from 40 to 31; Sudbury ceased operation; Toronto suffered a major decline from 76 to 57.

The 1971 resolution did not put the abortion issue to rest for Council. There has been no change in the organization's stance, and the resolution has rarely been brought forward for formal debate since. Nevertheless, access to abortion is an issue that is still frequently discussed among Council members. This is not surprising since it is, after all, one of the most fundamental questions for women's organizations. Even to attempt to summarize the argument is to invite dissension, since moral passions on both sides tend to generate emotional language. Essentially, however, the debate is between those who feel there can be no such thing as a "legal abortion," since any abortion procedure is a form of murder, and those believing that access to medically safe abortions must be provided if society does not wish to see the problem solved in economic terms alone, with poor women denied access to a procedure which can, was, and would be, bought by those with the necessary financial resources. That Council has stood firm over a woman's right to choose shows a remarkable tenacity of purpose.

---

[41] *Yearbook*, 1972, p. 84.
[42] *Ibid.*, p. 12.

Equally remarkable, during the seventies, was Council's refusal to turn
away from the broad issue of community welfare as a whole to more narrow
concerns. It continued to pay a great deal of attention to a broad spectrum of
social concerns while maintaining a strong commitment to many feminist
policies. At the 1972 annual meeting which took place in Regina, May
29–31, Mrs. Hnatyshyn gave an impassioned address on the need for women
to "become active in politics, where they could wield influence where it
counts — in the administrative bodies of this nation."[43] She remarked that
the Prime Minister and cabinet seemed genuinely interested in the issues
Council brought before them, and emphasized her belief that while "much of
our effort in this area probably has an intangible effect: [nevertheless] it is
safe to say that through the years there has been a great deal of Legislation
enacted for which we can claim direct responsibility."[44] She turned to the
issue of women in politics and sounded a little depressed as she noted that
"at no time since 1918, when Canadian women got the vote, have there been
more than six women in the House of Commons at one time." She went on
to say that "in the 105 years of Confederation, there have been two women
Cabinet ministers." Her conclusion was that "more women must go into politics, and more important, that more women [must] support those who do."
Unless this occurred she felt women would never really be part of the decision-making process, and therefore never gain equal status with men.

The standing committees continued to report widespread community
involvement by members of Council. The issue of drug abuse was once more
an issue for the committee on Health, as was the alarming increase in venereal diseases. These forms of disease which, from the founding of Council to
the end of the forties, were reported on annually, once more became a matter
of concern to members. The issues of treatment centres and confidential services for patients were raised again.[45]

Under the chairmanship of Mrs. Brigadier I. Halsey, the Social Welfare
Committee had the distribution and organized completion of an ICW ques-
tionnaire on "Senior Citizens — Their place in the Family and the
Community." It was pointed out that the current age structure of the
Canadian population signified that the country had a relatively small number
of aged people.[46] A study of the reports of local councils, however, shows

43 *Yearbook,* 1971, p. 37.
44 *Ibid.,* p. 35.
45 *Ibid.,* p. 53.
46 *Ibid.,* p. 59.

their very considerable involvement in programs such as "Meals on Wheels" for the elderly, in lobbying for free public transport for seniors, and in discussing their particular health and housing needs.

Among the twelve resolutions brought forward and accepted, four dealt with clearly feminist issues. The first and second of these concerned, respectively, equality for women in pension plans and affirmative action to provide employment opportunities for women. Both were brought forward by the Provincial Council of Manitoba.[47] Resolution no.8, proposed by the Saskatoon Council of Women, asked "the government of Canada to seek ways and means of officially recognizing the contribution to the Canadian economy and to Canadian society of the homemaker."[48] Resolution no.9, brought forward by the Saskatoon, Regina and Burnaby Local Councils as well as the Provincial Council of British Columbia, wanted "the participation by homemakers in a contributory Social Security Program" made possible. Other resolutions included one brought forward by the Provincial Council of British Columbia, proposing that the R.C.M.P recruit women. Both Montreal and Ottawa Local Councils were concerned with the preservation of Canadian heritage; Montreal asked for a federal archive to be established for film footage and other audio-visual material. There were three resolutions dealing specifically with social welfare matters: Ottawa Local Council asked for the proper enforcement of building safety codes, especially where these affected handicapped people; the Regina Council of Women asked for an increase in the Basic Old Age Security pension (in 1973 it was $82.88 per month); the White Rock and District Council brought forward the whole issue of child abuse and asked that legislation be enacted to make the reporting of known abuse obligatory.

There were six "emergency resolutions" adopted. These dealt with the perceived need to control begging; the need to monitor Canada's population growth and for Canada to participate fully in the United Nations efforts to make family planning a major issue for world attention; a request to the federal government to fund the National Council of Women of Canada; to ban phenoxy herbicides, such as 2,4–D, 2,4,5–T and Silvex; and to make federal funds available to municipalities to study the proper treatment of waste water.[49]

As far as individual reports of local councils were concerned, 1971–72

---

[47] *Yearbook,* 1973, pp. 105-6.
[48] *Ibid.,* p. 108.
[49] *Ibid.,* pp. 110-12.

had been very much the year of the Report of the Royal Commission, with most local councils devoting more than one meeting to discussion of the issues raised. However, many councils also paid considerable attention to international matters, organizing seminars on a wide variety of international questions. Hamilton Local Council went further and organized an International Christmas Festival which brought together "fifteen ethnic groups" and raised money for a piano for the new theatre auditorium.[50] A large number of Councils reported their continued support of UNICEF. For the first time in a decade, one Local Council, West Pictou, reported that children were provided with milk in schools.[51] In the course of the seventies Council would find its members turning once again to the relief of immediate needs in their communities.

Mrs. Hnatyshyn's final legacy to the Council was her backing of the final report of the "Committee on Structure, Organization and Goals of the NCWC," particularly the recommendation that work start immediately "on a manual of guidelines for all officers and chairmen, clerical staff and others for whom such help would be beneficial."[52] This has since evolved into a most useful compendium of instruction and information concerning the means by which the National Council tries to work. It has been kept up to date and the most recent edition was published in 1988. The volume consists primarily of the Constitution, By-Laws and Standing Rules of Council, but it also contains such items as the terms of reference for standing committees and a précis of the history of the organization. One of its most useful sections to anyone interested in the work of Council is the "Index of Policy Resolutions." This catalogues most of the resolutions passed since 1963. It is followed by an equally interesting section listing the briefs presented to the federal government since 1967.

In the spring of 1972, Laura Sabia and many who had worked with her on the Committee on Equality for Women, organized the "Strategy for Change conference." This gathering, which brought together approximately 500 delegates representing more than forty women's organizations, did two things. First, it presented a brief to the federal government asking for "the expansion of day-care, insertion of 'sex' as a prohibited basis of discrimination under Canadian human rights provisions, and decriminalization of abortion."[53]

---

50 *Yearbook*, 1971, p. 89.
51 *Ibid.*, p. 102.
52 *Yearbook*, 1973, p. 58.
53 Prentice, et al., *Canadian Women*, p. 350.

Secondly, it took steps toward the formation of the National Action Committee on the Status of Women (NAC). The aim of the new organization was to ensure that all the recommendations of the Royal Commission would be implemented, except the proposal for status of women councils to be appointed at all levels of government. From the outset, NAC obtained government funding for its work. In the years following it would become a very powerful organization and by 1984 claimed "458 member groups, 70 of which were pan-Canadian."[54]

It is important to understand what was happening here. In the period under consideration, membership in the National Council of Women of Canada fell; it was accorded less publicity by the media; and the federal government gradually paid it less attention. At the same time the National Action Committee developed and flourished, gained important recognition as a powerful voice for women's views, was accorded a growing importance by bureaucrats and politicians at both the federal and provincial levels, and obtained significant federal funding. There is undoubtedly some correlation between the two processes; the question is: How much?

An examination of the associations affiliated to the two umbrella bodies does not show any very great overlap. Annual listings of NAC membership for the seventies are difficult to come by, but the NAC membership in the eighties consisted predominantly of women's unions, women's resource and crisis centres, status of women groups and women's ethnic groups. At the national level, the associations included the Anglican Church of Canada, the Canadian Association of Women Executives, the Canadian Association of Women in Science, Economists, Sociologists and Statisticians, the Liberal Party of Canada and the Women's Liberal Commission. Some of these groups might well have been members of the Council in the past, and one or two — such as the Elizabeth Fry Society and the Y.W.C.A. — would be members of both NAC and Council.[55] However, many associations linked to NAC would not automatically have sought affiliation to Council. The Canadian Textile and Chemical Union and the Feminist Party of Canada are not, for example, obvious affiliates for an umbrella organization of volunteer associations such as NCWC.

---

54 Jill Vickers, "The Intellectual Origins of the Women's Movement in Canada," in *Challenging Times...* p. 43.
55 "Member Groups of NAC," *NAC Brochure*, May, 1968; in Christine Appelle, "The New Parliament of Women: A Study of the National, Action Committee on the Status of Women," unpublished M.A., Institute of Canadian Studies, Carleton University, 1987, App. A.

What happened was not so much the growth of one body at the expense of the other, as the recruitment of many women into supporting new forms of public action. NAC became, and remains today, the home of women's groups oriented towards changing, immediately, laws and societal practices which oppress women as a sex in any way. While NAC has experienced, as much as Council, chronic debate on how it should be run, its members agree, fundamentally, that NAC must engage in all the political processes of Canadian society to argue the case for women's rights. For over twenty years NAC has been the arena for dialogue between women of all political persuasions, and has incorporated the most vigorous of the new feminist collectives into its ranks: those of young socialist women, the many consciousness-raising groups, and at least some of the wilder, counter-culture women's associations. The growth of NAC took place at the expense of the Council of Women in so far as a number of new adherents, especially of the younger generation, felt the former's strategy and tactics were more suited to the times than those of the more conservatively paced organization. But many of the women who sought to strengthen their political positions in the public arena would not have been easily recruited to the Council.

As was customary, Mrs. Hnatyshyn reviewed the aims and achievements of the National Council during her term of office in her last presidential address, given to the eightieth annual meeting of the NCWC, held in Toronto, June 11–15, 1973. While Council inevitably devoted a great deal of its time to the Report of the Royal Commission on the Status of Women, Mrs. Hnatyshyn considered that attention focused on "the Human Rights of children" was of equal moment. Her summary of issues brought before the Prime Minister and Cabinet, at annual meetings accorded to Council, went far beyond the rights of women *per se*, although she also summarized the work of Council in this area. Her first listing of the matters of specific concern that she had presented on these occasions included:

> The plight of federal women prisoners; appointment of a senior officer, preferably a suitably qualified woman, for the treatment of women offenders; pollution, preservation of the Canadian heritage, youth hostels, the quality of Canadian broadcasting programmes, law reform, legal aid, urban development, housing; prescription restrictions for amphetamines and methadone; treatment centres for drug addicts, and the establishment and preservation of National Parks.[56]

---

[56] *Yearbook*, 1973, p. 30.

28. Mrs. Gordon B. Armstrong, President 1973–1976

In her second list she enumerated specific matters relating to the status of women:

> Appointment of more women to Boards, Commissions, the Senate and other policy making bodies. At successive meetings with the Cabinet, Council has reiterated the request that "government ensure for women equal opportunities with men in all aspects of Canadian Society." Repeated requests have urged government to amend the Pension Plan, so that the spouse who remains at home can participate in the Plan. This is particularly desirable for the protection of the homemaker, and would give recognition of her social and economic contribution to society.[57]

What is clear, from this speech, is that while many of the concerns of NAC and the National Council overlapped, the latter had a different perspective on the role of women in society.

To sum up, the focus of Council action had always been the combined pursuit of three major goals: to act as a channel for the public voice for women engaged in a wide variety of volunteer work for society; to persuade Canadians that women ought to be given a status equal to that of men in the social and political life of the country; to lobby governments, at all levels, in support of policies on which the broad membership of Council had come to a workable agreement. While both the second and third goals were important, Council's history has been shaped particularly by the volunteer work of its membership. The reports of both the standing committees and local councils show the extent to which women worked to design a particular texture for Canadian life. Whether they were involved in art exhibits and local concerts, or the organization of lecture series on matters of international concern or citizens' rights, Council women worked — for a wide variety of personal reasons — for the community as a whole. With regard to health matters, housing, educational issues or the need for recreational resources, local councils followed local proposals, commented to the relevant authorities and, often enough, had their suggestions incorporated into the final plans.

Yet even these traditional aspects of Council work were not beyond question in the seventies. Ever since 1940, the state, and particularly the federal government, had become an increasingly powerful player, not only in

---

[57] *Ibid.,* p. 31.

the arena of social welfare but also in culture. However one might argue about the adequacy of the welfare assistance provided, by the beginning of the seventies the state had become the major mechanism for the distribution of aid to the needy, the young or old, the ill or unemployed. Through official programs ranging from mothers' allowances to universal old age pensions, from medicare to unemployment insurance, Canadians were caring for one another through government bureaucracy. Society's compassion was being exercised primarily through paid community workers instead of individual acts of generosity. Similarly, since the founding of the Canada Council in 1957, all levels of government had provided occasional funding for the development of theatres, concert halls, orchestras, opera, ballet and modern dance companies. While there was a continuing need for volunteers to raise additional funds, the mainstream cultural life of Canada now obtained its major support from government agencies.

Mrs. Catherine (Gordon B.) Armstrong was President of the National Council from 1973–1976. She had graduated from the University of Toronto in 1965, with a B.A. in Political Science and Sociology, and was the President of the Provincial Council of British Columbia from 1969–1971. During her term of office, Council faced not only the challenges inherent in the development of NAC and in the ever-increasing government role in social welfare and culture, but also those presented through the emergence of a government bureaucracy to advise both the federal and provincial governments on women's issues. The Canadian Advisory Council on the Status of Women was brought into being on May 31, 1973. It was a thirty-member board reporting to the Minister responsible for the Status of Women. Three Council members were among the first appointees.[58] Ontario and Quebec also established Provincial Advisory Councils that year, Laura Sabia being appointed to head the former.[59] The activity of Council as an independent lobbyist was not precluded by the emergence of these bodies, but lobbying from this point on would be pursued in a different context, as new establishments found their place in the complex network of the civil service.

After 1973, Council was confronted on all sides by the need to justify its existence. What could it do, that was not being done with more energy or more efficiency by other bodies within the polity? Part of the answer can be

---

[58] *Ibid.*, p. 37.
[59] Saskatchewan followed suit in 1974, Prince Edward Island in 1975; Nova Scotia and New Brunswick in 1977; Manitoba and Newfoundland in 1980; Alberta in 1986; the Northwest Territories in 1990.

found in the report of the 1974 annual meeting, held in Moncton, New Brunswick, from June 3 through 6. Here the links between the National Council of Women of Canada and the International Council of Women were once more stressed. Mrs. Armstrong had a long-standing interest in international matters, had worked for the Canadian Commission for UNESCO, and had been Council's representative to UNICEF. In 1973 she was appointed to the UNESCO committee on the proposed International Women's Year, to be celebrated in 1975. In 1973, Mrs. Armstrong also participated in the twentieth triennial meeting of the International Council of Women in Vienna. In 1974, she stressed the importance of making all the preparations necessary for 1976, when Canada would host the twenty-first meeting of the International Council in Vancouver. During the rest of her presidency, the international links of Council would receive considerable attention from its membership.

But while the Moncton meeting gave more attention to International Council meetings, the crucially important actions of Council were still those reported by standing committees and by the local councils themselves, and the lobbying, at all levels, for official acceptance of resolutions. Both the strength of the Council as an organization, and its complementary weakness, can be seen in the multiplicity of actions chronicled. The very diversity and breadth of concern which made the Council at all three levels — local, provincial and national — an accurate reflection of the myriad concerns of women in a complex society, also made it difficult for the organization to present a coherent image of its activities. The Local Council of Chilliwack, for example, spent most of its time and energies on the visit of two Zambian women, who wanted "to learn skills that would benefit the women and families at home." Chilliwack paid all their expenses and felt that it had learnt as much as its visitors.[60] The Local Council of Niagara Falls concentrated its efforts, over the same period of time, on ensuring that it was represented on organizing bodies within the community. It reported its representation on the Conservation Authority Committee, the Charitable Appeal Review Board, and the Landlord-Tenant Advisory Bureau. Mrs. Alfred Dane, the President, was on the Social Planning Board of Council and on the Steering Committee of the Information Centre. Honourary Vice-Presidents were involved in the United Appeal and the Chamber of Commerce and one was a General Vice-President of the Canadian Union of Public Employees (CUPE).[61]

---

[60] *Yearbook,* 1974, p. 97.
[61] *Ibid.,* p. 103.

While it is difficult to decide which particular actions are most illustrative of the nature of Council from among the abundance of good, if discrete, projects carried out by its members, some endeavours dating from this decade of change seem particularly rewarding. The report of Mrs. W.T. Kennedy, the Chair of the Arts and Letters Committee, shows the type of action members could still usefully perform. She noted that:

> At the National level, Council took a look at the way interest in native art is being exploited. Facsimile reproductions, mass produced, resulting in no benefits to native artists, are being sold as "genuine" in stores considered to be reputable. Letters were written to those corporations suggesting an approach to purchasing which would encourage Indian and Eskimo carvers and artists.[62]

She concluded by saying that the CBC had provided Council with the details of this activity "and also the names and addresses of artists creating objects in traditional symbolic styles of the native peoples." The whole tangled issue of marketing the artistic work of Canada's First Peoples involves close analysis of how very different cultures can interconnect without undue exploitation of one by the other. At least the sort of action that Council pursued resulted in a greater measure of native influence over their art than might otherwise have been the case.

Activities reported through Mrs. R.E. Beach, who chaired the Environment Committee, demonstrate the extent to which Council moved early, and often most effectively, on environmental issues. The establishment of a Royal Commission of Inquiry into the use of Pesticides and Herbicides by the Minister of Health in British Columbia was attributed in the press to the work of Council members, in particular Merriam Doucet and Thelma McAdam.[63] Other activities reported were the work of the Ontario Provincial Council to preserve trees threatened by highway construction, the Saskatchewan Provincial Council's work on pesticides, and the general support of local councils for environmental action. The 1974 annual meeting adopted resolutions from the Halifax Local Council on the need to plan land use effectively, and from the British Columbia Provincial Council on the need to survey all research being carried out on weed and pest control by chemical means.

---

[62] *Ibid.*, p. 43.
[63] *Chatelaine*, 1974, cited in *ibid.*, p. 46.

The Report of the Health and Welfare Committee to this meeting was
lengthy, and dealt with two major issues: alcoholism and venereal disease.
The focus of Council members on both these problems related to the need
for prevention, through education, treatment centres, and counselling.
Resolutions against the advertizing of alcohol and tobacco were passed.
Other matters reported to this Committee included the Toronto Local
Council work on nutrition for pregnant mothers and preschool children in the
inner city, the continuing support of "Meals on Wheels" by a number of
councils, and the survey of nursing homes and the extended care programs
by the Ontario Provincial Council. The Local Council of Montreal reported
that it had held a major workshop on the theme of "Your changing
Community — Responsible Participation," organized so that 210 participants met in twenty-two discussion groups under the general headings of
"Education, Environment, Health, Welfare and Social Responsibilities..."[64]

Two of the issues reported on by a number of councils arose out of
recent rulings by the Supreme Court on the rights of native women and the
rights of farm wives. The first of these rulings concerned the application of
the notorious clause 12 (1)(b) of the Indian Act, which gave Indian status to
wives and children of Indian men, but denied it to Indian women marrying
non-status men. In 1973, the Supreme Court found that Indian women were
entitled only to "equality in administration and enforcement of the law." The
Bill of Rights enacted in 1960 did not forbid "inequality within a group or
class by itself, by reason of sex."[65] The Canadian Association in Support of
the Native Peoples had became an affiliate of Council at the national level in
1973. It represented some 5000 people and made it very clear that it was not
a native organization but a citizens' support organization whose members
were almost all of non-native descent.[66]

The resolution brought forward by the Provincial Council of Nova
Scotia, concerning the rights of native women, was given unanimous support. It read as follows:

Whereas present legislation denies an Indian Woman

(a) the right to be called Indian if she marries an non-Indian;

64 The Montreal Council of Women/Le Conseil des Femmes de Montréal, *Eightieth Year Book Annual Report 1973-1974*, p. 40.
65 Prentice, et al., *Canadian Women*, p. 397.
66 *Yearbook*, 1973, p. 69.

(b) the right to return to the Reservation if she loses her husband through death, divorce or separation; and

(c) if she is an unwed mother, the right to determine whether or not she shall keep her child, and whether or not it shall be brought up as an Indian; and

Whereas none of the above need involve any property rights or settlements to her, or rights of any kind to a non-Indian husband or children;

Resolved, The Provincial Council of Women of Nova Scotia requests the NCWC to request that legislation be enacted to rectify the situations noted in (a),(b),(c) in consultation with the Indian women.[67]

The issue concerning the rights of farm wives was highlighted by the case of Irene Murdoch. Her marriage had broken down in 1968, and she claimed a share in the value of the family ranch on the basis of her working contribution over the years. She had participated in "haying, raking, swathing, mowing, driving trucks and tractors and teams...dehorning, vaccinating and branding." The Supreme Court, with one dissenting opinion from Chief Justice Bora Laskin, felt that she did the work "of any ranch wife" and that such work should not "give any farm or ranch wife a claim in partnership."[68] Throughout the hearings on the case, women from the Local Council in Calgary walked with Irene Murdoch to and from the court room,[69] and also set about establishing a trust fund to finance her legal costs.[70]

Mrs. Murdoch's experience led to many members of Council expressing views similar to those of Mrs. M.W. Menzies, the President of the Provincial Council of Manitoba. She remarked on three specific events of the past year that demonstrated the urgency for continued work by members of Council. She noted:

First, the Manitoba election in June 1973 in which several outstanding women candidates for the provincial legislature were all defeated, leaving the provincial parliament a male preserve; second, the

---

[67] *Yearbook*, 1974, p. 114.
[68] Dranoff, *Canadian Life Law*, pp. 51-55.
[69] Personal testimony: interviews in Calgary, June 1991.
[70] *Yearbook*, 1974, p. 60.

court cases before the Supreme Court concerning Jeanette Lavell, the Indian woman and Irene Murdoch, the farm woman which demonstrated the injustice of the law; and finally the Reports of the Task force on Equal Opportunity in the Manitoba Public service which disclosed discrimination against women in the Manitoba Public service of a most extreme nature.[71]

The resolutions brought forward at the eighty-second annual meeting, held in Montreal in 1975, provide continuing evidence of the diversity of Council interests. The sixteen resolutions may be grouped into four main areas of concern:[72] the first dealt with general cultural life, and a resolution on "Satellite Transmission and Copyright Problems." The second area of concern was community planning, and resolutions presented addressed the need to enforce building codes; the transportation of hazardous cargo; the control of firearms; and the need for non-polluting sources of energy. The third group of resolutions had to do primarily with the welfare of the family in general, and children and the elderly in particular, and the subjects of resolutions were the legal system and the need for family courts; the control of advertising directed at children, the education of children and the need to plan, immediately, for the well-being of the elderly. Finally, there were resolutions which centred, particularly, upon the rights of women, and these dealt with such matters as spousal benefits under the Canada Pension Plan and the extension of rules respecting registered retirement savings plans to cover contributions paid for a spouse.

One of the most important activities of the 1975 meeting was the planning meeting for the following year when the eighty-third annual meeting of the Canadian Council coincided with the twenty-first triennial conference of the International Council of Women, June 21 to July 4. Mrs. Armstrong's opening speech in Vancouver emphasized the amount of work that had gone into organizing the gathering which brought together sixty-eight national councils[73] and representatives from nine major world agencies, including the United Nations and the World Bank. She reported the commendation Prime

[71] *Ibid.*, p. 91.
[72] *Yearbook*, 1975, pp. 94-104.
[73] Since 1963 the following countries had established Councils: Bahamas, 1966; Ghana, 1973; Guatemala, 1966; Ivory Coast, 1970; Madagascar, 1970; Malaysia, 1966; Malta, 1966; Mexico, 1966; Morocco, 1970; Nepal, 1970; Saudi Arabia, 1966; Surinam, 1973; Syria, 1966. *Vision ICW: Centenary 1988*, p. 11. This publication is a single issue journal published by the ICW to celebrate its Centennial Year.

Minister Trudeau had given to Council when their annual brief, on the widening Council interest in "those matters which affected the home and community in other countries,"[74] was presented to him and members of cabinet.

The business of the triennial meeting of the International Council, as distinct from that of the Canadian Council's annual meeting, concerned the issue of clean water; the importance of women as an economic factor in the community; and the broad spectrum of access to education for both young men and women.[75] Its main work was the interchange between women from across the world of views on these matters, and the organization of briefs which would enjoy support world-wide, and would be presented to the major international bodies on the status of women. Mrs. Armstrong was able to bring to the triennial meeting news of the founding in Canada of MATCH, the "non-governmental International Centre designed to match the resources and needs of Canadian women with those of women in the third world."[76] Three members of the National Council became members of its first board of directors: Helen Hnatyshyn, a former President, Catherine Armstrong, who would become past President of Council at this meeting, and Ruth Hinkley, who was about to be elected President.

With regard to the actions of the National Council at this meeting, the most significant report came from the Provincial Council of Manitoba on the issue of rape. Rape is sexual intercourse by force, without the voluntary consent of one party. As far as the Manitoba Council of Women was concerned, there were two major difficulties with the state of the law, of almost equal importance. One involved the attitude of the police and the legal profession towards the victim, and the other, the question of categorizing rape as a sexual crime, as opposed to a crime of assault. It had been observed under the first heading, that the victim's private life was as much a matter of trial as her testimony that rape had taken place. As Linda Dranoff has written:

> The accused rapist's lawyer had almost unlimited scope to cross-examine the victim on her previous sexual experience in an effort to prove her consent or possible seduction, even though it may have been irrelevant to the particular rape in question.[77]

---

74 *Yearbook*, 1976, p. 28.
75 The report of the Triennial Conference of the IWC is to be found in *Yearbook*, 1977, of the NCWC, pp. 26-43.
76 *Yearbook*, 1976, p. 25.
77 Dranoff, *Canadian Life Law*, p. 101.

The Criminal Code was amended on January 27, 1976 — again in the words of Linda Dranoff—

> to no longer permit the accused's lawyer to cross-examine the victim on her previous sexual conduct unless a judge concluded in the absence of a jury that such questions would produce evidence necessary to a "just determination of an issue of fact" in the proceedings.[78]

This reform by no means satisfied those working in Manitoba, nor many women elsewhere. The report of the Provincial Council of Manitoba was circulated among members of Council for some two years, and in 1978 a resolution was passed which read, in part, as follows:

> Whereas, the Present Criminal Code related to rape does not reflect the moral and social values of the Canadian public, but continues to view rape as a sexual crime and not as an assault; therefore be it
> Resolved that NCWC recommend to the Government of Canada that legislation should be further enacted to describe Rape as a sexual assault under the general heading of Assault:
>
> (1) Various forms and degrees of assault should be specified e.g.,
> (a) indecent assault
> (b) assault under threat of bodily harm
> (c) sexual assault with bodily harm
> (d) assault with sexual penetration of an orifice of the victim's body, etc.;...[79]

Changes reflecting this resolution were finally brought about by a bill passed in 1984.

The Vancouver meetings mark the high point of Council action in the seventies. From that point until the end of the decade, the problems confronting members, at all three levels, became increasingly clear and intractable. While there was no doubt that women who worked through Council were accomplishing a great deal for their communities and for themselves, it was also obvious that Council no longer held the position in

---

[78] *Ibid.*
[79] *Yearbook*, 1978, p. 138.

29. Mrs. Ruth (Charles) Hinkley, President 1976–1979

Canadian public life that it had occupied even a few years earlier. The temper of the times encouraged the growth of NAC, which drew to it those organizations most specifically interested in the rights of women, and hindered the growth of volunteer organizations, whose major interest was some form of service to the community. Mrs. W.C. (Ruth) Hinkley, the first Ontarian to be elected President of Council since Mrs. Marshall, (1946–1951) had this brought home to her with particular sharpness during her term of office. She was born in Belleville, Ontario.[80] Her mother, Minnie Lynn Lovell, had been born in Galt, Ontario, in 1891, of Scottish and United Empire Loyalist parents; Ruth's father, Arthur Barlow, arrived in Canada, from England in 1904. He was eighteen at the time and married his wife in 1909. The young couple settled on a farm in Foxboro, Ontario, but after the First World War, in which Arthur Barlow served overseas in the Canadian Expeditionary Force, the farm was given up and the family moved to Belleville. While never enjoying more than reasonable financial security, Ruth's parents brought up seven children, two of whom were adopted. Ruth graduated from high school in 1932, and worked in a local business until 1939, when she married Charles Hinkley. He saw service overseas in the RCAF during the war and only returned in 1946, being posted that year to RCAF Trenton. As the Hinkleys, with their young son, John, who had been born during the war, coped with the many moves attendant on service life, Ruth brought time and energy to various volunteer organizations. When John became a high school student, Ruth took up full-time work and became the first woman supervisor of the Canadian Division, Accounting and Administration, of the international pharmaceutical firm of Smith Kline and French. Further postings ensued and in 1966, when Charles retired, the Hinkleys moved to Ottawa, where Ruth was drawn into work for the Ottawa and District Association for the Mentally Retarded. This brought her, inevitably, into the Ottawa Local Council, and from 1973 to 1985 she was one of the stalwarts of that body. She served on the national executive of Council for four years, from 1972 to 1976.

Ruth Hinkley's first address as President was given to the eighty-fourth annual meeting, held at Carleton University, in Ottawa, from June 5 through 9, 1977.[81] She remarked upon the links that had been established between the Office of the Co-ordinator of the Status of Women and the National Council of Women. What neither she, nor any one else at the time perceived, was that the very strength of this connection would tend to prevent the federal gov-

[80] The author is indebted to Ruth Hinkley for the biographical details that follow.
[81] *Yearbook*, 1977, pp. 22-25.

ernment from recognizing how wide the range of activity undertaken by the National Council actually was.

Within the year it became apparent there was a down-side to the relationship between the National Council and the federal government offices instituted to oversee the status of women. At the eighty-fifth annual meeting, held in Banff, Alberta, from May 14–18, 1978, Mrs. Hinkley related the difficulties that had occurred when she had attempted to set up an appointment for the traditional meeting with the Prime Minister and cabinet for the presentation of the Council's "yearly brief to the Government of Canada." She was informed that any group that had participated in the previous spring meeting between the Prime Minister, cabinet ministers and national women's organizations, would not be allowed a second meeting. Through the efforts of Senator Neiman,[82] a meeting did take place with members of the cabinet, on April 14, 1978, but it was clear the government no longer attributed a pre-eminent position to the Council among the women's groups in Canada. At this meeting in 1978 there were four cabinet ministers, Marc Lalonde, John Roberts, Monique Bégin, Jeanne Sauvé and the Parliamentary Secretary to the Minister of Justice, Roger Young. Although Marc Lalonde gave assurances that "the Council would meet with the government each year, either on Consultation Days or through special meetings arranged through his department,"[83] Mrs. Hinkley understood that "new consultative processes [were being] initiated by the government."

It was plain that however much the work of volunteers might be praised, the wide-ranging work of the Council was not understood by government. Mrs. Hinkley had opened her speech to the eighty-fifth Council meeting with a quotation from Prime Minister Trudeau. He had remarked earlier in 1978 that:

The not-for-profit and voluntary sectors of our society could be made to flourish. Historically they have been the source of the humanizing social movements, which were the life-blood of our liberal democracies. They have employed the creative energies of many of our people. Surely we need this sector...on a broad second front

82 Joan (Bissett) Neiman was born in Winnipeg, Manitoba on September 9, 1920. She graduated from Mount Allison University before joining the WRCNS in 1942. She retired with the rank of Lieutenant Commander. She attended Osgoode Hall and was called to the Ontario Bar in 1954. She married Clemens Neiman in September 1953. They had two daughters and one son. She was appointed to the Senate by Prime Minister Trudeau in September 1972.
83 *Yearbook,* 1978, p. 27.

we must give encouragement and sustenance to these efforts.[84]

What had happened was that many in government had made a simplistic equation of associations of women being associations for women. That is to say, groups of women were considered, *ipso facto*, to be concerned, solely and exclusively, with the interests of women as women rather than with the broad interests of women as equal citizens with men in the community.

In some ways this can be seen as, once more, an attempt to categorize and marginalize women. No one paying close attention to a Council brief to government could take the view that this body was an association solely interested in the rights of women as women. The 1978 brief covered the following topics: the question of Canadian unity; the necessity of a guaranteed annual income for all citizens; the rights of Indian women; the need to pay more attention to the sexual abuse of children; the need to consider rape as assault; matters concerning aerosol containers, the proper packaging of food and the use of pesticides; aspects of the recognition of the work of homemakers, and their inclusion in the Quebec/Canada Pension Plan.[85]

In many ways this breadth of vision was itself a handicap for Council at the close of the seventies. Senator Neiman made the point clearly, in the address she gave to the eighty-fifth annual meeting. She analyzed the structure and program of Council, asking members to consider whether: everything they did was equally worthwhile; the participation of each of the member groups really supported the work of the Council; the use of time and energy could not be put to better purpose in a Canada which "was vastly different" in economic and social terms from what it been eighty-five years earlier when the Council had been formed. She remarked:

Over the intervening years the economic and social conditions of women have changed, their spheres of activity and influence have widened and the pace of change has accelerated quite dramatically in the last fifteen to twenty years. Women still want to serve their communities and their country on a voluntary basis, but, whether they are at home looking after a family or out in the working force or combining both activities, they must be able to do *what* they can *when* they can. Are you ready to change your procedures, the hours

---

[84] *Ibid.*, 24.
[85] *Yearbook*, 1977, pp. 113-18; *Yearbook*, 1978, p. 27.

your meetings are held, the times in the week or the year they are held, the way your business is conducted, the services you offer to your community, so that energetic and intelligent but busy people will realize that they should belong to their Local Councils because they have benefits to offer one another?[86]

At the eighty-sixth annual meeting held in Halifax, which took place June 10 through June 14, 1979, Council began to search for ways to answer the questions posed by Senator Neiman. In her last presidential address, Mrs. Hinkley began by stressing the need for "Council to adjust to changing Government processes if it is to remain an effective force to bring about improvements in our Canadian society."[87] This need to reconsider the way in which Council brought its influence to bear at the federal level was a major concern of many of the reports, as was the need to decide what were the present and future goals of Council.

Though the decade ended with a situation obviously requiring Council to engage in some soul-searching, the President and Executive continued to lobby the government on a number of topics. However taken aback Mrs. Hinkley may have been by the government's attitude towards Council, she oversaw the presentation of seventeen briefs to government departments.[88] As the organization began, once more, to look for the best way to make a positive difference in Canadian society, it could build upon a heritage by almost three generations in the form of intelligent efforts towards the realization of such a goal.

---

[86] *Yearbook*, 1978, p. 74.

[87] *Yearbook*, 1979, p. 1.

[88] The titles of the briefs were as follows, the body to which the brief was presented is given immediately after the title:

"Educational Leave and Productivity," Statement to the Commission of Enquiry;

"Voluntary Action-People in Action," Response to National Advisory Council;

"Disarmament," Statement to Federal Government in respect to Special UN Session on Disarmament;

"Canadian Unity," Brief to Task Force;

"Financial Situation of Older Women," Submission of NCWC Report on the Survey to Minister of National Health and Welfare;

"Pornography, Child Abuse and Parental Kidnapping, Treatment of Drug Addicts," Response to Bill C21 (previously Bill C51);

"Provisions Dealing with Rape," Response to Bill C52;

"Sex Stereotyping," Submission to CRTC;

"Personnel Management and the Merit System," Submission to Special Committee, Review of Personnel Management and the Merit System in the Public Service;

"Voluntary Code of Good Employer Practices," Submission to Labour Canada;

"Retirement Policies," To Senate Committee on Retirement Policies, Co-ordinator and Minister Responsible for the Status of Women;

"Women in the Urban Environment," Submission concerning National Capitol Commission Report on Concerns of Women in the Urban Environment;

"Employment," Brief to Task Force on Employment opportunities in the 1980's;

"Children in Canada," Overview of Children in Canada: Today's Child-the World's Future (released in preparation for the International Year of the Child, 1979);

"Marijuana," To the Senate Committee urging that marijuana not be legalized;

"Women's Programme Report on Survey," To Secretary of State concerning availability of space in Ottawa Buildings to house Voluntary Organizations;

"Canadian Council on Rural development," To Government concerning the disbanding of the Canadian Council on Rural Development.

CHAPTER 11

Years of Ambiguity
1980–1988

ON MAY 20, 1980, the government of Quebec, under the leadership of René Lévesque, held a referendum on the proposal to negotiate a new constitutional structure for the relationship between that province and the rest of Canada. It was a request by the Quebec government for a mandate to discuss "sovereignty-association" with the federal government, then headed by Prime Minister Trudeau. In a heavy turn-out of voters, the federalist option won, if not overwhelmingly, at least handily: 60% to 40%.[1] During this same week, the Council was holding its eighty-seventh annual meeting in Winnipeg. Mrs. Amy Fowler Williams had been elected president of Council the previous year. In her first presidential address, she commented on the extent to which members of Council felt helpless as they watched events in Quebec. She expressed, as a Montrealer, her appreciation for the supportive telegrams which had been sent to Quebec women by various women's organizations, in Toronto and elsewhere. The result of the referendum was not known at the time of the Winnipeg meeting, and Mrs. Williams took care to stress that "no matter what the outcome of the referendum, it is important to respect the decision of the population of Quebec, and in all free societies to guard the precious privilege of a vote without fear."[2]

Born in Bellavista, Peru, on August 3, 1927, to Canadians of Irish ances-

---

[1] Morton, "Affluence," p. 532.
[2] *Yearbook*, 1980, n.p. The imperfect state of the 1980 *Yearbook* reveals the fact that the Executive of Council, and the Head Office, were struggling with some financial and internal difficulties this year. However, though a dishevelled volume, the annual report contains, as usual, much important information.

try — her mother was a nurse and her father an engineer — Amy Fowler remained in that country until her mother's death in 1940. At that point her father brought her back to Quebec to be educated at King's Hall, Compton. She recalls that there was never any doubt in her mind that she would attend McGill University, which she did, graduating with a general B.A. in Economics and Psychology in 1949.[3] She married Jack Williams in 1929 and his work for Northern Electric as Wire and Cable Sales Manager took them to Vancouver, where their son was born. After their return to eastern Canada, two daughters were added to the family. Her introduction to volunteer activity came early, and she undertook church work in exchange for baby sitters. Her first major administrative responsibility was the result of her support of the Montreal Lakeshore University Women's Club and she served for six years, from 1973 to 1979, on the executive of the Canadian Federation of University Women. Other volunteer commitments included work for the Montreal Y.W.C.A., the Girl Guides of Canada, the Fédération des Femmes du Québec and the Canadian Federation of University Women. She first became linked to the Montreal Local Council of Women in 1971, as a joint representative of community associations of English, French, and Jewish women. From 1975 to 1978 she was the President of the Local Council. Looking back over her long career as a community activist, Mrs. Williams has ventured the opinion that work through the Council was the most exciting of all, since "it seemed to be a place where women worked to improve social conditions instead of complaining about them."[4]

The constitutional issue of Quebec provided more than a context for the first annual meeting at which Mrs. Williams presided as President; it was the pervading issue and of grave concern to members. It was obvious that Canadians would still be wrestling with constitutional problems in the immediate future. During the referendum debates, Prime Minister Trudeau had promised both Quebec and Canada a new constitutional deal. Early in October 1980 he proposed to patriate the constitution, cutting away the last vestiges of British legal authority over Canada. Furthermore, Trudeau was determined to insert a workable amending formula into the constitution, and to entrench in the document a charter of rights and freedoms.

At the eighty-eighth annual meeting of Council, held in Saint John, New Brunswick, from June 8 to June 11, 1981, it was clear that during the past

---

[3] The author is indebted for these biographical details to Mrs. Williams herself, who sent me a marvellously vivid letter about her life.

[4] Mrs. Williams to author: April 21, 1993.

twelve months a great deal of Council energy had been spent on constitutional issues. The Council had worked both through the ad hoc
Constitutional Reform Committee, chaired by Mrs J. (Evelyn) Harrington of
Quebec, and through action by the Executive. The Constitutional Committee
based its position on the statement issued by the previous President at the
annual meeting held in Banff, in 1978, which stressed the support of Council
for "the survival of our country as a culturally vibrant, independent whole
nation."[5] In September 1980, Council sent a statement to the Prime Minister
and the ten provincial premiers, then meeting in Ottawa, urging:

> that they refrain from making any precipitate or unilateral decisions
> due to pre-imposed time limits or other pressures; rather that they
> concentrate on the development of a negotiating strategy for a new
> Canadian constitution.[6]

Council presented policy statements on the general issues of Human Rights,
Freedom of Movement, Family Law, the Monarchy and Canadian Unity.

As the weeks passed, this communication was followed up by further
letters to both the federal and the provincial governments, emphasizing the
Council's stand on the proposed Charter, and in particular on the
"Fundamental Freedoms of Conscience and Religion, etc., Democratic
Rights, Mobility Rights, Language of Education, Legal Rights, Non-
Discriminatory Rights and Undeclared Rights." On November 25, 1980 the
Council delivered a prepared statement to the Joint Senate-Commons
Committee on the Constitution, with particular criticisms on a number of
specific matters, including Article 24, which, in Council's opinion, did not
provide sufficient protection for native women.[7]

With the opening of the new year it became obvious that the entrench-
ment of protection for women's rights in the constitution was in trouble. In
January 1981, the Justice Minister of the day, Jean Chrétien, announced that
Article 15 of the Charter would read as follows: "Every individual is equal
before and under the law and has the right to equal protection of the law and
equal benefit of the law."[8] At about the same time a conference on Women
and the Constitution, organized by the federal Advisory Council on the

---

5   *Yearbook*, 1978, p. 30.
6   *Yearbook*, 1981, p. 42.
7   *Ibid.*, p. 44.
8   Cited in Prentice, et al., *Canadian Women*, p. 402.

Status of Women, was cancelled. The chair of the Council, Doris Anderson, resigned. The result was an ad hoc meeting, held on February 13 and 14, 1981. Members of the National Council attended. The publicity created, especially by women journalists such as Michele Landsberg and Penny Kome, made the government think again. By early spring, it had been decided that the guarantees of equality, in Article 15, would be backed up by Article 28, which stated that "Notwithstanding anything in this Charter, the rights and freedoms referred to in it are guaranteed equally to male and female persons."[9]

The tumult and affray was not yet concluded for, in the autumn, a federal-provincial conference met to work out an "override" provision that would allow provinces to pass special, time-limited legislation in any areas "notwithstanding" the guarantees of the Charter. When it became clear that the override would apply to Article 28, there was a country-wide outcry. Protest came not only from women's pressure groups, such as NAC, but also the women's bureaucracy within the government, including the advisory councils on the status of women, and a very large number of individual women. The objections were also supported by the newly appointed Minister Responsible for the Status of Women, Judy Erola.[10] As Mrs. Williams reported in her address to Council, at the annual meeting held in Saskatoon, June 7-11, 1982, "Councils of Women across Canada took an active part in the lobbying process which was initiated by the Ottawa- and Toronto-based Ad Hoc Committee of Canadian Women." Provincial Councils lobbied their respective premiers and many members wrote to their own M.P.s. Changes were finally made and Article 28 was exempted from the override. Mrs. Williams commented to Council that she knew of no issue:

which has rallied Canadian women as much as the question of equality provisions in the Charter of Rights. The time had come when the most moderate of women would not accept being used as pawns at the bargaining table.[11]

One of the reasons for the strength of opinion voiced by women over

---

9   *Ibid.*
10 She was born in Sudbury, Ontario, January 16, 1934, the daughter of Nils and Laura Jacobson. She married on August 27, 1955 and had two daughters. An effective journalist, she was elected to the House of Commons in 1980 and served as Minister of Consumer and Corporate affairs as well as Minister Responsible for the Status of Women, 1980-1984.
11 *Yearbook,* 1982, p. 25.

this issue was the fact that many, who had spent their time and energy fighting for improvements in the status of women during the seventies, were facing the new decade in full awareness that the battle was far from won. In 1979, Doris Anderson had put the matter succinctly:

> ...the fundamental fact that women at the end of the 1970s are still economically disadvantaged at every level in society means the struggle for change must continue well into the 1980s and beyond. And the struggle continues to be about a change in attitudes as well as for an equal slice of the economic and social pie. Many women still believe what men say about them — that they are good only for a *Playboy* centrefold or work at the sink...For women [there has been]...the slowness of Canadian society to accept and adapt to their rights and needs, [the pain] of being the lowest priority when austerity hits, and the scapegoats on which many economic and other problems in society are often pinned.[12]

The eighty-ninth annual meeting of Council took place in Saskatoon, from June 7–11, 1982. Its theme was "Widening Our Horizons." Perusal of the reports presented at this meeting by nationally organized associations, by provincial and local councils, and consideration of the number of topics included in the resolutions passed by the general assembly, might suggest that the theme was redundant. There was scarcely a contemporary Canadian issue that did not appear somewhere as a matter of importance for some members of Council.

One which received a great deal of attention, and was the subject of the first resolution, was the economic situation. Economists have judged "the recession experienced in Canada, beginning in the spring and summer of 1981, marked the country's most dramatic economic crisis since the Great Depression of the 1930s. For six consecutive calendar quarters, the Gross National Product declined in real terms, shrinking by over 7 percent in total."[13] In terms of human livelihood this meant that "by early 1983, when the first faint glimmers of a recovery in production had appeared, over 1.5 million Canadians, almost 13 per cent of the labour force, were officially out

---

[12] Doris Anderson, "Women in Society," in Anne Porter and Marjorie Harris, eds., *Farewell to the 70s*, (Toronto, 1979), p. 169.

[13] Dan Butler and Bruce D. MacNaughton, "More of Less for Whom?: Dealing Directions for the Public Sector," in Michael S. Whittington and Glen Williams, eds., *Canadian Politics in the 1980s*, 2nd edition, (Toronto, 1984), p. 1.

of work."[14] At the national level, the Council requested government to consider a variety of means to control inflation which, in its view, was the major cause of contemporary distress. In addition, during the 1981–82 year, three of the four briefs taken to government departments by Council were on issues related to the impact of the economic situation on the social sphere. There was "An expression of Concern to the Minister of Finance as to decrease of growth in Federal Programs expenditure" and a "Request to the Parliamentary Task Force on Federal Provincial Fiscal Arrangements for consideration of Council Resolutions on Medicare and Health and Welfare Services." These resolutions stressed the need for continuing government support of such programs. Council also sent a brief to the Department of Employment and Immigration, commenting on a recent publication of the department on labour market developments. It stressed the importance of ensuring the economy could absorb new workers.[15]

The particular impact of this recession on women was discussed in the report given to the annual meeting by Sandra Kloss, who chaired the Committee on Women and Employment that year. She underlined the fact that women were still a long way from achieving "equal employment opportunities with equal pay and benefits, due in part to lack of adequate day care; inadequate or non-existent pension plans, lack of equal pay for work of equal value legislation and ambiguities in legislation related to maternity leave."[16] She wrote with feeling of the stress and fear many women felt in uncertain economic times, pointing out that:

> there are numerous women in the workforce who would like to "drop out" for a period of time to raise their families but hesitate to do so for fear of not being able to obtain work when they wish to re-enter. Many women fear the future. If they drop out of the workforce for any length of time, what retraining opportunities will exist, how can they keep themselves updated, and can they survive on a husband's pension or a minimal pension income of their own?[17]

Local councils, such as London, also emphasized the fact that the year 1981–82 had been "a time of increasing economic hardship," in a city that

---

[14] *Ibid.*
[15] NCWC, Council Year, 1981-82, *Handbook*, p. 5.
[16] *Yearbook*, 1982, p. 38.
[17] *Ibid.*

had "a poor support record on social issues."[18] What is interesting about this report, and others from towns and cities all over Canada, is that emphasis is upon barriers to employment for women, rather than upon direct welfare aid to the indigent within communities.

Mrs. Williams was succeeded as President in 1982 by Mrs. Margaret Harris. She grew up in Galt (now Cambridge), Ontario and from an early age was interested both in the position of women and in community service. In 1947 she moved to Saskatchewan. As a young mother, in 1958, she found time to accept the presidency of her church group and to work for the Saskatoon City Hospital's Women's Auxiliary. She recalled, in her first presidential address, that she had attended her first annual meeting in 1970. She was President of the Local Council of Women of Saskatoon from 1972 to 1974. In this position she ensured that the report of the Royal Commission on the Status of Women was carefully studied throughout the province and out of this disciplined work six resolutions came forward for presentation to the provincial government. These included 1) the concept of equal partnership in marriage in relation to the division of matrimonial property, 2) the establishment of a family court, 3) the adoption of textbooks with diversified role portrayals for women, 4) the provision of qualified guidance counsellors for both boys and girls at all levels, 5) encouragement to both boys and girls to consider all occupational fields, and 6) the establishment of day care centres and other day care programs.

In the tradition of many Council Presidents, Mrs. Harris spent much time and energy during her first year in office visiting local and provincial councils, including the Provincial Councils of Ontario and Manitoba, both of which were celebrating their sixtieth year of existence. Her first address as President was to the ninetieth annual meeting of Council, held in Toronto, from May 22 through 27, 1983. In it she stressed the courteous reception of the Council brief by the federal government committee to which it had been presented. In the course of a visit to the Provincial Council of British Columbia, Lucie Pépin,[19] then the President of the Canadian Advisory Council on the Status of Women, also made a comment on the federal gov-

---

[18] *Ibid.*, p. 74.

[19] Born in St. Jean d'Iberville, Quebec, September 7, 1936. She qualified as a Registered Nurse at the St. Jean d'Iberville Hospital in 1959, and later studied at the University of Montreal and at McGill University. She was a pioneer in the Birth Control-Family Planning Clinic, University of Montreal, 1966-1970; she served as the National Co-ordinator, Canadian Centre for Fertility Research, 1972-79. She became Vice-President of the National Advisory Council on the Status of Women in 1981 and almost immediately succeeded Doris Anderson as President, when the latter resigned. Lucie Pépin was elected as a Liberal M.P. for Outremont in the 1984 general election.

ernment's "respect and admiration" for the "concentrated expertise and research" that Council briefs represented.[20] Mrs. Harris underlined the contacts that she had had, as President, with a large number of other nationally organized women's groups, and the links National Council had maintained with a variety of organizations in the international field including the International Council of Women, the Canadian International Development Agency's International Non-governmental Organizations Section, and UNESCO.[21] A considerable amount of time this meeting was spent discussing the conference to be held in Nairobi in 1985, to mark the conclusion of the United Nations "International Decade of Women."

It was also at this annual meeting that firm plans were laid to carry out an idea, first explored at the meeting of 1982, of making the Council a visible presence in the field of international development. By 1984, the hard work of a number of members, especially Dorothy Milligan, had led to the presentation of a proposal for the establishment of the Canadian Council of Women Development Organization — the name being changed in 1986 to The National Council of Women of Canada Development Organization (NCWC-DO).[22] The stated objects were threefold: first, the establishment of an organization which would allow the Council to "develop and support education and social welfare programs." The second and third objectives were as follows:

2. The advancement of literacy and basic education and provision of skills training for women and girls in the Third World Countries and Canada, and, when deemed necessary, the provision of accommodation and meals during prescribed periods of training.

3. Contribution to the general well-being of all members of a designated community through specific projects such as a well in a Third World Country to provide pure water; a social or cultural facility to be available for recreation, health clinics, crafts and adult education including health, nutrition and sanitation courses.[23]

---

[20] *Yearbook*, 1982-83, p. 50.
[21] *Yearbook*, 1983, pp. 24-26.
[22] NCWC, "National Councils of Women of Canada Development Organization," *NCWC Handbook*, (1988), III.1.
[23] *Ibid.*

30. Mrs. Amy (Jack) Williams, President 1979–1982

Since the establishment of this organization, the Council has channelled approximately $6000 a year to projects in Cameroon, these monies being augmented by additional funding from the Canadian International Development Association.

In addition to this international initiative, of great importance for the future, very effective Committee work was reported to the 1983 annual meeting. One of the lengthiest and most comprehensive reports brought forward at this time served as the basis for a number of resolutions taken by Council to the federal government, and was presented by Elizabeth MacEwen, from the Status of Women Committee. Her reports also covered the work of the Women and Employment Committee and that of the Economic Committee. Local councils had been energetic. There was widespread concern over pensions, the issue having been studied by a number of local councils, especially in Manitoba, where the government had recently released its "Proposals to Amend the Pensions Benefits Acts."

Computer technology was an equally popular study. During the past months there had been a growing awareness, among council members, of the implications of computer technology for working women. Many universities had provided information sessions both about health concerns relating to the use of video-display terminals, and about the probable impact of word processors on women's employment. In the light of this information, Council requested that the government of Canada take a number of steps "to protect the health of persons working with video-display terminals," including the implementation "of the recommendations of the Labour Canada Task Force on Microelectronics and Employment with regard to health and safety measures...(research, standards, interim measures)."[24] It also requested that the government of Canada provide:

the Public Service of Canada and those agencies and institutions under federal jurisdiction, as word processors and other technological changes are adopted, with:

1. special opportunities for the integration and upgrading of women in their employment;
2. training and retraining operators of VDT's in computer skills...

---

24 *Yearbook*, 1982-83, p. 99.

Council also brought forward another resolution dealing with the need to educate young women in mathematics, physics and the other sciences, in order that they be properly prepared for the new technology of the workplace. Among the other points stressed by this resolution was the need to:

> promote and facilitate the participation of young female public servants employed at any level of scientific and technological job, in school career-related programs to provide role models, particularly for female students.[25]

Elizabeth MacEwen also reported that most local councils were involved in supporting both community-sponsored shelters for victims of abuse and rape crisis centres. As well, the issue of rehabilitative services for female prisoners was addressed. Here the work of a national affiliate, the Elizabeth Fry Society, provided the mainspring for Council activity. In line with the support which local councils gave to the Elizabeth Fry Society, the National Council itself accepted a resolution requesting that post-secondary courses, previously provided at nine penitentiaries by the Universities of Victoria and Manitoba, Queen's, and Laval Universities and the Collége Marie Victorin, be reinstated.[26] Another concern had to do with the question of language instruction for immigrant women. Local councils reported that, on the whole, the needs for language training were being met by government services in their communities. The final issue Elizabeth MacEwen brought to the attention of the general meeting was the variation in the actions of provincial governments relating to the status of women, some good, some bad. Montreal Local Council reported to the Status of Women Committee that it had expressed concern to the Premier of Quebec over the fact that the Minister responsible for the status of women was no longer a member of the provincial cabinet's Priorities Committee. On the other hand, the government of British Columbia had finally established a Women's Bureau, and the Manitoba Council on the Status of Women, dissolved for a brief time, was once again reported as active.

There were other resolutions considered by the 1983 annual meeting. One of the most interesting dealt with Canada's national anthem. In the preamble to the proposal, it was noted that when the official English version of

---

25 *Ibid.*, p. 101.
26 *Ibid.*, p. 98.

the anthem was proclaimed in 1980, "feelings of dissatisfaction were expressed by a number of women that our national anthem still only referred to Canada's sons." This dissatisfaction arose, it was explained, firstly from the idea that patriotism "was and still is, associated with bearing arms and going to war," when true love of country was something much more patriotic, and felt by women as well as men. It was suggested that the words could easily be changed from "True patriot love in all thy sons command" to either "True patriot love in all thine own command" or "True patriot love in all of us command."[27] It was also pointed out that the words "O Canada, our home and native land" could well be changed to "O Canada, our home and cherished land."[28]

The ninety-first annual meeting was held in Vancouver, from May 11 to May 15, 1984. In her presidential address, Margaret Harris gave a very full account of the work carried out over the past year. She had managed to obtain the traditional meeting with members of the federal cabinet. This took place on February 23, 1984. The resolutions presented included, in addition to those already listed as resulting from particular actions at the general meeting of 1983, one on the need for an education program relating to Fetal Alcohol Syndrome; two requesting better rail service and one asking the government to change its attitude to prostitution. The Council was convinced that prostitution was "generally repulsive to most of our society" and, above all, that it was a practice including a "double sexual standard." The Council therefore requested the government of Canada to:

1) amend the Criminal Code to remove the prohibition of soliciting (except in the case of adults soliciting from minors) from the code; and
2) increase penalties for procuring and living wholly or in part on the avails of prostitution of another person.[29]

In addition to the extensive briefs on each topic presented at this meeting chaired by Judy Erola, at the time Minister responsible for the Status of Women, detailed representations were made by letter to the particular ministers. Thus correspondence was exchanged with the Minister of National Health and Welfare on the need to protect the delivery of services through

---

[27] Or even "True patriot love in all our hearts command."
[28] Yearbook, 1982-83, pp. 95-6, pp. 104-5.
[29] Ibid., p. 102.

Canada's health care system; with the Minister of the Environment, requesting that the Pacific Rim National Park be designated as such in law; and with
the Minister of Employment and Immigration, on necessary amendments to
the Unemployment Insurance Act with regard to Maternity Benefits.[30]

The issue of pornography was one the Council felt strongly about, and
Mrs. Harris reported on correspondence with both the Ministers of Justice
and Communications on this subject. The Council position was very much a
reflection of the general feeling of people, that both matters of free speech
and individual taste were involved, as well as the prescriptions of social
mores. In the resolution which the four Provincial Councils — British
Columbia, Manitoba, Nova Scotia, and Ontario — had accepted the previous
year, 1983, it was admitted that "the line between pornography and art
becomes subjective and prohibitive legislation runs counter to the area of
human rights." Nevertheless it was felt that "any extended visibility of
pornographic material is completely unacceptable to women insofar as it
belittles them; it works against the movement for equal social, financial and
cultural equality of the sexes; and it encourages wife battering and other violent acts."[31] The real issue for Council was the accessibility of pornographic
materials to children, and in particular, pornography which glorified violence
and degradation. Most members wanted, above all, to make municipal councils responsible for limiting the access of children to pornography, whether
audio, pictorial or printed.[32]

The major concerns brought forward at the 1984 meeting were expressed
in resolutions dealing with aspects of the environment, including the preservation of South Moresby Park, the reduction of lead levels, and the improvement of fire safety precautions. Matters of social behaviour were addressed,
particularly drunk driving and the need to amend the Criminal Records Act
to ensure that those who are given an "absolute or conditional discharge" not
be afterwards labelled as having been convicted. Problems of research policy
were considered and resolutions brought forward requesting increased support for Canadian universities and general access to plant genetics resources.
Canada's international relations were addressed, firstly, by a resolution concerning the need for Canada to produce a policy for its military, to ensure
that the country would have the proper strength to meet its peacetime obligations. Other resolutions requested that Canada adhere to the principles con-

---

[30] *Yearbook*, 1983-84, p. 27.
[31] *Yearbook*, 1982-83, p. 103.
[32] *Ibid.*, p. 97.

tained in the Food and Agricultural Organization program, and that it support the International Year of the Family. A further resolution was accepted, requesting the Canadian government to reconsider its methods of dealing with refugees and, to do this, undertake a reform of the Refugee Status Advisory Committee and the Immigration Appeal Board.

In the area of social affairs there was a resolution concerning the need to ensure the proper payment of alimony and another dealing with further proposed reforms to the Canada/Quebec Pension Plan.[33] The resolutions concerning the South Moresby National Park, the maintenance of alimony payments, and drinking and driving were submitted not only in the spring of 1984 but again in September following the federal election, which brought a change of party at the federal level.[34]

The diversity of problems addressed by these Council resolutions, in a decade characterized by increasingly frequent recourse to single-issue pressure groups to effect political change, deserves particular attention. In the rapidly emerging world of the narrowly focused lobby group, the continuing broad concerns of the Council were often seen, by government and public alike, as indicative of some major flaw in the organization. The fundamental belief of those who worked through Council, however, has always been that community action requires recognition that human society is a complex, intricate, multifaceted phenomenon beset by more than one urgent need. Member organizations were, and are, dedicated to such diverse aims that Council has consistently acknowledged that these are goals which are good and yet competing, and occasionally contradictory. It has rarely, if ever, made distinctions of importance among issues raised by its members. It has implicitly based its action on the broad, if bewildering, agenda of public concern. It has sought to make Canadian communities civilized by according importance to the needs and rights of children, men, and women, in respect to such things as aesthetic nourishment, clean water or equal treatment before the law. Perhaps Council has limited its effectiveness in the current age by refusing to be confined to one single ideology, but in so doing it has supported the development of a pluralistic and tolerant society.

Brian Mulroney's victory on September 4, 1984 brought him, and the Conservative Party, 211 seats, the Liberals retaining only 40 seats and the NDP capturing 30 seats. Moreover, Mulroney's share of the popular vote rivalled that of "Robert Borden's Unionists in 1917 and Diefenbaker's Tories

---

[33] *Yearbook*, 1983-84, pp. 121-25.
[34] *Yearbook*, 1984-85, p. 28.

in 1958."[35] While the Conservatives slowly accustomed themselves to the discipline of government, it seemed as if the stranglehold of the recession had been broken. As the decade continued, however, it became clear that there were sufficient economic problems to halt any marked improvement in social programs, including the introduction of a national day care system. The last years of the eighties, which brought a second term for Prime Minister Mulroney, also brought high taxes, stagnating labour productivity, and unemployment, not only in the Atlantic and Prairie regions of the country, but also in Quebec and Ontario. In March, 1993, unemployment stood at 11% of the declared labour force and Canadian recourse to food-banks had reached unprecedented levels, making the economic situation of the early nineteen-eighties seem benign by comparison.

In the course of the decade, there were considerable changes in the social life of the country, some of which had begun to make their appearance even earlier. The population increased from 24,221,300 in 1981 to 26,840,900 in 1991.[36] The total number of families increased by 16.3%. Within this increase, the growth in the number of two parent families was only 6.2%, while single-parent families and common-law unions increased by 33% and 103.6% respectively.[37] In the plethora of data provided in Statistics Canada publications, which paint a picture of considerable social change, two figures are particularly striking. First, the fertility of Canadian women increased every year between 1986 and 1990: "the 1990 level of 1.83 children per woman represents a return to a level not seen in fourteen years (since 1976)."[38] The figure offers a contrast to the earlier years of the decade, when the fertility rate had been in decline, dropping to 1.7 in 1984.[39] Secondly, in 1991, 68.4% of women with children at home were in the labour force, 16% more than in 1981. Marriage brought about an automatic cessation of employment for women during their childbearing years, as it had frequently done in the sixties and seventies.

These demographic changes tell only part of the story of the alteration in Canadian society in the eighties. Constitutional issues came again to the fore, leading to the abortive Meech Lake and Charlottetown accords. Debate over Canadian-American relations took on a particular acerbity during the 1988 election campaign, when the question of free trade between the two coun-

[35] Bothwell, et al., *Canada Since 1945*, p. 435.
[36] Dumas and Lavoie, *Demographic Situation*, p.8.
[37] *Ibid.*, p. 27.
[38] *Ibid.*, p. 2.
[39] Prentice, et al., *Canadian Women*, p. 369.

tries was publicly debated. Growing deficits made the management of the economy an important issue in federal-provincial relations and debate between the parties was marked by a bitter rhetoric, the more so as the political party in power at the provincial level was hardly ever the same as the one holding the reins in Ottawa. At the same time, single-issue pressure groups began to attract significant public attention. This last development caused Robert Stanfield, Leader of the federal Conservative Party from 1967 to 1979, considerable disquiet. He argued that:

> It is one thing for individuals to pursue their own interests as they always have: it becomes a qualitatively different kind of society when individuals organize to pursue their individual interests collectively.[40]

By 1985, the National Council had become acutely aware that it must take account of the temper of the times, or accept a considerable decline in prestige and effectiveness. The situation was complex. Over the previous five years, six local council presidents had had to face the situation of Eileen Zamilinski, of Moose Jaw, who, in 1984 had opened her report with the following words:

> It is with humility that I present this annual report. While I value being your president, I am not proud to be going down in history as your LAST president, for I believe in the principles of the Council of Women and would be much happier to be seeing new members replacing those who have already served in one or more of the many positions.[41]

Chilliwack, Fredericton, Orillia, Owen Sound, and West Algoma had come to an end during these five years. But while the number of local councils had declined from thirty-eight to thirty-two, the total number of affiliates linked to local councils had remained almost the same: 918 in 1981 as against 919 in 1985.[42] Further, the actual number of nationally organized associations affiliated to Council had increased from twenty in 1980 to twenty-four in

---

[40] Robert L. Stanfield, The Fifth George C. Nowlan Lecture, Acadia University, February 7, 1977, cited in A. Paul Pross: "Pressure Groups: Talking Chameleons," in Michael S. Whittington and Glen Williams, *Canadian Politics in the 1980s*, 2nd edition, (Toronto, 1984), p. 306.

[41] *Yearbook*, 1983-84, p. 72.

[42] Membership figures are notorious for causing disputes; these are based on figures published in the relevant yearbooks.

1985, although there had been a change of membership. The Canadian Association of Hospital Auxiliaries had left. The newcomers were the Canadian Addiction Foundation, the Canadian Congress for Learning Opportunities for Women, the Canadian Pensioners Concerned Inc., the Canadian Council on Smoking and Health, and the Polish Canadian Women's Federation.

Furthermore, as President, Mrs. Margaret MacGee reported at the ninety-second annual meeting, held in Montreal in May of 1985, that the meeting with the Hon. Walter McLean, Minister responsible for the Status of Women, was well attended by other members of cabinet. This meeting took place on January 30, 1985. It had been followed by meetings with some members of the Official Opposition, and for the first time, with members of the NDP.[43] Mrs. MacGee, who was elected President at the 1984 annual meeting, had been born Margaret Bunner in Brampton, Ontario, on December 30, 1930, the middle child of three daughters.[44] She completed her high school years in London and went to work for the Bell Telephone Company in 1949. She met her husband in 1954 and in 1961 became a full-time homemaker. She immediately became involved in the Home and School Association and was one of the first organizers of the Ontario Block Parent Program. This led naturally to her membership in the Local Council of Women of London and she was its President from 1979 to 1982.

Margaret MacGee's first year in office was made particularly busy by preparations for the Nairobi meeting, and the visit to Ottawa of the President of the International Council of Women, Dame Miriam Dell of New Zealand, from March 17 through 19, 1985. Moreover, the creation of the NCWC Development Organization the previous year required that Mrs. MacGee devote time to the organization of the first board meeting of this new body, and to the coordination of its first presentation to government.[45]

In spite of these obligations, Mrs. MacGee also found time to visit a number of local councils in Ontario, and it was partly because of this experience that she made sure a report would be given to the 1985 meeting on the general position of Council as a public body. It was prepared by Mary Howell, with the assistance of Jean Scott and Trudy Wiltshire and a number of other members of Council. Its opening paragraphs included a quotation from the history of Council that Rosa Shaw had published in the fifties.

---

[43] *Yearbook,* 1984-85, p. 31.
[44] The author is indebted to Margaret MacGee for the biographical details which follow.
[45] *Yearbook,* 1984-85, p. 31.

"Council," she had written, "might not have existed for all the attention the press paid to it."[46] The report continued with general comments on the visibility of the organization, something which, it was admitted, was generally poor. Penny Kome, in a book published in 1985, under the title *Women of Influence: Canadian Women and Politics*, had little to say about the Council. In the 1983 publication issued by the Canadian Advisory Council on the Status of Women, *As Things Stand: Ten Years of Recommendations*, there was not a single reference to the National Council of Women of Canada. Council was also overlooked in contemporary articles in *Chatelaine* and the *Toronto Star*.[47] And this indifference was not confined to the Press: the National Action Committee rarely took notice of the existence of Council, and the Advisory Councils on the Status of Women, at the federal and provincial level, gave only minimal recognition to Council action.[48]

Mary Howell and her advisors attempted both an analysis of Council's problems and an outline of possible solutions to perceived difficulties.[49] An examination of Council assets was presented. These were listed as:[50]

1. Our heritage
2. Our great leadership — coming directly from the volunteer women's movement
3. Shared constitutions with local and provincial councils
4. Communication with women
5. Membership not political
6. The democratic process
7. Educational features
8. Annual presentation to Government
9. Our International connection
10. Our new development project

An additional factor mentioned was that when Council was considered at all, its image was seen as that of "a political interest group with a quiet voice that makes haste slowly."

46 Shaw, *Proud Heritage*, p. 184.
47 Mary Howell, et al, "Discussion paper on ways to Improve the Image of the NCWC," *Yearbook*, 1984-85, p. 130.
48 Writing in the *London Free Press*, Sunday February 9, 1986 Helen Connell reported that Chaviva Hosek, then the President of NAC, remarked that "because the national council is perceived as an old-line organization, it lends credibility when it comes out in support of the same issues as NAC."
49 May Nickson, Pearl Dobson, Gwen Bower-Binns, Charlotte England, Trudy Wiltshire, with Mary Joyce and Jean Scott communicating by telephone.
50 *Yearbook*, 1984-85, p. 130.

31. Mrs. Margaret (Arthur) Harris, President 1982–1984

Mary Howell and her companions were of the opinion that Council urgently needed a focus. Currently, there was no way that the press could sum up the organization's work in a one-liner. Indeed, Council methods seemed best characterized as the "buckshot approach."[51] This might have been a valid course to take in past years, it was suggested, when there were no other groups lobbying for women's economic and social concerns, but the field no longer had just one occupant. The paper stressed, however, that there were areas in which Council was still playing a unique role in Canadian society. The report noted that:

The Council structure has been the vehicle for lessons in civics and the experience of direct contact with how government works. It offers the opportunity to represent organizations, to learn about issues and develop them into resolutions and to see these resolutions reach to the highest levels of influence.

Because of this structure, it was emphasized, women who became members of Council had every opportunity for the personal development which would make them informed voters with considerable knowledge of world affairs. But, Mary Howell remarked, this benefit was almost completely overlooked, not only by outsiders but by members of Council itself. For this work to be properly carried out, "officers and 'other ranks' need to understand their roles as they relate to the needs of council women so that the democratic process in which our Councils act is the personal experience of all our membership." [52]

In commenting on this issue, the discussion paper touched on a most important Council role: the organization served as an educational and training ground for women in many, if not most, aspects of community politics. During the summer of 1990 the present author had the good fortune to meet with the Local Councils of Victoria, White Rock, Vancouver, Burnaby, New Westminster, Calgary, Edmonton, Saskatoon, Regina, Winnipeg and Truro. The women she met stressed, over and over again, that Council meetings had been an education for them. Not only did they obtain information, they also had the experience of seeing women speak in public, with solid information, about questions of the day, and, sooner or later, came to address the monthly

[51] Howell, et al, "Discussion Paper," p. 131.
[52] Ibid., p. 132.

meetings of the local council themselves. One of the constitutional provisions respecting local councils is that there should be an annual general meeting at which every single affiliate is required to present a report of its activities over the year. On this occasion, if on no other, delegates from small groups have to speak to the larger organization. Finding themselves delegated to Council by a church organization or a volunteer association, many women have had to learn how to report the activities of their own group to a much larger assembly of women, most of whom were unknown to them. Subsequently, a report of the local council meeting has had to be carried back to their own particular association.

Over and over again, women have related how terrified they were at first by these responsibilities and how confidence came from learning Council procedures. Margaret MacGee has remarked that the "biggest push forward" she ever received came from her local council president, Barbara Menear. It was through the latter's encouragement that Mrs. MacGee felt she could speak with confidence to the Premier of Ontario, Bill Davis, and to his cabinet, on Council concerns about fire safety regulations for highrise buildings.[53] In many cases, work through the local council has led women directly into memberships on school boards and hospital boards, and then to running in municipal, provincial and federal elections.

It is important to distinguish the way in which this work of Council has differed from what is done by consciousness-raising groups and by NAC. In the case of the former, the object of meetings is to enhance the psychological well-being and the political perceptions of individuals who attend. While such groups have differed, and still differ, radically from one another, their common aim is to make their participants understand the crippling impact of the real world on women's lives. They attempt to make women see that "the personal is political," that their difficulties, at home or in the work-place, are not just individual experiences but part of a larger pattern. As far as Council meetings are concerned, the issue of women's perception of themselves is never explicitly on the agenda. It is frequently addressed, implicitly, through the discussion of abused children, battered wives, and the need to support changes in the laws concerning marriage and divorce. Consciousness-raising groups have very effectively helped many women to understand how much of their lives is, indeed, a reflection of social demands. Local council meetings enable women to comment upon, and to shape, the demands of society.

---

[53] Margaret MacGee to author, letter, May 1993.

With regard to the NAC, there is a considerable difference between its organization and that of the Council, even after the reorganization of NAC in 1988.[54] NAC does not have the "local council" level as an active component of its constitution. The major structural difference between the two groups can be expressed as one of alternative patterns for umbrella organizations. NAC, in the words of Jill Vickers, is an affiliation of:

(1) pan-Canadian chapter based (top-down organization),
(2) pan-Canadian groups based on individual memberships,
(3) alliance umbrellas which focus on the provincial state and which re-group organizations of disparate sizes,
(4) national federations of local groups,
(5) national regional/provincial networks of service groups,
(6) single-issue coalitions,
(7) local groups, collectives, centers, services.[55]

The single coordinating force in NAC is the national level itself. Within NCWC the local and provincial councils play a major role in bringing together affiliates as diverse as those of NAC. However, it is clear that many of the groups which support NAC have a younger and, politically speaking, a more radical membership than those linked together by Council.

Nevertheless, the cumbersome pathways of communication between the National Council Executive, the provincial councils, and the local councils, provided by a threefold pattern of consultation and elected representation, have constituted a very strong link, made up of people as well as reporting structures, between the grass roots of Council and its national leadership. While, as is a Canadian custom, one region or another of the country has muttered about the way in which another region has dominated leadership positions, the reality is that the officers of Council, both those in charge of the implementation of policy and those who see to its formulation, are drawn from local council memberships across the country.

In 1985, for example, the President of Council was from Ontario, and the seven vice-presidents came from British Columbia, Saskatchewan, Manitoba, Ontario, Quebec, New Brunswick and Nova Scotia. There were

54 On this see Lorraine Greaves, "Reorganizing the National Action Committee on the Status of Women, 1986-1988," in Jeri Dawn Wine and Janice L. Ristock, eds., *Women and Social Change: Feminist Activism in Canada*, (Toronto, 1991), pp. 101-16.
55 Jill Vickers, "Bending the Iron Law of Oligarchy," in Wine and Ristock, eds., p.88.

thirteen standing committees that year, and two British Columbian women, Mary Higgins and Evelyn Fingarson, chaired the Committees on Arts and Letters, and Legislation respectively; Tina Rogers from Alberta, chaired the Committee on the Child and the Family; Anne Cholod from Saskatoon, Saskatchewan, chaired Education, and Margaret MacGee, that on the Environment. Manitoba was represented by three women, all from Winnipeg: the Committee on Health and Welfare was chaired by Elizabeth Feniak; that on Physical Education and Recreation by Michelle Meade; and Women and Employment was the responsibility of Elizabeth MacEwen. Ontario also had three Committees chaired by residents of the province: Citizenship and International Affairs was entrusted to Olha Zawerucha of Toronto; Economics was the responsibility of May Nickson of Ottawa and, also from that city, Gwen Bower-Binns chaired the Mass Media Committee.[56] Similarly, responsibility for the twenty-two "Administrative and Special Committees" was shared across the country, with members who accepted these responsibilities coming from Quebec and New Brunswick as well as the other provinces.

Amy Williams summed up the value of this structure when she said, in 1984, that "the debate on resolutions [at the annual general meeting] is where the year's work of thousands of Canadian women takes a major step towards the traditional presentation of the Annual Brief to the Government of Canada."[57] There is no doubt that this intricate set of arrangements has often made Council a slow-moving organization, but it has also allowed Council to develop a second and distinctive role for itself. It is a role described in the discussion paper as one of "looking ahead, anticipating needs, identifying problems, then acting on them in formulating resolutions and seeing them through to presentation to government."[58] This aspect has been a particular distinguishing mark of Council, as compared with the Canadian Advisory Council on the Status of Women and similar provincial bodies. It has been possible to bring recommendations and resolutions of members of Council forward to the appropriate level of government, municipal, provincial or federal. This process meant, implicitly, that where an issue, such as town planning or education, was of nation-wide concern but not in federal jurisdiction, members of Council could, and did, coordinate their actions when lobbying local or provincial authorities.

---

[56] *Yearbook,* 1984-85, pp. 12-13.
[57] *Ibid.,* p. 27.
[58] *Ibid.,* p. 131.

The discussion paper concluded with recommendations classified under three headings: general, specific and long-term. Under the category of general recommendations three major initiatives were suggested: first, a way should be discovered, by looking at how other organizations such as NAC and the Science Council operated, to react quickly to controversial public issues on which Council policy had not yet been formulated. Secondly, it was recommended that a major effort be made to improve knowledge of Council, through women's study programs at universities in conjunction with other women's organizations. Thirdly, when the work of Council warranted public recognition, a major effort should be made to nominate them for major achievement awards, such as the Léger Fellowship and the Thérèse Casgrain Award.

The specific recommendations in the paper concentrated upon the need to know who members of Council really were and to ensure that they, in turn, knew what Council was about. Finally, the long-term recommendations included the following: to revise the Council *Newsletter* and increase its distribution; to consider the production of a new history of the Council, as a source of information; to produce an effective guidebook on the policies supported by Council; and, finally, to set about organizing the financial basis. During the following years, many of these suggestions were put into practice but the future of Council remained a matter of concern to members, as it still does in 1993.

But, however much Council was concerned with its image in 1985, it was even more preoccupied by the usual demands of its committee work and the preparation of its briefs for presentation to appropriate authorities. The provincial councils reported good relationships with their respective premiers. Ontario in particular noted that Premier Davis and his cabinet, meeting with the Provincial Council on November 14, 1984, listened attentively, especially to the resolutions concerning the recognition of mid-wives. The Provincial Council of Ontario also met with the Liberal Opposition.[59] Similarly, Saskatchewan Provincial Council reported that their provincial government took seriously the issues brought to them, especially alcohol abuse.[60]

The reports given by local councils in 1985 described the usual wide variety of concerns. Calgary's report includes the first mention of food-banks[61] in local council reports. Several councils noted their involvement

---

[59] *Ibid.*, p. 66.
[60] *Ibid.*, p. 67.
[61] *Ibid.*, p. 68.

with women's centres. A significant note is struck by the Edmonton and Chatham Local Councils. In reporting on the discussion of the Cameroon venture, both councils mentioned a reluctance on the part of members to contribute to the project. This reaction ought not to have been unexpected. Women in attendance at local councils were, almost without exception, already involved in supporting one or more charitable enterprises. Their membership of local council was for the betterment of their own chosen activity, as much as anything else. To refer once more to the oral testimony from 1990, many women have admitted that they accepted the task of representing their association on Council in order to make other women aware of the pre-eminent importance of the needs of their own affiliate. While membership in a local council very often brought about a general understanding of the good works done by all present, most members nevertheless retained a fundamental loyalty to their own association. It was the Elizabeth Fry Society, or the Salvation Army, or many another worthy organization, that had first claim on time, energy, and money. Local councils, throughout the years, had acted as fund-raisers for particular purposes, but such action was usually for a very obvious community need: libraries, art galleries, women's shelters, and funds for food and clothing for immediate distribution. Consequently, requests for funds for a distant cause made a number of members uncomfortable. However, both Chatham and Edmonton voted, as councils, to subscribe to the Cameroon project.

The work of the standing committees of Council produced the usual number of resolutions for presentation to the federal government. There were two specifically concerned with social policies, one of which was a request for non-publication of the names of accused and/or arrested persons, and the other a proposal that at least part of the Alcohol Duties and Taxes should be used for treatment centres for alcoholics. General environmental concerns came to the fore, with resolutions on the need to formulate a policy for national river basin management; on the provision of safe drinking water and on the safe storage and disposal of hazardous products. A resolution on measures to ensure some standardization and reduction of package size for common goods could also be classified as springing from environmental concerns as much as from consumer needs. There was also a resolution dealing with the expanded use of mediation in labour disputes and with standards for mediation professions.[62]

62 *Ibid.*, pp. 137-41.

There were five "emergency" resolutions, which were presented on the floor of the General Meeting. These covered the possible deregulation of the telephone industry; maintenance of Radio Canada International services to those countries which had little free access to the world media; participation of Canada in the development of a "Star-Wars" technology program (which the resolution opposed); and the need for the reinstatement of a number of environmental programs including monitoring the effect of agricultural pesticides on prairie wetlands and water fowl. Finally, there was a request to the government of Canada and the International Council of Women to support the agenda item, at the Seventh United Nations Congress on the Prevention of Crime and the Treatment of Prisoners, stating that "every person has an intrinsic dignity and value regardless of condition and apart from institutional or social objectives."[63]

Another international activity of Council had an important place at the ninety-second annual meeting. This was the review given by former President Kay Armstrong of the work of the American Regional Council of Women/Consejo Regional de las Américas. Kay Armstrong had herself taken a leading role in the formation of this organization in 1977, after the triennial meeting of the International Council of Women in Vancouver. By the mid-eighties members included Canada, Chile, Columbia, the Dominican Republic, Ecuador, Guatemala, Surinam, Uruguay and the United States.[64] English and Spanish had been adopted as working languages. The organization had allowed representatives of Councils of Women in those countries that were members of the Organization of American States to lobby the OAS for the right of a married woman to obtain passports without first obtaining the consent of her husband, and for the general recognition of the parental rights of women.[65]

The ninety-third annual meeting of Council took place in Halifax, from May 25 to 29, 1986. It had been an extraordinarily busy year on the international scene: in July of 1985 there was the United Nations Conference in Nairobi to mark the end of the Decade for Women, and in April 1986, the twenty-fourth Plenary Conference of the International Council of Women took place in London, England. Canadian Council President, Margaret MacGee, presented a report on the latter. Some 400 women from thirty-four nations were present, the theme being "Women and International Understanding."[66]

---

63 *Yearbook*, 1985-86, p. 28.
64 *Ibid.*, p. 95.
65 *Yearbook*, 1984-85, pp. 115-16.
66 *Yearbook*, 1985-86, pp. 126-30.

But while the connection with international organizations was particularly important in 1985–86, the normal lobbying work of Council continued. The annual meeting with members of government took place on February 10, 1986, presided over by Walter McLean, the Minister responsible for the Status of Women. As well as the resolutions brought forward from the annual meeting, reference was made to such matters as the establishment of pensions for homemakers; Council's support for Canada's decision to stay in UNESCO; increased funding for family planning and some enforcement mechanisms in the area of employment equity.[67]

At the same time, Council carried on correspondence with the appropriate federal government departments, or committees, on a number of matters of immediate concern to the membership. There was a submission to the Special Senate Committee on Youth; a brief to the Task Force on Broadcasting; a submission to the Commission of Enquiry on Unemployment Insurance; a response to the Task Force on Refugee Determination in Canada; a submission to the Joint Committee on Senate Reform; a response on the Report of the Canadian Radio-Television and Telecommunications Commission on Sex-role Stereotyping in the Broadcast Media; a submission to the Secretary of State on the situation of indigenous and visible minority women in Canada; a response to a Housing Consultation Report; and a submission to Consumer and Corporate Affairs on children's sleep wear.[68]

The effective coordination of lobbying efforts was only part of the work carried on by Pearl Dobson in cooperation with the Executive and President of Council. She served as the executive director of the National Council of Women during the terms of six presidents, from April 1973 to September 1989. Her work during these years stands as a model of the dedication which many of those who held this position gave to Council. Pearl Dobson managed to carry out the many duties involved in running the national office of Council with great efficiency and economy. At the same time, she raised a family and supported the Local Council of Women of Ottawa, while still finding enthusiasm and time for work with the Canadian Citizenship Federation, the Boy Scouts of Canada, the United Church of Canada and Canadian Seniors for Social Responsibility. In recognition of her work she was named an Emeritus Life Member of the National Council of Women at the annual general meeting of 1989. She answered the question "why work

---

[67] *Ibid.*, p. 31.
[68] "Council Year, 1985-6," *NCWC Policy Manual 1988*, pp. 3-4, *Yearbook*, 1985-86, p. 29.

for the Council?" by saying "that the aims and objectives [of Council] are issue-oriented and the constant dialogue with other women for what we deem to be an improved society, has (forever) fascinated and invigorated me."[69]

Pearl Dobson was one of those who helped to implement the suggestions of Mary Howell's discussion paper. An effort was made both to nominate women for major awards and to celebrate and publicize the achievements of women actually honoured. The names of a number of women were put forward for government positions: Estelle Matthews, as representative of Saskatchewan to the Canadian Advisory Council on the Status of Women; Ruth Hinkley, as a liaison person for the study teams set up by a ministerial task force to consider the national voluntary organizations; Doreen Kissick as a director for the Canadian Institute for International Peace and Security; and, for the new Advisory Committee on the Appointment of Women to Boards and Commissions — Margaret MacGee and Beverly Clark.[70] Congratulations were sent to Past President Amy Williams and to Thora Mills, a long-standing member of the Toronto Local Council, both of whom were awarded the Order of Canada. At the same time, Past President Pearl Steen and Nazla Dane, who had been a long-time representative of the Canadian Federation of Business and Professional Women's Clubs, were congratulated on receiving Person Awards by the federal government.

As well as attending the meetings in Nairobi and in the United Kingdom, Margaret MacGee managed to travel more than 5000 kilometres within Canada, visiting local councils in Nova Scotia, New Brunswick, Saskatchewan and Alberta. These journeys raised the morale of members considerably, bringing an increased knowledge of the efforts at the national level to local councils across the country and encouraging them in their efforts. In their reports the local councils expressed their pleasure at these visits.

A significant development in the organization of Council affairs, during the 1985–86 year, was the visible care and attention given to the nationally organized societies. Council had always taken the affiliation of societies at the national level very seriously, and at annual meetings representatives of these societies had often been accorded special time and attention. However,

---

[69] Officially, in 1993, Pearl Dobson has "retired": but at the annual meeting of 1993 she was occupying the registration desk and coping with tangled problems of accommodation. She is currently a Director of the Canadian Citizenship Federation; the first Vice-President of the Ottawa and Area Local Council of Women; and Vice-President of the Provincial Council of Women of Ontario. Source: private letter to author, April 14, 1993.

[70] *Yearbook,* 1985-86, p. 32.

32. Mrs. Margaret MacGee, President 1984–1987

in 1986, there was a special luncheon during the annual meeting for those representatives of nationally organized societies who could attend. This category of membership had grown in importance since the opening of the decade. In 1986 the roster of organizations affiliated at the national level increased with the addition of the Canadian Congress for Learning Opportunities for Women and the Palliative Care Foundation. By 1992, the Media Club of Canada, the National Women's Liberal Commission, the Relief Society of the Church of Jesus Christ of the Latter Day Saints, the National Association of Women and the Law and the Federation of Medical Women of Canada had also joined, bringing the number of such affiliates to twenty-seven. At this time, the number of local councils in affiliation was twenty-four.

This changing balance between local councils and nationally organized societies brings the structure of the NCWC closer to the pattern set by national councils elsewhere in the world. While countries such as Australia, New Zealand and, to a certain extent, both the United States and the United Kingdom, have seen vigorous local councils, no other country has ever attained the number established in Canada. Margaret Oke, who served the Council as its archivist for a period of years, considers that, at one time or another, there have been 113 different local councils in existence.[71] Elsewhere, and especially in Europe, the strength of the National Council came, and still comes, predominantly, from the welding together of nationally organized societies. The Canadian experience, where local councils became the marketplace for the exchange of information and ideas among women's volunteer organizations, has not been repeated. The more usual model is that of a National Council whose policy and agenda is set through meetings of the leadership of nation-wide associations, each with its own focused objectives. The Canadian pattern, while demanding considerably more time and patience, has resulted in the handling of an extraordinary amount of public business by women from many walks of life in many different parts of the country. Further, the Canadian model has included the recruitment of leaders of Council women from an equally broad sector of society. Officers of the National Council of Women of Canada are by no means invariably women who hold executive positions in another organization. Very often, they have been solid, effective supporters of a particular volunteer activity at a local level, and have then become involved in Council

---

[71] *Yearbook,* 1988-89, n.p. See Appendix E for this list.

work at the provincial and national level through the committee structure.

In any case, local councils, as such, are in no real danger of extinction. In 1993, the Councils of Halifax, Montreal, Ottawa, Toronto, Winnipeg, and Vancouver can be described as flourishing; those of Niagara Falls, and Moncton, New Brunswick are holding their own; Hamilton, Kingston, London, St. Catharines, and Windsor are well supported and greatly helped by a lively Provincial Council; the Saskatchewan Local Councils at Saskatoon and Regina are vigorous, as is the Edmonton Local Council. The Calgary Local Council has experienced some difficulties in recent years. British Columbia boasts Local Councils at South Peace Regional, Fort St. John, Burnaby, White Rock, New Westminster, and Victoria in healthy circumstances. Thus, while the NCWC is certainly very different from what it was formerly, even in the late seventies, it is still an organization that commands considerable support.

The attention paid to the nationally organized societies at the ninety-third annual general meeting was only one of many actions taken at that time. Resolutions were, as usual, prepared for the annual brief of Council to the federal government. This took place on January 27, 1987. It departed from the traditional format. The Hon. Barbara McDougall, then Minister responsible for the Status of Women, offered both a challenge and a change. The challenge was to agree to discuss emerging issues (a difficult task for a body which speaks only on established policy); the change was that the Council met with ministers one at a time at thirty-minute intervals. Members of Council who presented the resolutions included Estelle Matthews, Regina, Saskatchewan; Trudy Wiltshire, Ottawa, Ontario; Margaret McKee, North Vancouver, British Columbia; Marianne Wilkinson, Kanata, Ontario; Irene Brown, Richmond, British Columbia; and Margaret Oke, Montreal, Quebec. Once more, Council provided evidence of its broad-based regional representation. It was noted in the report to the annual meeting that "every chair in the Senate Committee was filled with observers" and the President thanked those who had travelled to Ottawa from across the country, at their own expense, for this show of solidarity. She remarked that the "overflow crowd impressed the government and bolstered the spirits of those who dialogued with cabinet ministers."[72]

It was during this meeting that the place of the National Council within the spectrum of women's organizations was debated. An application for gov-

---

[72] *Yearbook*, 1986-87, p. 34.

ernment funding by the National Council had been recently turned down by
the Women's Program, on the grounds that the Council was not a status of
women organization. As President, Margaret MacGee asserted that the mandate of the Women's Program, when it was established, had been:

> to promote the full participation of women in all aspects of Canadian
> society and to increase the capacity and effectiveness of women's
> groups working to improve economic and social conditions for
> women.

She went on to argue, successfully, that such a mandate obviously encompassed the work of Council, which fell perfectly within the characterization
of women's issues given by the Hon. Barbara McDougall: "social issues,
family issues, societal issues and social justice issues."[73] Following up on
this meeting, Margaret MacGee, as President of Council, together with Vice-
President Estelle Matthews, managed to obtain a grant of $45,000 to Council
for the operation of the national office.

The ninety-fourth annual meeting of Council took place in Regina, May
16 through 21, 1987. Two factors combined to give the meeting a strong
international flavour: first, the outgoing President Margaret MacGee reported on her journey to India, where she had attended the triennial conference
of the National Council of Women of India, and the International Seminar on
the International Year of Shelter for the Homeless, held in New Delhi, India,
from February 25 through 27. Secondly, preparations were put in hand for
the 100th anniversary of the International Council of Women, to be held in
Washington from June 26 to July 4, 1988. The direct involvement of
Canada's National Council in the International Council of Women in 1987
included the work of Past President Amy Williams as Recording Secretary;
Past President, Pearl Steen as a member of the ICW Committee of Honour,
and of Doreen Kissick — elected in 1987 as the next President of the NCWC
— as Convenor of the ICW Standing Committee on Migration. Other toilers
in this vineyard included Past-Presidents Kay Armstrong and Ruth Hinkley.

The agenda of the ninety-fourth annual meeting was, as always, very
full, revealing both the perennial problems of Council structure and organization as well as Council's interest in the full range of Canadian public life.
The financial situation of Council was presented by Trudy Wiltshire, who

[73] *Ibid.*

outlined its problems: rising expenses, falling revenues, little real government aid and increasing demands for more services by member organizations. As the first century of Council activity drew to its conclusion, the
financial difficulties remained grave, but an extraordinarily generous bequest
from the estate of Mrs. Hardy's daughter, Alison Hardy, in 1992 has given
the organization some time in which to find solutions.

The usual wide variety of concerns was addressed both by the convenors
of the standing committees and through the reports of local and provincial
councils. Tina Rogers, reporting for the Standing Committee on the Child
and Family, noted that local councils were involved in discussions of a possible definition of "the family." No final conclusion was reached but all agreed
that the word represented a complex and changing series of problems, ranging from the difficulties that arose when there were children gathered together from previous and present marriages, to questions that arose when parents
"of the same or opposite sex [shared a house] in order to provide emotional
and financial support for each other."[74] On a related topic, Nina Bigsby
referred in her report from the Bioethics Committee to the issues of *in vitro*
fertilization, questions of surrogate motherhood and the use of embryos in
experiments, as well as to problems raised by the possibilities of recombi-
nant DNA research.[75] The report concluded with the proposed resolution that
the Bioethics Committee, "with input from the NCWC federates, identify
and study specific bioethical issues in which it is felt that council should
develop policy." Later on during the meeting, the general assembly passed a
resolution to recommend to the International Council of Women that it:

1. organize seminars and information programs on the subject of
   women and reproductive technology

2. urge National Councils to ensure that legislation is developed in their
   respective countries to protect women from social and economic
   exploitation in the area of advanced reproductive technology.[76]

In all there were seven resolutions passed by the ninety-fourth annual
meeting of the NCWC which were forwarded to the International Council of
Women. The remaining five dealt with "Women as Users and Producers of

[74] *Ibid.*, p. 56.
[75] *Ibid.*, pp. 65-73.
[76] *Ibid.*, p. 140.

Statistics," "Reproductive Health in Employment," the participation and representation of women in the work of the United Nations, "United Nations Standard Minimum Rules for the Treatment of Prisoners" and the "Irradiation of Foods." As well, it was asked that resolutions adopted as far back as 1973, dealing with acid rain and air pollution, be reiterated.[77]

There were ten resolutions formulated that year for presentation to various government bodies within Canada, covering the need of elderly women for improved benefits, the importance of the CBC, the necessity of armaments reduction, the crucial importance of making proper treatment available to sexually abused children, the case for thorough investigation of the issue of irradiating food, improvement of the tax treatment of child care expenses, the proper usage of car restraints for infants, legislation for the protection of non-smokers, and the need to ratify the United Nations Convention on the Law of the Sea.

However, while these resolutions, and those framed for presentation to the ICW, are important, the most significant work of this annual meeting was contained in the "Emergency Resolution" brought directly to the floor, on the subject of child care. Containing references to eighteen different and specific policies which the National Council had been developing since 1972, this resolution formed the basis of the National Council of Women's response to the Report of the Special Committee — set up by the federal government — on Child Care: Sharing the Responsibility.[78] It called for action by the appropriate authorities on a very wide-ranging front. It requested the extension of maternity and paternity benefits; the evaluation and monitoring of day care subsidy programs; the funding and licensing of non-profit day care centres; the provision by the CBC of films and programs dealing with the development of parenting skills and healthy family life; the consultation of Indian peoples' groups and organizations about the particular child care issues within their families, and particularly, the need for proper consultation with native women's organizations on the same issues; the provision of preschool multicultural programs and the provision of funds for transition homes with child care facilities. The most radical demand was for the establishment of a new Secretariat within Health and Welfare Canada to administer the Family and Child Care Act, which would include the development and enhancement of services such as:

---

[77] *Ibid.*, pp.141-44.
[78] *Ibid.*, pp. 136-39.

33. Mrs. Doreen Kissick, President 1987–1990

i.   parent education, including guidelines on ways to select quality non-parental care;
ii. work-related child care arrangements with employees, business and labour groups;
iii. preschool multi-cultural resources and culturally sensitive early childhood programs;
iv. care and supervision of school-age children;
v.   family day care homes;
vi. rural child care programs;
vii. educational upgrading of caregivers working with disabled children; and
viii. development of home support services for the purpose of providing relief to the parents of disabled children.

At this meeting, Doreen Kissick succeeded Margaret MacGee as President. Mrs. Kissick is now a New Brunswicker but was raised in Toronto by parents who had immigrated from England. Her involvement in Council began when she became representative for the Girl Guides in 1955, after she and her family had moved to the Maritimes. In her first presidential report, at the ninety-fifth annual meeting, held in London, Ontario from May 13 to 18, 1988, Doreen Kissick reported on the difficulty she had experienced in arranging any schedule of meetings with specific cabinet ministers to whom the resolutions, passed the previous year, had been addressed. In most cases Council members in charge of lobbying a particular minister could only reach a parliamentary secretary. Mrs. Kissick said that, in the end, the only cabinet minister she met was the Hon. Barbara McDougall. But she felt she had been able, at this meeting, "to establish the difference between the NCWC and the National Action Committee and to emphasize NCWC policy is initiated and approved from the ground up."[79]

1988 was the year that the lobbying opportunity Council had enjoyed over the decades, in the form of an annual meeting with a significant number of federal cabinet ministers, often including the Prime Minister, came virtually to an end. The result was that even greater care was given by the President and Executive of Council to the presentation of briefs by mail. After the annual meeting, all resolutions were meticulously prepared so that they would be taken seriously by the government departments concerned

[79] *Yearbook*, 1987-88, p. 29.

with the problems they addressed. The Council received detailed replies, from the appropriate ministers, to its submissions. The answers to the lengthy resolution concerning child care shows that, while the lobbying opportunity offered by face-to-face discussion was now restricted, Council presentations were nevertheless considered very seriously. Council received a reply on its proposals from the Department of National Health and Welfare, commenting that many of the elements in the NCWC resolution were being addressed through the new Special Initiatives Fund; from Statistics Canada, noting that a full scale survey was planned for the fall of 1988 in support of the survey undertaken by Health and Welfare for a national strategy on child care; from the Department of Communications, suggesting that Council lobby private and public broadcasters themselves, in order to ensure that major social issues were addressed by their programming decisions; from Central Mortgage and Housing, noting that discussions were underway with the provinces on the issue of special housing needs; from the Department of Employment and Immigration, rejecting any idea of responsibility for child care service under the terms and conditions of the Immigrant Settlement and Adaptation Program; from the Treasury Board, indicating that the government was considering the establishment of a significant number of new child care centres in appropriate federal buildings over the next few years; from the Department of the Secretary of State, mentioning that funding for child care programs was available through the Native Friendship Centre Program; and, finally, from the Canadian Council for Multicultural and Intercultural Education, announcing that it was discussing with early childhood educators ways to ensure that multiculturalism was promoted within early childhood curriculum and school systems.[80]

Doreen Kissick went on, in her opening address, to stress two other matters: the report of Rosslyn Tetley on *Homelessness in Your Home Town* and the coming celebration, in June, of the 100th anniversary of the International Council of Women. Rosslyn Tetley's work had arisen directly from the designation, by the United Nations, of 1987 as the Year of Shelter for the Homeless. Her report was linked with study sessions on this subject by local councils, from one end of Canada to the other, and with the attendance of Elizabeth Fleming, as Council representative, at the "Canadian Urban and Housing Studies Conference," held at the University of Winnipeg, from February 18 to 20, 1988.[81] Reporting for the Standing Committee on

---

[80] *Ibid.*, pp. 27-28.
[81] *Ibid.*, pp. 69-74.

Housing and Community Planning, Gracia Janes noted that those initiatives had led to widespread discussion of the need for land for both non-profit housing development and shelter for the psychiatrically disabled.[82] Further, the annual meeting passed a resolution on "Housing, a National Emergency," which was forwarded to the Canada Mortgage and Housing Corporation as well as to the Prime Minister and members of cabinet.

The impact of the 100th anniversary meeting of the International Council of Women on the Canadian Council was three-fold: it increased the enthusiasm of members who attended for Council work at all levels; it required detailed reports from Canada, not only on the situation of the Canadian Council but also on the status of women, generally, in Canada; and it brought to the notice of Canadian Council members who attended, the work being carried on in other ways, in other countries, for similar objectives. In her official report submitted to the International Council, Doreen Kissick, as President of NCWC, listed the topics on which representations had been made to the government of Canada:

> pornography; media sex role stereotyping; legalization of midwives; palliative care; sexual abuse of children; conservation of Canada's Arctic heritage; Chemical [products] and the Ecosystem; Reduction of Armaments; retention of present provision for licensing and manufacturing of Generic Drugs, and Banning of the use of the Drug Depo-provera as a contraceptive until new research is done.[83]

She also noted that Council was continuing to monitor government policy and legislation on equality for women.

1988 was an election year in Canada and the Council played its usual role in such circumstances: that of providing as much information as possible about the issues of the campaign without publicly aligning itself with any political party. Questions relating to the North American Free Trade Agreement and the Meech Lake Accord were both addressed by Council, through ad hoc committees supplying information for study sessions. Members of Council were as deeply concerned as the rest of the country about these issues, and similarly divided. As the ninety-fifth year of

---

82 *Ibid.*, p. 67.
83 *Ibid.*, p. 33.

Council's life came to a conclusion, it was as involved in the mainstream concerns of the Canadian polity as it had ever been.

CHAPTER 12

Continuity and Change

DOREEN KISSICK ENDED her presidential report to the ninety-sixth annual meeting of Council, held in Edmonton, Alberta from May 12–17, 1989, with a quotation from Thérèse Casgrain: "We will emerge from our struggle weakened if we remain turned in upon ourselves with no other horizons but those we have always known and if, led by false teachers, we remain attached to the old traditions alone."[1] During the last five years of the first century of Council, its membership sought, continuously and with considerable critical imagination, to take stock of what their organization had achieved and of what should be changed so that the challenges of coming years could be effectively addressed. While it is clear that Council has been conscious of the need to ensure that both its structure and its agenda were appropriate to contemporary circumstances, there was an unusually intense preoccupation with these matters during this period. The process of reflection culminated at the 100th annual general meeting, held in Ottawa, from May 13 to 17, 1993.

As in any healthy organization, decisions about future action included a reiteration of past principles which had proved their worth. The effort devoted during the mid-eighties, under the chairmanship of Ruth Hinkley, to the production of a new *Handbook* and the *Policy Manual* had assisted the process. Ruth Hinkley had been aided in this tedious but indispensable work by Pauline Beal, Pearl Dobson, Margaret Harris, Margaret MacGee, Dorothy Milligan, Margaret Oke, and Amy Williams. The final product consisted of

---

[1] *Yearbook*, 1988-89, n.p.

two loose-leaf binders, one containing the legal documentation of Council, its Act of Incorporation, and Constitution, as well as the list of federated associations, general information about membership categories and selected historical data. The other binder included an alphabetical listing of all resolutions presented to governments since 1963, together with a chronological grouping of the resolutions, and a general subject index. As Council began a determined effort to articulate reasons justifying continued support from its members, and what goals should be set for its second century of life, the retrospective of its work contained in these manuals proved to be of inestimable value.

The reader would, however, have a very false picture of the last five years of Council's first century if this self-examination were to be seen as the major work of Council during this time. For one thing, Canada was in the middle of discussions leading up to the Charlottetown Accord and Council, at all levels, played an active part. As might be expected, the Montreal Local Council was one of the first to articulate its views, submitting a strong brief, in November 1990, to the Quebec Commission on the Political and Constitutional future of the province.[2] In the spring of 1991, other local councils discussed and wrote about Canada's constitution, preparing briefs for the Spicer Commission. At the same time, members of the National Executive attended the Senate hearings. May Nickson conducted a survey of Council opinion, to which over fifty groups and 300 individuals replied.[3] Concerns voiced by Council members ranged from the possible impact of the accord on the economic situation, to the degree of multicultural diversity Canadian culture could accept. While opinions differed, especially on the last issue, most Council members supported the assertion of the Provincial Council of Saskatchewan that what was wanted was the preservation of "a Confederation from sea to sea, keeping all parts intact."[4] In its Brief to the Special Joint Committee on a Renewed Canada, Council expressed strongly its commitment to the recognition of:

> the distinct status of Quebec in Canada as having a French-speaking majority population, with rights to preserve its language, culture, and the Civil Code as the law of the province, such designation and rights to be entrenched in the constitution.[5]

---

2 *NCWC NEWS*, vol. 37, no. 3, Spring 1991, pp. 1-2.
3 *NCWC NEWS*, vol. 38, no. 3, Winter 1992, p. 3.
4 *NCWC NEWS*, vol. 37, no. 4. Almost the whole of this issue is devoted to constitutional matters.
5 Printed in *NCWC NEWS*, Vol. 38, no. 3, Winter 1992, p. 2.

Council took a clear stand in this document on the issues relating to aboriginal peoples and wanted:

> all of the following ... entrenched in the constitution:
>
> 1. the inherent right of the aboriginal peoples to self-government;
> 2. a constitutional process to deal with outstanding aboriginal issues; and
> 3. any self-government agreements as negotiated.

Overall, Council reacted to the Charlottetown Accord in much the same fashion as it had to the Meech Lake proposals: by examining the document in information meetings, and by discussing in public what exactly its provisions might mean. While Council members were not highly enthusiastic about the proposals as a whole, they, unlike the members of NAC, gave it their support.

Constitutional questions absorbed a considerable amount of time and attention, but Council members continued to clarify their own ideas about other problems facing Canadians and to convey their views to politicians and opinion makers at all levels. There were meetings between Council's Committee of Officers and members of the federal government. Although Council members found the meetings often left much to be desired,[6] their briefs were nevertheless accorded attention by all three political parties and lengthy, if unsatisfactory, replies were given to their requests. Apart from an examination of the organization itself, the topics receiving the greatest attention at the annual meetings included the rights of women, child care, the general level of public education, with special reference to illiteracy, and environmental issues. At the same time, resolutions were brought forward on gun control and the functioning of refugee boards.

The position of women within the Canadian polity was a theme addressed, in various ways, at all the annual meetings between 1989 and 1993. Elizabeth Kennedy, convenor of the Council Committee on the Status of Women, considered that the three most important issues for women in the nineties were, freeing society from violence; ensuring that "jobs traditionally done by women are valued correctly" and providing homemakers with access to adequate pension coverage; and, above all, securing the full repre-

---

6   Doreen Kissick, *NCWC NEWS*, vol. 36, no. 4, April 1990, p. 1.

sentation of women on decision-making bodies.[7] This latter theme was
shared by the 1989 report from Pat Beck, at that time Vice-President for the
Business and Professions section of Council. The year 1988–89 had been
filled with a crowded schedule of meetings with federal and provincial
politicians, other women's groups, and a wide variety of general community
associations. Her conclusions were an echo of the patient lobbying tradition
of Council. "We [Council members] are seen in the Province of
Saskatchewan as a good middle-of-the-road group with a lot of common
sense." She went on:

> For the coming year I would like to see some work done in the
> area of promoting women on boards, and also in the area of manage-
> ment positions in the university setting, school boards, principal-
> ships both at the elementary and high school level, and in business-
> es. There is need for a greater thrust in this area due to the fact that
> we are experiencing difficult economic times in most areas of
> Canada and it will be harder in the next few years, not easier, for
> women to succeed. We must also support women who are seeking
> public office.
>
> More pressure must be brought to bear on governments and
> large corporations and unions to provide work place and child care
> facilities. More lobbying for tax credits and tax relief for child care
> expenses must be considered if women are to make progress toward
> equality in the work force.[8]

This clear understanding of the fact that women had not achieved equality in Canada at the conclusion of the nineteen eighties, was repeated in many
of the reports presented in 1989. Elizabeth Kennedy's own presentation contained particularly gloomy news from both the Nova Scotia and the
Saskatchewan Provincial Councils. The main points of the Nova Scotia
report were:

> that the goal of equal pay is far from being achieved in that
> province;
> that there is an increasing trend to part-time work — resulting in

---

7   *Ibid.*, p. 4.
8   *Yearbook*, 1988-89, n.p.

reduced full-time job openings and benefits for working women;
that the minimum wage was raised to $4.50 an hour — with 75 per
cent of workers on minimum wage being women;
that women are under-represented in such professions as educational
administration...

The concluding point made by this report was to warn of the social and economic problems that would have to be addressed because of the imbalance
of women among the aged population. "In 1986 Nova Scotia had 15,675
more women than men over 65."[9]

Saskatchewan's tale of woe was equally bleak. The major points made
were that:

adequate day care is getting short shrift;
pay equity is almost at a standstill;
the need for part-time benefits for part-time workers is not being
addressed at all;
farm women have great need for day-care and good job training;
the removal of health and dental services from the school means
women often have to take an entire day off work for their children's
dental appointments;
the unequal treatment of women and men prisoners means poorer
facilities, job training programs and educational opportunities for
women.

Elizabeth Kennedy's overall conclusions were worded differently from those
of Pat Beck but carried the same message. She wrote that "after 10 years of
operation," the Canadian Human Rights Commission confesses in its Annual
Report for 1988 that "it is manifest that historical factors have distorted the
distribution of employment and pay to the disadvantage of certain groups, it
is out of the question to think that the problem can be dealt with purely in
terms of individual, complaint driven remedies. This is a different ball game
and it calls for a different approach." She went on to say:

Women told the government that 10 years ago — and the phrase
'the feminization of poverty' hadn't even been coined then.

---

9   *Ibid.*

In the year ahead we must be actively involved in ensuring women's equality — in the workforce, in the home, in retirement, in public life — everywhere — is advanced. No government agenda can justify delaying the achievement of equality for over half its citizens.

The same note was struck in the following year, during the ninety-seventh annual meeting held in Hamilton, from May 4 to 8, 1990. At this general meeting two resolutions were passed on the subject of the unequal treatment of women in and by the Canadian court system. The first resolution was concerned with the "special needs of women as victims of violence and degrading crimes."[10] It was addressed to the federal government and the respective provincial governments, and asked that all judges, legal counsel, and police receive education focused upon:

a. The context of women's lives and the impact of violence in homes across Canada.
b. The various aspects of sexual assault including the nature of the crime of sexual assault, the psychology of abuse, the prevalence and seriousness of sexual assault by acquaintances...and the difference between vigorous cross-examination that protects the defendant's rights and questioning that includes improper sex stereotyping and harassment of the victim.
c. Gender, class and race differences in order that they be better understood and deal [sic] with the crime in the context within which it is committed.[11]

The resolutions also requested that the criteria for the selection and appointment of judges include a demand for a demonstrated understanding of equality issues.

The second resolution dealt with three more general matters: the lack of understanding of the disadvantaged economic position of women with respect to "Spousal Maintenance, Child Custody, Access and Support, Marital Property Division and Personal Injury Awards"; the discrimination faced by women in the legal profession "with regard to job placement, university tenure, sexual harassment, lower pay scales and lack of reasonable

---

10 *Yearbook*, 1989-90, p. 132.
11 *Ibid.*

accommodation in working conditions during child bearing years"; and the paucity of appointments of qualified women to positions in the judiciary, to government boards and to other public bodies. In light of these concerns the NCWC asked for a national task force to examine the extent to which gender discrimination exists in the Canadian legal system and to make recommendations with a view to eliminating any such discrimination. Council also reiterated its 1980 resolution asking that women be appointed in proportionate numbers to federal decision-making bodies.[12]

The ninety-ninth annual meeting, held in White Rock, British Columbia, from May 21 through 25, 1992, reiterated the resolutions passed concerning gender equality in the courts, and adopted new resolutions on violence against women and children.[13] The President's Report of 1993 noted that a total of six resolutions on the status of women within the Canadian legal system — covering plea bargaining, sentencing and contempt proceedings — had been presented that year to the federal government, but that no response to any of the issues raised had yet been given.[14] This emphasis on continuing discrimination against women is to be found in reports brought back from the Sixteenth Plenary Conference of the International Council of Women, held in Thailand, from September 23 through 30, 1992. One of the resolutions passed by that body, requesting national councils to bring pressure on their governments to support action in favour of women's rights, noted that all around the world "the position of women...has scarcely improved and in some areas has actually deteriorated." A second resolution at the same meeting, asking for improved treatment of elderly women, observed that longer life for women frequently meant increased helplessness, inaction and feelings of utter uselessness.[15] At all levels of Council work, local, provincial, national and international, members continued to collect and collate data on the situation of women, to exchange information, and to suggest ways in which those in power could be brought to improve women's lot.

Council resolutions concerning child care had been brought forward since 1989. Council had, that year, pointed out that it had been urging the govern-

---

12 *Ibid.*, p. 134.

13 *Yearbook*, 1991-92, p. 21 *et seq.*

14 President's Report presented at the annual general meeting, Carleton University, May 13-18, 1993. The report of this meeting not being published at the time of writing, the author is indebted to the National Office for allowing complete access to their records.

15 The *Yearbooks* for the 1991 and 1992 annual meetings were not available until 1993. In both cases, they are much less full than usual. The author is indebted to the National Office for allowing access to their records. All citations without footnotes in this chapter come from the loose-leaf binders for the respective years held by the National Office.

ment of Canada since 1972 to implement a national policy on child care. It argued that the federal government, in its proposed child care legislation (1987–88) had not set any national objectives for child care services and that unless this was done, there was no real possibility of establishing at least a minimum level of services across the country.[16] In 1991, the tragedy of child poverty was further addressed. A resolution deploring the fact that "1.2 million children live in poverty in Canada today and Canadian children are the largest category of users of food-banks" asked the government "to move with haste to amend Canada's laws that violate the Articles of the United Nations Convention on the Rights of the Child," and requested provincial governments to adopt as a government goal "the reduction of the number of families in poverty, by providing more adequate income support and by improving opportunities for self-support."[17] At the same time, Council showed an awareness of the problems of young adolescents, and asked for funding to support counselling services for 12–14 year old girls about their sexuality.

Council interest in general educational matters and in the problems of illiteracy surfaced in three ways: through the reports submitted by the Standing Committee on Arts and Letters, the Standing Committee on the Mass Media, and the local and provincial councils. Again, the subject was first raised in 1989. Marion Beck, as convenor of the Committee on Arts and Letters for 1988–89, focused her attention and that of members of her committee on the conflict between free speech and expression, and the desire to suppress pornography and prevent the exploitation of children. She referred to the Canada Council resolution of 1985 which affirmed the right of artists to present their work directly to the public. She quoted, with approval, the statement of that body that:

> the requirement that works of art in literature, film, video, painting and other media be approved before the public is allowed access to them can rarely, if ever, be justified; it denies, to the artist on one hand and to the public on the other, the protection to which they are entitled within the laws and before the courts of this country; it obliterates that exercise of responsible judgement which is the right and duty of every citizen in a free society.[18]

---

[16] Resolution #5, *Yearbook*, 1988-89, n.p.
[17] *Yearbook*, 1990-91, p. 25.
[18] *Yearbook*, 1989-90, n.p.

34. Mrs. Joan De New, President 1990–1992

Among all the issues brought forward during these years the protection of the environment roused some of the strongest effort. In 1989 resolutions were passed concerning "the emission of ozone depleting chemicals," "ground-water quality contamination," "energy conservation," and "forest management." In 1990, two more resolutions dealing with similar issues were brought forward, the first dealing with the need to "promote renewable and alternative sources of energy," to restrict environmental damage from the burning of fossil fuels, and the second asking for government support for urban transit, in order to limit the use of the automobile in cities.[19] Briefs were also submitted that year which led, in many instances, to resolutions addressing the issues of "global warming," "radiation dose limitation," and the need for environmental assessment for projects such as the Grande Baleine (Great Whale River) hydro-electric development.[20] In 1992 resolutions concerned with the environment asked for a ban on the "production and export of tetraethyl lead"; for action by the government of Canada to increase the general protection of Canada's ecosystems, and national parks by proceeding "without delay to produce targets, timetables, and maps of areas to be protected in the '12% by 2000' campaign"; and for stronger measures, provincial and federal, to be taken to protect Canadian wildlife from poaching and trafficking for profit.[21] In all there were seven resolutions on environmental issues, either new or reiterated, brought forward in this year. All such briefs, with their accompanying resolutions, were forwarded to the appropriate government agencies at the federal and provincial levels. Regarding the issue of global warming, for example, the Minister of Mines and Resources in 1991, Jake Epp, noted that Canada had recently signed the Convention on Climate at the recent United Nations Convention on the Environment and Development, as well as Agenda 21 for preserving forests. In 1993, detailed replies from this Minister were received by Council on concerns brought to his notice in their briefs.

It was at the ninety-seventh annual meeting, held in Hamilton from May 4 to May 8, 1990, that Joan De New was elected President. She was born in Toronto in 1938, and graduated from McMaster University in 1959, taking a degree in English and History. She went on to study at McMaster Divinity College, receiving a diploma in Christian Education and Leadership Training from that institution in 1960. She met her husband while he was studying to

---

19 *Yearbook*, 1990-91, pp. 32-33.
20 *NCWC NEWS*, vol. 39, no. 1, September 1992, p. 5.
21 *Yearbook*, 1990-91, pp. 25-27.

become a psychologist at McGill University and they were married in 1962. It was during this time that Joan De New became involved with the Student Christian Movement. In 1964 the De News moved to Hamilton, where her husband opened his practice, and raised a family of three sons and one daughter. Joan De New became interested in the issue of violence on television and helped to form C-CAVE — Canadians Concerned About Violence in Entertainment — in 1983. Work on this project led to her recognition as Hamilton Woman of the Year in Communication. In 1985 she was elected as President of the Hamilton and District Council of Women.[22]

She brought to NCWC a strong conviction that one of the most important roles of Council was the way in which it involved its members in public life. In her first presidential report she remarked that "in a time when public apathy appears to be growing about politics in general, our concern and our ability to involve people in constructive action may never have been as important as it is now."[23] Her particular interest centred upon the structure of Council: would this structure allow the organization to continue to play a positive role "in a time of rapid social change...in a multicultural, multi-organizational multi-discipline bureaucratic era where it [Council] no longer was the main government source of the awareness of women's concerns."[24]

The general attitude of Council towards the changing demographic mix of Canada was made clear in that year, 1990, through a poll taken at the general meeting by Decima Research Associates on the attitudes of those attending to immigration to Canada. Decima was engaged at that time in a survey of the attitudes of the Canadian public as a whole on this question. The results were published in *The Decima Quarterly Report*,[25] and showed that "NCWC members appear to be significantly more accepting of the differing cultural, racial and religious backgrounds of recent newcomers to Canada and...significantly more willing to support increasing numbers of new immigrants entering the country." The greatest difference between the Council members and the general public was shown in the answers given to the question as to whether the current level of immigration to Canada should be reduced, increased or maintained at its 1990 level. Just over half of Canadians (54%) looked for a reduction in immigration; a significant majority of Council members considered that immigration should be increased.

---

[22] The author is indebted to Joan De New for these biographical details.

[23] *Yearbook*, 1990-91, p. 11.

[24] Private letter: Joan De New to author, April 13, 1993.

[25] Reprinted, *NCWC NEWS*, vol. 37, no. 2, Fall 1990, p. 5.

With regard to its own structure and financing, Council had begun to consider ideas for change when, at the ninety-eighth annual general meeting in Halifax, it became clear that there were considerable, and immediate, problems over the current account budget. As a result the Council was without an executive assistant from that time until early spring 1993. In May, 1993, the Committee of Officers accepted the resignation of Joan De New, and asked Ruth Brown to serve as interim president. Her account of this occurrence, given at the ninety-ninth annual general meeting, follows:

> It was discovered after the last Annual Meeting that many of our financial records were missing from the office or had not been completed properly. As a result of this discovery, our Executive Assistant resigned. With very incomplete records, it was not easy to piece together the details of our financial situation and we owe a debt of gratitude to May Nickson, this year's Vice-President Administration, and to our Treasurer, Diane Hoskins, for the hours which they spent on this over the summer months, working together with Leo Brierley, our new Chartered Accountant. In the end, they were able to produce a financial statement for 1990–91 which was acceptable to the Department of the Secretary of State as a basis for payment of the rest of this year's operating grant. The evidence of irregularities has been turned over to the police but their investigation has not yet been completed.[26]

Ruth Brown concluded this account by paying tribute to the contribution which Joan De New made to the work of Council. She said:

> I have worked with her over the last two years in my position as convener and later vice-president and have come to appreciate her openness, her energy and enthusiasm, and her communication skills, including her contribution to the Newsletter, both as Editor and later during her term as President.[27]

The essential strength of Council appeared during these trying months, as its members faced the financial crisis and also built upon work started by

---

26 *Yearbook,* 1991-92, p. 9.
27 *Ibid.,* p. 10.

the outgoing president. The theme of the ninety-ninth annual meeting, held at White Rock, British Columbia, from May 21 through 25, 1992, had been selected by Joan De New and was given as "Visioning our Future, Facing Realities, Building on our Heritage." The first action of Council was to elect the Interim President, Ruth Brown, as President.

She came to the office with a background in social work and considerable experience of life as a foreign service wife. She was born in Sunkist, Saskatchewan, once a hamlet on the prairies, now a wheat field. She attended school in Owen Sound and Sarnia, where her father taught and became a high school principal. Ruth attended the University of Toronto and graduated in 1945, from Victoria University, University of Toronto with an Honours B.A. in Modern Languages. She went on to earn a Master's degree in Social Work from Toronto and later on a Diploma in Social Welfare through the International Graduate Year program at the University of Stockholm. Between her husband's five foreign postings, and while bringing up four children, Ruth Brown worked with the Ottawa-Carleton Children's Aid Society, both as a staff-member and as a volunteer. Her experience with Council began with work on the Ottawa Local Council, of which she was president from 1987 to 1990.

In 1992, the year of her election as President of the NCWC, there were twenty-six nationally organized societies, four provincial societies and twenty-eight local councils.[28] The national organized societies included the Anglican Church of Canada; the Relief Society of the Church of Jesus Christ of Latter Day Saints; the Hadassah-Wizo Organization of Canada; the Presbyterian Church in Canada, the Women's Missionary Society; the Ukrainian Women's Association of Canada; the United Church of Canada; the Salvation Army; the Victorian Order of Nurses; the Canadian Mental Health Association; the Planned Parenthood Federation of Canada; the Girl Guides of Canada; the Federation of Junior Leagues of Canada; Na'amat Canada; the Canadian Congress for Learning Opportunities for Women; the Canadian Association of Elizabeth Fry Societies; the Canadian Federation of Business and Professional Women's Clubs; the National Association of Women and the Law; the Media Club of Canada; the Polish Canadian Women's Federation; the Ukrainian Women's Organization of Canada; the

---

[28] These statistics are from the *Yearbook*, 1991-92, pp. 6-7 and also from the data given by the National Office, May 1993. Since 1992 Truro, New Glasgow, and the Woodstock study group have ceased operation.

Women's Association of the Canadian League for the Liberation of the
Ukraine; the National Women's Liberal Commission; the Canadian Home
Economics Association. The Provincial Councils were Ontario, Manitoba,
Saskatchewan and British Columbia. The local councils reported to be in
operation were Halifax, Moncton, Saint John, Montreal, Ottawa and area,
Kingston, Toronto and area, Hamilton and District, Niagara Falls, St.
Catharines, London, Windsor, Winnipeg, Regina, Saskatoon, Prince Albert,
Calgary, Edmonton, Fort St. John, White Rock and District, Burnaby,
Vancouver, Victoria, and New Westminster.

The 1992 meeting accepted the proposal brought forward by the
Executive that an assessment of Council, and proposals for its restructuring
be a major matter of business during the coming year. An Ad Hoc
Restructuring Committee, later called the Ad Hoc Strategic Planning
Committee, was struck, and on June 29, 1992, Joan Butcher was confirmed
as its chair. Other members were Pat Rustad from Nova Scotia, Elizabeth
Hutchinson from Montreal, Monika Feist from Winnipeg, Pat Beck from
Saskatoon, Tina Rogers from Alberta, and Bette Pepper from British
Columbia, as well as Ruth Brown, Council President, and Katherine Tait,
who had become Executive Assistant in November, 1991.[29] A funding proposal was submitted to the Secretary of State on October 7, 1992 and was
approved in December, 1992. A survey was undertaken by Shelley Malkin, a
human services consultant based in Winnipeg, of the twenty-six nationally
organized societies affiliated to Council. Four main areas were investigated:
the understanding which these associations had of the National Council of
Women of Canada; their sense of the quality and nature of their relationship
with Council; their opinion of the particular strengths and weaknesses of the
organization; and finally, any suggestions which the affiliates might have for
the Council's future action.[30]

Fourteen societies gave some form of reply[31] and Shelley Malkin
summed up their perception of Council as being:

---

[29] *NCWC NEWS*, vol. 39, no. 3, February 1993, p. 5.

[30] The information brought together in the following paragraphs is a précis of Shelley Malkin, BA,
BSW, MSW, *National Council of Women of Canada Survey (of Nationally Organized Societies):
Report and Analysis of Data*, January 10, 1993.

[31] Canadian Association of Elizabeth Fry Societies; Canadian Home Economics Association; DES
Action Canada; Federation of Medical Women of Canada; Girl Guides of Canada; Mediawatch;
Media Club of Canada; National Consultation of Women of the United Church; Planned
Parenthood Federation of Canada; The Salvation Army; Ukrainian Women's Association of
Canada; Ukrainian Women's Organization of Canada; Women's Missionary Society of the
Presbyterian Church of Canada; Young Women's Christian Association.

a non partisan, unified (umbrella) organization working to improve the quality of life of women, families, Society (State) and for the equality of women by lobbying, educating and communicating.[32]

The majority of the societies who responded considered their association with Council worthwhile: the benefits being the information which Council brought to their notice, the support of Council for their own particular initiatives, the connection to other organizations which Council membership automatically furnished, and the strong voice which Council could provide as lobbyist on issues of general agreement.

The survey listed four reasons which nationally organized societies gave for their membership of Council: the continuance of an historical relationship; the communication with other women's groups which Council provided; the strength in numbers derived from membership, when federal and provincial governments were being lobbied on women's issues; the support that Council gave for the particular area of primary concern to the member association; and, finally, general support for Council work.[33] Seventy-five percent of respondents considered that they participated effectively in Council business, and while about a third wished for greater involvement in the administration of Council, most felt the running of their own organizations stretched their present resources to capacity. The majority of nationally organized associations considered that "participation on relevant issues through local or provincial councils" should be developed.[34] Questions about what Council and the nationally organized associations could do for one another were answered, to a very large extent, with suggestions for sharing information and for provision of networking opportunities.

Question 7 of the survey asked "What are the most important public policy issues for NCWC to address in the next three years?" A total of thirty-three public policy issues were suggested by ten of the respondents, reflecting concerns relating to violence against women and children, the broad needs of children, the struggle for better conditions for the poor, and the preservation of the environment. Other issues mentioned related to need for quality education, preventive health care, aboriginal issues and the proper delivery of social services.[35] Seventy-five percent of respondents viewed the

---

[32] Malkin, *Survey Report*, p. 4.
[33] *Ibid.*, p. 8.
[34] *Ibid.*, p. 10.
[35] *Ibid.*, pp. 13-15.

work being done by NCWC as relevant to contemporary society, with less than half (42%) expressing concern that there was a duplication of effort in the work of the NCWC and that of other women's organizations.[36]

Questions 12 and 13 of the survey respectively read as follows: "How might NCWC become more effective? Do you see a reason for NCWC to continue? Reversing the order in which the report gave these questions, the response to question 13 was most positive. Seventy-five percent of respondents considered that NCWC ought to continue since its history gave it credibility; it provided a forum for dialogue, increased awareness and understanding of issues; it filled a valuable societal role; it was a federation made up of diverse women, concerned with matters affecting Canadian women generally; it was seen as a grass-roots organization having access to government and, at the same time, international involvement.[37]

Only five societies responded to question 12, and those were fairly critical. The lack of response can be variously interpreted. As Shelley Malkin points out, it could mean:

> that the nationally organized associations view NCWC as being sufficiently effective
>
> or
>
> that they had no opinion as to its effectiveness
>
> or
>
> that they were reluctant to offer criticism.[38]

Criticism from the responding societies included the expression of some discomfort with Council's conservative, traditional image and advocacy of a sharper definition of its role. There was some perception that its resources were not well managed and it was suggested that Council discuss its mandate with NAC and the Canadian Advisory Committee on the Status of Women. Some respondents considered that Council needed more contact with feminist and labour organizations in order to increase its effectiveness.[39]

While the survey of the nationally organized associations was being carried out, members of the Ad Hoc Committee came to the conclusion that there was a need for a clear articulation of the mission, values and vision of

---

[36] *Ibid.*, p. 22.
[37] *Ibid.*, p. 24.
[38] *Ibid.*, p. 23.
[39] *Ibid.*

Council. As a result it was proposed that the Committee meet with Shelley Malkin in Winnipeg, on January 29 and 30, 1993, in order to prepare a strategic plan for presentation to the 100th annual meeting of Council. This step was taken with the help of further funding from the Secretary of State.

The proposals, which were brought to the 1993 annual meeting under the rubric "Proposed Strategic Plan for the National Council of Women of Canada" represented an attempt to articulate the why and wherefore of Council's existence. A hundred years earlier, the Council had been created by women who shared so many assumptions — about the ideals that animated them, about the problems they saw in the society in which they lived, about the way society worked, politically, economically and socially — that an explicit "strategic plan" would have been both divisive and redundant. Late twentieth-century Canada was not so closely knit a community.

The diverse beliefs of Council members became apparent, not only during preparation of the Strategic Plan by the consultant and the Ad Hoc Committee, but also during the meeting of the Committee of Officers called to discuss it, on March 6, 1993, and at the annual meeting in the spring of that year. On the whole, however, there was a general consensus to the effect that the dedication and hard work of the planners had produced an acceptable and important proposal for Council's future. Their aims had been to: compose a document which would help the NCWC to see its current situation clearly; involve its members in deciding where the organization should expend energies in the future; establish priorities for its agenda of action; and to ensure that its organizational structure could react quickly.

As is usual in strategic planning, the Ad Hoc Committee began its work with an attempt to state clearly, the "mission, values and vision" of Council. It was decided that, although many members had a clear sense of what the organization did, no one was able to define its activity in a few words. Consensus was reached, however, on the following wording, as an expression of the "raison d'être" of Council:

To empower all women to work toward improving the quality of life for women, families and society through a forum of member organizations and individuals.[40]

---

[40] Shelley Malkin, BA, BSW, MSW, *Proposed Strategic Plan for the National Council of Women of Canada*, March 1, 1993, p. 9.

While an articulation of the mission statement had been achieved fairly easily, a common declaration of the values of Council members presented greater difficulty. It was the view of the Ad Hoc Committee, however, that "the absence of clearly articulated values which reflect what the organization stands for perpetuates confusion about the NCWC."[41] Such confusion, it was felt, led to the negative comments made by some of the nationally organized societies. The task was seen as one of bringing together those values which could reasonably be identified "as representing the organization's culture" and characterizing fairly the work done by members of Council. The Ad Hoc Committee sought to list those values which truly reflected the attitudes of the membership and assembled the following list:

JUST and DEMOCRATIC SOCIETY	ADVOCACY
EQUALITY SEEKING	CARING
INCLUSIVITY	VOLUNTEERISM
EDUCATION	CIVIC RESPONSIBILITY
MUTUAL RESPECT	'ESPRIT de CORPS'
RESPECT for the ENVIRONMENT	GRASSROOTS[42]

After considerable argument, the Committee could not agree on the inclusion of FEMINIST PERSPECTIVE in this list of core values. It was decided that Council itself had to determine whether it wanted to declare itself a feminist organization. The debate over the inclusion of feminism as a value for the organization, in 1993, stemmed from contemporary argument over the meaning of the word. It is clear that if the word is understood to mean "a belief in the equality of men and women," then Council members would be happy to subscribe to it. The idea that the word stood for the affirmation of women as normal human beings, as females of a bisexual species, as individuals as necessary and as valuable as the male, with the same social, economic, intellectual and cultural rights, was applauded vigorously by the members when they gathered together at the 1993 annual meeting. However, the contemporary representation by the media of feminism as a set of beliefs incompatible with a view of stable marriages, child care and homemaking as honourable occupations for women, made many Council members uncomfortable about the use of the term itself.

---

41 *Ibid.*, p. 10.
42 *Ibid.*

35. Ruth Brown, President 1992 –

The Ad Hoc Committee found it easier to describe what the vision of an ideal Council would be. It proposed the following:

A vibrant, pro-active, credible council of women, reflecting the diversity of society, influencing political decision making and public attitudes for the well-being of society through education and advocacy.[43]

The Committee next turned to the task of deciding to what extent Council was in a state to embody the ideals expressed. Its analysis of the organization's health was a confirmation of the strengths and weaknesses which had been clear to Council since the appearance of the report of the Committee to Study Means of Improving the Image of the NCWC, in 1985. The Ad Hoc Committee agreed that Council must reflect the following general elements of late twentieth-century Canadian life:

1. The reality of the Electronic/High Tech Age — akin to the impact of the Industrial Revolution.
2. The changing climate of Aboriginal peoples — positive role models, human rights.
3. Greater cultural diversity in Canada — no longer an Anglo-Franco dominance but one that is a broad mosaic.
4. Global Economics — fiscal responsibility, dismantling of health and social services in Canada, diminished Canadian funding-sources.
5. Impact of the USA on Canada — Political and financial.
6. Changing roles for Women — enhanced profile as leaders and professionals, decrease in volunteerism.[44]

Having defined the principles that should infuse Council action and presented an analysis of the context in which Council must work, the Committee next outlined six "goals" for immediate consideration by members:

1. To examine the decision making processes of council
   with reference to Policy Development
   with reference to governance

---

[43] *Ibid.*, p. 11.
[44] *Ibid.*, p. 13.

2. To define and clarify the roles and responsibilities of the organization
3. To improve communication
   internal to the organization
   external to the organization
4. To enhance the image and to improve the visibility of the NCWC
5. To strengthen the membership of the organization
6. To maximize relationships with organizations external to NCWC's memberships.[45]

For each goal, the Ad Hoc Committee produced a detailed operational plan, outlining the type of task force to be appointed for its accomplishment, the process by which the task should be accomplished, and the time frame for the undertaking.[46]

For some members, particularly the Local Council of Women of Calgary, the whole process was a disturbing and threatening venture rather than an exhilarating exercise in self-knowledge. The report they sent to be read into the record at the 1993 annual meeting, revealed a considerable fear that the strategic plan would turn Council into some kind of ideological movement.[47] In essence, of course, the reception of the "Strategic Plan" by the general membership in no way alters either the traditional aims of Council or its program of action. Strategic plans, by their nature, are an explicit statement of the rationale for the operations of an organization, and their implementation depends upon the day-to-day acceptance of this rationale for the better deployment of resources and the logical assignment of priorities. Council has defined, in the plan, a process for more effective translation of the wishes of its members into concrete action.

In any case, the traditional core of Council action in Canada remains the same: the discussion of concerns raised by its members so that collective action may be taken. The fear of some members that the "Strategic Plan," in some undefined manner, will erode the essential grass-roots control of Council may be understandable but is not grounded in the document itself. Further, the substantial weight of historical tradition and precedent would

---

45 *Ibid.*, p. 15.
46 *Ibid.*, pp. 18-35.
47 "Report on the 'Strategic Planning Report' from Calgary Local Council of Women," documentation circulated at the 100th annual meeting.

hinder any such development. The Council movement in Canada, over the last hundred years, has bound together women of very different beliefs on many diverse issues by tackling problems on which a consensus for action could be created. The mark of Council meetings, at all levels, has been the clear understanding that members have accepted one another's right to differing opinions. What has mattered has been the existence of agreement on a particular problem and on what could be done in the immediate future to provide some kind of remedy. Council policies on major issues have developed with "all due speed." For example, the final adherence of Council to the suffrage movement took place sixteen years after Council's founding — and even then, there were a minority, still remaining as members of Council, who felt that votes for women were unnecessary.

The essence of Council action lies in the fact that its membership is made up of women involved in volunteer work, women convinced of their right to comment upon the public life of their communities and their country, and committed to accepting responsibility for the improvement of that life. The strength of each local council is quickly apparent when one considers not only the record of past achievement but the plans for the future. During a visit to western councils, in 1991, the author found a common pattern: pride in the past, plans for the future, and concern because volunteer work in Canada seemed to be in decline. Members of the Victoria Council recalled the work their group had done on the Report of the Royal Commission on the Status of Women, its present concern with the lives of street kids in British Columbia's capital, and its wish to have a membership whose average age was not over sixty. The Local Council in White Rock, with a number of members in their late forties and representing business and professional interests, considered its efforts for the preservation of heritage buildings in the community. It listed twenty-six federated associations as members in 1991–92: ATIRA Transition House Society; two Business and Professional women branches; the Canadian Red Cross Society; the Canadian Federation of University Women; the Catholic Women's League; the Come Share Society; the Fraser Valley Peace Council; the I.O.D.E.; the Jane Doe Renascence Society; the Kiwanis Club; the Liberal Women; the Modern Centre Service for the handicapped; the New Horizons Peacemakers; the Peace Arch Community Services and the Peace Arch District Hospital Auxiliary; the Salvation Army Women's Organization; the Semiahmoo House Society and the Semiahmoo Peninsula Youth Support Society; the Soroptimists; the South Surrey/White Rock Women's Place Association; the Surrey Community Services; the Ukrainian Women's Association; two

United Church groups; and the White Rock and District Garden Club. This local council has a strong commitment to bringing the expanding Council membership to include those on welfare, to listening to those in trouble and to providing ways of making the social net a help towards a new life rather than just a prop for survival. At the time of the author's visit, the Council, partly because of the leadership shown by Bette Pepper and Mary Ozolins, was seeking to find a means of reaching out to women who were not linked either to churches or to other organized social action groups.

At the time of the author's visit, the Local Council of Women of Vancouver, with twenty-eight federated societies, was flourishing under the presidency of Joy Scuddamore. Its members were proud of the way they had worked for the Vancouver Orchestra in particular, and for the general civic amenities of the city in general. They recounted with pleasure the way in which Council had helped women fight for equal treatment by banks in the matter of mortgages during the nineteen seventies, and was still fighting for women's pension rights. Some members recalled the work done in getting the city to establish the 911 service. All of them were pleased that the tradition had been established, and still continued, whereby those standing for election to City Council addressed a special meeting of the Local Council of Women. Confronting the problem of membership, this Council felt that by recruiting retired people into volunteer work, the crisis would be solved. The good health of men and women in their sixties and seventies meant that there were a number of intelligent, energetic, and willing volunteers, with leisure time, whose talents had yet to be properly exploited. In addition, such people would have a long experience of community affairs that could only enrich the council movement.

The Local Councils of Burnaby and New Westminster were small but vigorous operations, both flourishing through the personal recruitment of members. The agenda of both bodies was a mix of local civic action and concern for the agenda of the National Council. The provision of citizen scholarships for local students was as much a priority at their meetings as the business carried out at the provincial and national levels. It was a long-time member of the New Westminster Local Council who, in a personal interview, brought out one of the great strengths of Council when she said that her membership in the organization was due, above all, to the fact that she, as a member of the Elizabeth Fry Society, wanted the broadest possible support within the community for that particular charitable organization. She was quite willing to listen to others, even to support their programs. Her most important goal, however, was to ensure that other Council members knew about the projects of the Elizabeth Fry Society, and would support them wherever possible. Her view of the organization as a whole was that it was a market place of causes, where efforts were made to ensure a maximum of cooperation among volunteer groups and a minimum duplication of effort.

In 1991, Freda Hogg was the capable President of the Provincial Council of British Columbia which included at that time, in addition to the local councils visited by the author, the Local Council of Fort St. John. Besides the local councils, the Provincial Council included seventeen other affiliates: the Alcohol and Drug Education Service of British Columbia; the B.C. Association for Community Living; the B.C. Liberal Women's Commission; the B.C. Social Credit Women's Auxiliary; the B.C. Synodical Women's Missionary Society, W.D. Presbyterian Church; the Business and Professional Women's Clubs of B.C. and the Yukon; the Canadian Daughters' League, Provincial; the Canadian Mental Health Association, B.C. Division; Hadassah-Wizo B.C.; the Licensed Practical Nurses' Association of British Columbia; Planned Parenthood Association of British Columbia; Salvation Army British Columbia Division; the Ukrainian Association Provincial Council; the Victorian Order of Nurses; the Women's Christian Temperance Union of British Columbia; the Health Action Network; and Mothers Against Drunk Drivers.

It is clear from the records of the Provincial Council of British Columbia, that the process of action through the preparation of resolutions, while often seeming exasperatingly cumbersome and slow, was also found to be particularly effective by local council members. The complex two-way street of communication, where common topics were chosen for study by all councils as part of the agenda for the year in combination with local problems raised by individual councils, necessitated much hard work. Briefs had to be written, bringing together information and opinion, resolutions were formulated for discussion at the meetings, then lobbying would be undertaken. Lobbying might invoke a local council working on the provincial level for support to a motion that it wanted to raise at the national level, or it might take the form of direct action at the municipal level by the local council, or representations to members of the provincial legislature through the Provincial Council. Perhaps because of the extraordinary beauty of their surroundings, many council members in British Columbia see the environment as the most fundamental issue for future Council action. Given the strength of the British Columbian membership in Council, and its diversity, it would be difficult for any other group in the country to monopolize the process of grass-roots consultation and make the National Council the tool of any single ideological view-point.

It is, in fact, two of the elements most often criticized about the structure of Council that account for its enduring strength: first, the acceptance of the very diverse interests of its affiliates, and secondly, the lengthy, convoluted process of consultation and deliberation over policy resolutions. Work at the local level provides not only a bulwark against a take-over of Council by a single-issue group, but also a rich source of suggestions for the agenda of Council at the national level. The exception appears to be the Local Council of Women in Calgary. In 1993 it reported twelve affiliated members. This council has had a long, distinguished and, frequently, stormy history. It has a heritage of considerable achievement, not only through its impact upon municipal affairs, but also its involvement with topics of national concern. At the opening of the nineteen nineties, however, it was in the midst of considerable internal dissension about its future course. The debate seemed to centre on the need felt by some for a commitment to a series of general principles rather than to an issue-oriented agenda. Its survival is debatable, but Calgary is a Council that has occasionally ceased to exist and then, like the phoenix, reappeared with new strength.

Edmonton Local Council was a strong organization of seventeen affiliates, bringing together Canadians of many different heritages: those of Jewish faith, those who were members of the Ukrainian Orthodox Church, those who supported the Church of Jesus Christ of the Latter Day Saints and those for whom organized religion was of minor significance. All cherished the past achievements of their Council and all were concerned for its future, while at the same time making plans for work on immediate projects, such as the services needed by new immigrants from Asia who were arriving in the city. There was general consensus that "there were single-issue groups out there in their hundreds" and that this made Council's cooperative mode of action even more necessary, and more difficult to maintain, than in the past. The networking among different pressure groups, always a major strength of local councils, was seen as something that must be preserved as Council struggled to confront the problems of the late twentieth century, especially those relating to the care of children and the elderly. Edmonton Local Council desired particularly that Council should be able to work, effectively, at binding together the many different peoples who are Canadians.

The strength of the Provincial Council of Saskatchewan is attributable, in particular, to the Local Councils of Women in Saskatoon, Regina and Prince Albert. These bodies have consistently devoted their energies to coordinating the volunteer work of their communities while at the same time

commenting on national issues actively and intelligently. In 1991, the
Provincial Council of Saskatchewan included thirteen societies as well as the
local councils and their various affiliates. Organizations linked at the provin-
cial level included the Elizabeth Fry Society; the Planned Parenthood
Association; the Presbyterian Church women; the Salvation Army; the
Saskatchewan Association for Community Living; the Business and
Professional Women's Clubs; the Saskatchewan NDP Women; the
Saskatchewan Society of the CCC Therapists; the Saskatchewan Women's
Agriculture Network; the Saskatchewan Women's Institutes; the
Saskatchewan Women's Liberal Commission; the Ukrainian Women's
Association of Saskatchewan, and the Church in Society Committee of the
United Church. The Saskatoon Local Council had twenty-four affiliates,
among them the Progressive Conservative Association of Saskatchewan, and
the Saskatoon UNICEF Committee. Regina's Council numbered twenty-two
affiliates, including five Roman Catholic parish organizations as well as the
Spiritual Assembly, Baha'i Faith of Regina.[48]

Saskatchewan Council members stressed how important the organization
was in helping volunteer groups tackle issues, without becoming tangled in
ideological differences. However, much the membership might be divided on
matters of abortion, the need to provide for better education for living children
was a subject which concerned them all. However much they differed on what
actions merited jail sentences, the needs of women in jail were recognized by
everyone, and work for better prison conditions, job-training, and counselling
for inmates brought unified lobbying support for the Elizabeth Fry Society. As
one person put it, "Council was a net of people talking over things that matter," a net that educated and sustained its members. The report given in 1993
by Lynda Newsom, President of the Saskatchewan Provincial Council,
stressed the work that had been done the previous year on the provincial government's announcement that it intended to cancel the Saskatchewan Pension
Plan — a welfare provision especially important to women and strongly supported by them. Energetic lobbying on the part of the Provincial Council of
Women of Saskatchewan helped to bring about a revision of the proposal. The
Saskatchewan government agreed to leave the plan in place but removed its
matching funding and allowed members to transfer funds from it.[49] This quick

---

48 Owing to the unfortunate interruption in the traditional good recording work carried on at the
    national level, detailed membership information is not fully available as of late spring 1993.
    However, these listings are accurate in themselves, even though the information about some local
    councils is unavailable at this time.
49 Saskatchewan Provincial Council of Women, Report, 1993.

reaction by the Saskatchewan Council, on a provincial government matter, is an example of its traditional lobbying expertise.

In Manitoba, the Council movement rests upon the existence of the Winnipeg Local Council and the Provincial Council of Women of Manitoba. Should rules be strictly applied, the Provincial Council ought to be in recess until other Manitoban Local Councils are either revived or founded. The anomalous situation seems, however, to be extremely productive, giving the urban women of Winnipeg a unified strength while providing women throughout the rest of the province with a channel for making their own views known. It also ensures an annual meeting between Council members and provincial cabinet ministers. Pride in past achievement here centres upon the changes in the law concerning the property rights of married women and on the subject of rape. At both Council levels, there has been considerable praise for the way in which Council has helped women gain experience in public speaking, familiarity with how the political world works, and reliable information on the issues of the day.

The Manitoba Councils were less worried than others about recruitment and more concerned about working effectively on contemporary problems. Nevertheless, the members, who represent a wide variety of organizations, often confessed that their work for Council had begun because someone had told them it was time for them to be involved — together with their affiliate — in Council work. Many related stories of finding in Council a welcome source of strength in a daily struggle with a generally sexist society, in which it was socially acceptable for a man to remark that "anybody who thinks it appropriate that a women be a plumber has lost all claim on my courtesy," or again, as one member said, "I don't need to be told about the attitude of the European, Catholic male towards women — I'm married to one." There was a general conviction that women's social, economic and intellectual rights were effectively represented by Council.

Far more than any other group, the Manitoban members reflected explicitly on their lobbying tactics, remarking that they developed a dress plan for their meetings with official bodies: hats and gloves for the Conservative party, casual for the NDP and full regalia for the Salvation Army members when appropriate. The presence of immigrant women's organizations within the Winnipeg Council and the involvement of the native women's organization, Ikwewak, in the Provincial Council had come about because of deliberate action by Council members. Their recruitment was seen as essential for proper continuation of Council in Manitoba. Members saw the organization as a marvellous tool for civic action by women, to be used as such, and not as something that represented any particular ideological stance or specific political program.

All but one of the western Councils had little doubt about their value to their communities, the importance of the work undertaken, and the appropriateness of their methods of action. This self-confidence was certainly part of the Ontario Provincial Council and its nine Local Councils: Ottawa and Area; Kingston: Toronto and Area; Hamilton and District; Niagara Falls; Woodstock Study Group; London; St Catharines, and Windsor. Ottawa was the largest Local Council in the province in 1992–93, with forty-seven affiliates; London and Area Council came next with forty-one affiliates, among them the Congress of Black Women, London Chapter and the London Status of Women Action Group. In reporting to the national office, this Council gave the membership whenever its affiliates supplied the information. According to its conservative estimate it represented 10,000 women.[50]

Much time was devoted during these years by all local councils to preparing for Council's centennial celebrations in 1993. Muriel Beatty of the Kingston Local Council coordinated a gala evening to open the annual meeting of 1993, for members at Government House, when Council was presented with its official armorial bearings by the Governor General; photography during the annual meeting itself; and the lecture given on the centennial history at that National Library of Canada. Her committee members came from across the country and their work included not only the organization of the many celebrations taking place during the 100th Anniversary meeting, but also the support of local council initiatives.[51] The production of a magnificent quilt had been undertaken by Doreen Kissick, all local councils working on separate sections which were sent to Fredericton to be assembled. Each section was to show the particular city crest or emblem of the local council in question. Archives were organized and exhibitions prepared. In particular, Ruth Brown, Ruth Bell, and other members, both of the Ottawa Local Council, and the NCWC, organized an exhibition at the National Archives of Canada to celebrate Women's History Month, October 1992. Kay Stanley, Co-ordinator of the Status of Women, addressed the gathering on opening day and congratulated organizers for preparing this tribute to "the work of

---

50 Because this is one of the few listings of a local council to give such membership numbers, the membership role is printed as Appendix E.

51 The committee included Ruth Brown, President, NCWC (Ottawa); Lynne Berthiaume, Treasurer, NCWC (Wakefield); Shirley Brown (Ottawa); Margaret Harris and Helen Hnatyshyn, both Past Presidents of NCWC (both from Saskatoon); Bea Leinback (Vancouver); Sheila Pepper (Nepean); Shirley Post (Ottawa); Gertrude Tynbes (Dartmouth); and Trudy Wiltshire (Ottawa).

36. The National Council of Women of Canada 100th Annual Anniversary meeting. Carleton University, Ottawa, May 17, 1993.

MIKE PINDER — PHOTOGRAPHY

Canada's oldest and most distinguished women's organization."[52] She mentioned that:

> The idea for a Women's History Month was initially suggested to the Hon. Mary Collins, Minister Responsible for the Status of Women by a number of women from the academic community and...current members of the Victoria Council of Women.

Toronto Local Council also worked in this area, spending time and energy attempting to bring together the lost archives of the early meetings of the International Council of Women. It succeeded in tracking down four of the seven volumes of the proceedings of the 1899 meeting, held in London, England.[53]

All the Ontario Local Councils described, in the annual reports and the *Newsletter*, a varied program of activities during the period 1990–93. The work of Margaret MacGee, as editor of the *Newsletter* and President of the Provincial Council of Ontario, was of great importance. Her editorials pointed out that Council had always existed with little money and too few volunteers, and that these difficulties had never prevented Council from functioning effectively.[54] The spirit she wrote about was evident in the programs carried out by local councils. There were some topics of general interest that were an essential part of the agendas of almost all Ontario Local Councils: pension rights for women, global warming, and support for the cultural life of communities. At the same time, there was an individual flavour in the agendas reported to the provincial and national levels. Hamilton, for example, cooperated with other organizations on December 10, 1992, in sponsoring a candlelight vigil for the victims of wartime violence. Ottawa and Area Council held a public seminar on the possibilities of solar energy.[55] St. Catharines invited Catherine Sly, Past President of the Montreal Local Council, to speak to a joint meeting of their local council and the Woodstock Citizens' Committee about the Postponing Sexual Involvement Program, developed in Atlanta, Georgia.[56] Meanwhile, all councils continued to moni-

---

[52] *NCWC NEWS*, vol. 39, no. 2, November 1992, p. 1.

[53] Even the British Library does not have this resource. The Toronto Council is considering placing the volumes in the Doris French Library at Waterloo.

[54] See, in particular, *NCWC NEWS*, vol. 38, no. 3, Winter 1992.

[55] *NCWC NEWS*, vol. 39, no. 3, February 1993.

[56] *Ibid.*, p. 2.

tor municipal affairs and to inform themselves on issues of general interest.

It is pleasant to report that the Ontario Provincial Council has managed to maintain a strong profile with the Ontario Government and that the tradition of annual meetings between cabinet ministers and Council members is still alive and well. In 1993 ministers attending the occasion included the Hon. Marion Boyd, then Minister of Community and Social Services and the Minister responsible for Women's Issues; the Hon. Howard Hampton, Attorney General of Ontario; Margaret Harrington, Parliamentary Assistant to the Minister of Housing; Jenny Carter, Parliamentary Assistant to the Minister of Citizenship with responsibilities related to Seniors' Issues; and representatives from the Ministries of Health, Labour, Municipal Affairs, the Environment and National Resources. The only portfolio not represented was that of Education.

The President of the Ontario Provincial Council, Margaret MacGee, noted that the Council's brief stressed most particularly the needs of Ontario children living in poverty and concern over the increase of violence in the school system. In addition, resolutions on the environment, women's legal disabilities and the need for improved treatment for women with AIDS were submitted.[57] In concluding the Provincial Council's report, Margaret MacGee drew the attention of Council members to the way in which the organization works. Her words underline the responsibility for Council action and policies residing in the membership at the local level:

> It is your study, your meaningful resolution debate, your input on matters of importance to Council — *it is your participation* which provides Council's strength and its diverse and grassroots voice.

Similar strength was apparent in the Montreal Local Council, which had seventy-four affiliates, the largest number in the country. The 1993 report by its President, Amy Williams,[58] covered an extraordinary range of membership activities. Whether they were involved in cultural events, which brought together Montrealers of "French, Scottish, English, Irish, Jewish, Black, Greek, German, Ukrainian, Polish, Indian and Haitian" origin, or in making representations to municipal, provincial and federal governments, or work-

---

57 Report of the Provincial Council of Women of Ontario, 1993, n.p. n.d.
58 The way in which former presidents such as Ruth Hinkley, Margaret MacGee and Amy Williams are willing to continue work for Council after their term in office, is a remarkable testimony to their commitment to the ideals of the organization.

ing for the National Council, the Montreal Local Council of Women strove to ensure their participation in the life of their community. Their council managed to obtain a grant, from the Secretary of State, for a second edition of its booklet on pornography, which it hopes to see in print in 1993. It will be published in French and English and its title will remain the same: *Pornography — A Human Rights Issue which Affects Both Men and Women.*

In the Atlantic provinces, Councils in Moncton and Saint John, New Brunswick continued to flourish, with Moncton bringing together seventeen affiliated societies and managing to hold eight full Council meetings a year. In the report from the Local Council of Saint John it was noted that the membership had decided not to endorse the stand taken by the National Council on the referendum, since, in their view, the matter was a "personal one, not a group decision especially where we represent federates with different political views."[59] This action was consistent with Council tradition that members might choose openly not to support a Council decision. It should be noted, however, that it is a condition of membership of a local council in the national organization, that it shall not campaign for a view opposed to that of the National Council. This requirement dates back to 1893, the founding year. In Nova Scotia, New Glasgow, and Halifax Councils continued to function effectively, with Halifax counting thirty-nine affiliates, including the Black Professional Women's Groups and the Halifax Hadassah-Wizo Council.

In addition to activity which local and provincial bodies described in their particular reports, the energy and interests of members of Council is also apparent in the reports of standing committees. In 1993 the convenor for the Standing Committee on Child and Family summarized some fifty replies to a questionnaire she had sent out, asking people what they understood by the term "family values." The responses showed that Council members were no clearer about the matter than they had been a decade earlier. At the same time, respondents considered that the issue was critically important because the term was so misused. In her concluding remarks Christina Rogers noted that:

> Many responses indicated that "family values" have been used to subjugate women and children, that sometimes family loyalty is seen as the most important and certainly overrides individual rights allowing wife battering, child abuse and other abuses. Others stated

---

59 Report of the Saint John Council of Women, 1993.

that family values is a catch phrase evoking a false sense of nostalgia for an earlier simpler time.

The report leaves no room for doubt that the issue aroused very complex
feelings and that respondents gave very thoughtful replies. There was a general understanding that the need to allow maximum individual freedom in
matters of religious belief and cultural practices, had to be balanced with the
public consensus about norms of acceptable behaviour.

Freda Hogg, convenor of the Citizenship and Immigration Committee,
reported on the status of proposed federal legislation effecting both immigrants and refugees, as well as the work of local councils, whose agendas
included study sessions on AIDS and immigration (Toronto) and support for
the work of citizenship courts (Halifax, Regina, New Westminster,
Vancouver). The convenor of the Committee on Education, Gertrude Tynes,
summarized lengthy reports from the Local Councils of Ottawa, London,
Moncton, and Halifax. Common themes were the need to support initiatives
to encourage the young to remain in school, to address problems of violence
in schools, and to handle the question of racism. Mary Lemrye, convenor for
the Environment Committee, and Gracia Janes, convenor for the Land Use
and Housing Committee, both found considerable interest in their fields
among local councils. Global warming and pure water were the most common topics for the former, and aboriginal and inner-city housing for the latter. Council was also engaged, in 1992–93, in a cooperative, twenty-eight
month program with the Department of the Environment on alternative energy sources, with Gracia Janes acting as coordinator of the project. This activity included a common program for local councils across Canada on alternative energy sources and the publication of a quarterly newsletter, *The
Conserver*.[60]

As convenor for the Committee on Health and Welfare, Pat Eglinski
brought together four reports. These addressed the issues of domestic violence; substance abuse, including cigarette smoking in particular and drug
abuse in general; the de-medicalization of prenatal care; and the financial
problems of Canada's health care system as a whole. A significant insight
from this committee was that, since government had taken over the care:

of the infirm, disabled, and elderly, they adopted an "all or nothing"

---

[60] President's Report, 1993.

approach. Even healthy seniors were often "ghettoized" in a variety of sequestered accommodation...The integration of older people into our society has, to a great extent, been lost.

Bette Pepper, reporting for the Committee on International Affairs drew attention to the broad spectrum of problem areas brought together in this portfolio: the environment; the manufacture of, and trade in, arms, and war generally; the chaotic global economic system and resultant problems of poverty; and the need to come to grips with AIDS. Stella Ohan, responsible for the Legislative Committee, drew up a précis of federal legislation tabled in the House of Commons. Rose Dyson, reporting for the Media Committee, raised the question of how "Canadian culture or what we have come to regard as unifying experiences and values" will be affected by "consumer-driven, multi-channel television." The main issue for Loretta Norton and the Committee for Public Safety was safe driving, especially by young persons. Ruth Bell, for the Archives Committee, Pat Beck, as Status of Women convenor, and Elizabeth MacEwen, as Resolutions convenor, all reported full schedules of activity in their areas of responsibility. Margaret MacGee reported for the Committee on Women and Justice Issues. Topics included the proposed legislation on stalking, the rape shield legislation, the need for regional correction centres for women, and the question of judicial recognition of the "battered women's defense." As well, proposed gun control legislation was discussed, together with the protection of society from "dangerous offenders." Whether through the local council organization or via the standing committees, members of Council in 1933 addressed most of the major concerns facing Canadians at the close of the twentieth century.

To sum up: at the time of the 100th anniversary of the National Council of Women of Canada, the organization was in a strong position to adapt to the challenges facing its membership. The annual meeting was given an impressive opening reception by Govenor General, the Right Honourable Ramon John Hnatyshyn and Mrs. Gerda Hnatyshyn at Rideau Hall, on Thursday May 13, where the new coat of arms was presented to the Committee of Officers. At the banquet, held on Sunday, May 16, at the National Arts Centre, Lady Jessamine Harmsworth, the granddaughter of Lady Aberdeen was present. She had spoken at the dinner, on May 14, about her memories of her grandmother. During the banquet itself telegrams of congratulation were read, among them messages from the Prime Minister of Canada and the Premier of British Columbia, and there was a presentation by Canada Post of a painting representing the commemorative stamps, issued in

March 1993, to celebrate the 100th year of Council.

In the midst of the justifiable pride and joy at the anniversary celebrations, the annual meeting continued with business as usual. It discussed eight major resolutions brought forward for discussion, as well as a number of emergency resolutions, and the need to reiterate and update four previously accepted resolutions. The roster of subjects addressed reflected the traditional concerns of Council. There were resolutions on international policies relating to the environment, women, and development. Others dealt with issues of the environment in North America, in particular the relationship of Canadian water resources to the North American Free Trade Agreement. Three resolutions were concerned with the problems of women and children respecting equality of treatment by health services, and under the provisions of the Income Tax Act and the Criminal Code. There was the reiteration of past resolutions concerning women and employment. The issue of protecting federal civil servants who report wrongdoing was discussed, as was the matter of M.P.s' pensions. The need of Canada's native people for new programs was addressed in a resolution which noted that, "despite [federal] expenditures which now run to $4 billion per year, [native] poverty and dependency still exists." It was requested that the federal government make:

> self government the basis for change in the knowledge that native peoples will find better ways to speed economic development, educate children, supply the skill training that is needed and address social problems...

The unique blend that has marked the annual meetings of the National Council of Women of Canada for a hundred years was once more evident in this agenda of resolutions. It was a mix of the concerns of women about general issues of public policy, and about issues which are often considered to be matters of self-interest for women. In reality, given the equal importance of both sexes for the human species, even those issues which are seen as areas of special pleading for women are of moment for all citizens, men as much as women. What members of Council have occupied themselves with has been the reality of people's daily living, the public aspect of people's private lives. In areas such as town planning and civic health measures, the functioning of the legal system and the operation of laws governing conditions of employment, conditions in jails and hospitals, provisions for children in schools and the quality of care given by public bodies to those without power, the weak and the old, the poor and the outcast, Council women have established their right, and the rights of all women, to be consulted on the conduct of affairs, and have demonstrated their own sense of responsibility for the running of their communities.

The sharpest complaint about the National Council of Women of Canada represents its most remarkable attribute: its kaleidoscopic, fragmented focus, its diffuse program of causes. Its force is its representation of the normal, myriad concerns of Canadian women, whose daily experience is that there is always one more urgent issue to be dealt with. Even though one cause will be particularly dear to a member, Council maintains its concern for the many general problems faced every day by its members. Its unspoken rule is "you listen to my problem and I'll pay attention to yours." The women who worked through Council in the past often did so because it was the only way for them to have a significant voice in the governing of their communities. Women who continue to work through Council today do so because it is an effective way to play a role in civic affairs. As Council moves on, it will retain the broadest agenda of issues, and will comment, knowledgeably, on all the complex links between the lives of individuals and the life of a society.

APPENDIX A

Presidents of the National Council of Women of Canada

1893-1898: Lady Ishbel, Marchioness of Aberdeen and Temair

1898-1899: Lady Edgar (Acting President)

1899-1902: Lady Taylor

1902-1906: Mrs. Robert Thompson

1906-1910: Lady Edgar

1910-1911: Lady Taylor

1911-1918: Mrs. F.H. Torrington

1918-1922: Mrs. W.E. Sanford

1922-1926: Miss Caroline C. Carmichael

1926-1931: Mrs. J.A. Wilson

1931-1936: Miss M. Winnifred Kydd

1936-1941: Mrs. George O. Spencer

1941-1946: Mrs. Edgar D. Hardy

1946-1951: Mrs. R.J. Marshall

1951-1956: Mrs. Turner Bone

1956-1959: Mrs. Rex Eaton

1959-1961: Mrs. G.D. Finlayson

1960-1961: Mrs. C.W. Argue (Acting President)

1961-1964: Mrs. Saul Hayes

1964-1967: Mrs. M.F. Steen

1967-1970: Mrs. S.M. Milne

1970-1973: Mrs. John Hnatyshyn

1973-1976: Mrs. Gordon B. Armstrong

1976-1979: Mrs. Ruth (Charles) Hinkley

1979-1982: Mrs. Amy (Jack) Williams

1982-1984: Mrs. Margaret (Arthur) Harris

1984-1987: Mrs. Margaret MacGee

1987-1990: Mrs. Doreen Kissick

1990-1992: Mrs. Joan De New

1992-   : Ruth Brown

The form for the listing of names is the form chosen by the Presidents themselves in the reports of the *Yearbook*.

APPENDIX B

The Foundation Fund[1]

This fund was begun in order to cope with the financial difficulties encountered by the NCWC. Since the organization was an amalgamation of volunteer associations, all of which had their own financial obligations, the problem of core funding — for a national office, for aid for attendance by members at annual meetings, and for the necessary travelling expenses of officers of the Council — soon became urgent. Lady Aberdeen was a generous patron in the early years of the NCWC, but by the mid-twenties it was clear that a new initiative had to be undertaken of the Council was to continue, let alone expand. In 1925, Mrs. W. Bunday, Finance Convener, suggested that an annual investment income of $10,000 would cover the expenses of a Head Office, executive secretary's salary, some support for travel by Local Council Presidents to annual meetings and the out-of-pocket expenses of the Executive.

Mrs. Patrick Etherington of Kingston, suggested that the National Council establish a Foundation Fund of $200,000, which, at the current rates of interest, would yield the $10,000 needed. The capital sum was to be raised, in the first place, by bequests of $10,000 each, the interest of which was to be paid into the fund annually during the life of the donor. It was hoped that such bequests would provide half the sum needed. Mrs. Etherington volunteered to establish and chair a committee to run the campaign and contributed the first $10,000 bequest.

It was decided that each Local Council would be asked to raise a particular amount, ranging from $100 to $25,000, according to their size. The response was good and the annual meeting of 1928 was one of the best held in years, owing to the assistance given delegates for their travel expenses. As well, Mrs. Etherington showed great generosity by paying the accommodation costs of the Local Presidents who attended.

By the annual meeting of 1929 the sum of $50,000 had been collected which yielded an annual revenue of $3,100. However, the Depression brought an immediate halt to the growth of the fund and it was only in 1946 that a further, major, effort was undertaken to reach the original goal. On the completion of her term as President, Mrs. Edgar D. Hardy took over responsibility for the Foundation Fund. By 1952, the capital invested had reached

---

[1]   The information in this appendix has been taken from the NCWC *Handbook* and from a small pamphlet on the origins of the fund compiled by Mrs. A. Turner Bone, Mrs. F. Etherington and Mrs. Edgar D. Hardy. This pamphlet is held by the head office of the NCWC.

$114,750. In 1953, Mrs. W.P. Fillimore of Winnipeg succeeded Mrs. Hardy and by 1956, the fund had increased to $124,300. Over the next decades, the Fund increased slowly and in 1993 Council had $240,354 invested in this portfolio. A large bequest from the Estate of Alison Taylor Hardy, daughter of Mrs. Edgar D. Hardy, will go a long way towards insuring the survival of Council from a financial point of view.

APPENDIX C

Affiliated Societies of Local and Provincial Councils
1956

ALUMNAE ASSN. COLLEGE, (CONSERVATORY, SCHOOL): Halifax 3, Kingston, London 2, Montreal 4, New Westminster, Toronto 6, Saint John, Windsor 2, Fredericton.

ALUMNAE SCHOOLS OF NURSING: Brantford, Kingston, London, Montreal 4, New Glasgow, New Westminster, Ottawa 3, Owen Sound, Peterborough, Toronto 3, West Algoma, Winnipeg 3, Chatham, Edmonton, St. Catharines, Orillia.

ALTRUSA CLUB: Halifax, Hamilton, Montreal, Toronto, Vancouver, London, Victoria.

AMERICAN ASSN. MEDICAL SOCIAL WORKERS: Montreal.

AMERICAN WOMAN'S CLUB: Kingston, London, Montreal, Regina 2, Toronto, Windsor, Winnipeg, Vancouver.

ANTI-T.B. ASSN.: Halifax, West Pictou.

APARTMENT & ROOMING HOUSE OPERATORS ASSOC.: Vancouver.

ARTS AND CRAFTS, HANDICRAFTS, NEEDLEWORK GUILDS: Brandon, Brantford, Montreal, Kamloops, West Algoma, Georgetown.

ART ASSN. GROUPS: Montreal, Moose Jaw, New Westminster, Owen Sound, Hamilton, Peterborough, Fredericton, London.

ASSN. PROTECTION FUR-BEARING ANIMALS: Toronto, Vancouver.

ASSN. FOR HELP OF RETARDED CHILDREN: London, Hamilton, Vancouver, Windsor.

ASSOCIATED CHARITIES: Yarmouth.

AUX. ACT: Brandon.

AUX. ARMY, NAVY, AIR FORCE, SAILORS: North Shore, Portage, Saint John, Vancouver 2, Victoria, West Algoma, Winnipeg 2, Montreal.

AUX. ASSOC. PROPERTY OWNERS: Vancouver.

AUX. BOY SCOUTS: Toronto, Swift Current.

AUX. C.B.R.T.: Brandon.

AUX. C.B.R.E.: Winnipeg 4, West Algoma.

AUX. COMM. CENTRE: Winnipeg.

AUX. DENTAL SOCIETY: London.

AUX. ELYS: Brandon, Dauphin, Edmonton.

AUX. FIRE DEPT.: Nanaimo.

AUX. KIWANIS CLUB: Brandon, Ottawa, London.

AUX. B.C. ELECTRIC: New Westminster.

AUX. LOCOMOTIVE ENGINEERS AND FIREMEN: Kamloops, Medicine Hat, West Algoma.

AUX. NEIGHBOURHOOD HOUSE: Montreal, North Shore.

AUX. MUSEUM FINE ARTS: Montreal, Saint John.

AUX. OILWORKERS NAT. AOWU.: Moose Jaw.

AUX. OLD AGE PENSIONERS: Saskatoon, West Algoma, Nanaimo, New Westminster.

AUX. POLICE ASSN.: Peterborough.

AUX. RAILWAY CONDUCTORS: Medicine Hat.

AUX. PHARMACISTS: Toronto, Windsor.

AUX. ST. ANDREW'S SOCIETY: Ottawa.

AUX. UNITED COMMERCIAL TRAVELLERS: Ottawa, Regina, Saskatoon, Windsor, Brandon.

AUX. BALLET: Dauphin.

BARBERS AND BEAUTICIANS: Saskatchewan PCW, Regina.

BETA SIGMA PHI: Brandon, London, Montreal, New Westminster, Nanaimo, Ottawa, Portage, Saint John, Vancouver, Windsor, Fredericton, Peterborough.

BIG SISTERS' ASSN.: Toronto, Saint John.

B'NAI B'RITH WOMEN: Montreal 6, Ottawa, Halifax, Hamilton, Windsor.

BREAKFAST CLUB: Chilliwack.

BREHMER REST PREVENTORIUM: Montreal.

BRITISH WIVES' ASSN. OLD COUNTRY CLUB: Brantford, Winnipeg.

BUSINESS AND PROFESSIONAL WOMEN'S CLUBS: Brandon 2, Chatham, Brockville, Edmonton, Kamloops, Halifax 2, Hamilton, Kelowna, Kingston, London, Chilliwack, Montreal, Moose Jaw, Nanaimo, Niagara Falls, New Glasgow, New Westminster, Ottawa, Owen Sound, Peterborough, Regina, Saint John, St. Catharines, Saskatoon, Smiths Falls, Swift Current, Toronto, Truro, Vancouver, Victoria, Weston, Windsor, Winnipeg, Man. PCW, Ont. PCW, N.S. PCW, Fredericton, Orillia, Yarmouth.

C.A.C.: Montreal, Dauphin, London, Saint John, Saskatoon, Toronto, West Algoma, Sask. PCW, N.S. Prov. Fredericton, Halifax, Nanaimo, Regina, Truro, Victoria.

CAN. ARTHRITIS & RHEUMATISM SOC.: New Westminster, Kingston.

CAN. ASSN. SOCIAL WORKERS: Montreal, N.S. PCW.

CANCER RESEARCH SOCIETY AND AUX.: Kingston, Halifax, Montreal, Toronto, Winnipeg.

CAN. DAUGHTER'S LEAGUE: Brantford, Moose Jaw, North Shore, Ottawa, Regina, Toronto, Vancouver 6, Victoria, West Algoma, Winnipeg, Kingston.

C.G.I.T.: Halifax.

CAN. LADY FORESTERS: Brandon, Mission City.

CAN. HOME READING UNION: Montreal.

CAN. LEGION B.E.S.L.: Chilliwack, Dauphin, Georgetown, Edmonton, Medicine Hat, Montreal, New Glasgow, Ottawa, Owen Sound, Peterborough, Portage, Sackville, Swift Current, West Algoma 3, Winnipeg, Westville, Georgetown, Kingston.

CAN. MOTHERCRAFT SOCIETY: Ottawa, Toronto.

C.N.I.B. AND AUX.: Hamilton, Kingston, London, New Westminster, Peterborough, Saint John, Vancouver, Winnipeg, Montreal.

CAN. REPERTORY THEATRE: Ottawa.

CATHOLIC AUX.: Halifax 6, Windsor.

CATHOLIC GIRLS: Montreal, Ottawa.

CATHOLIC WOMEN'S LEAGUE: Brandon 2, Chilliwack, Dauphin, Halifax, Mission City, Moose Jaw, New Glasgow, New Westminster, North Shore, Portage, Saint John, Saskatoon, Swift Current, Weston, Yarmouth, Kelowna, Westville, West Pictou.

CHILDREN'S AID SOC.: Hamilton, Halifax, London, Peterborough, Orillia, Portage, West Algoma, Yarmouth, Winnipeg, Saskatoon, Saint John.

CHILDREN'S CENTRE: Kingston.

CHURCH WOMEN'S ORGANIZATIONS: Anglican, Adventist, Baptist, Catholic, D.V.V.S., Hebrew, Presbyterian, Ukrainian, Unitarian, United: Brandon 20, Brantford 9, Brockville, Calgary 2, Chilliwack 9, Chatham 3, Dauphin 5, Edmonton 5, Georgetown 2, Halifax 15, Hamilton, Kelowna 2, Kingston 9, London 4, Medicine Hat 4, Mission City 1, Montreal 12, Moose Jaw 6, New Glasgow 16, New Westminster 14, Niagara Falls 11, North Shore 2, Ottawa 31, Owen Sound 10, Peterborough 9, Portage 9, Regina 10, St. Catharines 7, Sackville 3, Sask.

PCW, Saint John 3, Saskatoon 14, Smiths Falls 3, Stellarton 2, Swift Current 6, Toronto 16, Truro 15, Vancouver 19, Victoria 8, West Pictou 4, Weston 13, Westville 9, West Algoma 18, Yarmouth 7, Weston 3, Windsor 10, Winnipeg 24, Man. PCW 2, Ont. PCW, Fredericton 6, Orillia 5, B.C. PCW.

CITY IMPROVEMENT LEAGUE: Montreal.

C.C.F. WOMEN'S COUNCIL GUILD: Brantford, Kelowna, Mission City, London, Nanaimo, North Shore, Regina, Sask. PCW, Swift Current, Vancouver, Victoria, Winnipeg, Windsor, Saskatoon, New Westminster.

CIVIL COUNCIL AND TOWNSWOMEN GUILD: North Shore, Sackville.

COUNCIL FOR PRE-SCHOOL EDUCATION: London.

COMPENSATION WIDOWS ASSOC.: Man. PCW.

CREDIT UNION, WOMEN'S AUX.: Hamilton.

CREDIT WOMEN'S BREAKFAST CLUB: London.

DAUGHTERS OF ENGLAND: Dauphin, St. Catharines, Vancouver, West Algoma.

DAUGHTERS OF SCOTLAND: London.

DAY NURSERY: Montreal, Ottawa, Winnipeg, Halifax, London.

DIETETIC ASSOCIATION: Toronto.

DIET DISPENSARY: Montreal.

ELIZABETH FRY SOCIETY: Kingston, B.C. Prov.

FACULTY WOMEN'S CLUB: Fredericton, London.

FED. AGRICULTURE, WOMEN'S SECTION: Dauphin, Man. Prov., Ont. Prov.

FRUIT AND VEGETABLE WORKERS' UNION: Kelowna.

GIRLS' COTTAGE SCHOOL: Montreal.

GIRLS GUIDES'S ASSOC.: Brandon, Brantford, Fredericton, Hamilton, Halifax, Kamloops, Kelowna, Kingston, London, Montreal, Moose Jaw, New Glasgow, New Westminster, North Shore, Ottawa, Regina, Toronto, Truro, Vancouver, Victoria, Weston, Windsor, Winnipeg, N.S. Prov., Man. Prov., Ont. Prov.

GIRLS' WORK BOARD: Kingston, Montreal, Brandon.

GRENFELL MISSION: Montreal, Ottawa.

HADASSAH: Brantford, Chatham, Halifax 2, London 2, Montreal, Moose Jaw, New Glasgow, New Westminster, Ottawa, Peterborough, Regina, Saint John, Toronto, Vancouver, West Algoma 2, Windsor, Winnipeg, Brandon, Fredericton, Victoria.

HANDICRAFT SCHOOL COMM.: Toronto, Windsor.

HEBREW BEN. SOCIETY SISTERHOOD: Niagara Falls, Ottawa, Regina, Yarmouth.

HELLENIC LADIES' BEN. SOCIETY: Montreal.

HERVEY INSTITUTE: Montreal.

HISTORICAL SOCIETY: Ottawa.

HOME ECONOMICS ASSN.: Edmonton, Halifax, London, Ottawa, Regina, Saskatoon, Saint John, Yarmouth, Winnipeg, N.S. Prov., N.B. Prov., Fredericton.

HOMEMAKERS' CLUBS: Regina, Swift Current, Sask. Prov., Hamilton.

HOMES FOR AGED: Hamilton, Ottawa 2, New Westminster.

HORTICULTURAL SOCIETY: Peterborough.

HOSPITAL AID, AUX. ASSN.: Brandon, Brantford, Chatham, Chilliwack 2, Dauphin, Halifax 3, Kingston 3, London 4, Montreal, Nanaimo, New Glasgow, New Westminster 2, Niagara Falls 2, North Shore, Peterborough, Portage, Regina 2, Saint John 4, St. Catharines 2, Saskatoon 2, Swift Current, Toronto 4, Truro, Vancouver 3, Windsor 2, Winnipeg, Victoria, West Algoma 3, Yarmouth, Man. Prov., Owen Sound 2, Fredericton, Orillia.

HOSPITAL BOARD: Smiths Falls, Hamilton.

HOSPITAL STAFF: Toronto.

HOTEL GREETERS OF AMERICA: Vancouver.

HUMANE SOCIETY, S.P.C.A.: Moose Jaw, New Westminster, Ottawa, West Algoma, Peterborough, Yarmouth, Toronto, Edmonton, Kingston, Vancouver 2, Fredericton, Winnipeg.

INNER WHEEL WOMEN OF ROTARY: Halifax, Montreal, Ottawa, Vancouver.

INTERNATIONAL LEAGUE FOR PEACE AND FREEDOM: Toronto, Winnipeg.

INTER-CHURCH COUNCIL: Hamilton.

I.O.D.E.: Brandon 2, Brockville, Chilliwack 3, Dauphin, Fredericton, Georgetown, Halifax 5, Kelowna 2, Kingston, London 2, Medicine Hat, Montreal, Nanaimo 2, New Glasgow 3, Ottawa 9, Owen Sound 2, Peterborough 2, Portage, Regina, St. Catharines, Saskatoon 2,

Smiths Falls 2, Stellarton, Swift Current, Toronto, West Algoma 5, Yarmouth, Winnipeg, Windsor 2, Truro, New Westminster, Orillia.

ITALIAN WOMEN'S CLUB: Windsor.

INTERNATIONAL WOODWORKERS OF AMERICA: Vancouver, New Westminster.

JAYCEE-ETTES: Owen Sound, New Westminster, London, Windsor.

JOHN HOWARD SOCIETY: Saskatoon.

JUNIOR LEAGUE, MAY COURT CLUB: Chatham, Halifax, London, Montreal, Ottawa, Winnipeg, Windsor, Hamilton.

KING'S DAUGHTERS: London, New Westminster, Ottawa, Owen Sound, Saint John, Vancouver, Windsor, Fredericton.

KINETTES: Kingston, Moose Jaw, New Westminster, Chatham, Windsor.

KIWASSA: New Westminster, Vancouver.

LATTER DAY SAINTS' RELIEF SOCIETY: Chatham.

LEAGUE OF WOMEN VOTERS: Vancouver, Winnipeg.

LEPER MISSION: Georgetown.

LIBRARIES, PUBLIC AND CHILDREN'S: Montreal, Yarmouth 2, Hamilton.

LIFE MEMBERS' CLUB: Peterborough.

LIONS LADIES' AUX.: Kingston, London 2, Ottawa 2, Vancouver, Saskatoon, Halifax, New Westminster.

LYCEUM CLUB AND ART ASSOC.: Owen Sound, Toronto.

L.O.B.A. AND ORANGE LODGES: Mission City, Nanaimo, New Westminster, Peterborough, Portage, Regina, Saint John 2, Chatham, Vancouver, West Algoma, Brandon, Westville, Victoria.

MOTHERS' UNION: Toronto, St. Catharines.

MEDICAL WIVES SOCIETY: Kingston.

MENTAL HYGIENE: Halifax, N.S. Prov.

MFAC WOMEN'S COMM.: Man. PCW.

MORRISON LAMOTHE WOMEN'S ASSN.: Ottawa.

MULTIPLE SCLEROSIS SOCIETY: Winnipeg, Regina.

MUSICAL CLUBS AND SYMPHONY ORCHESTRA SOC.: Dauphin, Brandon, Kelowna, London 2, Ottawa, Regina, Saskatoon, Toronto, Vancouver, Kingston, Ottawa, Winnipeg, Saint John.

MUSICAL TEACHERS' SOC.: West Algoma.

NAT. COUNCIL OF JEWISH WOMEN: Calgary, Edmonton, Hamilton, Kingston, London, Montreal 2, Ottawa, Regina, Saskatoon, Toronto, Vancouver, Winnipeg, West Algoma, Owen Sound.

NATIVE DAUGHTERS OF B.C.: Nanaimo, Victoria, Vancouver, New Westminster.

NEIGHBOURHOOD SERVICES: Ottawa.

NURSERY SCHOOL ASSN.: London 2, Victoria.

NURSES' ASSN. AND REG. NURSES: Brandon, Brantford, Chilliwack, Orillia, Dauphin, Edmonton, Halifax, Hamilton, Kamloops, Kelowna, London 2, Owen Sound, Mission City, Montreal, New Glasgow, New Westminster, North Shore, Ottawa, Peterborough, Regina, Moncton, Saint John, St. Catharines, Sask. PCW, Saskatoon, Swift Current, Toronto 2, Yarmouth, Windsor, Winnipeg, N.S. Prov., Owen Sound, Vancouver 2, Moncton, Fredericton, Nanaimo, Orillia, Portage, Victoria.

OPTI-MRS.: Saskatoon, Kingston, New Westminster.

ORDER OF MOOSE: Medicine Hat, Nanaimo, Peterborough, Windsor.

ORDER OF ROYAL PURPLE: Regina, West Algoma, Mission City, Dauphin, New Westminster.

ORPHANS AND CHILDREN'S HOMES: Montreal, Ottawa, Winnipeg, Saint John, Edmonton.

OVERSEAS WIVES CLUB: Fredericton.

PARKS AND PLAYGROUNDS ASSN.: Montreal, Yarmouth.

PARENT'S COUNCIL FOR RETARDED CHILDREN: Toronto, Ont. Prov.

PHYSICAL THERAPISTS'S ASSN.: Sask. PCW.

PILOT CLUB: Windsor.

POLIO PATIENTS COMFORT CLUB: Toronto.

PROTECTION OF WOMEN AND CHILDREN: Montreal.

PROT. WOMEN'S FED., GIRLS' CLUB: Ottawa 2, Toronto Ont. PCW.

PUBLIC HEALTH NURSES' SERVICE: Chilliwack, Halifax.

PUBLIC LIBRARY STAFF: Toronto, Windsor, Yarmouth.

PYTHIAN SISTERS: Halifax, Montreal, New Glasgow, Saint John, Truro, Regina, Westville.

QUOTA CLUB: Montreal, Medicine Hat, Moose Jaw, Ottawa, Vancouver, Swift Current, London, Saskatoon, Brandon, Owen Sound.

REBEKAH LODGE: Kamloops, Kelowna, New Glasgow, Portage, Regina, Saskatoon, Vancouver 2, West Algoma, Winnipeg, Sackville, Chilliwack, Westville.

RED CROSS: Kingston, New Westminster, Smiths Falls, Weston, West Pictou, Windsor, Ottawa, London.

ROSICRUCIAN ORDER: Windsor.

SALVATION ARMY: Brantford, Dauphin, Kingston, London, Montreal, Moncton, New Westminster, Peterborough, Portage, Edmonton, Halifax, Saint John, Toronto, Vancouver, Yarmouth, Winnipeg, Truro, Ont. Prov., Halifax 3, Regina, Westville 2, Windsor, Fredericton, Orillia, West Pictou, N.S. PCW.

SCHOOL FOR CITIZENSHIP: Vancouver.

SCOTTISH DANCE SOCIETY: Vancouver.

ST. JOHN AMBULANCE: Brantford, Kingston, London, Montreal, New Westminster, Ottawa, Regina, Saskatoon.

SENIOR CITIZENS ASSOC.: Vancouver.

SILVER CROSS WOMEN: Brantford, Halifax, Kingston, London, Montreal, Niagara Falls, Peterborough, Toronto, Winnipeg, Vancouver, Brandon, Nanaimo, New Westminster 2, Vancouver 2, Victoria.

SOCIAL CREDIT WAS.: Victoria 2, Vancouver 4, New Westminster, Kelowna, North Shore.

SOCIAL SECURITY COUNCIL: Medicine Hat, Calgary.

SOC. HANDICAPPED CHILDREN: New Westminster.

SOLDIERS' WIVES LEAGUE: Montreal.

SOROPTIMIST CLUB: Brantford, Chilliwack, Edmonton, Halifax, Kamloops, London, Montreal 2, New Westminster, Ottawa, Regina, Vancouver, Victoria, Windsor, Kelowna, Fredericton, Nanaimo.

TEACHERS' WIVES' ASSOC.: Toronto 2.

TOC H (WOMEN'S SECTION): Montreal.

UKRAINIAN WOMEN'S ORG.: Regina, Windsor, Winnipeg.

UNITED NATIONS SOC.: Toronto, Halifax, Regina.

UNIVERSITY SETTLEMENT: Montreal.

UNIVERSITY WOMEN'S CLUB: Brandon, Brantford, Chatham, Chilliwack, Halifax, Kingston, London, Medicine Hat, Montreal, Moose Jaw, Nanaimo, Mission City, New Westminster, Niagara Falls, Ottawa, Regina, Sackville, Saskatoon, Swift Current, Smiths Falls, Toronto, Truro, Victoria, Windsor, Winnipeg, Vancouver, Peterborough, Fredericton, Saint John.

VETERANS' KITH AND KIN, NON-PENSIONED WIDOWS: Brantford, Montreal, Vancouver.

V.O.N.: Hamilton, Kingston, Edmonton, Halifax, London, Montreal, Moose Jaw, New Glasgow, North Shore, Ottawa, Owen Sound, Peterborough, Regina, Saint John, Saskatoon, Smiths Falls, Truro, Vancouver, Victoria, Yarmouth, Weston, Windsor, Winnipeg, Orillia, Nanaimo, West Pictou.

WELFARE ASSN. COUNCIL LEAGUE, SERVICE BUR.: Hamilton, Halifax, Kingston, London, Brantford, Montreal, Peterborough, Saskatoon 2.

WOMEN'S BR. ANTIQUARIAN AND NUMISMATIC SOC.: Hamilton, Halifax, Kingston, London, Brantford, Montreal, Peterborough, Saskatoon 2.

W.C.T.U.: Brantford, Brockville 2, Chatham, Dauphin, Edmonton 2, Halifax 2, Kamloops, Kingston, London 2, Mission City, Montreal 4, Moose Jaw, Nanaimo, New Glasgow, New Westminster, Niagara Falls, North Shore, Ottawa 4, Owen Sound, Peterborough, Portage, Regina 2, St. Catharines, Sask. PCW, Saskatoon, Saint John 4, Toronto 2, Truro, Vancouver 10, Victoria 2, West Algoma, West Pictou, Yarmouth, Weston, Windsor, Winnipeg, B.C. Prov., Man. Prov., Ont. Prov.

WOMEN'S CANADIAN CLUB: Brandon, Chilliwack, Hamilton, London, Montreal, Moose

Jaw, Ottawa, Saskatoon, Smiths Falls, Victoria, West Algoma 2, Winnipeg, Halifax, Saint John.

WOMEN'S CLUBS STUDY GROUPS: Brandon, Dauphin 2, London 3, Montreal 14, Moose Jaw 4, New Westminster 4, Niagara Falls, North Shore 2, Ottawa, Portage, Sackville, Saskatoon, Smiths Falls, Swift Current, Toronto 6, Vancouver 6, West Algoma, Yarmouth, Weston, Windsor 2, Winnipeg, Regina, Chatham, Fredericton, Nanaimo 2.

WOMEN'S CO-OPERATIVE GUILDS: Saskatoon, Swift Current, Winnipeg, Moose Jaw, Sask. Prov., Man. Prov., Regina.

WOMEN'S INSTITUTES: Brockville, Calgary, Chatham 3, Chilliwack 3, Brandon, Kelowna, Kingston 3, Mission City, Montreal, Niagara Falls, Penticton, Peterborough, Portage, Vancouver, Victoria 3, West Algoma, Yarmouth, Weston 4, Man. PCW, Nanaimo, Fredericton, London, Orillia.

WOMEN'S LIBERAL CLUB ASSN.: Brandon, Brantford, Chatham, Calgary, Halifax, Kelowna, Kingston, London, Montreal, Nanaimo, New Westminster, North Shore, Ottawa, Peterborough, St. Catharines, Saskatoon, Smiths Falls, Toronto 2, Vancouver, West Algoma, Winnipeg, Regina, Ont. PCW, Fredericton.

WOMEN'S PERSONNEL GROUP: Montreal.

WOMEN'S PROGRESSIVE CONSERVATIVE ASSN.: Brandon, Brantford, Dauphin, Edmonton, Hamilton, Kelowna, Kingston, London, Montreal, New Westminster, Niagara Falls, Toronto 2, Vancouver, West Algoma, Winnipeg, Windsor, Ont. PCW, Man. Prov., Calgary, Moose Jaw, Fredericton, Orillia.

WOMEN'S TEACHERS ASSN. FED.: Brantford 2, Chatham 2, Dauphin, Edmonton, Halifax, Kelowna, Kingston, London, Montreal, Moose Jaw 2, Ottawa, Owen Sound, Peterborough, Regina, Saskatoon, Toronto, West Algoma 2, Windsor 2, Winnipeg 3, Ont. PCW, Orillia.

W.V.S.: Montreal.

Y.M.C.A. AUX.: Kingston, Chatham, London 2, Moose Jaw, St. Catharines, Yarmouth, Brandon, Fredericton, Orillia, Saint John, West Algoma.

Y.W.C.A.: Brandon, Brantford, Edmonton, Halifax, Kingston, London, Medicine Hat, Montreal, Moose Jaw, New Westminster, Ottawa, Owen Sound, Peterborough, Regina, St. Catharines, Saint John, Saskatoon, Toronto, Vancouver, Victoria, Weston, Windsor, Winnipeg, West Algoma, Fredericton.

Y.M. AND Y.W.H.A.: Montreal.

ZONTA CLUB: Brantford, Kingston, Montreal, Ottawa, Windsor, Vancouver, St. Catharines, Halifax.

APPENDIX D

Terms of Reference for the standing committees
1956

The reforms undertaken by Mrs. Turner Bone led to the most structured organization of the committee structure of Council that it had known. The listing that follows includes the names and addresses of those who were their conveners in 1956. The present-day committee structure of Council is to be found in the 1988 *Handbook*.

CHAIRMEN OF STANDING COMMITTEES

(Representatives on I.C.W. Standing Committees)

ARTS AND LETTERS — Miss Beatrice Brigden, 1175 Dominion St., Winnipeg, Man. (1952).

Terms of Reference:
1. To encourage talent wherever found, and to stimulate popular interest in Art, literature, drama and music, by the promotion of libraries, exhibits, concerts, plays, etc.
2. To support UNESCO and other agencies promoting international co-operation and goodwill by more widespread and sympathetic understanding of the cultures of other people.

ECONOMICS — Mrs. F.E. Underhill, 260 Victoria St., London, Ont. (1955).

Terms of Reference:
1. To study and appraise our economic policies including taxation as related to national and international trade;
2. To study our natural resources and industries with a view to maximum production and prevention of waste of materials and human resources;
3. To work for full recognition of the economic and social contribution of the homemaker;
4. To recommend appropriate action on the above.

EDUCATION — Mrs. Jean Newman, 65 Rochester Ave., Toronto 12, Ont. (1954).

Terms of Reference:
1. To work toward full opportunity for education, through study and constructive recreation, for all children and adults;
2. To support better training for teachers, and remuneration commensurate with the importance of their service;
3. To spread information regarding the work for universal education by UNESCO and other international agencies;
4. To recommend appropriate action on the above.

FILMS — Mrs. A. L. Caldwell, 807 University Drive, Saskatoon, Sask. (1955).

Terms of Reference:
1. To assess the value of films available, and to promote the use of films of artistic, educational and recreational value, whether produced commercially or otherwise;
2. To assemble and spread information regarding such films as are available through the Children's Film Library, the National Film Board and other agencies.

HEALTH — Dr. Marguerite Bailey, 256 Oriole Parkway, Toronto, Ont. (1955).

Terms of Reference:
1. To conduct inquires into all matters affecting the physical and mental health of the people with a view to taking necessary action;
2. To spread information regarding WHO and other international health authorities.

HOUSING — Mrs. R.G. Gilbride, 7 Brock Ave. N., Montreal, Que. (1954).

Terms of Reference:
To examine the general conditions of housing and community planning with a view to:
1. Improving conditions of living for family units and single men and women;
2. Encouraging new methods of building leading to more rapid production of reliable dwellings at lower cost;
3. Supporting CAC and other bodies working towards more artistic and functional design in housing and equipment.

INTERNATIONAL AFFAIRS — Dr. Myrtle Conway, Ste 3, Blackstone Apts., Winnipeg, Man. (1956).

Terms of Reference:
To keep up to date on all matters concerned with international relations, and inform members on developments in the following three fields:
1. On peace problems;
2. On United Nations, its work, and the work of its specialized agencies;
3. On the work of ICW and NCW in relation to UN.

LAWS — Mrs. Wilhelmina Holmes, 39 Notre Dame E., Montreal Que. (1956).

Terms of Reference:
1. To consider all bills, orders-in-council and other forms of legislation, and in consultation with the Parliamentary Secretary to make recommendations for the amendment of existing or proposed legislation, and the promotion of new, by suggesting amendments and bills, and otherwise;
2. To consider recommendations on legislation sent in by the other NCW Standing Committees and report to the Chairman of the Resolution Committee;
3. To unite women in their efforts to work for legal reform;
4. To report developments in International Conventions and necessary action by NCW, especially those affecting the status of women.

MIGRATION AND CITIZENSHIP — Mrs. J.R. Hoag, 2651 Angus Blvd., Regina, Sask. (1955).

Terms of Reference:
1. To impress on women the duties and responsibilities attached to citizenship;
2. To suggest practical methods whereby women may discuss the fundamental principles of democracy, and may participate in programs which will afford them opportunity for the full development of qualities commensurate with the needs of the rapid growth of our population and the contribution expected of us internationally;
3. To work for the election of women to parliament and all other public offices;
4. To consider the problems and responsibilities connected with the immigration and social integration of newcomers;
5. To keep informed on the policy of our government's relation to migration and citizenship, and to recommend NCW action, when advisable.

RADIO AND TELEVISION — Mrs. John Bird, 372 Lewis Street, Ottawa, Ont. (1956).

Terms of Reference:

1. To emphasize the responsibility of broadcasting to contribute to Canadian unity, and the cause of peace and international goodwill;
2. To support and defend freedom of speech on the air, and fair comment;
3. To publicize programs of quality, and work for the accessibility of such programs to all Canadians;
4. To work for the appointment of more women to policy making positions in Canadian broadcasting.

SOCIAL WELFARE — Mrs. Muriel Milligan, 236 Queen St. S., Hamilton, Ont. (1956).

Terms of Reference:

1. To collect and distribute information on problems connected with the welfare and protection of all citizens, young and old, including society's dependents and malad-justed and immature people of all ages;
2. To provide an opportunity for study and promote conferences on such problems;
3. To press for more women police, juvenile courts, the rehabilitation of prisoners, etc.;
4. To work separately, or in conjunction with the Health, Housing and Community Planning, Laws, and Education Standing Committees, as occasion demands.

TRADES AND PROFESSIONS — Miss Eleanor Morley, 1155 Robson St., Vancouver, B.C. (1956).

Terms of Reference:

1. To study the economic and social status of the woman worker in all trades, professions and unskilled jobs;
2. To work for equal pay for equal work, and equal opportunity for advancement;
3. To educate public opinion on the dignity of human labour;
4. To investigate and, where possible, promote improvement of industrial conditions;
5. To collect information and spread knowledge concerning the existing legal rights — such as unemployment insurance, health certificates, safety regulations, workman's compensation, child labour, etc.

TERMS OF REFERENCE — AS APPROVED AT SPRING EXECUTIVE

Constitution Committee

1. To be responsible that newly made amendments are written into the Constitution and By-laws, and that Federated Associations are advised of them.
2. To give rulings as required through the year, and at meetings of the Council.
3. To receive and review, proposed changes in Provincial and Local Council Constitution and advice [sic] N.C.W. Executive.

Finance Committee

1. To study the finances of N.C.W. in relation to its program of activities and to the finances of its federated associations.
2. To consider and make recommendations on measures for raising funds which will establish and keep the finances of N.C.W. on a satisfactory basis;
3. To set up a close liaison with the Treasurer and the Chairman of the Foundation Fund, so that facts relevant to the progress of current money raising projects may be available to the Finance Committee.

I.C.W. Committee

To work for full co-operation with I.C.W.
1. By encouraging two-way exchange of information relevant to I.C.W. policies and activities.
2. By briefing all N.C.W. delegates to I.C.W. Conferences and meetings.
3. By welcoming all visitors accredited by I.C.W. or other N.C.W.'s and studying the means of maintaining cordial relations with other National Councils.

Public Relations and Publicity Committee

1. To make known the work and scope of the N.C.W. of Canada to its members, its federated associations and the general public.
2. To publicize action taken by the N.C.W. of Canada, its President, or any other N.C.W. Officer authorized to take action on behalf of N.C.W.
3. To spread information about I.C.W.
4. To encourage provincial and local Councils to take similar action regionally and locally.

APPENDIX E

Local Councils of Women, 1893-1993

This listing was compiled by Margaret Oke, during her term as Archivist of the National
Council of Women of Canada, from the *Yearbooks*. She presented her work at the annual
meeting of 1989. Since that time Fort Saint John, B.C. has been organized. Where dates are
missing, records are incomplete.

ALBERTA:

    Calgary — organized November 1895; 12 October 1912

    Edmonton — organized March 1908

    Fort St. John and District — organized 1961

    Lethbridge — organized June 1914

    McLeod — organized April 1916

    Medicine Hat — organized 15 March 1916

    Olds — organized 1916

    Pincher Creek — 1917

    Ponoka — organized April 1917

    South Peace

    Virden — organized 1918

BRITISH COLUMBIA:

    Abbotsford — organized 1959

    Burnaby — organized 1959

    Chilliwack — organized 1927; 1936

    Comox Valley — organized 1959

    Courtney

    Dawson Creek — organized 1961

    East Kootenay

    Fernie — organized 1919

    Kamloops — organized 1933

    Kelowna — organized 1950

    Mission City — organized 1951

    Nanaimo — organized 1919

    Nelson — organized 22 July 1898

    Penticton — organized 1951

    North and West Vancouver — organized 1930; 1937

    White Rock — organized 1960

Vancouver — organized 1950
Victoria — organized 1894
Vernon — organized October 1895
New Westminster — organized July 1898

MANITOBA:

Brandon — organized November 1895; 1952
Dauphin — organized 27 April 1917
Mather — organized 1923
Portage La Prairie — organized February 1917
Winnipeg — organized 24 February 1894

NEW BRUNSWICK

Fredericton — organized 18 October 1903; 1946
Moncton — organized 1920
Saint John — organized 14 August 1894
Sackville — organized 1918

NEWFOUNDLAND:

St. John's — organized 1974

NOVA SCOTIA:

East Pictou — organized May 1899; 1914
Halifax — organized 24 August 1894
New Glasgow — organized 1899
North Sydney — organized 1920
Stellarton — organized 1931
Truro — organized May 1912
Westville — organized 1921
Yarmouth — organized 28 August 1894, 1914

ONTARIO:

Brampton — organized 1931
Bradford — organized 29 May 1908
Brockville — organized 1951
Chatham — organized 1921; 1937
Chapleau — organized 21 June 1911
Berwick — organized 1919
Galt — organized 1918

Georgetown — organized 1921

Guelph — organized 1923

Hamilton — organized 17 November 1893

Hailebury

Ingersoll — organized May 1903

Goderich — organized 1937

London — organized 14 February 1894

Lindsay — organized May 1903

Kingston — organized 26 April 1894

Moncton — organized 1920

Niagara Falls — organized 1919

North Bay — organized 1915

Orillia — organized 1915

Ottawa — organized 16 January 1894

Oshawa — organized 1920

Owen Sound — organized 1920

Pembroke — organized 10 May 1914

Peterborough — organized February 1913

Petrolia — organized 1921

Port Hope — organized 12 November 1902

Port Colbourne

Renfrew — organized May 1909

Sarnia — organized February 1913

Smith's Falls — organized 1922

St. Catharines — organized 1918

St. Thomas — organized 1917

Sault Ste. Marie — organized 1917

Strathroy — organized 1917

Stratford — organized 1922

Toronto — organized 3 November 1893

Trenton — organized 1917

Temiskaming — organized May 1915

Sudbury and Copper Cliff — organized 1922

Weston — organized 1930; 1952

West Algoma — organized September 1894

Welland — organized 1918

Woodstock — organized 1910; 1920

Walkerville — organized 3 December 1909

Whitby — organized 1954

York Township — organized 1930

Rat Portage (Kenora) — organized 3 December 1895

PRINCE EDWARD ISLAND:

Charlottetown — organized January 1898

QUEBEC:

Quebec City — organized 13 April 1894; 1919

Montreal — organized 30 November 1893

SASKATCHEWAN:

Estevan — organized 1923

Moose Jaw — organized 14 November 1916

Regina — organized October 1895

Saskatoon — organized 1916

Swift Current — organized 1918

Prince Albert — organized November 1916

Weyburn — organized 1923

Yorkton

APPENDIX F

Nationally organized societies presently affiliated with the N.C.W.C.

Anglican Church of Canada, Women's Unit
Canadian Association of Elizabeth Fry Societies
Canadian Congress of Learning Opportunities for Women
Canadian Federation of Business and Professional Women's Clubs
Canadian Home Economics Association
DES Action Canada
Federation of Junior Leagues of Canada
Federation of Medical Women of Canada
Girl Guides of Canada
Hadassah-Wizo Organization of Canada
League of Ukrainian-Canadian Women
Mediawatch
Media Club of Canada
Na'amat Canada
National Association of Women and the Law
National Consultation of Women of the United Church
National Women's Liberal Commission
Planned Parenthood Federation of Canada
Polish Canadian Women's Federation
Relief Society of the Church of Jesus Christ of Latter Day Saints
The Salvation Army
Ukrainian Women's Association of Canada
Ukrainian Women's Organization of Canada
Victoria Order of Nurses
Women's Missionary Society, (W.D.), (Presbyterian Church of Canada)
Young Women's Christian Association

APPENDIX G

Present Provincial and Local Councils

In 1993 there were four Provincial Councils of Women: Ontario, Manitoba, Saskatchewan, and British Columbia.

Local Councils of Women in existence were:

Maritimes: Halifax, Moncton, and Saint John;

Quebec: Montreal;

Ontario: Ottawa and area, Toronto and area, Hamilton and district, Niagara Falls, St. Catharines, London, and Windsor;

Manitoba: Winnipeg;

Saskatchewan: Prince Albert, Regina, and Saskatoon;

Alberta: Calgary and Edmonton;

British Columbia: Fort St. John, White Rock and district, Burnaby, Vancouver, Victoria, and New Westminster.

APPENDIX H

**Excerpts from the current Constitution and By-Laws
of the National Council of Women of Canada**

NCWC CONSTITUTION

PREAMBLE

We, the women of Canada, sincerely believing that the best good of our homes and nation will be advanced by our greater unity of thought, sympathy and purpose, and that an organized non-sectarian and non-partisan movement of women will best conserve the highest good of the family and State, do hereby band ourselves together to further the application of the Golden Rule to Society, Custom and Law.

NCW BY-LAWS

PREAMBLE

The By-Laws of the National Council of Women of Canada (NCWC) set out how the Purpose Stated in the Act of Incorporation is to be accomplished.

The National Council of Women of Canada is part of a world-wide Federation of women and men dedicated to the betterment of conditions pertaining to the family and the State. Through its affiliation with the International Council of Women (ICW), a non-governmental organization in consultative status (category 1) with the Economics and Social Council of the United Nations (ECOSOC), NCWC may give support to the endeavours of ICW on behalf of the National Councils around the world.

NCWC is a founding member of the American Regional Council/Consejo Regional de las Americas and, through affiliation in this organization brings the special concerns of National Councils in the Western Hemisphere to the attention of the International Council of Women.

The National Council of Women of Canada Development Organization/Organization de Development du Conseil des Femmes Canadiennes (NCWCDO/ODCFC), a subsidiary of NCWC, provides the vehicle whereby NCWC develops and supports educational and social welfare programs in the Third World and Canada.

NCW STANDING RULES

PREAMBLE

NCWC Standing Rules are intended for procedural direction and to implement the By-laws. A Standing Rule may be adopted at an NCWC Annual Meeting by a majority affirmative vote if previous Notice of Motion has been given or by a two-thirds (2/3) affirmation vote if previous Notice of Motion has not been given. Standing Rules may be adopted by the Committee of Officers or Executive with ratification requested at the Annual Meeting of the Council.

NCWC CONSTITUTION
Section 2

No society entering into federation with the Council shall thereby lose its independence or aim or method or be committed to the principles of any other federated society in the Council.

NCWC CONSTITUTION
ARTICLE III
MEMBERSHIP

The Council shall be composed of Local and Provincial Councils of Women of Nationally Organized Societies, which shall be designated Federated Associations.

a) **Local Councils** shall be composed of at least the required number of societies and associations of women (or of men and women) in any locality, as regulated by the By-laws, federated for the purpose of carrying out the objects of the Council and having a constitution in harmony with that of the Council.

b) **Provincial Councils** shall be composed of at least the required number of local councils, as regulated by the By-laws, together with such societies, institutions and associations as are organized on a provincial basis AND provincial branches or divisions of nationally organized societies which are federated with the Council. This federation shall be organized for the purpose of carrying out the objects of the Council and shall have a constitution in harmony with that of the Council.

c) **Organizations** of women (or men and women) having branches in not less that three provinces, whose work is national in scope, and whose objects are in harmony with those of the Council, shall be considered to be Nationally Organized Societies.

d) **Individual women** may become members of the Council as regulated by the By-laws.

NCW BY-LAWS
ARTICLE 111
MEMBERSHIP

Section 1: Nationally Organized Societies

A.   **Application** for membership in NCWC shall be in the form of a motion, passed by the organization asking for federation. A copy of this motion shall be sent to the Executive Secretary of NCWC together with a copy of the Constitution and the names of the officers of the organization desiring federation.

B.   **Election** to membership shall be by a vote of the Executive Committee. Every application shall be submitted to the Committee of Officers and shall be referred by it to the Executive Committee for a recommendation for action.

Section 2: NCWC Patrons

Patrons of the Council shall be those persons who have been accepted as such at an Annual Meeting of the Council, following payment of an amount as approved from time to time by the membership.

Section 3: NCWC Individual Members

A.   **Honourary Life Members** may be elected from those who have rendered signal service to the Council. Candidates for election to this membership shall be proposed by six (6) federated associations, and shall be elected at any Annual Meeting. Any federation wishing to propose a person for Honourary Life Membership shall first submit the name to the Committee of Officers before approaching other associations for endorsement. Retiring Presidents of the Council may be proposed for Honourary Life Membership by the Committee of Officers and/or the Executive Committee and shall be elected at any Annual Meeting. Honourary Life Members shall receive the Year Book and regular mailing of the Council and Executive Committee, and have the right to vote when present, the vote count to be established by current Standing Rules.

B.   **Emeritus Life Members** of the Council shall be those endorsed by a federated association which has contributed an amount, as approved from time to time by the membership, to the Foundation Fund. They shall be elected at an Annual Meeting and conferred with Emeritus Life Membership. They shall be entitled to purchase a Life Membership pin with bar, stating "emeritus" and to receive the Year Book and notices of meetings. They shall have the right to vote when present at Annual Meetings. The vote count shall be established by current Standing Rules.

C.   **Life Members** of the Council shall be those members who have contributed an amount to the Foundation Fund as approved from time to time by the membership and, who have been elected Life Members at an Annual Meeting of the Council. They shall be entitled to purchase a Life Membership pin and to receive the Year Book and notices of meetings. They shall have the right to attend Annual Meetings, to take part in the proceedings, but not to vote.

D.   **Sustaining Members** shall be those persons who annually contribute an amount to Council, as approved from time to time by the membership. They shall receive the Newsletter, Flash Sheet, notices of meetings, shall have the right to attend Annual Meetings of the Council, to take part in the proceedings, but not to vote.

NCW STANDING RULES
ARTICLE III
MEMBERSHIP

NOS Membership

Each applicant for membership with NCWC shall be required to send a copy of their Constitution and By-laws to National Office along with the official application. The Constitution and By-laws shall be forwarded by the Executive Secretary the **Constitution Convenor** for review by her Committee. The Convenor shall advise the Committee of Officers whether or not the Constitution Committee considers the Constitution and By-laws of the Applicant to be in harmony with that of NCWC. The Extension and Membership Convenor will be responsible for approaches to National Organizations which, in the opinion of the Extension and Membership Committee, have aims and objectives in accordance with those of NCWC.

NCWC Patrons

A Patron or Patroness may be elected on payment of $500. or more. Patron status may be granted following payment of $500. over a period of five (5) years or in one payment.

When a Federated Association wishes to Honour and/or endorse a current NCWC Life Member, thereby conferring Emeritus Life Member status on said Life Member, it is necessary effective 1 January 1987 for a payment of $150. to be made to the National Council.

Life Members

An individual receiving a Life Membership shall be named within one year of payment of Life Membership Fee.

All inquiries should be addressed to:
   NCWC
   270 MacLaren St., Suite 20
   Ottawa, Ontario
   K2P 0M3
   Tel.: (613) 233-4953   Fax: (613) 232-8419

INDEX

A

Aberdeen Association: 48, 51, 56, 85, 113

Aberdeen, Countess of (Lady Ishbel Marjoribanks Gordon): 9-10, 15, 23, 26, 27, 28, 29, 47, 49, 58, 79, 122, 152, 167-168, 195, 205, 206, 212, 273, 298, 416; annual address, 1897, 52-54, 1898, 65-68, 1899, 74; concept of feminism, 51; conditions of employment for women, 35; election as first President, NCWC, 22; idea of tolerance, 27; importance to Council, 50; reply to London Council, 32

Aberdeen, Lord: bio. 16-17, 43

Aberdeen Mutual Benefit Association: 56

Adams, Miss Roberta: 300

Agnes Baden Powell Girl Guides: 111

Alcohol and Drug Education Service, British Columbia: 406

Altar Society: 155

Alumnae Association of the Ontario Medical College for Women: 90, 111

American Regional Council of Women: 368

Ames, Herbert Brown: study of poverty in Montreal, 62

Anderson, Doris: 287, 346, 347

Anglican Church of Canada: 325, 395

Anglican Church Women: 320

Anthony, Susan B.: 7, 76

Anti-Tuberculosis League: 51

Archibald, Mrs. Edith Jessie: 56, bio. 56, ftnt. 53

Argue, Mrs. C. W.: 272, 276

Armstrong, Mrs. Catherine/Kay (Mrs. Gordon B.) Pres.: 329, 334-5, 368, 374; bio. 329

Armstrong, Mrs. R. H.: 262 L'asile Bethlehem: 32, 56

Atira Transition House Society: 404

Auxiliaries for the Police Association: 251

Auxiliary of the Railway Conductors: 251

Auxiliary of the United Mine Workers of America: 252

B

Ba'hai: 408

Bailey, Dr. Marguerite: 266

Barber, Miss Beatrice: 223, 234

Barber, Marilyn: 38, 97

Beal, Pauline: 383

Beatty, Muriel: 410

Beck, Marion: 390

Beck, Pat: 386, 387, 396, 416

Bégin, Monique: 288, 292, 294, 313-339

Bell, Ruth: 410, 416

Bennett, R. B.: 194, 203, 215

Bigsby, Nina: 315

Bird, Florence: 290, 291, 293

birth control: 122

Blackstock, Barbara: 184

B'nai B'rith: 213, 252

Boll, Baroness: 240

Bone, Mrs. Turner (Enid Margaret) Pres.: 249, 251, 256, 257, 258, 259, 262, 268, 276, 299; bio. 250

Boomer, Mrs. Harriet: 89; attitude towards servants, 40; bio. 39, ftnt. 50

Bower-Binns, Gwen: 365

Boy Scouts of Canada: 369

Boys Home: 30

British Columbia Association for Community Living: 406

British Columbia Social Credit, Women's Auxiliary: 406

British Columbia Synodical Women's Missionary Society: 406

British Women's Emigration Society: 96

Brown, Irene: 373

Brown, Ruth, Pres.: 394, 396, 410; bio. 395

Bruneau, Mrs. Theodule: 220

Burwash, Eva T.: 205

Business and Professional Women's Association/Club, (Canadian Federation of): 110, 190, 194, 209, 227, 234, 254, 260, 261, 289, 290, 318, 370, 404, 406, 408

Business Women's Association: 112

Butcher, Joan: 396

C

Campbell, Mrs. Roy: 235

Canada: population of: 17, 82, 83, 94, 159, 213, 244, 357

Canadian Addiction Foundation: 359

Canadian Advisory Council on the Status of Women: 329

Canadian Association for Adult Education: 274

Canadian Association in Support of Native People: 321, 332

Canadian Association of Consumers: 218, 250, 274; formation of, 236-9

Canadian Association of Hospital Auxiliaries: 359

Canadian Association of Trained Nurses: 132

Canadian Association of Women Executives: 325

Canadian Association of Women in Science: 325

Canadian Branch of the King's Daughters and Sons: see Canadian Order of the King's Daughters and Sons

Canadian Brotherhood of Railway Employees: 235

Canadian Centenary Council: 274

Canadian Citizenship Federation: 254, 361

Canadian Committee for the Control of Radiation Hazards: 274

Canadian Congress for Learning Opportunities for Women: 359, 372, 395

Canadian Council on Smoking and Health: 359

Canadian Daughter's League: 406

Canadian Dietetic Association: 227

Canadian Dominion Council of the Mother's Union: 194, 227

Canadian Federation of University Women: 273, 287, 344, 404

Canadian Girl Guides Association: 152, 193, 227

Canadian Highway Safety Council: 274

Canadian Home Economics Association: 395

Canadian Home Reading Association/Union: 273

Canadian Institute for International Peace and Security: 370

Canadian Manufacturers' Association: 162

Canadian Mental Health Association: 274, 395, 406

Canadian Nurses' Association: 193, 299

Canadian Order of the King's Daughters and Sons: 7, 15, 21, 48, 56, 74, 111, 193, 22, 228

Canadian Patriotic Fund: see First World War, Patriotic Fund

Canadian Pensioner's Concerned Inc.: 359

Canadian Red Cross Society: 37, 114, 125, 128, 155, 404

Canadian Seniors for Social Responsibility: 369

Canadian Social Hygiene Council: 163, 193

Canadian Society of Superintendents of Training Schools for Nurses: 90, 111

Canadian Suffrage Association: 111, 163

Canadian Welfare Council: 274

Canadian Women's Press Club: 84, 90, 111, 163, 176, 188, 215

Cantacuzene, Princess: 239

Carmichael, Miss Carolyn. E., Pres.: 160, 167, 168, 172, 177, 178; annual address; 1924, 176, 1926, 176; bio. 166, ftnt. 41

Carson, Rachel: 277

Casgrain, Thérèse: 288, 385

Catholic Daughters of America: 192

Catholic Young Ladies Literary Society: 55

Catholic Women's League: 192, 252, 318, 404

censorship: 355, 390; immoral literature, 68

Central Women's Christian Temperance Union: 32

Cholod, Ann: 365

Children of Mary Society: 55

Children's Aid Society: 56, 99, 103, 128

Childrens' Home: 32

Christian Endeavour Society: 70

Church of England Auxiliary to Missions: 30

citizenship rights: 68, 115, 116, 139

Clark, Beverly: 370

Come Share Society: 404

Comfort Fund: 203

Congregation de Nôtre Dame: 32
Congress of Black Women: 410
Convalescent Home: 30
Convent of the Good Shepherd: 32, 56
Cook, Ramsay: 84, 197, 198, 222
Council of Social Service of the Church of England: 185
Creighton, Donald: 214, 232
Creighton, Mrs. Robert: 300
Cummings, Mrs. Emily Willoughby: 10, 15, 25, 135, 173; bio. 141, ftnt. 165

D
Dandurand, Josephine: 101, 135, 136; bio. 101, ftnt. 54
Dane, Nazla: 370
De New, Joan (Pres.): 392, 394, 395; bio. 392-3
Derick, Carrie: 108, 114, 135, 136; bio. 107, ftnt. 69
Depression: see Chapter VI
Diefenbaker, John: 195, 208, 270, 278
Dignam, Mrs. J.S. (Mary): 30, 168, 195, 208; bio. 35, ftnt. 60; comment on Canadian taste, 36-37;
Dobson, Pearl: 369, 370, 383
Dominion Labour Party, Women's Section: 190
Dominion Order of the King's Daughters and Sons: see Canadian Order of the King's Daughters and Sons
Dominion Women's Association of the United Church of Canada: 227
Dominion Women's Enfranchisement Association: 15, 33, 34, 36, 52, 55, 80, 83, 111
Doukhobors: 99
Dyson, Ruth: 416

E
Eastern Star: 155
Eaton, Mrs. Rex, (Pres.): 268, 271; bio. 270
Edgar, Lady Matilda, (Pres.): 84; bio. 85
education: 140, for health, 37; manual training for girls, 41, 60, 65-66
educational governing bodies, women as

members of: 68
Edwards, Henrietta Louise Muir: 173, 175, 188, 189; bio. 19, ftnt. 12 and 136, ftnt. 76
Eglinski, Pat: 415
Elizabeth Fry Association/Society: 299, 325, 353, 405
employment, 60; conditions of, 35, 40, 61, 62-65, 187, 188, of children, 117, 118; of immigrant women as servants, 97-98; of servants, 37-39; of women, 115, 116, 185-188, 234, 259-261, 310-11, 315-316, 353, 367, 386, 387, 408; of women during Depression, 198-202; of women during Second World War, 219-220; opportunities for, 140; participation of women in labour force, 245-246
England, Dr. Grace Ritchie: 131, 168; bio. 134, ftnt. 74
English, Mrs. John: and ideology of NCWC, 25
Epworth League Society: 70
Erola, Judy: 346, 357; bio. 354, ftnt. 10

F
factory inspectors, appointment of women as: 42, 60, 116, 117
Fairclough, Ellen: 289
Fallis, Iva: 215
Federated Women's Institutes of Canada: see Women's Institutes
Fédération des Femmes de Québec: 288, 344
Federation of French Canadian Women: 192
Federation of Junior Leagues of Canada: 395
Federation of Medical Women of Canada: 372
Feist, Monica: 396
feminism, discussion of idea and belief in: 42, 49, 50-51, 60, 93, 107-108, 168-170, 172, 233-234, 307, 309-310, 313-314, 400
Feniak, Elizabeth: 365
Ferguson, Muriel: 261, 365
Findlay, Jessica: 315
Fingarson, Evelyn: 365

Finlayson, Mrs. G.D. (Isabel): 249, 273, 274, 276; bio. 272

First World War: 123-4; Conscription Crisis and, 133-35, 137-139; Local Councils and, 126, 128, 129, 130; National Council and, 124-26, 130, 131; Patriotic fund in, 125-127, 129, 130

Fisher, Miss Kathleen: 220

Fleming, Elizabeth: 379

Food and Agricultural Organization: 240

Fortnightly Club: 157

Fraser Valley Peace Council: 404

Freedom from Hunger Committee: 274

Free Kindergarten: 32

Freiden, Betty: 289

Friends of the Poor Society: 128

Froebel Union: 56

G

Gelber, Sylva: 315; bio. 315, ftnt. 26

Gerin-Lajoie, Marie Lacoste: bio. 101, ftnt. 54

Girl Guides of Canada: 190, 195, 235, 344, 395

Girls' Friendly Society of Canada: 7, 14, 15, 33, 34, 74, 111, 163, 193

Girls' Industrial Institute: 30

Gorman, Ruth: 284

Graduate Nurses' Association: 190

Grant, Reverend Principal: 34; speech to Council, 45

Great War Veterans' Auxiliary: 155

Gullen, Mrs. Augusta Stowe: 105, 173, 193; as Chair of the Committee on Citizenship, 169

gun control, 115

H

Hadassah Organization of Canada: 163, 176, 190, 193, 209, 227, 252, 406

Hadassah-WIZO Organization of Canada: 395

Hamilton Health League: 115

Hardy, Mrs. Edgar Drury, (Pres.): 223, 234, 235, 236, 250, 375; bio. 221

Harmsworth, Lady Jessamine: 416

Harris, Margaret (Pres.): 348, 350, 354, 355, 383; bio. 349

Hayes, Mrs. Saul (Beatrice) Pres.: 266, 276, 278, 279; bio. 277; ideas on race, 280, 284

Health Action Network: 406

Health League of Canada: 272, 273

Hebrew Benevolent Society: 252

Hebrew Ladies' Aid: 177

Hebrew Women's Society: 30

Higgins, Mary: 365

Hill, Jennie S.: 185

Hinkley, W.C. (Ruth) Pres.: 335, 339, 370, 374, 383; bio. 338

Hnatyshyn Mrs. John (Helen) Pres.: 306, 319, 322, 323, 325, 335, 341; bio. 308

Hnatyshyn, Ramon John: 416

Hogg, Mrs. W. (Freda): 406, 415

Home for Incurables in Montreal: 51

Home for the Aged: 56, 86

Homemakers' Club: 163

Hoodless, Adelaide: 22, 34, 42, 56; attitudes regarding women's education, 42-45; bio. 20-21; comment on Council organization, 88-89, 91-92; defense of manual training for girls, 55-56

Hoskins, Diane: 394

Hospital Aid, Auxiliaries Association: 254, 273

Howe, C.D.: 233, 259

Howell, Mary: 359, 360, 362, 370

Humane Society: 30, 56, 70

Humphrey, John: 290, 292

Humphries, Charles: 126, ftnt. 44, 128

Hutchinson, Elizabeth: 396

Hyndman, Margaret: 289

I

Ikwewak: 409

Ilsley, J.L.: 216
immigration, 94-97, 99, 116, 120-21, 140, 142; and women, 97-98, child, 98-99; representation of women on committees dealing with, 115

Imperial Order of the Daughters of the Empire: 90, 111, 126, 130, 155, 172, 176,

185, 190, 193, 227, 254, 318, 404
Independent Order of the Foresters
(Women's Branch): 90, 111, 163
Industrial Rooms Association: 30, 55
Infants' Home and Infirmary: 30
International Alliance of Women for
Suffrage and Equal Rights: 197
International Council of Women: 24, 50, 52,
74-76, 85, 90, 122-123, 146, 166, 178,
211-213, 276-278, 330, 334-5, 350, 368,
374, 375-6, 380, 389; and aftermath of
Second World War, 239-241 and anti-
semitism, 212-13; constitution of, 8-9;
first Quinquennial (1898), 20, Toronto
meeting (1909), 105-9; founding of, 7-9,
15; influence on NCWC, 20, 196-197;
membership, 74 ; and suffrage, 105
International Labour Organization: 239
International Ladies' Garment Workers'
Union: 200
International Typographical Union, Women's
Auxiliary: 190
International Woodworkers of America: 252

J

Jamieson, Mrs. Alice: bio. 131, ftnt. 61
Janes, Gracia: 415
Jane Doe Renascence Society: 404
Jewett, Pauline: 289
Jewish Ladies: 177
Jewish Society of Kingston: 55
Jewish Vocational Service of Montreal: 276
Johnson, Mrs. A.: 234

K

Keefer, Bessie Starr: 15
Kennedy, Elizabeth: 385, 386
Khaki Leagues: 126, 128
Kindergarten Department of the Hamilton
Teachers: 31
King, William Lyon Mackenzie: 173, 203,
214, 222, 233, 243
Kissick, Doreen (Pres.): 370, 374, 379-380,
383, 410; bio. 378
Kiwanis Club: 404
Kome, Penny: 359

Kydd, Miss M. Winnifred, (Pres.): 105, 197,
212, 250, 276; bio. 195-6

L

Laberge-Colas, Rejane: bio. 288
Ladies Aid Society: 56, 70, 128, 155, 185,
190
Ladies Aid Society of Spanish and
Portuguese Jews: 31, 55
Ladies Betterment League: 155
Ladies Curling Club: 155
Ladies Guild: 155
Ladies Hebrew Benevolent Society: 55
Ladies Hospital Auxiliary: 155
Ladies of the Maccabees: 80, 90, 104, ftnt.
61, 111
Ladies Sewing Society of Spanish and
Portuguese Jews: 31, 55
Lamarsh, Judy: 288, 290
Landsberg, Michele: 346
Lang, Mrs. R.W.: 217, 236, 238, 250
Langford, Mrs. Frederick: 132
Lapointe, Miss Jeanne: 290
Laskin, Bora: 333
Lavell, Jeanette: 334
Leacock, Stephen: 251
League of Nations: 188, 196
League of Nations Society: 211, 212
Lefaucheux, Mrs. Marie Helene: bio. 277,
ftnt. 9
Lemrye, Mary: 415
Liberal Party of Canada: 325
Liberal Women's Association: 192, 404
Librarians and Civil Service Association: 31
Licensed Practical Nurses' Association of
British Columbia: 406
Local Councils: affiliates of, 112, 114, 315,
358 and Appendix C; character of, 72,
74, 80, 90, 104-105, 110; committee
structure of, 72, 104; membership of,
154, 190, 192-193, 228; organization of
affiliates, 103-104; programs of, 130-
131, 156-157, 159-161; relationship with
provincial councils, 255-256; urban planning, 284-285, 307

Local Councils, specific (see also Appendix
E and G):
Abbotsford: 273
Alberni: 273
Brampton: 193, 202, 208
Brandon: 48, 56, 112, 251, 282, 321
Brantford: 89, 112, 130, 208, 228, 254,
258, 321
Burnaby: 273, 321, 323, 362, 373, 396,
405
Calgary: 89, 98, 103, 112, 160, 176, 189,
190, 203, 208, 220, 228, 234, 252, 284,
285, 321, 362, 366, 373, 396, 403, 407;
Jewish membership in, 177
Chapleau: 89, 112, 162
Charlottetown: 48, 55, 72, 89, 318, 321
Chatham: 193, 28, 267, 321, 366, 367
Chilliwack: 162, 205, 228, 254, 296, 321,
330, 358
Comox: 273, 321
Dauphin: 128, 176, 183, 190, 208, 228;
Jewish membership in, 177
Dawson Creek: 321
East Kootenay: 48
East Pictou: 48, 56, 112
Edmonton: 48, 89, 112, 183, 189, 190,
202, 203, 208, 238, 252, 267, 285, 321,
362, 366, 367, 373, 396, 407
Fort St. John: 373, 396, 406
Fort William: 220, 235
Fredericton and area: 89, 112, 251, 254,
268, 358
Galt: 128, 162
Georgetown: 162, 228
Guelph: 89, 162
Halifax (and Dartmouth): 47, 55, 60, 64,
65, 70, 72, 96, 107, 112, 130, 140, 176,
192, 194, 208, 218, 228, 252, 285, 321,
331, 373, 396, 414, 415; Jewish member-
ship in, 177
Hamilton (and District) Local Council:
56, 71, 112, 170, 183, 185, 187, 192, 193,
200, 228, 234, 252, 258, 282, 321, 324,
396, 414, 415; founding, 31
Ingersoll: 89, 112, 162
Kamloops: 190, 228, 252

Kelowna: 251, 299
Kenora: see Rat Portage
Kingston: 55, 60, 64, 112, 170, 178, 185,
202, 208, 227, 228, 252, 266, 321, 373,
396, 410; founding of, 33, 47; resolution
concerning employment conditions of
girls and women, 62
Kitchener: 187, 193, 208, 226, 228
Lethbridge: 89, 112, 130, 190
Lindsay: 89
London and Area: 35, 56, 64, 72, 112,
129, 192, 193, 228, 252, 254, 321, 348,
359, 373, 396, 410, 415; founding meeting, 32; challenge to principles of
NCWC, 32
McLeod: 128, 165, 190
Medicine Hat: 89, 128, 189, 190, 228,
251
Mission City: 251, 299
Moncton: 162, 192, 202, 228, 255, 282,
321, 373, 396, 414, 415
Montreal: 55, 65, 96, 101-2, 112, 129,
130, 133, 160, 176, 187, 194, 203, 208,
218, 220, 227, 228, 251, 252, 264, 266,
321, 323, 332, 344, 353, 373, 384, 396,
413-414; action on child mortality, 71;
establishment of committees, 31; found-
ing meeting, 31; Jewish membership in,
176
Moose Jaw: 128, 183, 190, 192, 202, 208,
228, 321, 358
Nanaimo: 162, 228, 252, 321
Nelson: 48, 56, 112
New Glasgow: 205, 228, 321, 414
New Westminster: 48, 73, 112, 193, 185,
190, 200, 221, 226, 228, 282, 321, 362,
373, 376, 405
Niagara Falls: 183, 228, 236, 252, 282,
321, 330, 373, 396, 410
North and West Vancouver: 196, 321
North Bay: 126, 128, 162, 193
North Shore: 228, 266, 275
North Sydney: 162
Olds: 128, 162
Orillia: 251, 258, 321, 358
Oshawa and District: 313

Ottawa and Area: 28, 55, 56, 61, 71-72, 100, 102, 104, 112, 129, 181, 193, 199, 202, 228, 249, 252, 321, 323, 369, 396, 410, 412, 415; accommodation of Roman Catholic affiliates, 31-32; founding meeting, 31
Owen Sound: 162, 228, 285, 358
Pembroke: 89, 128, 193
Peterborough: 89, 112, 228, 285, 321
Pincher Creek: 128, 155, 162
Ponoka: 128, 155, 162
Port Arthur: 170, 218
Port Colbourne: 273
Port Hope: 89
Port St. John: 321
Portage La Prairie: 128, 228, 285
Prince Albert: 312, 396, 401
Quebec: 56, 72, 89, 112, 162; founding, 32
Rat Portage (Kenora): 48, 56, 70, 89
Red Deer: 128, 162, 273
Regina: 48, 70, 71, 96, 103, 137, 184, 187, 190, 199, 226, 228, 235, 252, 280, 286, 321, 323, 362, 373, 396, 407
Renfrew: 89, 112, 130, 183, 193
Sackville: 128, 155, 165, 184, 228, 234, 312
St. Catharines: 128, 202, 228, 321, 373, 396, 410, 412
Saint John: 47, 55, 72, 73, 112, 130, 165, 192, 218, 228, 285, 321, 396, 414
St. John's: 299, 321
St. Thomas: 128, 228
Sarnia: 89, 112, 228
Saskatoon: 112, 128, 160, 321, 323, 349, 362, 373, 407
Sault St. Marie: 128
Smith Fall's: 162, 228
South Peace Regional: 373
Stellarton: 192, 228, 312
Strathcona: 89
Stratford: 162
Strathroy: 128, 162
Sudbury: 89, 313, 321
Swift Current: 128, 155, 170, 190, 228, 321

Sydney: 89, 112
Témiscaming: 126, 162
Toronto: 55, 60, 61, 71, 72, 86, 96, 103, 112, 120, 123, 129, 176, 183, 184, 186, 187, 192, 193, 202, 203, 208, 227, 228, 236, 252, 254, 260, 321, 332, 370, 373, 396, 412; action regarding filtration plant, 118; affiliate societies of, 30; founding of, 30; Jewish membership in, 176; resolution on unemployed in, 29
Trail: 273, 312
Trenton: 128, 193
Truro: 89, 112, 156, 208, 228, 321, 362
Vancouver: 48, 55, 103, 112, 130, 160, 183, 190, 194, 202, 208, 228, 252, 254, 268, 321, 362, 373, 396, 405; and founding of VON, 69-71, 74
Vernon: 48, 56, 112, 156, 162, 273
Victoria: 48, 55, 73, 112, 115, 130, 160, 190, 194, 202, 228, 321, 362, 373, 396, 404
Virdin: 162
Walkerville: 89
Welland: 154
West Algoma: 48, 56, 72, 112, 226, 228, 251, 358
West Pictou: 112, 226, 228, 251, 321, 324
Weston: 193, 228, 299
Westville: 162, 228, 321
Whitby: 89
White Rock and District: 273, 321, 323, 362, 373, 396, 404
Windsor: 193, 228, 252, 254, 258, 285, 321, 373, 396, 410
Winnipeg: 72, 96, 112, 149, 160, 164, 165, 168, 183, 185, 187, 192, 194, 202, 203, 208, 228, 252, 282, 299, 321, 362, 373, 396, 409; founding of, 32, 33; withdrawal from NCWC, 150, 151: petitions for readmittance, 168
Woodstock: 410
Yarmouth: 89, 112, 228, 298
Yorkton: 193, 312
Long, Mrs. Elizabeth: 285, 198

M

McClung, Nellie: 138, 188, 211
Macdonell, Mrs. Mary: 10, 15
McDougall, Barbara: 373, 374, 378
MacEwen, Elizabeth: 352, 353, 365, 416
MacGee, Mrs. Margaret (Pres): 359, 363, 365, 368, 374, 383, 412, 413, 416; bio. 359
McGibbon, Pauline: 312; bio. 312, ftnt. 13
MacGill, Elizabeth Muriel Gregory: 290
McKee, Margaret: 373
McKinney, Mrs. Louise: 188
McKivor, Evat: 187, 197
Maclachlan, Ethel: 131
McLarty, Norman: 223
MacLellan, Margaret: 289, 295
Machar, Agnes Maule: 63; bio. 62, ftnt. 36
magistrates, appointment of women as: 131-133
Manitoba Grain Growers' Association, Women's Section: 132, 162, 176
Manus, Rosa: 239
marriage: 50, 51-52, 59, 91, 171, 177, 310-311
Marsh, Leonard: 233
Marshall, Mrs. R.J. (Pres.): 236, 238, 247, 248, 249, 338; bio. 236
MATCH: 335
Matthews, Estelle: 370, 373, 374
Meade, Michelle: 365
Media Club of Canada: 372, 395
Medical Alumnus of Toronto University: 111, 193, 227
Menzies, Mrs. M.W. (June): 301, 207, 333
Methodist Women's Missionary Society: 30
Mess, James: 228
Milligan, Dorothy: 350, 383
Mills, Thora: 370
Milne, Mrs. S.M. (Pres.): 300, 305, 306, 307; bio. 299
Ministering Children's League: 30
Model School Association: 56
Modern Centre for the Handicapped: 404
Montreal Coordination Council on New Immigrants: 277
"Moral Purity" movement: 114

Morrisey, Kathleen C.: 296
Morton, Desmond: 55, 123, 148, 243, 278
Moses Montifiore Benevolent Society: 30
Mothers Against Drunk Drivers: 406
Murdoch, Irene: 333, 334
Murphy, Mrs. Emily: 115, 131, 188; bio. 114, ftnt. 9
Mutual Benefit Association of Working Women: 56

N

Na'amet Canada: 395
National Action Committee on the Status of Women: 312, 338, 346, 360, 363, 364, 366, 378, 398; characteristics of, 325; formation of, 324-325, 385; membership of, 325
National Association of Women and the Law: 372, 395
National Council of Women of Canada: 21, 23, 39, 43, 50, 74, 108, 136, 145, 146; and abortion, 320-321; Ad Hoc Planning Committee, 396, 397; articulation of Council values, 400; proposed aim, 402; proposed goals, 402-3; survey of, 397-8; affiliated associations and societies, 359-59, also Appendix F; and Canada's constitution, 345-346, 384-5; characteristics of, 10-12, 14, 24-25, 37-39, 49, 52, 110, 206-209, 223-224, 243, 274, 286, 328-329, 372, 393, 404, 405, 408; committee organization, 14, 59, 176, 414; concerns voiced at annual meetings, 182, 185-188, 189, 204, 206, 247, 256-258, 296, 322-323, 330, 344, 340, 347-8, 352, 354-55, 356, 367-8, 369, 375-6, 378-9, 388, 389-90, 415-16, 417-18; constitution of, 23-26, 32, 52, 93 [see also Appendix H]; committee organization, 14, 59, 176; definition of aims, 360-362, 366; difference from National Action Committee, 363-364; environmental concerns, 277, 392; Executive Committee of, 22, 23, 33, 34, 60, 86, 132, 134, 135, 173, 178, 364; federal government, relations with 173-4, 248-250, 300, 339, 373-374, 378, 385;

fees, 34, 86-88, financial statements, 34, 86-88; formation of, 15; founding meeting of, 21-22; Foundation Fund, 178 (see also Appendix B); ICW, relationship with, 15, 168; Local Councils, relations with, 100, 149, 151-153, 160; membership of, 111, 158, 176, 227-228, Jewish membership in, 252, within Quebec 101; manuals of, 383-384; and National Anthem, 353-354; officers of, 34; provincial governments, relations with, 406; on rape, 335-336; post war planning meeting, 229-232; public opinion, 91; Special Committees of, Maternal care, 182-183; Property relations of husband and wife, 175; Standing Committees of, 14, 58, 59, 92, 158-159 (see also Appendix D), Citizenship, 169-170, Finance, 57-58, Household Economics, 131, Laws Concerning women and children, 175, 364-365, Parliamentary, 173, Public Health, 118; structure of, 14, 34, 56-58, 79-82, 86-88, 194-195, 254-255, 258-259, 265; surveys of, aged poor, 68-69; views on family values, 414-415

National Council of Women of Canada Development Organization: 350-352, 359

National Council of Jewish Women: 190, 192, 194, 209, 213, 227, 252, 289

National Council of the Y.W.C.A.: 193

National Employment Committee/Commission: 203

National Equal Franchise Union: 132

National Girls Work Board of the Educational Council of Canada: 194, 227

National Historical Society: 90

National Home Reading Association/Union: 59-60, 111

National Parks Federation: 176

National Union of Women's Suffrage Associations: 7, 111, 132

National Women's Liberal Commission: 372, 395

Native People, and Council: 91, 282-284, 300, 331, 332; Council study concerning, 267-268; federal policies in Far North and, 272; rights of women, 332-333, 417; right to control education, 248; right to vote in federal elections, 247-248, 271; right to pensions, 248; status as Canadian citizens, 270-271

Neiman Joan (Bissett): 339, 340-341; bio. 339, ftnt. 82

New Horizons Peacemakers: 404

Newman, Mrs. Jean D.: 266

Newsboy Club: 31

Newson, Lynda: 408

Nickson, May: 365, 384, 394

Nurses' Association: 254

Norton, Loretta: 416

Nutt, Elizabeth: 208

O

Ogilvie, Mrs. Robert: 290

Ohan, Stella: 416

Oke, Margaret: 372, 373, 383

Ontario Horticultural Association: 90, 111

Ontario Women's Citizen Association: 132, 162

Ontario Women's Liberal Association: 132

Order of Allied Mothers in Sacrifice: 163

Orphan Home Girls' Home: 30

Orphanage of St. Joseph: 32

Ottawa Home for Friendless Women: 35, 56

Ottawa Refuge Branch of the Protestant Orphans' Home: 35

Ottawa Protestant Home for the Aged: 5

Ozolins, Mary: 405

P

Palliative Care Foundation: 372

parental rights: 113, 115, 368

Parlby, Irene: bio. 188, ftnt. 24

Parsons, Lydia M.: 186, 197

Peace and Arbitration Association/Society: 90, 111, 163

Peace Arch Community Services: 404

Peace Arch District Hospital Auxiliary: 404

Pearson, Lester B.: 248, 250, 278, 289, 300

pensions, mothers: 139

Pépin, Lucie: 349-350; bio. 349, ftnt. 19

Pepper, Bette: 396, 405, 416

Person's Case: 188-189
Pickering, Miss Mildred: 234
Pioneer Women's Organization: 299
Planned Parent Federation of Canada: 395,
406, 408
Plumtre, Mrs. Adelaide: bio. 148; special
report on maternal care, of, 175, 182, 183
police matrons, appointment of: 60
Polish Canadian Women's Federation: 359,
395
Polish Gymnastic Society: 192
Presbyterian Church in Canada: 395, 408
Presbyterian Ladies College: 56
Presbyterian Women's Foreign Missionary
Society: 5-6, 395
Primary Sunday School Teachers' Union: 30
Prisoners Aid Association: 60
prostitution: 354; control of 114
Protestant Orphans Asylum: 86
Provincial Councils: 251, 261, 262
Provincial Councils (specific)
Alberta: 189, 273, 300
British Columbia: 190, 251, 254, 262,
268, 281, 282, 323, 331, 349, 355, 396,
406
Manitoba: 190, 251, 252, 254, 261, 262,
299, 310, 323, 333, 335, 336, 349, 355,
396, 409
New Brunswick: 192, 251, 264
Nova Scotia: 192, 251, 254, 261, 264,
355, 386-7
Ontario: 193, 220, 221, 236, 251, 255,
262, 300, 331, 349, 355, 366, 396, 410,
412-413
Saskatchewan: 251, 254, 262, 331, 366,
386-387, 396, 407, 408
public health, 117-19, 129, 139, 140, 281;
and insane, care of, 116; and pasteurization, 115;
public ownership: 142

Q
Queen's University Alumnae Association:
132, 194, 227

R
Rebekah Assembly: 155
Rebekah Lodge: 155
Redmond, Miss Jessie: 235
Registered Nurses: 254
Reid, Helen: bio. 129, ftnt. 53
Relief Society of the Church of Jesus Christ
of the Latter Day Saints: 372, 395, 407
Ritchie, Lady: 28-29; bio. 28, ftnt. 29
Rogers, Tina: 365, 375, 396
Roman Catholic Woman's Work: 30
Ross, Dr. Phyllis: 286
Routhier, Madame: Pres. of Quebec Local
Council, views on illegitimacy, 36
Royal Commissions: on Bilingualism and
Biculturalism 279, Council attitude
towards 279-280; on Divorce, 296, on
Mills and Factories, 1882, 19; on
Relations between Capital and Labour, 1889,
19; on the Status of Women, 1967, 287-
9, 311-312, 313, 319, 324, 325, 349, 404,
appointment of commissioners, 290, ide-
ology of, 314, impact on public opinion,
293-5, 316-318, implementation of 318,
recommendations of, 314, press reaction
to, 291-3, terms of reference for, 293-5
Royce, Marion: 315
Rustad, Pat: 396

S
Sabia, Laura: 287, 288, 289, 290, 324
Sacred Heart of Jesus Society: 70
Saint Boniface's Ladies Aid Society: 55
St. Bridget's Sewing Circle: 32
St. John's Ambulance: 37
Saint John's Auxiliary: 155
St. John Guild: 155
St. Patrick's Orphan Asylum/Home: 32, 56
St. Vincent de Paul Society: 60
Salvation Army (in Canada): 96, 104, 115,
163, 194, 227, 367, 395, 404, 406, 408;
re abortion, 320
Salvation Army Social Workers: 115
Sandford, Mrs. W.E. (Harriet Sophia) Pres.:
135, 148, 166, 167, 168, 172, 195; bio.
146

Saskatchewan Association For Community
Living: 408
Saskatchewan Grain Growers' Association,
Womens Section: 132, 162
Saskatchewan N.D.P., Women: 408
Saskatchewan Society of the CCC therapists:
408
Saskatchewan Women's Agriculture
Network: 408
Saskatoon City Hospital's Women's
Auxiliary: 349
Saywell, Jack: 55
School for the Blind: 55
Schwart, Julia: 189
Scott, Jean: 359
Scuddamore, Joy: 405
Seaman's Mission: 55
Second Book Section of the Hamilton
Teachers' Association: 31
Second World War: 213, 214; capital volun-
tary services division, 215-216; conscrip-
tion in, 222-223; War Savings
Certificates, 216; Wartime Nutrition,
216-217; War Time Prices and Trade
Boards, 217-218; women in the Forces
in, 218-219, 220-221, 228-229
Semiahmoo House Society: 404
Semiahmoo Peninsula Youth Support
Society: 404
Senate, appointment of women to: 142 (See
also Person's Case)
Senior Mission Circle: 155
Senior Section of the Hamilton Teachers'
Association: 31
Sewall, May Wright: 7, 9
Shand, Miss Gwendolyn: 267
Sharp, Mitchell: 232
Shaw, Rosa L.: 274, 359
Shipley, Ann: 268
Shortt, Mrs. Adam: 89; views on
Canadianization of, 121
Siemenska, Mrs.: 239
Silver Cross Women of the British Empire:
227
Single Tax Association: 90, 111
Sly, Catherine: 412

Society for Prevention of Cruelty to
Animals: 31
Society of French Canadian Women in
Manitoba: 192
Soroptimists: 404
South Surrey/White Rock Women's Peace
Association: 404
Spencer, Mrs. George O.: 204, 205, 214, 221
Stanfield, Robert: 358
Stanton, Elizabeth Cady: 7
Steadman, Miss S.M.: 318
Steen, Mrs. H.H. (Pearl) Pres: 285, 286, 296,
299, 370, 374; bio. 285-6
Stowe, Dr. Emily Howard: 21, 36, 169; atti-
tude towards servants, 40; bio. 15, ftnt. 3
Strong-Boag, Veronica: 3, 37, 60-61, 93,
103, 118, 131, 148, 199
suffrage: 105, 135-139, 142, 143; NCWC
resolution on, 1910, 106-7

T
Tait, Katherine: 396
Taylor, Lady Margaret (Pres.): 84, 107, 135;
bio. 85-6
Tetley, Rosslyn: on homelessness, 379-380
Third Book Section of the Hamilton
Teachers' Association: 31
Thompson, Sir John: 34, approval of
Founding of Council, 44
Thompson, Mrs. Robert (Pres): 84; bio. 86
Thorburn, Mrs. C.H.: 195, 272
Toronto and Women's College Hospital and
Dispensary Board: 86
Toronto Relief Society: 30
Toronto Union of King's Daughters: 30
Torrington, Mrs. F.H.(Pres): 84, 135, 138-
139, 206; bio. 86
Trades and Labour Congress: 55, 65, 117,
178; links with NCWC, 64
Trudeau, Pierre-Elliott: meetings with
Council, 305-6, 335, 339, 344
Tynes, Gertrude: 415

U
Ukrainian Labour-Temple, Women's
Section: 190

Ukrainian Women's Club: 192
Ukrainian Women's Association of Canada: 395, 404, 406, 408
Ukrainian Women's Organization of Canada: 194, 227, 395
Underhill, Mrs. F.E.: 265
Unemployed Women's Association: 190
United Church of Canada: 188, 194, 227, 228, 252, 273, 379, 395
United Empire Loyalist Association: 85
United Farm Women of Alberta: 132, 162, 188
United Nations: 239, 241, 249, 270, 274, 275, 276, 295
United Nations Conference on Trade and Development: 240
United Nations Development Program: 240
United Nations Education, Scientific and Cultural Organization: 240, 274, 330, 369
United Nations Environmental Program: 246
United Nations Industrial Development Organization: 240
United Nations International Children's Emergency Fund: 267, 330
United Nations Society of Canada: 274
University Women's Club: 236, 252, 273

V
Van Ginkel, Mrs. H.F.D.: 306; vision for Council, 302-304
Vanier Institute: 318
Vautelet, Madame H.E.: 239
Veterans of France: 185
Victorian Order of Nurses: 37, 48, 84, 194, 227, 252, 395, 406; establishment of, 69-71, 73, 86, 111
Visiting Committee Protestant Hospital: 56

W
Walker, Mrs. B.W.: 279
Walsh, John, Archbishop of Toronto: letter supporting founding of Council, 43-44
Watt, Mrs. Alfred: 239
Wentworth Historical Society: 31
Wesleyan Female College: 31

White Rock and District Garden Club: 405
Whitton, Charlotte: 99, 183, 211; complaints about other members of Council, 183-4
Wilkinson, Marianne: 373
Williams, Mrs. Amy Fowler (Pres.): 343, 346, 365, 370, 374, 383, 413; bio. 343-344
Wilson, Cairine Reay: 211, 239
Wilson, Mrs. J.A. (Henrietta) Pres.: 178, 195; bio. 178
Wiltshire, Trudy: 359, 373, 374
Winnipeg General Strike: 164, 165
Wise, S.F.: 49, ftnt. 3; 146, 148
women reformers, characteristics of, 19-20, 116, 163-164; and volunteer work, 140
Women's Alliance: 50
Women's Art Association of Canada: 14, 30, 33, 34, 74, 85, 111, 194, 227
Women's Association of the Canadian League for the Liberation of the Ukraine: 395
Women's Auxiliaries of the Locomotive Engineers and Firemen: 251
Women's Auxiliary, Anglican Church: 15, 235
Women's Auxiliary Missionary Society: 155, 235
Women's C.C.F. Club: 190
Women's Canadian Club: 86
Women's Canadian Historical Association: 56, 85
Women's Christian Temperance Movement/Union: 6-7, 14, 15, 21, 27, 30, 32, 36, 49, 52, 55, 56, 70, 80, 114, 115, 138, 152, 155, 165, 176, 185, 188, 190, 193, 227, 254, 321, 406
Women's Christian Union: 32
Women's Civic Council: 155
Women's Conservative Club: 190, 192, 193
Women's Educational Union: 56
Women's Enfranchisement Association: 21, 30
Women's Foreign Missionary Society: 56, 70
Women's Historical Association: 51
Women's Hospital Aid Society: 32, 155

Women's Institutes: 4, 83, 162, 163, 185,
    190, 252, 318; of Alberta, 132, 162, 183;
    Manitoba, 162; Ontario, 90, 111;
    Saskatchewan, 408
Women's Labour League: 190
Women's League of Health and Beauty: 194
Women's Liberal Association: 193
Women's Liberal Club: 190, 193, 254
Women's Literary Society (Toronto
    University): 30
Women's Missionary Society of the
    Presbyterian Church of Canada: 155, 190
Women's Morning Musical Club: 56
Women's Musical Club: 155
Women's Platform: 114, 115, 160, 171
Women's Progressive Conservative
    Association: 254
Women's Protective Immigration Society: 31
Women's Stenographic Club: 31
Women's Welcome Hospital: 86
Woman's Work Exchange: 55
Working Girls Association: 19, 136
Working Woman's Protective Association:
    30
World Health Organization: 240, 267

Y
Yeomans, Letitia: bio. 6
Young Men's Christian Association: 27, 86
Young Women's Christian Association: 4, 6-
    7, 15, 21, 30, 32, 56, 115, 132, 155, 176,
    227, 235, 325
Young Women's Christian Guild: 30

Z
Zamilinski, Eileen: 358
Zawercha, Olha: 365
Zonta International: 236